T0289154

FILMING DIFFERENCE

F I L M

D I F F E R E N C E

N Actors, Directors, Producers,
and Writers on Gender, Race,
G and Sexuality in Film

Edited by Daniel Bernardi

University of Texas Press
Austin, TX

Copyright © 2009 by the University of Texas Press
All rights reserved
Printed in the United States of America
First edition, 2009

Requests for permission to reproduce material from this work
should be sent to:
Permissions
University of Texas Press
P.O. Box 7819
Austin, TX 78713-7819
www.utexas.edu/utpress/about/bpermission.html

⊗ The paper used in this book meets the minimum requirements
of ANSI/NISO Z39.48-1992 (R1997) (Permanence of Paper).

Library of Congress Cataloging-in-Publication Data

Filming difference : actors, directors, producers, and writers on gender, race, and sexuality in film / edited by Daniel Bernardi. — 1st ed.
    p.   cm.
Includes bibliographical references and index.
ISBN 978-0-292-71923-1 (cloth : alk. paper)
ISBN 978-0-292-71974-3 (pbk. : alk. paper)
    1. Social problems in motion pictures.   2. Sex roles in motion
pictures.   3. Race relations in motion pictures.   4. Motion
picture producers and directors—United States—Interviews.
5. Motion picture actors and actresses—United States—Interviews.
6. Screenwriters—United States—Interviews.   I. Bernardi,
Daniel, 1964–
    PN1995.9.S62F55   2009
    791.43'6355—dc22
                                                    2008049869

I dedicate this book to my former students, particularly:

Rachel "God Is in the Details" Adams
Kathryn "In and Out of the Rabbit Hole" Bergeron
Mike "Anything But a Flash in the Pan" Burk
Leigh "The Nose" Baltzer
David "Hardest Working Man in the Business" Carol
Andrea "Design on a Dime" DeFrancisco
Young Eun "Help Me Get You Out of My Way" Chae
Colorful Chiara Ferrari
Michael "New Jack" Green
Jorge "I Don't Do Hugs" Jake
Judith's Lacertosa
Leslie "Trek Star" Lamb
Michelle "Momma" Martinez
Barry "Extraterrestrial Timeline" McGuire
Michelle "It's All About MySpace" McCormick
Jana "Alien Hybrid" Minka
Crystal "You Talking to Me?" Quintero
www.Eliza/Robinson
Callen's "A Punk" Shutters
Katherine "Reaching for the Stars" Warner
Ayanna "You Better Not Be Talkin' to Me" Whitworth-Barner
Yang "Just Do It" Xiang

Thank you for pushing me to be a better teacher!

Contents

Acknowledgments

I thank the contributors to this volume for sticking with the project as it went through four years of revision. I also thank the research assistants who helped put this project together: Michael Green, Deydra Linares, and Alexis Cabrera. I appreciate the help and extra effort! Finally and especially, I thank my wife, Helen Na, for giving me room to finish this  and other projects as we started raising our ItKoRican son, Sojin Rock Soto Bernardi (a.k.a. El Jefe).

Sojin Rock Soto Bernardi

FILMING DIFFERENCE

Different Visions, Revolutionary Perceptions

RACE, GENDER, AND SEXUALITY IN THE WORK OF CONTEMPORARY FILMMAKERS

Daniel Bernardi

(Arizona State University)

Difference, I learn—whether gendered, racialized, or otherwise defined through the body—is often enforced by society, defined by those with power, and maintained by law, doctrine, and culture.

LAURA KISSEL

Story

Most of us have heard George Bernard Shaw's famous line, "He who can, does. He who cannot, teaches." Although Shaw's line has to do with revolutionaries, I have heard film students use a variant to chide film and media educators.[1] It goes something like this: "Those that can make films, do. Those that cannot make films, teach." A stereotype of sorts, the film school perversion of Shaw's quote suggests there is but one kind of filmmaking—the kind that takes place outside of teaching. Similarly, it implies that the work of filmmaking isn't also the work of teaching—and that teaching isn't "doing." Yet for better or worse, films influence our views about things even when we don't want to learn or when the filmmaker is not interested in education. Indeed, people often learn about other cultures and countries—about difference—from what they see in movies. We might even say that films instruct us about difference in much the same way that teachers do. They act on audiences in ways that are indirect and direct, didactic and subtle—at times, even revolutionary.

Those of us who teach critical and cultural studies face an equally simplistic charge that we read too much into the films we study. The line I hear early in almost every class on Hollywood film that I have taught goes something like, "It's only a film. It's just entertainment."

DANIEL
BERNARDI

The point, I think, is to suggest that by critiquing cinema, we give it more power than it actually wields. It also seems to suggest that the process of questioning a film—of reading a film critically, for example—undermines the pleasure we get from being entertained by cinema. I suppose these would be fair charges if moviegoers only rarely watched films. What impact can one or even a few films have on a person's consciousness, let alone culture and society? But, of course, moviegoers do not "only rarely" watch films—none of us do. We have an almost insatiable desire to watch films, to read the stories they stem from and read and view the forms they give rise to. Hollywood films in particular are based on older stories, from novels to other films, and they are often repackaged for television, video games, and other venues such as entertainment and star magazines. Television works much the same way. An example is the life outside television enjoyed by the *Star Trek* franchise. *Star Trek* evolved from a low-rated series in the 1960s into an animated series, numerous feature films, and four spin-off television series, along the way engendering a universe of fan conferences, fanzines, and memorabilia. In the course of all this activity, it also created a myth that equates race with alienation.[2]

The point I'm trying to make is that storytelling is an enduring feature of films, and thus it is naive to think that watching films, if only for entertainment, has a value-neutral impact on society and culture. Films are powerful because they help direct our perceptions of each other and of difference. The goal of critical studies is to reveal this power. And that pursuit need not be unpleasurable.

The experience of viewing a film becomes especially powerful when we stop questioning the work of cinema. Indeed, films are particularly ideological—engaged in troubling, even ugly discourses—when they intend only to entertain or when we watch them only to escape. Yet many filmmakers are thoughtful artists and storytellers who want to move their audiences to think critically, to feel passion, to experience something unique. At a basic level, watching a movie is not unlike listening to a lecture: it is an active and creative process that, at one extreme, can lead to boredom or, at the other, critical catharsis. The results, and the myriad of viewing experiences between these extremes, depend as much on the filmmaker as on the audience.

Sometimes cinematic catharsis is based on personal experience. We may better understand a friend, a family member, or a personal experience through the performance of an actor in a film. Sometimes it opens up new ways to think critically about society: watching a film may make us question how we think about and treat others. And some times the catharsis is about the medium itself, as when a film makes us realize that cinema speaks in a wide array of beautiful languages and poignant dialects. The most captivating films—revolutionary films—speak simultaneously to the individual, our culture, and cinema itself.

Spike Lee's *Do the Right Thing* (1988) affected me at all three levels. It taught me something about the diverse makeup of the place where my Puerto Rican mother and Italian father grew up and got married, New York City; the complexities of urban racism; and the way the Hollywood style, particularly cinematography and sound, can be as enlightening and explosive as character and narrative.

The contributors to this book speak to audiences in these ways, yet, like Spike Lee, they are not critical theorists in the academic sense. They are working filmmakers. In their craft and words they demonstrate a desire—a work ethic—directed by a passionate commitment to social change. They might not call it revolution, but their awareness of and allegiance to the pedagogical dimensions of film—including those that entertain us—speak volumes about the power of cinema. Students of film, be it film production or critical and cultural studies, have much to learn from their ideas and experiences.

Different Visions, Revolutionary Perceptions

Plot

In giving voice to working filmmakers, this book addresses a series of fundamental but profound questions about the production of difference in film. How do filmmakers deal with the heterogeneity of their own identity when representing the complex identities of others? How do they deal with the history of stereotyping in attempts to construct deeper and fuller representations of difference? More practically, how do filmmakers plan and design films that feature difference? How do they use the tools of cinema, from cinematography to lighting, from sound to editing, to represent gender, race, and sexuality? Why do they elect to work in specific modes, from experimental and documentary to the big screen and television? For that matter, how do they grapple with the economic pressures involved in filmmaking as they pursue their goal of telling thought-provoking, conscientious stories?

In addressing these questions, some of the contributors to this book confront the role race plays in their work and the films that have informed their visions. In the interview conducted by Yuri Makino, for example, Chris Eyre talks about the tensions he faced as a Native American making a film, *Smoke Signals* (1998), about Native Ameri-

4

cans. Eyre had to confront stereotypes behind the scenes at the same time that he had to confront the potential to stereotype the people whose story he was telling:

> There is a polarization where people love me for my ethnicity, or they think I'm less than human. I can have dinner with Robert Redford, fly home, and in the air something happens at 35,000 feet, which is the perception that the world has of me changes. . . . Last year, while I was standing in a supermarket with my wife and daughter, a woman looked at me and said, "If you are going to use food stamps, you've got to go to the other line." What is the impetus for you to look at me and decide this is something nice to say?

BERNARDI It is this kind of polarization that informs Eyre's work. The student of film can thus learn a lot about racism behind- and on-screen by reading Makino's interview and screening Eyre's film.

Other contributors write about topics ranging from gender and misogyny to sexuality and homophobia. Some, such as Cristina Kotz Cornejo, talk about how race, gender, and sexuality intersect in their experiences as filmmakers working inside and outside of academia. Kotz Cornejo is, among other identities, a lesbian filmmaker from Argentina who teaches film production at Emerson College. Her essay addresses the matrix of ideologies she confronts when making films that don't always deal with Latinos, women, or lesbians:

> The characters in my films struggle to become more fully themselves. Often they must fight to reclaim their lives as well, and to pursue a better future. Long after the film is over, we might imagine, they will continue on this path, a work in progress.

Kotz Cornejo's essay asks us to question many things, including the value of labeling someone as a "woman filmmaker," a "lesbian filmmaker," or a "filmmaker of color." To some, these labels confront the social realities of inequality today. For others, they limit the filmmaker's vision—and in some cases our appreciation of her vision. Kotz Cornejo shows us why, like her films, the answer to these questions is a work in progress.

In addition to questions of race, gender, and sexuality, this book confronts questions of ableism, religion, and war. In a strikingly honest essay, Daniel Cutrara, a former Jesuit priest and Hollywood story analyst, addresses censorship and the Catholic Church in his contribution to this project. Cutrara talks about his experience writing a script, *Ka*

Danced, about the sexuality of priests in a story featuring missionary work in India. Jesuit priests have a long tradition of working for social justice and education, so Cutrara elected to write about homosexuality in the priesthood against the backdrop of abject poverty and class warfare in India. In the process, he faced Church censorship and psychic conflict as he struggled through the writing process:

> The choices I made . . . were influenced on the one hand by my fears concerning Church censorship and my relationship to the Jesuit Order, and on the other by my fears in regard to my own sexual identity. The struggle with these fears led to mixed results: compromises in my creative choices for the script that I later regretted, and with those regrets the realization that if I was to be free to create, I would have to forsake the Catholic priesthood after nineteen years of religious life, which, ultimately, I did.

We learn a great deal from Cutrara's essay, including what a writer endures when writing about truth in the midst of contradiction and hypocrisy.

As Cutrara's work demonstrates, "filmmaker" is not synonymous with "director." Although this collection features writings by and interviews with a number of directors, it also features the revolutionary work of writers, producers, and actors. Christopher Bradley, for example, talks about his experiences as a gay actor working in films that cast him as a gay character. After a fan of one of his films, *Leather Jacket Love Story* (1997), saw him waiting tables and shouted, "I saw you naked!" Bradley felt humiliated. His experience is, of course, personal and in some ways unique, but it raises a fundamental question: What are the political and artistic implications of reducing an actor to his sexual orientation? After all, the task of an actor is to act. The point, I think, is that we do actors a disservice when, whether inside or outside the gay community, we see their performance of sexual intimacy on-screen as natural rather than as craft. Bradley's essay confronts this issue with frustration, humor, and resolve.

Another craft featured in *Filming Difference* is that of the producer. Producers confront a unique labyrinth of tensions when launching a film, particularly when they aim to make both a difference and a profit. This can be clearly seen in the interview that Kathryn Galán, the executive director of the National Association of Latino Independent Producers, conducts with Moctesuma Esparza, the producer of such Hollywood hits as *Selena* (1997), *Gods and Generals* (2003), and *Walkout* (2006). As a student in the 1970s, Esparza participated in the

Chicano movement, a political and, for many, radical effort at social justice and equality. He is now a Hollywood producer with the credibility to get films like *Selena* made, and he lets us know how he goes about navigating the economic demands of Hollywood while staying true to the politics of the Chicano movement. "I made a commitment," he tells us, "to learn how to make movies that entertained and that also taught me about different aspects of the human condition." Esparza demonstrates that a producer committed to social justice and diversity can work inside the Hollywood system, and in Galan's interview he gives us tips on how that might be achieved.

Producers who work outside Hollywood also face these tensions. Aaron Greer, a producer and director who teaches at the Loyola University of Chicago, talks about his efforts to make narrative films that feature the complexity of the African American experience. His film *Gettin' Grown* does not feature sex, nudity, violence, drugs, or gangs. It does not star rappers, basketball players, or even A-list talent. "It is a fairly unglamorous, realistic portrayal of a black child's life in a Midwestern city," he tells us. "By design, it has little in common with any other films in the urban film and video market." Greer faced an uphill battle to get the film made and, once it was finished, to get it distributed. We learn a lot about his plight and, by extension, the struggles many independent filmmakers endure when crafting complex stories about their communities in ways that do not capitulate to sensationalism or stereotypes. Like Esparza, Greer shows us some of the ways we might navigate this particular labyrinth of creative tensions.

Filming Difference reveals the degree to which filmmakers think deeply about how they go about creating difference on film. These filmmakers are not simply creative decision makers. They are also critical thinkers and cultural practitioners, concerned about their words, their art, and their profession. Some use critical theory to guide their work. John Thornton Caldwell, for instance, confronts questions of authenticity that arise when a European American filmmaker and academic makes a documentary about Latino migrant workers living in squalor in the canyons of San Diego County. Caldwell, a professor in the School of Theater, Film, and Television at UCLA and author of *Production Culture: Industrial Reflexivity and Critical Practice in Film and Television,* offers his documentary, *Rancho California (por favor)* (2002), for our study.[3] He explains:

> In *Rancho California (por favor)*, I decided to shift away from any attempt at creating a pure ethnic space for expression and instead try to articulate the many material layers and symbolic boundaries used

by the public to construct and assign race. What emerged, on camera and in interviews, was a very real sense that the rural-suburban landscape in the area of the camps was meticulously managed.

Caldwell goes on to remind us that "filmmakers, academics, and activists owe it to themselves and their constituents to more carefully pick apart the layers of outside interests that commonly broach, exploit, and manage indigenous racial identities in public." In *Rancho California (por favor)*, he picks apart his own interests as well as those of the rich, the powerful, and the political, thereby showing us—his audience and students—how to confront complex political issues about identity and society in the process of making documentary films.

The potential for radical filmmaking crosses screens of all sizes: from multiplex theaters to regional festivals, from living rooms to classrooms, from network television to HBO. Celine Parreñas Shimizu, an independent filmmaker and critic at the University of California, Santa Barbara, interviews experimental filmmaker Machiko Saito, whose work you are most likely to have seen only at festivals or in classrooms. Like Caldwell, Saito is not Hollywood. She represents sexuality in ways that resist stereotypes about Asian women while offering insightful looks into diverse forms of intimate cinema. As Shimizu, who wrote a powerful book on the subject, *The Hypersexuality of Race: Performing Asian/American Women on Screen and Scene*,[4] explains:

Different Visions, Revolutionary Perceptions

> . . . because Asian Americans are overdetermined by an excessive and perverse sexuality, Asian American women filmmakers find the language and subject of sexuality necessary to their expression. As filmmakers, whether by accident or on purpose, we engage sexuality in order to transform established representation and create subjectivity in terms that demand recognition.

In reviewing Saito's work, the student of film might ask, in what ways do experimental styles work toward a filmmaker's vision to represent sexual difference radically different from the norm? The same can be asked of Shimizu, who also makes films that deal with these issues. In fact, Shimizu's interview with Saito makes headway in answering this question by introducing us to both Saito's and Shimizu's work.

In another contribution by an experimental artist, John Jota Leaños's essay, "Dead Conversations on Art and Politics: José Guadalupe Posada Interviews John Jota Leaños," experiments with the interview style itself while making a political statement about the pornographic nature of war and terrorism. Juxtaposing the infamous images of torture from Abu Ghraib during the U.S. occupation of Iraq with the image of football player Patrick Tillman as a war hero after he joined the army and died in Afghanistan, Leaños builds on the spirit of Días de los Muertos (Day of the Dead) celebrations as a way to provoke us to honor the reality of Tillman's tragic death by friendly fire, despite the army's cover-up of these facts in an effort to sell the invasion of Iraq. In reading his historic interview, done with wonderfully ironic creativity, we laugh, cry, and scream in indignation. A new media artist who has turned to narrative film to continue his politics of creativity, Leaños shows us one way to use history, art, and film to confront the nexus of racism, war, and propaganda.

Several of the contributors work in television, from documentary filmmaker Paul Espinosa, whose work on the border has been featured prominently on PBS, to Paris Barclay, who has directed episodes of *ER*, *Lost*, *NYPD Blue*, *The Shield*, and *The West Wing*, among other series. Conducted by Kevin Sandler, a professor of media industries at Arizona State University (ASU) and author of *The Naked Truth: Why Hollywood Doesn't Make X-Rated Movies*, the interview with Barclay is particularly telling for filmmakers and scholars interested in prime-time television.[5] Sandler asks Barclay poignant questions about representation, difference, and the messages he tries to articulate in his work. Barclay, a gay African American man, sees it as walking a very thin line:

> . . . it's tough to shove a particular agenda down people's throats; they tend to resist that. It's too obvious, too blatant. So I gave up on that whole concept a while ago, and what I try to do now is show humans that viewers can relate to (even if they disagree with them) so there's some way to get under their skin and maybe provoke some thoughts and consciousness, and in some way maybe shake down the stereotypes we may have of people.

Barclay's experiences, like those of several of the other contributors to this collection, show that difference behind the camera is potentially as diverse as difference on the screen, and that filmmakers working in television deal systematically with similar issues of difference as those working in feature film production. Students of cinema can glean a great deal from Barclay's insights, as he reveals the strategies he used to become a successful television director.

All of the contributions to *Filming Difference* focus in one way or another on the representation of difference from the filmmaker's point of view. The contributors are working actors, directors, producers and writers. They discuss identity and difference in detail and with

stunning candor, providing readers with insights into the representation of social identity from actual creative decision makers. They address representation and identity in a variety of production modes and
genres, including experimental film and documentary, independent
and mainstream film, and television drama. It is the contributors' collective hope that readers of this book come to a broad understanding
of how a range of practicing filmmakers engage a range of profound
social issues.

Characters

The first section of this book, Exposing Bodies, considers the diverse
ways in which representations of identities are located at the site of
the body. Laura Kissel, a professor at the University of South Carolina,
takes an in-depth look at how she went about translating her personal
experience into political filmmaking. Kissel's chapter, "Disability Is
Us: Remembering, Recovering, and Remaking the Image of Disability," traces images of disability across media and into her own work.
In the second chapter in the Exposing Bodies section, "'I Saw You
Naked,'" Christopher Bradley, who teaches screenwriting at ASU while
also working as an actor, analyzes his experiences as a gay man staring
in a gay independent film. In the last chapter in this section, Celine
Parreñas Shimizu interviews Machiko Saito, the experimental filmmaker whose work often focuses on the pain and pleasure of the flesh.
For the filmmakers contributing to this section of the book, the body
is the site at which identity is fleshed out.

The second section of this book, Border Visions, focuses on metaphoric and geographic borders. In "Framing Identities / The Evolving
Self: Beyond the Academic Director," Cristina Kotz Cornejo tells us
how she came to produce and direct her first feature film, *3 Américas*.
In the next chapter, "Indigenism, (In)Visibility: Notes on Migratory
Film," John Thornton Caldwell talks about how and why his films work
to confront the erasure of indigenous identity in American society.
Finally, my interview with Paul Espinosa, an Emmy award–winning
documentarian whom I also work with at ASU, reveals in detail the
strategies he uses to represent the border in films screened on PBS.
Espinosa also talks about the process one goes through in pitching and
making films for PBS, an important insight for all aspiring documentary filmmakers. The literal and metaphoric border becomes, for the
filmmakers contributing to this section of *Filming Difference*, the site
of both struggle and hope.

The third section, Global Identities, extends a discussion initiated

*Different
Visions,
Revolutionary
Perceptions*

by Kotz Cornejo to the international dimension of difference. In the first chapter, *"Del Otro Lado:* Border Crossings, Disappearing Souls, and Other Transgressions," C. A. (Crystal) Griffith, a film professor in the School of Theater and Film at ASU, talks about her journey as an African American filmmaker working in Mexico. Her film, *Del Otro Lado* (1999), tells "a story about love, friendship, Mexico's inability to deal with the AIDS crisis, and the problematics of U.S.-Mexico border policies." In the second chapter in the Global Identities section, "Faith in Sexual Difference: The Inquisition of a Creative Process," Daniel Cutrara, also a screenwriting professor at ASU, recounts his journey as a writer, teacher, and former priest. The final chapter of this section, "Dead Conversations on Art and Politics: José Guadalupe Posada Interviews John Jota Leaños," is by political artist and filmmaker John Jota Leaños, a professor at the California College of the Arts. We learn a great deal about the connection between creative choices and the politics of difference in relation to history, war, and racism from Leaños's work. In short, contributors to this section of the book see difference as a global representation that speaks simultaneously to local and universal concerns.

In the fourth section of this book, Independent Ambitions, filmmakers discuss the visionary and practical politics of working independent of Hollywood. In the first chapter, "Neither Color Blind, Nor Near-Sighted: Representation, Race, and the Role of the Academic Filmmaker," Aaron Greer discusses the film about black life he "became an academic to make." In the next chapter, "Preparing to Perform the Other: Developing Roles Different from Oneself," Sheldon Schiffer, a professor of film production and acting at Georgia State University, talks about how he directs actors to perform ethnic and racialized roles. In the final chapter in Independent Ambitions, "Cinematic Reservations," Yuri Makino interviews her NYU film school classmate, Chris Eyre. For the filmmakers featured in this section of the book, working independent of Hollywood is key to their creative goals in filming difference.

The final section of this collection, True Hollywood Stories, includes four interviews with established and successful Hollywood filmmakers. Many of the interviewers are themselves working filmmakers. In "'And Maybe There Is a Way to Give Hollywood the Kick in the Ass That It Needs:' An Interview with Karyn Kusama," Dan Rybicky, a working screenwriter who teaches at Columbia College, Chicago, asks Kusama how, as a woman working in a male-centric profession like Hollywood she came to make films as diverse as *Girlfight* (2000) and *Aeon Flux* (2005). The second interview in this section, "From *Selena* to *Walkout*

An Interview with Moctesuma Esparza," by Kathryn F. Galan, covers a range of important topics key to conscientious filmmakers aspiring to work in Hollywood. The next interview, "Negotiating the Politics of (In)Difference in Contemporary Hollywood: An Interview with Kimberly Peirce," is conducted by Denise Mann, director of UCLA's Independent Producers Program and author of *Hollywood Independents: The Postwar Talent Takeover*.[6] In the interview, Peirce opens up to Mann, detailing how she came to write and direct a film like *Boys Don't Cry* (1999). Finally, in the last interview in the True Hollywood Stories section, "Televising Difference: An Interview with Paris Barclay," Kevin Sandler and Barclay discuss the journey a gay African American director took from directing music videos to directing some of the most provocative prime-time television on the air today.

Audience

Like many of the contributors to this collection, I teach film and media studies. In fact, I have taught film in departments ranging from Film, Television, and Digital Media at UCLA to Transborder Chicanaō and Latinaō Studies at ASU. My research focuses on the representation and narration of race in Hollywood film, television, and online media. In addition to writing a book on whiteness in *Star Trek*, I have edited three books on whiteness in cinema and have published essays on racism in online pornography.[7] I have also worked in the entertainment industry as a consultant, writer, and producer, including a stint at the Sci-Fi Channel. In that experience I came to realize two things: first, media often segregate difference from whiteness in order to perpetuate racism, and second, many filmmakers, from executives to actors, work diligently to subvert racism, misogyny, and homophobia on and behind the screen. They work in documentary, experimental, narrative, and mainstream venues. They come in all shapes, sizes, and colors. Several offer their visions and strategies in this book.

All must overcome the historical and semiotic legacies of misogyny, racism, homophobia, and other dominating social ideologies found in Hollywood film and television. Indeed, what we sense in reading the contributions to *Filming Difference* is that the history of stereotypes looms large as an obstacle that conscientious filmmakers must endure and overcome. As we watch their films, we can see that some are more successful than others at combating cinematic "isms." We can also see that all of them work diligently to make a difference.

My hope is that the reader of this book will see in its essays and interviews a critical agenda. Some of the contributors, such as Kotz

Different Visions, Revolutionary Perceptions

DANIEL

BERNARDI

Daniel Bernardi on the set of *The Shield.* (Photograph by Little Man.)

Cornejo, Greer, Griffith, Kissel, Makino, Rybicky, and Schiffer, teach film production at major American universities. Their goal is to engage the future of cinema through both education and independent production. Others, such as Sandler and myself, teach only history, theory, and criticism, yet have worked in Hollywood. Our goal is to reveal the creative visions and production cultures of working professionals.[8]

Other contributors are former executives and producers, including Galan and Mann. They bring executive-level experience to our understanding of difference in film. Still others work in Hollywood itself, including Barclay, Esparza, Eyre, Kusama, and Peirce. They aspire to change the system of Hollywood from the inside out. Finally, contributors such as Caldwell, Espinosa, Leaños, Shimizu, and Saito work outside Hollywood. They document social life and experiment with cinematic form, expanding both our appreciation of political cinema and our understanding of social difference.

The contributors are critically astute professionals aware of the revolutionary power of cinema. They think deeply about how to represent the diversity inherent in difference in our culture, and thus to tell stories that expand our consciousness in the hope of making a difference through film. In the process, they challenge viewers and students of film alike.

Notes

1. In this introduction, I mean "film" broadly to include television (which is often shot on film), digital "film," and media in general. As I discuss later in the introduction, I also mean "filmmaker" broadly to include actors, writers, producers, and directors—that is, the creative people who make films.

2. For a critical analysis of how *Star Trek* repositioned ideologies of race across its franchise, see Daniel Bernardi, *Star Trek and History: Race-ing Toward a White Future* (New Brunswick, NJ: Rutgers University Press, 1998), and Michael Pounds, *Race in Space: The Representation of Ethnicity in "Star Trek" and "Star Trek: The Next Generation"* (Lanham, MD: Scarecrow Press, 1999). For gender in *Star Trek*, see Robin Roberts, *Sexual Generations: Star Trek: The Next Generation and Gender* (Urbana: University of Illinois Press, 1999).

3. John Thornton Caldwell, *Production Culture: Industrial Reflexivity and Critical Practice in Film and Television* (Durham, NC: Duke University Press, 2008). See also *Televisuality: Style, Crisis, and Authority in American Television* (New Brunswick, NJ: Rutgers University Press, 1995).

4. Celine Parreñas Shimizu, *The Hypersexuality of Race: Performing Asian/American Women on Screen and Scene* (Durham, NC: Duke University Press, 2007).

5. Kevin Sandler, *The Naked Truth: Why Hollywood Doesn't Make X-Rated Movies* (New Brunswick, NJ: Rutgers University Press, 2007).

6. Denise Mann, *Hollywood Independents: The Postwar Talent Takeover* (Minneapolis: University of Minnesota Press, 2008).

7. See Daniel Bernardi, *Star Trek and History*. For the edited works, see *The Birth of Whiteness: Race and the Emergence of U.S. Cinema* (New Brunswick, NJ: Rutgers University Press, 1996), *Classic Hollywood, Classic Whiteness* (Minneapolis: University of Minnesota Press, 2001), and *The Persistence of Whiteness: Race and Contemporary Hollywood Cinema* (London: Routledge, 2008). For my work on race in pornography, see Daniel Bernardi, "Interracial Joysticks: Pornography's Web of Racist Attractions," in *Pornography: Film and Culture*, ed. Peter Lehman (New Brunswick, NJ: Rutgers University Press, 2006).

8. Sandler and I are co-writing a book on the production of *The Shield* that connects what we see on screen in the FX police drama to the intent of filmmakers behind the scenes. See Daniel Bernardi and Kevin Sander, *The Shield, FX, and the End of the Network Era* (Berkeley and Los Angeles: University of California Press, forthcoming).

Different
Visions,
Revolutionary
Perceptions

PART 1 **EXPOSING BODIES**

CHAPTER 1

Disability Is Us

REMEMBERING, RECOVERING, AND
REMAKING THE IMAGE OF DISABILITY

Laura Kissel
(University of South Carolina)

We must stop at its very source the
pollution of the blood stream of the
nation by properly enforced, sane
eugenic laws. The Hope of The
Nation: Perfect Babies.[1]
THE BLACK STORK (1916)

Impairment is the rule and
normalcy is the fantasy.
LENNARD J. DAVIS, *BENDING*
OVER BACKWARDS

My brother, born two years before me, came into the world two months
too soon, and very sick. He stopped breathing when he was only a few
days old, and the delay of oxygen to his brain resulted in significant
cerebral palsy. When I was three and my brother was five, we shared a
bedroom, toys, a place at the dinner table, and almost everything else
in our small Texas town. I never thought of him as different from me,
of his body as different from mine, until I learned from others that he
was different.

I don't remember the exact moment that I learned this, and my
parents certainly didn't teach it to me. My growing recognition of the
insistent categorization of my brother as *different* paralleled my growing awareness of larger political and social struggles, namely the civil
rights movement and feminism. I remember the reactions to my
brother in the 1970s and 1980s, and the frequent refrain when people
learned of his disability: *I'm sorry.* Sorry? As I revisit these scenes of
segregation and pity, I find myself responding: *Why are you choosing to*
see my brother as less—as retarded, crippled, and impossibly different?

My brother was born in 1967, a year marked by race riots, Vietnam War protests, and the ongoing national struggle for racial equality and civil rights. The disability rights movement was in its infancy, emerging from other civil rights struggles in the year of my brother's birth. Affirmative action was extended in 1967 to include discrimination based on gender, yet civil rights legislation that addressed employment and equal access for people with disabilities was still twenty-three years away.[2] I was born two years later, the same year the now ubiquitous line drawing of a wheelchair user was introduced as the universal symbol for accessibility. My sister was born the year the Equal Rights Amendment (ERA) was ratified by Congress, the same year as the *PARC v. State of Pennsylvania* ruling, in which a U.S. district court declared unconstitutional state laws that barred disabled children from attending public schools.[3] In addition to this backdrop of social and political change, our parents were strong proponents of the Catholic doctrine of social justice. The concept flowed naturally from my parents to us that everyone deserved dignity and equal political, economic, and social opportunities.

LAURA KISSEL

My parents became adults during the emergence of civil rights for many people who had been marginalized and discriminated against because of their difference from the accepted norm—white, male, and able-bodied. When my brother was still very young, a doctor told them, "Put him in an institution and get on with your life." Institutionalization would have meant isolation, segregation, and the abandonment of my brother's care to a state-run, bureaucratic structure that was more like a prison than a family. Institutionalizing my brother would have denied him agency, choice, and dignity. For my parents, this was not an option.

In the 1970s and 1980s I learned about difference in subtle and powerful ways. My parents advocated with other parents for my brother's right to a public education. My mother supported passage of the ERA. She confronted our priest about restrictions against women in the Catholic Church. I was driven to the other side of town to attend an integrated school with Hispanic and African American kids. Difference, I learned—whether gendered, racialized, or otherwise defined through the body—is often enforced by society, defined by those with power, and maintained by law, doctrine, and culture.

In 1982, my parents packed us into a station wagon and took us on a road trip out West. It is almost too easily dismissed as a mundane fact: the family on summer vacation. We trekked to the Rocky Mountains, Yellowstone National Park, Mount Rushmore, and the Badland of South Dakota during the high heat of summer. We were on the road for two weeks. During the trip, Dad handed me his 35mm SLR camera and I learned how to use it, an experience that solidified my professional fate. I remember this trip as if it were framed through the viewfinder of that camera, the needle of the light meter gesturing up and down, as if pointing out the content of each view.

Frame 1: the hugeness of the landscape, and our family in it.

Frame 2: navigating my brother's wheelchair over rocky paths and steep terrain.

Frame 3: all of us whitewater rafting down the Snake River.

The stacks of Ektachrome slides that archive this family experience tell only part of the story. The other part—the effort behind the family vacation, the navigation of a pre-ADA world—is, for the most part, beyond the frame.

In the late 1980s, when my parents moved to Georgia, there were few, if any, meaningful opportunities for my brother, then beyond school age. My mother, who spent day after day at home with him, became exhausted and then angry at his lack of options. She met with other parents and founded an independent living organization to serve people with disabilities in their own homes. I chronicled this struggle in the first of two films about disability, while I was a student at Ithaca College. One cold January day in Atlanta in 1991, I attended and shot my first ADAPT⁴ action with an Atlanta group protesting the government bias toward institutions and the lack of community support for people with disabilities. Several protestors were arrested for occupying a government building. I filmed all of it, including the arrest of a protestor, who, as he disappeared inside the police van, yelled out: "There's been a statement made by the federal government today that they'd rather have us in jail than living in our own homes and communities." I let him have the final word in my film, a personal and activist documentary that I called *Campaign for Full Citizenship*. Fifteen years later, there is still a social bias to segregate people with disabilities. My current film about disability civil rights addresses this problem.

Translating Personal Experience into Political Filmmaking: Form and Content

As far back as I can remember I have been politicized and political, in large part as a result of the epic battles my parents fought, and continue to fight, to ensure basic civil rights and an inclusive life for my brother. As an independent media maker, I am committed to deconstructing and exposing the power of images to reinforce dominant ideologies, specifically the capacity of images to structure ideas about and attitudes toward disability. Indeed, this is the objective of the film I am currently producing about disability civil rights. A number of questions guide me in the production of this work. When disability is the subject, how are bodies with disabilities represented in industrial, commercial, documentary, and newsreel footage from the last hundred years? How have historical and contemporary images of disability been used by the society that manufactured them to define and enforce institutional and individual responses to disability? If the archival record of disability is revealed, how can it help us understand disability's past? Released from the obscurity of the archive, how can these images and ideas inform the production of new images that counter, challenge, and ultimately change how disability is understood and received? When the footage I draw from and recycle is at best discriminatory and at worst dehumanizing, how can the effects of its reuse, through collage and juxtaposition, revolutionize awareness and promote new readings, rather than reify the image's original intent? Finally, how do my own images—interviews, protest footage, and oral histories—combine with and comment on the archive?

LAURA
KISSEL

The archival images I am using illustrate a broad range of negative attitudes toward disability, from horrifying, blatant discrimination to more subtle images that, when scrutinized, reveal patronizing, paternalistic responses that restrict our imagination and narrow potential responses to disability. It is painful to look at some of these images and films, and even more difficult to realize that the anonymous lives represented within them have been lost, abused, or managed into meaninglessness. I take a risk in reusing these images. Workers in institutions and nursing homes who provide care for people with disabilities should not be blamed; they are also victims of a system that narrowly interprets the abilities of individuals who have disabilities. Additionally, some might argue that we don't need to see horrible images that remind us of a past we want to forget. It is my position that addressing traumatic histories enables a transformation, and not only for those whose lives have been painfully compromised or lost but also for the vast majority who don't know that this is our history. For example, the Truth and Reconciliation Commission in South Africa was designed to allow victims and perpetrators of violence to face each other and recount their pain and suffering or their collusion with apartheid. What emerged from this process was an opportunity to face the past and move forward with a unified, collective memory that addresses horror and promises not to repeat it. Similarly, resurrected images of the mistreatment of people with disabilities make visible a history of recurrent dehumanization and the denial of human rights. This visibility urges audiences to assimilate disability history into our collective memory of civil rights struggles.

My primary goal is to make the invisible history of disability visible. This is a political objective and a guiding metaphor for the film. Many people with disabilities are segregated from society in institutions and nursing homes; just as the visual record of disability is hidden from view, so too are many lives. Opening the archive and releasing images of disability can establish the context for a scene of collective and politicized remembrance. Reexposing the trauma of eugenics, euthanasia, institutionalization, and forced obscurity of people with disabilities demands that we remember the past and, through it, attempt to create a new future. In my film, *Disability Is Us,* contemporary narratives that represent the disability rights movement interface with images   *Disability Is Us* from the archive to release the trauma of history into the present. The film offers an opportunity to reconfigure pity, objectification, and the "better dead than disabled" attitude into a new vision: people first, not disability or difference first. Oral histories and personal narratives are used to locate personal experience within recent memory, naming and articulating modern trauma—inequity, forced institutionalization, the struggle to stay alive and be visible. This contemporary witnessing collides with the archive's artifacts to produce an interpretation of the experience of disability that reaches from the past to the present.

Documentary historian and digital media theorist Patricia Zimmermann urges cultural practitioners to approach the archive as a place alive with potential to invoke remembrance and inspire change: "Witnessing and testimonial, image and artifact: together, they move and work through repetition to create memory that is collective and always forming, collaged and reconfigured. . . . [Artifacts] are mobilized to create a collaborative performative space for the imagination of new histories and new futures."[5] The recycling and reuse of these discarded images and ideas can reframe today's disability rights movement as a civil rights struggle by exposing the tragedy of segregation and the labeling of human beings as impossibly different.

Images from the archive objectify and demoralize. By contrast, new framings and oppositional narratives are necessary to undermine this history of objectification and dehumanization. This is the goal of the politically minded filmmaker, yet there is an additional challenge that emerges related to the acquisition of contemporary images, which include interviews, narration, voices, and illustrative images of people with disabilities. How should I shoot, edit, and narrativize disability so that I do not reproduce the attitudes and popular narratives that people with disabilities decry—namely, that living with a disability is either heroic, tragic, something to be pitied, or an obstacle to overcome? The second formal (and political) challenge is, how should I shoot and conduct interviews with people who have significant developmental or cognitive disabilities and utilize alternative modes of communication, such as eye contact or alphabet boards, rather than a standard "voice"? The experience of being silenced, talked down to, or otherwise overlooked is profoundly felt by many people with disabilities, especially individuals whose modes of communication are more closely attuned to gesture, eye contact, or sounds, or who rely on others to understand their wants and desires. Moreover, people with significant mental and cognitive disabilities are more often at risk of being segregated from others than people who are only physically disabled and can converse in typical fashion. What is it to be responsible and attendant to these voices and these perspectives?

Finally, when I turn the camera (and the audience's attention) on a person who cannot readily return such a gaze, I risk conjuring an image of spectacle, the history of which is bound up in the apparatus itself and in the history of looking at others. My film is directed primarily at an able-bodied audience, an audience unfamiliar with disability. This situates the audience as unknowing or unfamiliar and invites them to look *at* the person who is severely disabled. The risk I take is that the nature of looking at physical or mental difference draws attention away from the person and toward the disability. The challenge then becomes one of manufacturing an image that encourages an active, complex spectatorship rather than a passive viewing that is attuned to voyeurism and spectacle. I want to create a spectator position that challenges an audience to address its assumptions and attitudes about disability, especially significant disability. How can popularly accepted attitudes, such as *it is better to be dead than to be disabled*, be challenged, altered, and changed through the interview form? These questions wrestle with issues surrounding the representation of disability on the level of both form and content. At the same time, I want my film to challenge the ingrained ideological assumption that people with disabilities are different in the first place; I want my film to offer a critique of the very notion of difference.

Malleable Images and Bodies in Motion

A body that has a disability is a body that has been altered in some way, perhaps by accident, war, or disease. And bodies with disabilities are perceived as different from "normal" bodies. My film asserts that the categorization of people with disabilities as different is profoundly ideological, constantly reinforced by the social structures, policies, and attitudes of an ableist culture determined to see disability as other than "normal." *Ableism* is the term most often used to describe attitudes and power relationships that categorize and define a person's ability by the perceived limits of his or her body and mind. Just as sexism insists that women are less capable than men and racism insists that people of color are inferior, so too the assumption that twisted, hunched-over, drooling, wheelchair-using bodies are less valuable—even discardable—than bodies that do not limp or falter insists on an inferior status.

Since the emergence of eugenics 120 years ago,[6] the response to disability has ranged from its extinguishment, by way of calculated, government-sponsored euthanasia as carried out in Nazi Germany, to preventing reproduction of the "unfit" through forced sterilization, undertaken in many parts of the world and in the United States, to the institutionalization of disability by moving it behind walls and barbed-wire fences, out of the public's view. The sight of different bodies has provoked remarkable efforts to curtail, change, or make invisible that which does not conform to an ideal, to society's "normal." The consideration by many people today that people with disabilities are not normal is manifest socially and politically in a variety of ways.

As I began working on preliminary ideas for my film, an article was published in the town newspaper in Calhoun, Georgia, that illustrates these pervasive attitudes. The article summarizes a town meeting to discuss construction of a new institution "to treat and house mentally retarded girls." Excerpts from the article reveal that the institution promises to be

> invisible to the surrounding areas . . . no one will be accepted who has a history of violence or criminal activity. . . . The girls will not be a burden on the local school system because they will be schooled in-house. . . . [name deleted] expressed dismay that her property values could go down because of this facility. She said residents at such facilities are prone to "end up on your doorstep or in your yards." [The county commissioners decided that] a chain link fence will be built around the facility to separate it from a nearby I-75 rest stop.[7]

At this meeting, residents expressed the view that they did not want to see, hear, or even educate girls with disabilities in their local schools. The facts of the article exhibit the fear surrounding disability, namely, that disability is commonly thought of as something to isolate and contain—behind a chain-link fence, no less. Ironically, three years before this community discussion took place in Calhoun, Georgia, the Supreme Court of the United States in *Olmsted v. L. C. and E. W.*, a case brought by two women with disabilities in Georgia, affirmed the right of people with disabilities to live where they choose, and not to be institutionalized. The ruling mandates that states integrate people with disabilities into the communities in which they live.

The public anxiety on display in the newspaper article illustrates the basis for an important social critique I encountered in my early research for this documentary, the interrogation of the concept of normalcy. Primarily a focus of cultural studies scholars, the critique of normalcy analyzes the capitalist, sexist, and racist fantasy that bodies can be perfected and made to conform to an ideal.[8] As scholars have pointed out, society's conception of what is normal often results in manipulation of the body to make it conform, through dieting or plastic surgery, for example. Moreover, the concept of normal is ideological. In the case of disability, the euphemism "special" is sometimes substituted for "not normal." My film asks, What *is* normal? And what does it mean to call someone special, other than another way to institutionalize the idea that people with disabilities are different, and that something must be done about them? The social critique of normalcy is also an effective tool for calling attention to what has become another socially accepted response to disability, namely, that it is a medical problem, a sickness to be cured, or a condition that needs to be fixed.

Disability rights activists and scholars have placed the medicalization of disability into a historical context that emphasizes the vestiges of eugenics. Medical testing, such as in utero screening for disability, deformity, and gender, allows parents the opportunity to abort a child if it doesn't conform to their standards. The deeply ingrained societal attitude "better dead than disabled" also informs the right to die movement and keeps alive the notion that to be disabled is to be living an unworthy existence, or that life with a disability is not worth living at all. The repercussions of these ideas in the lives of people living with disabilities are profound.[9] If the attitude that disability leads to a poor quality of life is widely accepted, and if newly disabled people are allowed to end their lives under these assumptions, the lives of those who choose to live are compromised, especially if euthanasia and assisted suicide become legalized or routine. In other words, if the societal response to my brother is that his life is not worth living, how will that belief inform the care that he is liable to receive the next time he needs medical attention?

Identity politics has been an efficacious way to deconstruct power as well as to describe and celebrate difference within a hegemoni-

culture that marginalizes difference, including disability. It has been pointed out, however, that identity politics embraces the very categorization of other that has been used to legitimate power over those who are marginalized. To identify someone as a person of color, as queer, female, transgendered, or disabled, means to embrace the very categories used to systematically oppress. In his book *Bending Over Backwards: Disability, Dismodernism & Other Difficult Positions*, literary critic and disability studies scholar Lennard Davis suggests that disability can offer a new understanding of difference that has the potential to reshape identity politics as well as our understanding of what it means to have a disability, what he calls the *dismodern*. In part because the category of disability is so large, unwieldy, and potentially inclusive (we all have vulnerable bodies), Davis suggests a reworking *Disability Is Us* of the exclusive "them" of identity studies into an "us" that recognizes our social collectivity[10] and the unstable and malleable category of disability. He writes:

> We should not go on record as saying that disability is a fixed identity, when the power behind the concept is that disability presents us with a malleable view of the human body and identity . . . The dismodern era ushers in the concept that difference is what all of us have in common. That identity is not fixed but malleable. That technology is not separate but part of the body. That dependence, not individual independence, is the rule.[11]

In other words, difference is us. Davis goes on to say,

> While there is no race, there is still racism. But dismodernism argues for a commonality of bodies within the notion of difference. It is too easy to say, "We're all disabled." But it is possible to say that we are all disabled by injustice and oppression of various kinds. We are all nonstandard, and it is under that standard that we should be able to found the dismodernist ethic.[12]

A new understanding of difference, one that is inclusive of the changeability of bodies and the diversity of disability, has been an influential idea in the shaping of my film.

Demystify Difference, Then Redefine It

This idea emerges from both the content and the form of the film in a variety of ways. First, the representational history of disability is revealed as the foundation for popular attitudes. Contemporary footage I shoot interrupts erroneous footage from the archive, extending the critique of this history into the present and setting a new goal of redefining difference through the device of the interview. This may seem obvious practice for a documentary, but when disability is the subject, it is not. In all the archival materials I have so far uncovered, the person with the disability is silenced on-screen, both by the discourse of the film and by the apparatus of the institution in which the film is set—doctor's office, state institution, or segregated school. It is common for people with disabilities to be overlooked by society or not addressed at all. In documentary practice, the formal interview signals authority. The person speaking on-camera not only speaks for herself, she shapes and directs the discourse of the film.

LAURA
KISSEL

I intend to shoot two types of interviews. First, I focus on oral histories, in order to construct a people's history of disability, to document how individuals have been subjected to confinement in an institution, for example, and how they have responded to this predicament through protest or other activist means.

These interviews may last for an hour or more when they are shot, with the goal of collecting the most information about the person's life as possible. Aspects of these interviews will be included in the final cut of the film to extend the histories reflected in the archival footage into the present. Moreover, the oral history interviews are important beyond my film, because they document a marginalized history of which the public is unaware.

The second type of interview I am conducting serves the purpose of redefining difference and challenging audiences to look at and listen to people with disabilities in new ways.

These interviews are shot at eye level, which involves a different camera height and orientation for each subject, depending on whether he or she is seated, lying down, or standing. In an effort to actively engage the audience, a three-quarters frontal profile (implying a single listener) is rejected in favor of direct address to the camera. Direct address implores an audience to remain active and responsive to what is being said, in effect, directly to them. Questions asked include: "What do you most dislike about the way in which people who don't know you claim to 'understand' you or speak to you? Why do you think this is the case?" And "Describe an ordinary day in your life." Because many people with significant disabilities rely on other people to interpret their desires, caretakers and friends may be in the frame with the person being interviewed. In these interviews, the able-bodied friend's responses and interactions help reveal the unique qualities of the re lationship. This strategy enables the audience to view an interaction between someone who is able-bodied and someone who has a disability; more powerfully, it begins to define the dismodern: we are a social collectivity; it is "us" and not "them," and difference is that which we all have in common. The nondisabled viewer is called on to see herself as part of the story, as part of the collectivity that is being expressed.

If voiceover is used at all, it will not be disembodied but locatable and definable, from a source within the frame. Each voice is associated with a unique person. This means that computerized voices are also used, mixed in with noncomputerized voices that are slow, careful, quiet, slurred, or otherwise unique. The use of voiceover with cutaway shots, or b-roll, is potentially problematic, because for many people with disabilities, technology is part of the body, and gesture is also part of the body and used as a language, to signify meaning. Technology enables bodies that have disabilities to be more mobile, upright, dialogic; battery-powered wheelchairs operate at the slight touch of a joystick, offering freedom and mobility; computers construct words and sentences, then speak. Technology of all kinds—be it communication or medical technology—means adaptability and freedom. In the absence of technology-enabled speech, gesture can suffice; eyes, sounds, and other nonverbal forms of communication are very much like speech. Interviews, then, must also show the malleability of *voice*. We all glance, sigh, look down, or otherwise pause; sometimes we are silent. What can and do these signals mean if we truly understand them as part of language? They are useful, expressive, and functional. By foregrounding gesture as a form of speech, the traditional voiceover becomes impossible. Cutaway shots detract from our engagement with the person in front of us; if we are not looking with attention, we might miss an expressive statement that is offered through gaze, gesture, or other means. My interviews privilege face-to-face interaction and closeness. They create intimate opportunities for listening, a simple act that is readily discarded in daily life when the person we face is someone with a significant disability.

Finally, I keep in mind throughout the process of filming and editing the idea that we are all potentially disabled. Perhaps it is this awareness that so disturbs people when they encounter a person with a disability; it reminds them of their own vulnerability. Lennard Davis offers another idea that I find compelling for my film, which has the combined goals of critiquing difference, examining the representational images of disability, and challenging the attitudes they foster. Davis names the nondisabled observer's encounter with disability as a kind of disturbance, "a disruption in the sensory field of the observer."

28   This is a guiding analysis for my film, equally as important as the interrogation of normalcy. People with disabilities do not commonly define themselves as different, as abnormal, with lives that are deficient. "Disability, in this sense, is located in the observer, not the observed, and is therefore more about the viewer than about the person using a cane or a wheelchair."[13] The private, individual observation of disability has been made public through the cinematic eye, through a history of looking at disability, a history that supports an equally disruptive image. Images have been used to shock and disrupt; more insidious is perhaps the observation of disability to manipulate ideas that breed harmful attitudes, especially when they are used to deny people with disabilities their civil rights.

LAURA
KISSEL
      The apparatus of the camera and the discourses that surround the act of gazing at others are implicated in the archival materials I use. I want to challenge this history of voyeurism, of looking in on difference in such a way that it is marginalized even further. Because I use the same device of the camera that is implicated in this history, my effort is not to look *at* disability but to look toward and with the person who is speaking. In so doing, I interrogate the reasons behind every shot, ask permission to take every shot, and get feedback from my subjects about how they'd like to be imaged on camera. I rely on my subjects to let me know how they'd like to be interviewed and what they'd like to be doing while the interview is conducted. Also, there are two unique forms of looking privileged in my film. First, people with disabilities look *with the audience* at the archive, in a gaze of shared witness, at *a mass of bodies* that have been compromised. We are all outside this deplorable history, yet the discourse of the film urges its acknowledgment. And in the process of gazing together toward the past, our spectatorship positions, disabled and nondisabled, then split: people with disabilities live each day of their lives in a struggle against narrow understandings that the archive reveals; able-bodied people, unaffected by this history, unknowingly allow ill-conceived attitudes about disability to continue. Both spectators witness history, but able-bodied audiences are urged to become active participants as they meet people whose lives articulate the desire to be visible and to stay alive, despite disability.

Production Concerns: Funding, Copyright, and Distribution Strategies

A pragmatic concern in the early stages of research and idea development for a documentary that relies on the archival record is, where wil the money come from to pay for this history? It is a well-known fact that the acquisition of rights to use archival footage is an expensive and often restrictive enterprise. The recent case of *Eyes on the Prize,* a documentary routinely characterized as our shared national memory of the civil rights movement, illustrates the conditional terms involved in the purchase of archival materials. The producers must now raise a half-million dollars or more to renew their license of the archival materials in order to continue to distribute the film. The cost to obtain archival material already impacts the research for my film. For example, a rare copy of *Are You Fit to Marry?,* a spin-off, re-release of *The Black Stork,* is now owned by an individual in New Jersey. This rights holder charges researchers a couple hundred dollars for a vhs transfer of the film with a burned-in time code. The use of only a few seconds of this footage, and the cost to obtain a transfer for postproduction work, are also excessive, likely precluding my use of this material. In the case of clips I intend to use from educational films produced thirty or forty years ago, I will have to undertake some detective work to locate current rights holders. If the copyright holders cannot be found, I will retain a record of my "good faith" effort and claim fair use of the material. In cases where I use popular Hollywood films that I would never be able to acquire the rights to, I will also invoke the fair use clause to cover my use because I am using popular films chiefly for the purpose of cultural and political commentary.[14]

Financing for the film will be creative, with funds derived from a combination of grants, individuals with a stake in the politics of the film, and state organizations mandated to change their systems of support for people with disabilities. Needless to say, meager personal funds are always used, and I try to find crews who will work for free or deferred pay; this enables funds to be used for travel expenses, equipment rental, and other production costs. Other avenues for funding include startup grants or seed money; there are a few fellowships and workshops for documentary productions in the early stages of production, to develop rough cuts, scripts, or trailers. A highly competitive production fund is allocated by itvs for projects produced in cooperation with a local PBS affiliate station. Local stations are often short of funds for independent productions but eager to provide in-kind services (equipment, postproduction facilities, closed captioning services, etc.) in exchange for the opportunity to exhibit, broadcast, or promote work that reflects in some way the interests of the station—be it support of independent producers or the subject matter of the film, which might have regional import as well as national significance. For *Disability Is Us,* I am investigating all of these options.

Finally, in the case of archival materials, festival rights are cheaper to acquire than broadcast rights. A budget might initially restrict the purchase of broadcast rights, but it can also force the filmmaker to en- vision a distribution strategy that continues the life of the film beyond the initial broadcast or a festival tour. A broadcast audience is usually captive and passive, yet an audience that views a film in a public place as a collective group can be given ways to respond to the message of the film that are meaningful, direct, and specific. My plan for *Disability Is Us* is to connect the film to the work of disability rights activists, with the hope that my film can be effectively integrated into campaigns that are already under way.[15]

LAURA
KISSEL

Recovering and Recycling the Past: The Work of Media Archaeology

Acting as both archaeologist and recycler in my hunt for the film record of disability, I am searching for and researching media images and their associated narratives, in the hope that their exposure, dissection, and repurposing will bring context, voice, and new political purpose to the disability rights movement. The reemergence of a storied past of segregation, pity, and euthanasia, when collaged with new images that witness and resist this past, sets the stage for a progressive politi- cal future. Like an archaeologist, I search for and reexpose artifacts; as a recycler (and editor), I reprocess these images and reuse them to bring about new, imaginative possibilities for the contextualization of the disability rights movement. My approach to these images is aca- demic and intellectual. I am interested in the archive as a repository of institutional and personal ideology, as a messy place that provides an opportunity to map histories that are submerged, invisible. Moreover, my strategy to reexpose these images creates an emotional import that influences audiences to challenge equally submerged attitudes, espe- cially when the images are mixed with contemporary footage from the disability rights movement.

I outline below a diversity of archival sources and contemporary im- ages that evidence popular attitudes and powerfully ingrained ideolo- gies about disability. Archival images not only provide visual counter point to my own images but, through their reuse in another context and through experimental techniques of collage, layering, looping and other forms of manipulation, they are turned into evidence o deeply held social, cultural, and political beliefs that the disabilit rights movement fights against. Contemporary images of protest wor.

in opposition to this history and provide context and import for the change in popular attitudes that my film promotes.

"Today you can't find freaks very easily. There aren't a great many of them left."

FAIRGROUND WORKER,
INTERVIEWED FOR A LOCAL NEWS
SHOW IN COLUMBIA, SOUTH
CAROLINA, 1967

Early newsreel camera crews were often dispatched around the world to capture the culture of the everyday. Camera crews for Fox News (after the coming of sound, Fox Movietone News) were directed to search for images of "oddities," the unusual or unexpected. For example, *Glass Eater* (1929) shows a man eating and swallowing glass. Unusual bodies, classified then as "freaks," are found in outtakes and stories such as *Major Mite, World's Smallest Man* (1922), and *Coney Island Freaks* (1924). In the Fox newsreel outtakes, there is significant footage documenting the history of disability. Examples include *Legless Automobile* (1922), a demonstration of an early motorized wheelchair, and *Legless Traffic Cop* (1923), featuring an amputee directing traffic from a skateboard-like device and later seen climbing a ladder and diving into a pool. Several stories and outtakes of famous Siamese twins and other well-known circus and carnival acts of the day are found throughout the collection, offering significant cultural views of disability from the early twentieth century. There are also films of historic import, specifically *Legless Automobile* (1922), which shows a demonstration of an early motorized wheelchair invented by Arthur M. Van Rensselaer. In the footage, Van Rensselaer is seen surrounded by a group of men on crutches as he climbs into the "automobile," shows off its hand controls, and drives it down a New York City sidewalk. According to Van Rensselaer's own press release announcing this demonstration, "The machine is a motor propelled three wheeled vehicle, 32 in. wide and 76 in. long, built to hold one person. It is operated entirely by hand control." The newsreel cameraman must have found this event interesting enough, because a record was made of it. Whether the draw was an assembled group of "crippled" men watching the demonstration, the machine, or Mr. Van Rensselaer himself, the film is an important document of disability history and possibly the first motion picture depicting a wheelchair user.

Disability Is Us

In the nineteenth century, people who had medically based physical abnormalities or otherwise exaggerated physical traits were highly
sought after for display in dime museums, fairs, and traveling freak
shows. The approach to disability was that unusual qualities of the
body were "freaks of nature" or the result of trauma suffered by the
mother when she was pregnant. Promoters of freak shows relied on
an audience's lack of knowledge as well as its curiosity and voyeuristic
tendencies to exploit the exhibition of people who lacked limbs or were
otherwise extremely shaped or sized. The exhibition of bodies began to
decline when disability became absorbed by the rise of medical profes-
sionalism and birth defects could be explained away by science; however, some shows remained viable well into the mid-twentieth century,
LAURA
KISSEL   as evidenced by a 1967 interview with a South Carolina fairground
worker, who stands in front of a sign painted with the words "FREAKS"
and "STRANGE" and exclaims, "I have a lead on an outstanding freak
that I hope to bring to Columbia next year. In the hinterlands of Ven-
ezuela, there is a girl I've been told about there who has a sister—she
should have been twins—but for some reason nature made a little
mistake and so she has another body growing out of the abdomen."
        This film and several others I have located are useful in portraying
this voyeuristic, display-oriented approach to disability. Others include
the Fox Newsfilm outtakes *Coney Island Freaks* (1924) and *Brockton Fair*
(1929), the latter an early sound film that allows the audience to listen in
on fair workers as they exhibit previews of the oddities inside the tent.
        One of the oddities shows a person with microcephaly performing
for the audience. People with microcephaly, a misshapen skull resulting in mental retardation, were commonly exhibited as "pinheads."
Coney Island Freaks (1924) contains a shot of the most famous micro-
cephalic exhibition, a man known as Zip, or What Is It? His popular
name alone affords an opportunity to critique the display of people
with disabilities as strange, a phenomenon that solidified the concept
of difference as it pertains to body shape, size, or ability. Finally, an
orphaned home movie I obtained will be useful as counterpoint to
these public newsreel views because it offers a rare inside view of a
freak show tent. This film shows a number of physically altered bodies, disabled or otherwise extreme, on a stage from the point of view
of the audience. It is a private view of disability that I make public, an
image that offers an opportunity to critique objectification and draw
attention to the construction of "us" and "them"—able-bodied and disabled. These early images serve the content of my film because they
reveal the multiplicity of ways that disability has been seen by those
outside its experience. They are also examples of the use of the cam

era to peer in on disability, to frame it as something strange, and to foreground difference. The camera is complicit in the construction of this difference by holding the image up to an audience as that which should be put on display.

> *You can blame the Black Stork for much of crime, poverty and misery. The White Stork brings us the babies that should make for a nation of power.*
> INTERTITLES, *THE BLACK STORK* (1916, PAPER PRINT)

The Black Stork was produced by Dr. Harry Haiselden, a Chicago doctor who became well-known across the United States for his refusal to treat disabled babies. A narrative propaganda film in support of eugenics, its exhibition began in 1916 with its initial release and continued as late as the early 1940s, and included a reedited version titled *Are You Fit to Marry?*, released in 1927.[16] There is one known exhibition print and research copy of the 1927 version; I have seen only a substantial paper print fragment of the 1916 version. I plan to reuse aspects of this paper print in my film, not only because it reveals the eugenic response to disability but because it is the perfect vessel for exploring the "better dead than disabled" attitude, which remains a popular response to disability.

I am intrigued by this paper print, by its narrative construction, its propagandistic intertitles, and even its physical appearance as a taped-, stapled-, and riveted-together fragile fragment hidden inside box no. 109 with the catalog number LC-MBRS, #LU-9978. My ideas about repurposing this fragment extend from reprinting it to animate parts of the story to using successive still frames of the intertitles and the people with disabilities represented to create an awkward, animated feel that is repetitive and mechanical. Many frames of this film lend themselves well to both visual and textual analysis. One frame affords an iris view of a hunched-over body, clearly disfigured. The iris motif, a black background with the disabled body encircled in the center of a field of blackness, guides the viewer to look toward the disfigurement, and objectifies the body. In another frame a doctor holds up a baby before the camera, rotating its body so that it can be studied and viewed from multiple vantage points. The narrative and intertitles surrounding these images argue that deformed individuals—whether disfigured, infected, or otherwise compromised—should not repro-

duce. "You can blame the Black Stork for much of crime, poverty ar
misery," exclaims an intertitle. The message is clear: blame the persc
with a disability for society's ills. Ultimately, *The Black Stork* argues f
the elimination of weakness through selective breeding and the dea
of disabled babies. At the conclusion of the film, a doctor stands over
woman and her newly born "defective" child: The doctor exclaims, "It
wrong to operate to prolong a useless life. . . . It was the will of God th
the child be born defective. . . . God does not want that child to live

As an outgrowth of eugenics, the attitude of better dead than di
abled remains common, as was recently illustrated in Clint Eastwood
film *Million Dollar Baby* (2005), which became a favored film of criti
and fans as well as of the Hollywood establishment, which voted it fo

Oscars. Critics profusely praised the film, specifically relishing i
"surprise" ending, which was often withheld in reviews. The protag
nist in the film, a down-on-her-luck waitress named Maggie, manage
to escape her impoverished, welfare-cheating, poorly educated (ar
deeply stereotyped) southern family to become a famous female boxe
Midway through the film, after the montage sequence detailing h
rise to glory, Maggie is seriously injured by an illegal blow to her hea
She falls, cracking her neck, and ends up a quadriplegic. Maggie's la
days in the nursing home that provides her care are dark, desolat
empty. She is barely moved from her bed, and receives no rehabilit
tion. Instead, in great melodramatic style, she asks her trainer-coac
Frankie, to kill her.

The disability this character incurs immediately crushes the figh
ing spirit that defined her rise as a boxer. Her disability is given e
traordinary power, so much so that the message portrayed when sh
asks for euthanasia is that it is better to be dead than to be disabled. A
disability rights activist Stephen Drake writes, "This movie is a corn
melodramatic assault on people with disabilities. It plays out killing a
a romantic fantasy and gives emotional life to the 'better dead than di
abled' mindset lurking in the heart of the typical (read: nondisable
audience member."[17] I envision a radical recombination of the deat
scene in *Million Dollar Baby* with animated sequences of *The Bla
Stork* death scene to illustrate how both films urge the extinguishme
of disability.

*"Pity? [If] you don't want to be
pitied because you're a cripple in d
wheelchair, stay in your house!"*
JERRY LEWIS, INTERVIEWED ON
CBS SUNDAY MORNING IN 2001

Most telethon shows manipulate an audience into giving money by 35
urging viewers to pity what is represented. Telethons routinely depict
the recipient of charity as helpless, situate the viewing audience outside the "trauma" being depicted, and plead to the unaffected viewer
for a donation to "save" a person's life. While the Jerry Lewis MDA—
Muscular Dystrophy Association—Telethon may have contributed
millions to research on neuromuscular diseases, it has done so at the
expense of humiliating people with disabilities. As disability rights
activist and lawyer Harriet McBryde Johnson, who leads an annual
MDA Telethon protest in Charleston, South Carolina, underscores in
her memoir, "the message [of the MDA Telethon] denies the worth and
value of such lives as they are."[18] Similarly, when people express to   *Disability Is Us*
me that they are "sorry" about my brother's disability, their attitude
is based on an assumption that his life is not okay as it is. Jerry Lewis
has continued to promote, well into his forty-plus years as spokesper-
son for the MDA, the attitude that people with disabilities are powerless
and that pity, rather than an agenda of rights for people with disabilities, should be the national response. The MDA message is antiquated,
and Jerry Lewis's message is virulent[19]; both ignore thirty-five years
of work of the disability rights movement. These ideas undergird this
scene in my film.

I introduced myself to Harriet Johnson after reading an article she
wrote for the *New York Times Magazine* about her debate with Peter
Singer, a prominent philosopher and animal rights activist who believes, among other things, that babies born with disabilities should
die. I asked her immediately to be a subject for my film, at which
point she hesitated, and rightly so. At the time, she was finishing her
memoir and other articles, keeping a busy law practice, and otherwise
committed to disability rights work. She did invite me to attend and
film her annual protest against the Jerry Lewis MDA Telethon, held
every year in Charleston, South Carolina, for the past fifteen years.
Hurricane Frances sidelined this shoot in 2004, but I kept in touch
with Harriet and filmed the protest in September 2005. Her memoir,
Too Late to Die Young, includes a chapter on the colorful history of
Charleston's telethon protest, which she expounded upon in person:
"In Charleston, our protests are very polite." When I arrived to shoot
the event, I found a handful of friendly supporters bearing colorful
handmade signs and handing out bright yellow fliers that summarized the grievances against Jerry Lewis. There was no shouting, and
most passersby took the fliers that were handed them, with a "thank
you, sir" or "yes, ma'am." Most seemed open to the message, though a
few responded with hostility of various kinds.

I asked a number of young people in Charleston what they thought of the Jerry Lewis MDA Telethon. The most common response was, "Who is Jerry Lewis?" Though clearly no longer the presence on television they once were, the MDA Telethon images have done their part to promote pity as a typical response to disability. My plan for this portion of the film is to showcase the work of Harriet Johnson's disability rights protest and to intercut images of action and protest with footage from past MDA Telethons, to enable and bolster the critique that is offered by Harriet and other protest participants. For example, one woman joining the protest in Charleston recalls watching Jerry Lewis force a child to walk across the stage at the telethon, to prove to the audience how he'd been made "victim" to a neuromuscular disease and to draw

LAURA
KISSEL

attention to his disability. She explains that her own daughter can't walk, and that this telethon scene was humiliating, not only to the child being depicted on national television as unable to walk but also to her daughter and to her personally. Ideally, I will intercut her story with images from the telethon that illustrate her argument. I envision this scene in my documentary as one that follows typical documentary form by setting up point and counterpoint with images and words.

Finally, images of protest, polite or otherwise, are exceedingly important to my film's argument. Because so many people with disabilities are fighting a history of segregation and invisibility, scenes of protest are far from typical. They are a necessary and vital part of the film's goal to make the invisible history of disability visible and to challenge the attitude that people with disabilities should be seen at all. In a protest I filmed in 2003, disability rights activists and their supporters marched for two weeks from Philadelphia to Washington, D.C., to draw attention to a Medicaid bill that would provide funding to support people in integrated settings, instead of the now mandated long-term care facility—a nursing home or a state institution. A common response of passersby when they saw 150-plus wheelchair users powering down the highway with protest signs and flags was, "Is this a parade?" The public assumption is that people with disabilities aren't dangerous or capable of dissent, and that if they are in public, they must be on display, perhaps for the public's enjoyment. *Is this a parade?* also highlights the surprise factor for nondisabled people when people in wheelchairs are suddenly visible, en masse. Harriet Johnson describes this visibility factor well when she writes, "If you're alone in a public place and you happen to be in a wheelchair, nondisabled people tend to assume something's seriously amiss—you're stranded, your nurse has run off, you're dazed and disoriented, you need to get back to the nursing home."[20]

"Few of these girls will know the normal experiences of childhood; few will know the pleasure of home and family life. The institution is the only place they have been happy."

VOICEOVER FROM *TOYMAKERS* (1963), A TELEVISION DOCUMENTARY

Numerous attempts to manage or control disability have been undertaken in the name of medical and social progress, including the warehousing of people with disabilities in large, state-run or private institutions, what Harriet McBryde Johnson has referred to as "the disability gulag." The support for institutions is prevalent in many industrial and training films from the middle to the latter half of the twentieth century. These films were used to educate a workforce and the public, and they define a response to disability that foregrounds and supports segregation and is often disguised as a humane response. Many of these training films urge support for the institutions they profile either outwardly, through voiceover, or indirectly, by portraying the institution as the only response to a hopeless situation. As the voiceover authoritatively proclaims in *Toymakers,* when the camera focuses on a child who has been picked up from the floor where a dozen or more severely disabled children lie, "There is no cure for Marie's condition." The children on the floor are looked upon by the camera and by the narrative of the film as a mass of bodies, abandoned and alone.

Disability Is Us

I have collected many clips from films like this one that establish and describe the setting of an institution. One film, *Teaching the Mentally Retarded: A Positive Approach,* shows a woman "training" a young boy to sit still, tie his shoelaces, and perform other tasks. She points around the room and he complies; at the end of each task he completes, she gives him a treat. It is an astonishing sequence: the interaction is grossly similar to how people interact with dogs when the dogs are being trained. I imagine constructing a rhythmic collage of shots of this woman mechanically pointing and feeding the child, over and over again. The shots might be edited together to emphasize not only the control she exhibits over the child but the way she demands responses and activities from him that have no meaning or agency behind them, such as "Sit in this chair." It is important to me that my use of training and educational films from the recent past clearly describe to the audience how the response they exhibit toward disability has no imagination, exhibits no effort to understand people as individuals who have passions, hopes, and dreams. Watching these films, I can't help but wonder what has happened to the people in these films. How many of them are dead? Do some still live in institutions? I cannot help but have a deeply personal response to these images from the 1960s and 1970s: this could have been my brother's life if my parents had taken their doctor's advice.

A New Conversation

LAURA
KISSEL

We do not have, have never had, and seem incapable of having, a realistic national public conversation about life as a severely disabled person. And so we have no way to really understand—no way to believe, as a society—that it is all right to be disabled. We have no social consensus that it's all right to live with a disability.

MARY JOHNSON, *RAGGED EDGE MAGAZINE*

I am deeply committed to making this film, not only because I have a personal stake in its message but also because there is a gap in our public conversation about disability, and little to no national press coverage of the disability rights movement. As I finish this chapter, activists in Tennessee are on their third month of a sit-in at the Tennessee governor's office to protest the institutional bias of their state's Medicaid funding, a bias that forces people to live in state institutions rather than in their own homes. It is the longest occupation of a government office in history, and it is not even in the news. Even as history is being made, it is being forgotten.

Once my film is finished and begins to circulate, it will take on a life and a meaning that I cannot now envision. I have hopes for the film. I want it to instigate the national public conversation that activists say we've never had. I want it to be useful, troubling, poetic, and deeply resonant. I want it to teach. I want it to challenge able-bodied people who have never thought creatively or critically about disability or difference. And, ultimately, I want it to motivate all of us to see disability as part of our own lives. Disability is *us*.

Disability Is Us

Laura Kissel at work on *Disability Is Us*. (Photograph by Mark Gamble,
Spare Room Media.)

Notes

The writing of this chapter was partially supported by a grant from the University of South Carolina Research and Productive Scholarship Fund.

1. This text is excerpted from two sequential intertitle cards on a paper print fragment of the film *The Black Stork*, a pro-eugenics film produced in the United States in 1916 and later re-released as the film *Are You Fit to Marry?* in 1927.

2. The Americans with Disabilities Act was signed on July 26, 1990, by President George H. W. Bush. The ADA is a civil rights bill that prohibits discrimination in employment and guarantees access to transportation, telecommunications, and public and private buildings.

3. For a digital timeline of events in the social, cultural, and political history of disability, see San Francisco State University's Institute on Disability Web site: http://www.instituteondisability.org/.

4. ADAPT is a national disability rights organization dedicated to the use of civil disobedience and direct action to bring about social change. Founded before the ADA, ADAPT stood for Americans Disabled for Accessible Public Transit. ADAPT has since changed its name to Americans Disabled for Attendant Programs Today and agitates for an end to institutionalization as a long-term care solution.

5. Patricia Zimmermann, "A Manifesto for Reverse Engineering: Algorithms for Recombinant Histories." I am inspired by Zimmermann's insistence to see the archive as never static but constantly moving, with the power to evoke new temporalities, possibilities, futures. Quoting further, "Histories and stories are always retold and retold

differently, moving from the speaker to the listener, from the state to the everyday, from the interface to the body, from the virtuoso to the amateur." This idea holds particular relevance for a film that is ultimately about bodies—recovering the history of their manipulation and destruction—and combining and collaging this evidence with the image of the modern, disabled body, a body that is fluid, redefinable, interfacing with technology: motorized wheelchair, feeding tube, digital alphabet board, speaking computers. Technology means freedom for people with disabilities.

6. The term *eugenics*, meaning "good birth," was coined by English scientist Frances Galton in 1883. Galton was a cousin of Charles Darwin, whose concepts of natural selection and survival of the fittest influenced the eugenic notion of selective breeding ("good marriage") and sterilization to weed out "degenerates."

7. Jeff Bishop, "County OKs Rezoning for Mentally Retarded Facility," *The Calhoun Times,* July 10, 2003.

8. Lennard J. Davis, *Bending Over Backwards: Disability, Dismodernism & Other Difficult Positions* (New York: New York University Press, 2002), 38 and 32.

9. For legal and social arguments about the euthanasia movement's impact on the rights of the severely disabled, the activist group Not Dead Yet (www.notdeadyet.org) is an excellent source.

10. Davis, *Bending Over Backwards,* 44.

11. Ibid., 26.

12. Ibid., 31–32.

13. Ibid., 50.

14. The Center for Social Media at American University has developed a "best practices" statement on fair use that clarifies the term and outlines how filmmakers can invoke fair use in their work.

15. Working Films (www.workingfilms.org) is a nonprofit organization that partners with filmmakers and activists to develop issue-driven, grassroots campaigns that merge the work of documentary film with the work of activists for the purpose of social change.

16. Martin S. Pernick, *The Black Stork: Eugenics and the Death of "Defective" Babies in American Medicine and Motion Pictures Since 1915* (New York: Oxford University Press, 1996), 6.

17. Stephen Drake, "Dangerous Times," *Ragged Edge Magazine* (online), January 11, 2005.

18. Harriet McBryde Johnson, *Too Late to Die Young: Nearly True Tales from a Life* (New York: Henry Holt, 2005), 51.

19. Jerry Lewis infamously expounded on his own attitudes toward disability in an article for *Parade Magazine* in 1990 in which he referred to wheelchairs as a "steel imprisonment" and to people with disabilities as "half persons." A chapter in Johnson' memoir, "Honk If You Hate Telethons," contains a summary of this article and her response to Lewis's and the telethon's messages.

20. Johnson, *Too Late,* 59.

CHAPTER 2 *"I Saw You Naked"*

"HARD" ACTING IN "GAY" MOVIES

Christopher Bradley
(Arizona State University)

I was starring in this independent film, *Leather Jacket Love Story*. It was playing at an art house on Sunset Boulevard in Los Angeles, and I was featured prominently on the poster displayed out front. With no clothes on. You couldn't see anything, really, but I was naked when we shot the photo. *Leather Jacket Love Story* was not a pornographic film, but the marketing seemed designed to make it appear that way.

At the same time, I was also a cater-waiter. Sweating, carrying four plates of coq au vin at a time to tables full of brittle rich people. This particular night, I was wearing a tuxedo I'd purchased to go to the Cannes Film Festival eight years before, when I was promoting another movie I'd hoped would be my breakthrough. It was a 1930s-style gangster movie called *Killer Instinct,* my first leading role. The film ended up going straight to video, but I was very proud of my work in it, and the other actors were great. Janusz Kaminski, who would soon win an Academy Award for *Schindler's List,* was our cinematographer.

But I was performing a far less glamorous duty in the tuxedo tonight. Serving from the right. Clearing from the left. Don't think. Just get the food out. Don't make eye contact with the customers. Customers were always trying to make eye contact. They wanted you to break ranks and go get them that cup of coffee *right now.* Or that salad fork or that dessert spoon or low-fat creamer. Once you'd made eye contact, you had to either make them mad by saying no or make the catering captain mad by breaking ranks and getting it for them.

But I accidentally did make eye contact. With this willowy, dark-haired aristocratic twinkie-boy. His eyes went wide when he saw me. He poked a long, creamy finger in my direction and shrieked, "I saw you naked!"

I froze.

"Didn't I? That was you, wasn't it? In that movie! I saw you in that movie! And you were naked! Isn't that you?"

Everyone at his table was waiting expectantly for my answer.

"Yes," I said, my jaw a little tight.

"Wow. Nice!" He sensed my discomfort. "What's wrong? Don't be embarrassed! If I had a cock like that, I'd want to show it off, too!" His tablemates laughed.

My face was on fire with anger and humiliation. I wanted to grind the food right into his bony little face.

But I didn't. I thanked him and gently placed his plate in front of him and retreated as quickly as I could. I meant the film to be much more than that.

As I walked back to the kitchen, a million thoughts ran through my mind. I thought about the huge risk I'd taken in making that movie—being gay and starring in a gay independent film, something that just wasn't done at that time. A film with a nude love scene, no less. There were casting directors over the years who had refused to call me in just because they'd heard that I *might* be gay. If this risk didn't pay off, things were going to be far worse in that regard.

I thought about the cover story interview I'd done for *Genre* magazine in which I'd spoken openly about being gay, when everyone would have understood (and even supported me) if I'd lied and said I had a girlfriend. How many gay actors have taken that route over the years? I thought about how my agent told me not to do *Leather Jacket Love Story* because it would ruin my career, and how I'd refused to budge. I thought about my bold plan to be the first gay actor to make it big while telling the truth right from the start, rather than after years of lying.

"The first gay actor to make it big telling the truth right from the start?" Where did this plan begin?

I was gay bashed in 1989. I couldn't believe it when it was happening. Halloween in West Hollywood. I was cornered, and I'd been kicked to the ground twice. I was yelling at the gay men obliviously passing by in wild costumes that I was being gay bashed. They looked at me as if I were screaming in a foreign language, and kept walking. It's hard to imagine that happening now, but this was before the political consciousness and rage of political groups like ACT UP.

My jacket was pulled over my head and I was being punched and kicked when a carload of lesbians heard me and stopped in traffic When these women started piling out of their car, the gay bashers ran

In the weeks and months that followed, I became filled with the strange courage that blossoms after something one has always feared finally happens. And I had an idea how to test that courage.

I'd known Stephen Kolzak, the openly gay casting director of the television show *Cheers,* for a couple of years at that time. He was in th

advanced stages of AIDS, and seemed full of the same rage I was. I read
an interview with him in one of the gay weekly magazines in which he
sneered at closeted people in the industry. He decried the cowardice of
these gay performers.

I called him and I told him what I thought was a brilliant idea. "No
actor has ever been 'out' right from the start and become a movie star
before," I enthused. "Some have come out, or been forced out, once
they got to the top, but no one's ever told the truth right from the beginning. I'm going to do that!"

I expected him to shout for joy.

He just got quiet.

He said, "I applaud you for being willing to take that on. I don't
know what would happen if you actually tried that, but I think it's great
you want to."

I was suddenly embarrassed, the way you feel when you notice a
cool breeze blowing through your open fly. I knew what I was suggesting was stupid. No one had to tell me that. But it was stupid in
that old-Hollywood, crazy-underdog-beating-the-odds kind of way. Not
stupid stupid.

I understand his reaction better now. It's one thing to suggest in
the abstract that someone, somewhere, toss his career on the bonfire
for "the cause." It's another to watch someone you believe in, and like,
actually do it. And he might have been a tiny bit embarrassed by my
"watch me single-handedly save the world" arrogance.

At the time, I thought, "Okay. Stephen Kolzak isn't going to be my
cheerleader. Maybe no one else will be, either. I don't need cheerlead-
ers! The first step in accomplishing anything is asserting that it *can* be
done, and I say that it can!"

Willing as I was to talk about being gay, it was a long time before
anyone asked.

In 1992 and 1993, I played Sheriff Dillon's son-in-law in two of the
five "reunion" movies based on the old *Gunsmoke* television series of
the 1960s and 1970s. Everything about my career at that time looked
great from the outside. I had fourth billing after three well-established
actors—James Arness, James Brolin, and Ali McGraw. I was being
paid almost $5,000 for two weeks of work, not much compared to the
astronomically high salaries some actors get, but far more than I'd
ever been paid before. And by playing Sheriff Dillon's son-in-law, I was
now part of the *Gunsmoke* "universe," which was thrilling.

The scripts for the *Gunsmoke* made-for-TV movies were not bad, but
they were standard television fare. Sheriff Dillon is framed for murder by an old enemy in one, and he teaches a teenager the dangers of

vigilante justice in the other—the kind of fare that doesn't challenge viewers in any way and keeps them on the couch long enough to sell them laundry detergent and fast food.

But I love working, and I love creating a character. In this case, no one seemed to care whether the acting was good or not, but *I* wanted it to be good. In one scene, we're riding in a stagecoach being attacked by bandits. I'm shot in the leg during a dramatic gun battle. Doing my character homework before the shoot, I would push a pencil eraser into the side of my thigh as hard as I could, until it really hurt, for as long as I could stand it, to get some sense of where the bullet wound might be, and to give myself some distant idea of what the pain might be like.

CHRISTOPHER
BRADLEY

This all backfired on me in a pretty funny way. Another character in this same gun battle scene is shot in the arm. Later, when I'm being pulled from the stagecoach in what looks like realistic pain, he jumps out with a bloodied arm, and he's just fine. The effect was not, "That first actor was very real and convincing." It was more, "That first actor is a cry-baby. Look—that other guy got shot and it didn't even hurt!"

The director didn't speak to me much during the filming. He and the producer seemed unhappy during the first film, and even more unhappy during the second. The tension trickled down to almost everyone. I didn't have access to any behind-the-scenes information, but later I read an article about the television show *Murder, She Wrote*. The article said that despite its high ratings, *Murder, She Wrote* was not loved by the studio executives because the advertising demographic skewed so old. The *Murder, She Wrote* viewers, despite their huge numbers, did not have the purchasing power of teenagers and young adults. I think something similar might have been going on with these *Gunsmoke* movies. The director and producer were perhaps being treated as unimportant by the network.

The first movie got a decent screening on the studio lot. It won its time slot by a healthy margin when it aired. One would imagine that the next movie would be given similar treatment, but it wasn't. It did equally well in the ratings, but there was no real screening. On the afternoon of the air date, CBS allowed the cast and crew to meet in an executive lunchroom at Television City and watch the satellite feed from New York, where it was airing first. The director and producer did not attend. I'm only guessing, but these sorts of slights may have been happening while we were filming.

At this same time, I had a commercial for Miller beer running. was playing a truck driver in the Arizona desert. There were no other actors in the commercial, just me and an animated cactus. Nothing

artistically satisfying, but the commercial ran consistently and kept
me afloat financially.

This may have looked good from the outside, but inside I was squirming. I had played a standard-issue "stalwart young man" in the *Gunsmoke* movies and was little more than a model in the beer commercial. It wasn't that I was ungrateful. I knew how lucky I was to be where I was, but there wasn't any passion in it. I felt uncomfortably off-track.

Part of my discomfort was that incredibly exciting things were starting to happen in independent film. Several gay-themed independent films came out around that time, including *Grief* and Greg Araki's *The Living End*. I was sick of watching the entertainment industry tiptoe around gay themes, and these films were unapologetic and groundbreaking and thrilling. The gay characters did not commit suicide at the end. They were not murdered. They were not clandestine saboteurs of the American family. Nor were they representative of the other extreme—noble victims of homophobia. The characters in *Grief* are flawed in authentic, funny, and fully human ways. The take-charge HIV-infected gay men in *The Living End* are angry, bold, and dangerous.

I looked across the chasm from where I was to where these films were. I wasn't sure how I was going to get there, but I knew where I wanted to go.

I'd heard a lot of these films were cast through the actors' and directors' theater connections. I joined an Equity waiver theater company called Mojo Ensemble, a company dedicated to producing only locally written plays. They were getting great reviews for their fresh and courageous work, including *Washington Square Moves,* a play about brilliant but drug-addicted homeless people winning chess tournaments in Washington Square Park, and *Lester and the Argonauts,* a play about a man trying to put his life back together after being released from jail, having been sentenced for running over a child while driving drunk. Keeping a small theater company going in L.A. is extraordinarily challenging, particularly one doing unknown plays by unknown authors, but Mojo Ensemble managed to scrape by for several years, and I was very proud to have been a part of it.

I also joined an improvisational comedy group that performed a brilliantly subversive gay comic soap opera called *The Plush Life* in the basement of a Mexican restaurant in Silver Lake. The show eagerly embraced the cheap glamour, the cheap sexuality, and the self-dramatizing martyrdom of American soap operas, and American society in general, to a point that was both hilarious and repulsive.

I loved the adrenaline shot of doing live improv. Tommy O'Haver, a director who a few years later would cast me in his breakthrough independent film, *Billy's Hollywood Screen Kiss,* was a fan.

Almost immediately after I joined these two companies, my mainstream work disappeared. The metaphysically inclined might say, "The universe knew you were looking for something else." The paranoid might say, "You got close enough to breaking through and the television executives started asking around about you and they didn't like what they heard." Both of those may be true, but I think it's more likely that when I found something I loved, something that felt right, my interest in going in the direction that *didn't* feel right just naturally fell away.

I enjoyed three artistically satisfying years of this mostly unpaid theater work, but I found myself no closer to my goal of being an independent film actor. It was time to retrench. There's an old proverb, "Ride the horse in the direction it's going." I was doing the kind of work in theater that I wanted to be doing in film, so if theater work and not film work was what was happening, maybe I should move to New York, where I might actually make a living at it. I gave up my apartment, agreed to move in with a friend in New York, and bought a plane ticket. Then my agent sent me the screenplay for *Leather Jacket Love Story.*

I read the character Mike for the director. He wanted me for the role right away. The producer, too. My agent got cold feet. "Don't do it, Chris. It'll ruin your career."

What? No! I hadn't worked in a film for three years. It was a great role. I was perfect for it. I'd never played anything like this character before. The story was about a gay man who has given up on intimacy and later opens himself back up to the possibility of falling in love. It was a story I believed in and wanted to tell.

In queer studies scholar David Halperin's essay, *What Do Gay Men Want? An Essay on Sex, Risk and Subjectivity,*[1] the author invites the reader to move beyond discussions of sexuality in terms of right/wrong or healthy/pathological dichotomies. Most gay films, and perhaps most films in general, deal with sexuality in these terms, particularly when dealing with less standard sexual practices. This screenplay was different.

For instance, the second time Mike and his love interest, Kyle, have sex, Mike pushes Kyle face down on the bed and brings out a pair of handcuffs. Kyle refuses to participate. This is not because of a moral objection. The screenplay has already established that Kyle has sadomasochistic fantasies. Kyle's objection is Mike's inability to authentically connect. When Mike angrily pulls away, Kyle tenderly brings hi

back, keeping firm eye contact and initiating a true, passionate sexual
connection. The story isn't making a judgment here, it's showing a
character opening up to a new possibility.

I knew my agent was concerned about the nudity and the subject
matter. So was I. But this was the kind of challenging, even scary,
independent film work I wanted to be doing. I wasn't going to walk
away from this role for fear of what mainstream Hollywood producers
might think. I signed the contract.

The director wanted to get the nude scenes out of the way first, fear-
ing that the other actor and I would get cold feet. We didn't. The nude
scenes were just work for the most part, though I do remember thinking as I dropped my pants, "Okay. No going back now." I knew this was
going to take my life in an entirely different direction.

The scene went fine. The whole film shoot went fine. We were on a
very tight schedule, and for many scenes I got only one take. My theater work served me well, as after all, you get only one take on stage.
The director pulled me aside several times and thanked me for my
good work, for being so prepared. It was fun, and we had the whole
thing finished, in the can, on schedule, in ten days.

I stuck to my plan to move to New York, not convinced that landing
this one film job was more than an anomaly. Some months later I was
sitting in a theater in Greenwich Village watching *Leather Jacket Love
Story*.

I was naturally concerned about the sex scenes, but I was excited to
see my work as an actor on the screen. When I read these scenes in the
script, I imagined them as the erotically intense but ultimately empty
acts of a lost soul. My character, Mike, has a strong underlying anger
to his sexuality. For example, late in the film, I openly flirt with other
guys in front of Kyle in a low-key, emotionally sadistic way. This same
anger is seething under the surface in the sex scenes. Because I know
what I was thinking during the filming, I can see it on the screen.
But as presented in the film, this emotional color is completely undermined by wacky, quick-cut editing and an underscoring that sounds
like xylophone music. For reasons I can't figure out, the scene keeps
cutting away to two smiling muscle-boy dolls in Speedos posed on a
nearby dresser under a plastic palm tree.

There was additional nudity shot when I wasn't on the set. A sex
club scene is briefly described in the script. Kyle takes a quick and unhappy trip to this sex club before he meets Mike and decides he wants
something more. The screenplay paints these sex club scenes as grim
and ugly, contrasting them to the beauty of the authentic sexual connection Kyle finds later. In the film, the sex club scenes go on forever,

the camera moving sensuously, lingering over warmly lit nude bodies. The theme of the screenplay is that the only sex worth having is sex with true intimacy, but the way the sex club scenes are shot completely undermines that theme, making what the screenplay tells you *not* to want—that is, empty, anonymous sex—beautiful and appealing. I can only imagine that this decision was made from a marketing perspective, not a storytelling perspective. Perhaps they decided that more graphic sex would mean more sales, even if it didn't make sense in regard to the story.

This scene was also repositioned in the final edit. In the screenplay, the sex club scenes take place before Kyle meets Mike. In the final edit, they happen late in the story, after Kyle and Mike have had a fight. Kyle says over and over that he wants intimacy, but after one fight with the man of his dreams he's off to a sex club? Again, the story's theme is significantly undermined.

As a professional, I knew this could happen. Scenes can be reedited and recontextualized to say something completely different from the original intention. It had just never happened to me. I got a taste of how it feels to lose control of your own image to marketing sensibilities, an editor's razor, and ultimately an audience's interpretation of your work.

I was eager to do publicity for the film, thinking I might be able to frame it for audiences and critics before they saw it, perhaps preventing them from seeing it as soft-core porn. I took a train from New York to Baltimore, where the film was playing in a gay and lesbian film festival. I was to be introduced before the screening along with Mink Stole, an actress who was also in the film, known mostly for her work with legendary independent film director John Waters. And John Waters himself was going to be there.

When I was introduced at the screening, the emcee asked if anyone had any questions. No hands went up. I took advantage of the silence to tell them some things I thought would be useful. I told them the film had cost only $90,000 to produce. I told them that when the producers didn't get a reasonable offer from a distributor, they formed their own distribution company and released it themselves. I said, "We don't have to wait for the approval of the mainstream. We don't have to suck up to them. We can tell our own stories the way we want to tell them. We can make our own films and release them ourselves!"

I searched their faces for any sign of someone being inspired. Nothing I could see.

I couldn't find John Waters afterward.

Ten years earlier, I had had a tiny four-line part in *An Early Frost* a brave 1985 TV movie about AIDS. At the gym the day after it aired, a 49 stranger came up to me and said, "I saw you in that movie last night. I called my parents afterward and told them I was gay. I felt like I had to."

That was the kind of impact I wanted to have in the world. That was why I wanted to be in gay independent films. I wanted to break things open for people, I wanted to show everyone there was nothing to be afraid of. I wanted to be the hero, the risk taker, the guy that stood up for social justice.

On the trip home from Baltimore I wrote in my journal, letting my mind wander. I wrote about small-town New Jersey whipping by the train windows. A church steeple among the trees blurring past. Old houses standing shoulder to shoulder. A brick chimney on a factory. Intrusive, confrontational, corrugated tin industrial buildings standing naked, flesh-yellow and seventy-five feet high. An office park nestled in a forest of leafy trees.

"Hard" Acting in "Gay" Movies

All a blur as they go by. There and gone too quickly to be more than glimpsed. Wooden palettes rotting in the sun. Two-thirds of a wooden box, burst open and spilling gravel. A scrap of a bright blue tarp. And so many people I'm overwhelmed. Graffiti tags cover the bridge supports, but we're moving too fast for anyone to read them, if anyone wanted to. Do the taggers even suspect this? They would have to write their names thousands of times before they registered with anyone, before someone said, "Hey, I've seen that tag before." But out here, even that would be pointless. Everything goes by too fast. It's all wasted effort. "See my name! Remember me! If only for the enormous, destructive mess I've made! At least it's something!" But one can only glimpse the blurred defacement. The identity of the person who did the defacing is lost. One bridge underpass has been hastily painted white, covering up the screamed names, but doing nothing so much as providing a clean, blank slate for the next demand for acknowledgment.

Like those taggers, I may have overestimated how many people would actually hear me, how many people would know I was there. Maybe fifty thousand people saw *Leather Jacket Love Story*. What percentage of them gave the performers any thought beyond the film? How many of the people who gave the performers any thought were filmmakers? *Genre* magazine has a readership of perhaps a few hundred thousand. Of those, how many people actually read the interview? Of those, how many thought about it later?

Another problem was that I seemed to be confusing gay identity with gay community. You don't have a choice for the most part about identity. A black identity or a gay identity is pretty much assigned by outside historical and social forces. The only real choice about identity is whether you're going to hide from the assigned label or lie about your qualifications for it. Community, on the other hand, is something in which you consciously participate. Community is a choice—a choice sometimes made from moment to moment.

Like a drunken rock star, I leapt off the stage of my career into what I saw as the gay community, certain their hands would grab me and hold me up. I hit the concrete hard.

I had a distorted expectation of the impact the actions of an individual are likely to have. Yes, the actions of individuals can sometimes effect enormous change, but the forces at play in a society are

CHRISTOPHER
BRADLEY

incredibly complex. An expectation that just because one has clarity of personal vision, everything else will fall into place, is bound to lead to disappointment.

As film theorist Geoff King says in his book *American Independent Cinema,* "Independent features offering alternative social perspectives are often dependent on the existence of niche audiences, rooted in particular social groups." However, "there is no guarantee that audiences defined in terms of one specific attribute according to which they are denied adequate representation in the mainstream (such as race or sexual orientation) are likely to have radical or alternative tastes in other respects."[2] It's not that the gay community doesn't exist but that it doesn't exist in the way I understood it. Communities are not homogeneous. The people who form communities around social issues and social identities will almost certainly have hundreds if not thousands of competing additional agendas moving like tectonic plates in all sorts of unpredictable directions. For better or for worse, gay people are all over the map politically and socially. Many consider their race, their cultural identity, their political affiliations, or their religious traditions to be much higher priorities than their sexual orientation.

So I hit the concrete. When I moved back to Los Angeles, the agent who had warned me not to do *Leather Jacket Love Story* turned me down for representation. I met with a number of other agents, who also declined. Was this evidence of a "ruined" career? Was it part of a quiet conspiracy not to sign gay actors who come out? I admit I had that paranoid fantasy then, but it seems unlikely now. I think it was simply that the work I'd been doing was not the kind of work that was likely to produce significant income for a talent agency.

I'd taken a huge risk and it hadn't turned out the way I'd hoped. Work was sparse, but I had something emotionally solid inside.

I arranged my life so that I could deal with the realities of where

I was. Maybe I'd never have an agent again. I'd make it work. Maybe it would be career winter forever. I'd build an igloo and just make it work.

My career wasn't ruined, but it did have to change. Actors must be persistent in the face of rejection. I continued to work through my own professional relationships, my own footwork, and some of the good fortune that has followed me throughout my life.

For example, a number of years after *Leather Jacket Love Story* came out, a director named Reid Waterer happened to see that film and *Billy's Hollywood Screen Kiss* on consecutive days. He said, "It occurred to me driving home, 'Hey! That was the same actor!'" He did some digging and started looking at my other work. "You're so different in everything you do!" He promised himself if he ever got a feature off the ground, he'd put me in it. He did. I played the wheelchair-bound Ivan in *The Deviants,* his independent film about a matchmaking organization for people who believe they're too bizarre for anyone to love them.

So what I dreamed would happen eventually did happen, just not with the speed or on the scale I'd hoped. But given how unlikely I now understand it all was, it was a nice little miracle.

And springtime did come.

The world changed. Ellen DeGeneres came out. Rosie O'Donnell came out. Chad Allen from the television series *Dr. Quinn, Medicine Woman* came out. Randy Harrison, one of the actors from the American version of the television series *Queer as Folk,* casually acknowledged he was gay. In queer theorist Richard Dyer's *Now You See It,* the author asserts that "the political aim of lesbian/gay representation should be to infiltrate popular culture in order to engage wider queer and straight audiences."[3] This aim was being realized. The ice broke up so suddenly it was hard to believe.

Recently I was at a party with a large gathering of gay men. I was introduced to a group of people. One of the guys pointed at me and said, "Hey, you're that guy in that movie. In *Leather Jacket Love Story.*"

"Yes?" I was afraid of where this might be going.

He said, "Dude, that's like a gay independent film classic!"

I smiled, relieved.

"You should be really proud of your work in that."

And another little miracle happened. Two casting directors who had always liked my work, Perry Bullington and Bob MacDonald, had dinner with the director of *Leather Jacket Love Story.* They asked him how I was doing. He told them I didn't have an agent. They sprang into action and started making phone calls. They set up a meeting for me with a new manager.

The manager I had back in the 1980s warned me that no one was to ever know I was gay. I told this new manager I wasn't going to lie about it. She looked at me with some confusion and said, "No one cares about that anymore."

Thirty years of tightness went out of my body.

About a month later, I booked a nice guest star part on a FOX TV show called "Standoff." It was a fun set, a good script, and the regulars on the show all took time to introduce themselves to the guest cast. I played a psychiatrist. A heterosexual psychiatrist. I've known the casting director for many years and he knows I'm gay. Every actor fears being typecast, but to my happy surprise, it wasn't happening.

The world changes. It changes by human volition. We are not passive pawns. Creating change in the world demands not only a sense of one's own power to effect change, but also humility, knowing that the work is bigger than any individual. It demands a trust that you are part of a community, but not the expectation that your community will act in one voice. This is not, perhaps, a romanticized version of the "gay community," with its rainbow-themed merchandise, but a real, invisible community. One of diverse yet common interests, diverse yet common concerns, diverse yet common values, and a history that includes both gay and straight people.

The fight is certainly not over.

About a year before he died, I heard Abraham Polonsky speak. Polonsky was one of the "Hollywood Ten," the screenwriters, directors, and performers who refused to name names in the infamous Joseph McCarthy communism trials in the 1950s. After the lecture, a member of the audience asked Polonsky, "Looking back at everything that happened, was it worth it? Was standing up to the House Un-American Activities Committee worth it?"

Polonsky didn't miss a beat. He said, "Absolutely not." I caught my breath. He said, "I lost my livelihood. I lost my home. I lost my outlet for creative expression. No. It was absolutely not 'worth it.'" But then his eyes twinkled. He said, "And I wouldn't have done it any other way. It was a losing battle from the start. But losing battles are the only ones worth taking on."

"Is it worth it?" is the wrong question. The question isn't "Will this pay off?" or "Will I get what I want if I make this sacrifice?" The question is, "Who am I in the world? What do I stand for? How am I going to humbly use my great power as an individual?" These are questions for actors, writers, producers, and directors—for all of us. An artist needs to answer those questions and make his or her choice accordingly.

CHRISTOPHER BRADLEY

We all run the risk that it won't be "worth it." But what fun is it to take on a battle you're sure to win? Losing battles are the only ones worth fighting. And we just might be winning this one.

I had an acting teacher who used to say, "Acting is telling lies for a living." If an actor is good, they take something invented—a "lie," if you will—and make it seem real. But, paradoxically, no art is worthwhile if it doesn't communicate truth.

Art is about communicating truths that create change. That's not to say the communication has to be heavy and serious. Ideas can be packaged in a million ways, from Shakespeare to sitcoms. If the ideas work, the changes they bring about can be as profound as shaking the foundations of a society or as simple as making someone laugh. But any artistic communication needs truth to work.

Actors are not the roles they play, but somewhere all of us want to believe that Harrison Ford really is Indiana Jones, that he could somehow actually do the things Indiana Jones does. If an actor's real-life actions conflict too strongly with his or her on-screen persona, it can spell doom for their career. Ingrid Bergman's adulterous affair conflicted too strongly with her saintly screen persona. It took years for her career to recover.

Any actor wants to protect his or her image. Building a career is difficult, and the prospect of losing everything because a hidden truth might be revealed is terrifying. For that reason, it's better to build a screen persona, and a life, that can encompass the truth rather than one that can be shattered by a simple revelation.

While the results for me personally have been a mixed bag, I stand by this as self-evident wisdom: Lies in your life will poison your art. Lies will endanger what you've built in your career. If you tell the truth from the beginning, things might not turn out perfectly, but everything you have is really yours. It can't be taken away.

You might manage to single-handedly change the world, but even if you don't, you're part of a larger tide that will.

"Hard" Acting in "Gay" Movies

Notes

1. David Halperin, *What Do Gay Men Want? An Essay on Sex, Risk and Subjectivity* (Ann Arbor: University of Michigan Press, 2007).

2. Geoff King, *American Independent Cinema* (Bloomington: Indiana University Press, 2005), 200.

3. Richard Dyer, *Now You See It: Studies on Lesbian and Gay Film* (New York: Routledge, [1990] 2003), 268.

CHAPTER 3

Pain and Pleasure in the Flesh of Machiko Saito's Experimental Movies

Celine Parreñas Shimizu

(University of California at Santa Barbara)

A photograph lying on the table at a curatorial meeting at the San Francisco Cinematheque features a figure that looks like the human incarnation of a whip—long, lean, and dressed in leather. Stick-like and twisted on a white floor—with the biggest, blackest, and longest hair in the world fanning her spread-eagled body. Who is that? Is it a woman or a man, Asian or Yellowface, or someone in between the established borders of recognizable gendered and racial identities? I search the face for expressions of pain, pleasure, or anything to help me understand the image. I see nothing definitive but something in between, with the long hair and sharp and lean physicality of a dragon lady Fu Manchu. It's simultaneously racial, genderqueer, and sexual. While she is not easily consumed, I find her nothing short of delightful.

The caption names the figure as the filmmaker Machiko Saito in a photo still from her film *Premenstrual Spotting* (1998). Because the intensely racial and sexual image is self-authored, the image becomes even more intriguing. Are viewers ready to see Asian American women making films that don't just protest the hypersexualization of Asian American women in Western cinema but engage such images as the filmmaker's own? Saito seems to use the legibility of the hypersexual Asian woman to articulate a new form of self. If film represents the embodiment of our desires and the power of the imagination to craft new realities, can hers be a world where Asian women can be highly sexual and not self-annihilating but celebratory and real? That is, how do self-authored sexual images present good possibilities for Asian American women within the long-established equation of sexual representation as misrepresentation by others? What's going on here? Why the trafficking in highly charged sexual and racial meanings in her racialized and gendered authorship? More precisely, how is Machiko Saito using difference—race, gender, and sex—and its visible elements to say something about her vision of self and the world? I needed to get hold of her work urgently, immediately, so I could better understand her mobilization of the power of race, sex, and the moving image.

Perhaps the image speaks to me because I'm also an Asian American woman filmmaker obsessed with sexuality—power, pain, and pleasure in its various forms—as feminist practice. In my own short films, I dwell on fucking and other sex acts to illustrate the dynamics of power, desire, and colonial history as they imprint themselves on Asian women. With intense pleasure, I direct a character to offer herself up like dessert in *Mahal Means Love and Expensive* (1993), name my characters versions of the Tagalog word for *vagina* in *Her Uprooting Plants Her* (1995), and shoot numerous vigorous interracial sex scenes in *Super Flip* (1997). Is my commitment to composing representations of Asian American women's sexuality and power—and my subsequent enjoyment of these entanglements in Machiko Saito's films— appropriate and proper to good racial and feminist politics? Meeting Saito in her films, I feel no longer alone; it's cathartic. Momentous! Does Saito, like me, stand alongside others like Margaret Cho, whose political tactics point to how the inappropriate and improper serve for productive expressions of subjugation and power?

CELINE
PARREÑAS
SHIMIZU

My latest video work, *The Fact of Asian Women* (2002–2004), explores how perverse sexuality unifies the representations of Asian American femme fatales in Hollywood. As I argue in my book, *The Hypersexuality of Race: Performing Asian/American Women on Screen and Scene,* as well as in my latest video, Anna May Wong's, Nancy Kwan's, and Lucy Liu's repertoire of roles each represent a different mode of perverse sexuality: dragon lady, prostitute with a heart of gold, and dominatrix. The perversity unifying their representations can be interpreted variously as strength, diversity, or pathology and thus can become a politically productive perversity. By examining what my gaffer Serene Fang called "sexual lighting," what my director of photography Yun Jong Suh described as the looming power of the male gaze in traditional shot compositions, and what my actors Lena Zee, Angelina Cheng, and Kim Jiang delivered in their performances, I locate the original Asian American femme fatales' performances somewhere between the wound of sexual racialization and the remedy of pleasure in visual and sexual representations of race. Their performances and our consumption express desire for identities that include radical expressions of sexuality as part of our very human desires, including authorial expressions and spectatorial needs of pleasure, pain, and power.

In this chapter, I examine the commingling of race, sex, and gender

difference in experimental cinema by Asian American women filmmakers. I show how Machiko Saito and I are Asian American feminist
filmmakers who dramatize the role of sexuality and eroticism in the
experience of race and cinema in order to create subjectivities for Asian
American women not solely constituted by race but also connected to
gender and sexuality, as well as representation. In other words, because the representation of Asian Americans is too frequently associated with an excessive and perverse sexuality, Asian American women
filmmakers find the language and subject of sexuality necessary to
their expression. As filmmakers, whether by accident or on purpose,
we engage sexuality in order to transform established representation
and create subjectivity in terms that demand recognition.

As such, this is simultaneously a response to and a critique of the interpretation of
racial and sexual images as simply tools to discipline, oppress,
and police. Such an interpretation places an unfair burden
on Asian American women. It
is a racist demand that Asian
American women abhor their
own carnal sexuality. A form
of docility is required in priori-
tizing racial subjectivity separate from gender and sex. An
example is the way critic Ben
Fong Torres is featured in the

Lena Zee, Angelina Cheng, and Kim Jiang perform various
forms of Asian American female perversity in *The Fact of
Asian Women*. (Photograph by Stephanie Chen, courtesy of
Filmmaker.)

classic Asian American feminist documentary *Slaying the
Dragon* (1989). In his interview,
he renders Asian women spectators as uncritical and powerless in the face of their sexual-
zed images when he draws a
cause-and-effect relationship
between the image and Asian
female desire for white men,
supposedly evidenced by many
out-marriages," or marriages
between Asian American
women and non-Asian Ameri-

Lena Zee performs Anna May Wong on the streets of San Francisco in *The Fact of Asian Women*. (Photograph by Stephanie
Chen, courtesy of Filmmaker.)

can men. In such an evaluation, sexualized images are all-powerful in their ability to disenfranchise and split men and women of color. This equation also romanticizes a "same" race or ethnic coalition without accounting for gender and sexual inequality. And the dynamics of fantasy and imagination in negotiating these images remain unaccounted for. Do all Asian women who out-marry enact racial treachery, as such a critique implies? In this case, sex and representation are marginalized in a diagnosis that prioritizes good, docile womanhood for Asian American women. Borrowing Eve Oishi's term "bad Asians" (whom she describes as frequently queer, and specifically those who refuse the model minority project as a positive one) and Elaine Kim's "bad woman" (her description of feminist Asian American artists who

go against the grain in their formal and political work), I claim the position of bad Asian womanhood in order to expand the roles of Asian American women to include perversity as well as normalcy.[1]

Framing Machiko Saito

Machiko Saito screens films and wins prizes in experimen-

Kim Jiang evokes Lucy Liu's image on the streets of San Francisco in *The Fact of Asian Women*. (Photograph by Stephanie Chen, courtesy of Filmmaker.)

tal film festivals all over the world while working as a filmmaker who eschews the markers of "independence" by barely distributing her own work and resisting the commercial, mainstream marketing of herself. Working in the San Francisco Bay area, she is prominent in the queer community, participating in the Gay, Lesbian, Bisexual, Transgender International Film Festival and other San Francisco international festival venues. Her experimental movies offer a powerful critique of the constraints of normalcy and normative scripts for racialized and sexualized people.

The intriguing photograph described at the beginning of this essay publicizes Machiko Saito's *Premenstrual Spotting*, her award-winning first movie. In this work, Machiko Saito's whiplike physicality hints at practices considered perverse and deviant, such as sadomasochism and bondage. Genderqueer and racially ambiguous in fetish wear, two characters in a subsequent film, *15 Minutes of Femme*, masturbate. One penetrates the other with a large black dildo until the recipient screams with pleasure. Saito does not shy away from "politically incorrect" rep resentations of explicit sexuality, compelling the question, are sexually explicit images made by women, particularly Asian American women filmmakers, dangerous, as products of false consciousness? That is, do sexual images have a negative impact on already marginalized and minoritized communities? Her film representations, dramatizing sadomasochism, bondage, and other women's practices, compel us to ask questions more complicated than whether these scenes are degrading or bad for women. In presenting these acts, she claims them as part of her expression and subjectivity. She says much more about the forms of race, gender, and sexual difference and how to represent what is traditionally considered not normal in cinema. Her goal of striving for representation reaches beyond the established and the normal in order to make space for diverse racial sexualities.

59

Machiko Saito's face appears superimposed on the cityscape in *Hart Schell und Schon.*

Machiko Saito's Movies

Making films that engage the complex dynamics of racialized sexuality in innovative experimental forms, Machiko Saito expands our notions of what film can do to expand what is acceptable in terms of race and sex. Her latest film, *Hart Schell und Schon,* features a blue fetish gear–clad Saito running through the streets of San Francisco, shooting herself in private and in her community. These sequences are intercut with quick shots of brilliant sculptures and images from the underworld of Berlin's art district. Scenes are shot in what appears to be a tenement. Focused on lives on the margins, *Hart Schell und Schon* celebrates a nomadic, cosmopolitan sexual being whose racial identity is not central in that it is only part of a constellation of identities.

Pink Eye documents and narrates Machiko Saito's process of filmmaking. She shoots herself in a pink wig and fetish gear breaking a camera in the middle of shooting. By shooting herself in the process of making film and negotiating her ability to use technology, Saito attempts to illustrate and articulate other facets of her life, including the celebration of sexuality and desire and the problematization of technology in visualizing race and desire. In *Pink Eye,* she takes the camera off the tripod and places it on the floor, then lies down on the floor to peer through the lens before deciding on the camera's final position. This sequence documents the intimate relationship between the woman and the camera. It's intimately part of her body. We see the decision making involved in production by a woman making a film solo. She demonstrates keen awareness of the camera in relation to her body and the power of her own body on screen. Just as in her solo performance as subject and filmmaker in *Premenstrual Spotting*, in *Pink Eye* Saito uses the power of the moving visual image to reveal the complexities and contradictions of gender, race, and sexuality. She experiments with the most visible forms such as cinematography—we watch her positioning the camera, deciding where to move her body in relation to it.

CELINE
PARREÑAS
SHIMIZU

In *15 Minutes of Femme*, selections of infamous moments from Saito's hourlong television show, *Femme TV*, Saito documents the queer community in San Francisco during a festival in which people are dressed in various forms of fetish wear. As a filmmaker she is clearly situated within the community she records, as various attendees holler her name and openly respond to her camera. The video then focuses on sexual relations between genderqueer and racially ambiguous women, a butch and femme lesbian couple, who engage in sex acts and role reversals. The video ends with a violent scene in which a black dildo is stuffed in one of the women's mouths. By focusing on intimate sexual acts that involve tenderness and violence as well as recognition, Saito pushes what is acceptable in queer representations. She does so to explore the relational dynamics expressed in sexual acts between people and to expand our understanding of what we experience during acts of sexuality. She exceeds the goal of simply documenting and recording a community but also shoots intimate sexual acts that help shape that community. She puts video at the service of representing that community and normalizing what might otherwise be considered perverse content and practice. Similarly, *Super Flip* dramatizes various interracial sexual encounters so as to eroticize difference, such as in Filipino-Latina or Filipino-white sex acts, where power shifts and flows.

Moreover, in terms of our films, our production design work intersects. Machiko Saito dons futuristic everyday astronaut wear in *Hart Schell und Schon*, looking into the camera as if into a mirror as she walks down a street in Germany. The image reminds me of my own *The Fact of Asian Women*, in which actresses wear costumes inspired by Hollywood Asian American femme fatales and walk on San Francisco streets in order to show their disjuncture. I attempted to reveal the production, construction, and fabrication of Asian American women on-screen crashing against everyday scenes in ways passersby found shocking and unacceptable in light of their other encounters with Asian American women. Machiko Saito's performance of the

screen version of the Asian woman dragon lady/femme fatale renders the problem differently. She wears the layers of Asian American
femme fatalism as her own. The screen is her, as we see in the scenes
of her own making. Machiko Saito's films focus on the visibility of
sexual, racial, and gender differences. In these examples, we can see
how Machiko Saito makes sexualized images of Asian women while
simultaneously critiquing injuries, harms, and social injustices.

Premenstrual Spotting

Premenstrual Spotting exemplifies the critique of making and looking
at racial and sexual films that attend to the complexity of the human
experience. The film features a racialized sexual subject whose history of family sexual trauma registers visibly in a playful, powerful,
disturbing, and defiant presence on-screen. Working with a definition
of sexuality that insists on the simultaneity of pleasure and trauma,
the Asian woman performing drunkenness in Saito's film renders the
damaging power of sexual abuse visible and the pain one must endure from it as necessarily emergent before any kind of transformation
or consciousness can be realized. In this powerful way, *Premenstrual
Spotting* challenges approaches to racialized sexuality in Asian American film and feminist studies that render sexual representations of the
racial experience as damaging rather than productive political practice,
even when seemingly perverse and thus falsely conscious and dangerous for women of color, who are always already rendered hypersexual
and thus sexually available, not normal and wrong. Her emphasis on
the pain of sexual experiences also amends sex-positive frameworks
that do not account for the different experience and history of racial
subjugation via sexuality.

The opening of *Premenstrual Spotting* suggests a traditional Asian
American autobiographical nonfiction film. The camera zooms into
the still image of family life, but this traditional revelation of the documentary subject is soon interrupted by the appearance of a tall, angular
female figure in leather fetish wear whipping her long body taut. She
is ambiguous: is this a drag queen or a woman playing at being a man
in female drag? The editing is cut fast, as if to the beat of a strobe light
that appears on screen. The cuts are set to jarring music, announcing that this is not a typical confessional. It provides a counterpoint to
what Lisa Lowe calls the generational framework of history-telling in
Asian American narratives.[2] Familiar images of family in home movie
footage are intercut as the strikingly tall, amazingly long-haired and

*Machiko Saito's
Experimental
Movies*

thin figure poses in the shocking white light: images of the father smoking at the dinner table and the mother in a 1960s haircut are juxtaposed with images of the daughter (the figure in drag). Dressed in evening gowns and then in fetish gear or naked, wildly made up, and flaunting a confrontational attitude with the camera, she belts out show tunes in full performance mode of arms flinging and long, long hair, big and teased, flying. In voiceover, the narrator describes getting drunk every night as an adult and the elaborate performance of fetish wear as rehearsing "child's play" through a "superhero" sexual persona. She plays with gender instability and ambiguity, so we never quite pin her down.

The movie is difficult to watch. There is a specter of violence throughout the film in her physical performance—drunken, she falls all over the place, simulating masturbation—and in her description of graphic sex acts when she recounts the sexual abuse by her father. She describes the comfort she feels in bathrooms, spaces that "lock—[so she can] breathe again." Show tunes from a Stephen Sondheim musical featuring the refrain "I'm Still Here!" register the coming together of terror and subjugation with self-acceptance of emerging from those very conditions. The ending of the film features, for example, the reinterpretation of fellatio and sodomy with her father, performed as a six-year-old girl, so that the final shots we see are a form of the money shot but with blood all over her face as she lies spread-eagled in the very bathroom in which she played and performed earlier in the movie. It is in the final moments of the movie that we understand the title as the misnaming of evidence in order to hide the crime. The mother deliberately classifies the blood on her daughter's genitals, evidence of sexual abuse committed by her father, as nothing but "premenstrual spotting." So premenstrual spotting actually refers to what her mother describes as her vaginal and anal bleeding at six years old. In this classification, designed to protect the integrity of the family and mute the daughter's pain and experience, we see the daughter as derivative, unimportant, negated. In the film, she becomes central. The film's language of sexual play and visual pleasure emerges from violence and intertwines with intense trauma regarding surviving sexual violence at home, at the hands of a loved one. The coexpression of the pain of trauma and the joy of survival reminds us of the formative power of sexual experiences. What we see is the collision of her two worlds: an old sexual terror that won't go away haunting her current world. The current subject explodes and overwhelms the past with expressions of pleasure in her body's movements and songs as the reclamation of that ugly, violent, and horrible experience as hers, something she owns, and a force that makes her so that a new subjectivity is born.

Premenstrual Spotting, which Saito shot almost entirely by herself, is the first of her four films, all of which engage with sexuality in experimental form. In our conversation-interview, she described her process of filmmaking:

> I shoot, direct, edit, and create, write, perform and act—whatever
> I feel like. I don't think that I have a specific agenda with my four
> [video] pieces. In *Premenstrual Spotting*, it was a big experiment,
> learning technology, learning how to shoot and edit. I played with
> myself on camera with no intent for anything other than what hap-
> pens in the moment: put on an outfit, put on a [lighting] gel.

For Saito, making the film is about engaging herself as a visual artist or finding another venue as an expressive person. She aims to capture what she sees that the camera does not always get. Because lives like hers are not represented well, she enacts film experiments. *Premenstrual Spotting* did not start out as a film about abuse, but abuse reared its head in the final moments of the film, when she records her voice-over to make sense of the images she captured.

A curator discovered her work when he passed by her editing booth at Artists' Television Access. He saw one frame, and asked to program her film. The incident was purely accidental, for she guarded the film fiercely: "I did not think about entering in film festivals." He saw a shot as she opened and closed the door of her editing room. In its premiere at the giant and highly regarded queer of color festival, MIX NYC, she "felt vulnerable" on seeing her image "staring back at me in the front row—it actually was surprisingly, quite uncomfortable and nauseating." She describes an intensely bodily response to the corpo-reality of the film itself. Her viewing in New York is informed by the context of the film's production in San Francisco. Saito explains the sexuality of the film is "not intentional. . . . Naked does not equal sexy. There's a line in *Premenstrual Spotting*, 'learning to enjoy my sexual-ity.'" In the celebration of sexuality in popular culture today, Saito says, "I feel I was doing it in a way but [also] not. This town [San Francisco] is so sex positive, sex parties. . . . Can we do other things than fuck each other on stage?" Her film is a critique in which pleasure is emphasized at the expense of pain and sexual trauma. In describing the film as a process of discovery rather than one intended to show sexual violence, Saito describes sexual trauma functioning like the return of the repressed. Her first film addresses sexual violence as something that rears its head in the final postproduction process. The work of making the film engages its haunting in the life represented on-screen. For Saito, sexuality is "an innate quality that should be protected, appreciated, enjoyed, and not exploited. . . . It's really unfortunate . . . happens to all women, we feel we have to mask sexuality to protect ourselves. . . . Sex should be fun, intense, and dramatic." Saito's engagements with race, sexuality, and visuality as forces central to life offer new forms of power and pleasure as she wrestles with the Asian woman's sexuality on-screen, making and unmaking her in ways that testify to her resilience in the face of her assignation as simply a derivative subject of race, sex, and gender.

CELINE
PARREÑAS
SHIMIZU

Interview with Machiko Saito

I met Machiko Saito for the first time in Café Flore, San Francisco, on May 29, 2004. She was dressed in cowboy-inspired gear—black hat, tiara, and black fitted ensemble that emphasized her tall, slender body. When we met again in Santa Barbara, where she screened the body of her work at the MultiCultural Center on April 20, 2005, she wore a pvc miniskirt and a plastic bag top emblazoned with "I love nyc"—an outfit she had made. Prior to the screening, the mcc announced that the material the audience was about to see might be difficult to watch due to explicit sexuality and violence. During the question-and-answer session, the crowd enjoyed a long discussion with the filmmaker. In person, she is even more striking, with attentive and aware eyes framed by big black hair. In both interviews, we discussed her process as a filmmaker, as well as her approach to filming sexuality and race.

MACHIKO SAITO: I shoot, direct, edit and create, write, perform and act—whatever I feel like. I don't think that I have a specific agenda with my four [video] pieces. In *Premenstrual Spotting*, it was a big experiment, learning technology, learning how to shoot and edit. I played with myself on camera with no intent for anything other than what happens in the moment: put on an outfit, put on a [lighting] gel. I play music, dance around and create compositions with different shots through movement, lighting, music, angles—almost as I photograph myself moving. I take the experience of [seeing myself] in still photography and make that live. To record in a very visual way the person with eyes open so as to remember them years later. [It's a matter of] documenting and creating why . . . to keep my sanity because I'm crazy, I'm hanging on to a piece of dental floss. [The process] is very isolating, the making of *Premenstrual Spotting*. I shot by myself, a lot of footage. It was difficult to set up, different angles, working alone—99 percent of it. A couple of shots I asked my friend to hold this angle. Most of it [was] shot in an isolated way, editing happened in a dark room twelve hours a day. It was spooky. I was sleep-deprived. I edited in the place at midnight and would hear bumps and creaks at night.

CPS: What about being naked in the movie?

MS: I forgot I was naked in the movie. That's right. How embarrassing. It was unintentional. It was more about how I got this camera and see what happens. I put footage on my shelf for a long time. After a while, I said I guess I should edit. So naive! Started editing, no sound, working exactly with what was live. I should get sound and music. Doing it that way: with no plan, no one guiding you. It was exciting. I picked some music, all very natural and unpredicted. With the rough cut, there was no sync sound. Loud scratching music on CD. I realized with my rough cut of about twenty minutes that it kind of did not make sense. I needed to do something here. With music selected, I added words. At Artists' Television Access, a curator working with New York City MIX festival as a curator asked me if he [could] put four minutes of my short in the show. What are you talking about, I asked him. He had walked by when I cracked open my editing door and said that my work looked good. He needed it in a few weeks. Four minutes! I don't even know what that is—I pretended to know what I was talking about. In two weeks, I busted my ass to get a six-minute work-in-progress. I screened it at New York's MIX. At the NYC Underground Film Festival, it made me sick and nauseated to hear the first monologue, really revealing—me high up there, naked, staring back at me in front row. Embarrassing! I felt vulnerable—it was actually quite painful. [When making my work,] I did not think about entering film festivals. I never thought about them except when I made *Femme TV* (1998)—a trailer for Oxygen Network. They were looking for shows—it sounded great. I stopped thinking about them [eventually], and started making it for myself and it turned into what it was—I made something not for them. It was clips of San Francisco city life—queer community specifically. Is it a movie? Is it a trailer? It remains ambiguous.

In making my work, I act on instinct. I pull from my own experiences and preferences. What I like, what I feel, what I know. My usage is not intentional: naked does not equal sexy. There's a line in *PMS*—"learning to enjoy my sexuality." There's acceptance of individual sexuality. I feel

Machiko Saito's Experimental Movies

like I was doing that but not as a predetermined intention. This town is so sexual, sex parties, sex positivity. Can we do other things than fuck each other on stage? Nothing shocks me—not about sex. I made this about the queer community—nothing like it on TV. Sexuality is more playful, empowering, not sexy. Maybe a hint of that. Sex positive is all great, but sexuality is all-encompassing—I want to depict a strong sense of humor about sexuality—humor is needed, to honor so much about sexuality more than what we see usually. Sex should be fun, intense, and dramatic.

CPS: How did you come to make *PMS*? What led to it?

CELINE
PARREÑAS
SHIMIZU

MS: I really played with myself. I love to shoot stuff and look through the viewfinder and see things. A way of communicating for me—I can never verbally describe what I see—document it, show it, how I want to be seen. Maybe in a distant way, when I do it I just get really excited about the process of shooting. Figure it all out later! All footage never really comes together until after shooting many hours. Every time, I try to learn a new creative skill. Move on to learning craft, sculpting the way a storyline comes about—later. Months between stuff—dinner party, home alone, shot in kitchen. I start with visuals, then add music and a layer of text. Sat there in front of the camera talking. The first mono-logue came off a voiceover tape. Solo theatrical piece, somehow compatible—scouring through paper of found text on my way to record—writing very quickly and rewriting. I need another hour × 3! Editing, writing, rewriting. No idea what I was doing in the mix, sound overlapping. It took only three takes. I used all of it. Editing words to pic-ture is very exciting. Music really works—did not know that was going to happen. I'm attracted to the medium. I began with fashion, design, pho-tography, theater, makeup. I love lighting and editing. Most artists work autobiographically, it would be very hard not to. Coming from yourself, work can be more honest that way. What I like, what I feel is right—that's what's happening. People respond to that.

CPS: I am excited about your future projects.

MS: I want to make more honest work. Not bombarded or discour-aged by technical or traditional ways of working. It's more exciting to learn. Part of the process is new to me—I possess a certain naiveté in my ability to make work. When discoveries are made without other influ-ences, it's not only more exciting, more inspirational. A freshness and an uninhibited edge come along with it rather than taking classes on how to write a feature. So I just watch any movie. It's more exciting to figure out in your own way. I'm really impressed with editing, the whole way it flies. I spend time doing it, figuring it out numerically. I think I can do that, I just feel it. I don't think about it, it's a more intuitive process for me. As an editor, I work on projects not like an operator. It's not cerebral or intellectual but felt. I feel the beat and rhythm of the picture—a lot of people miss the beat. Not everybody can feel that as a dancer, the editing is either too fast or too slow. There are a lot of people who are trained in school, but in editing, you can't really be taught. Film school? Not knocking it, can afford it but no patience. I live in San Francisco, by the seat of my pants. Very hand-to-mouth. How I feel about it is not always a good thing—not a lot of stability, but I live a simple life, [one] I make complicated. I have the desire to make something, it's possible for anyone.

CPS: Let's focus on Asian women and sex. Earlier you said you are not specifically influenced by Asian women. And from past experience, other Asian women hindered your expression and have stifled your creativity and sexuality.

MS: I took a production class with an Asian American teacher. She turned it [my film] off and did not comment on it. I was devastated, felt uncomfortable. There was no comment, really abrupt. This is not cool. I was in turmoil. What should I do? She was mean and not supportive. Asian women don't understand I am different, less traditional. [They] don't want a more original individual. I am less stereotypical. More aggressive and harsher. I don't have a high voice but a "fuck you" voice. No time or energy to be any other way.

CPS: Let's move on to sex. You've said sexuality is an innate quality that should be protected, appreciated, and enjoyed, not exploited.

MS: I am a very sexual person who's developed a harder edge. I would say my sexuality has been concealed, harassed, and violated—a terrible thing. I don't run down stigmatized [however]. In a sense, I am provocative, fun, funny, or comfortable. But it's really unfortunate, happens to all women, we feel we have to mask sexuality to protect ourselves. Some guy followed me home, for example, even if I was wearing sweatpants, sweatshirt, hoodie . . . how do you assess that? What we're wearing? We should be able to walk around in tube-top minis. Part of me thinks when I am more open, I am more normal and nonthreatening. Not bite his head off like I did when I felt hassled. Not like when I get dressed up. Thank God I live in San Francisco; it's more liberal and accepting than New York or Los Angeles. The vibe is still lighter even though we wear sexy stuff on street, I feel more annoyed than threatened.

Machiko Saito's Experimental Movies

C P S: I want to ask you again about the future.

MS: I don't want to talk about the future . . . I want to live in the moment. That's where I want to be: spiritual, soul-searching, stay-in-the-moment, live-in-the-moment approach to the day. I constantly strive for balance. Getting better at it. I combine my work for it to be easier to make. Ultimately it's for me. When it's for other people, it's about responsibility—like the Coalition on Homelessness. Not my regular stuff. With budget cuts, it's harder. I'm doing a couple of PSA's now. When I do work, news reporting, producing, Free Speech TV, music videos—I want to link them all. It's all so hard to balance.

CELINE
PARREÑAS
SHIMIZU

Making Bad Objects, Posing Good Questions

How to go about making sense of the power of Machiko Saito's work? She expresses the experiences of sexuality, sexual desire, acts, and identities in representation, in ways that need to be accounted for in current understanding of representations of racialized sexuality today. Her works defy the logic of race panics regarding sex and visuality by insisting on using explicit sex as the grounds for articulating and redefining their identities. If Asian women are overly determined by hypersexuality, she takes on that premise and shows how that sexuality needs to be considered in order to express and understand Asian women and others who exist in the margins today because of their relationship to unattainable constraints of normalcy.[3] She uses sexuality and representation to point to the inadequacies of frameworks that reject the importance of their experiences and expressions.

By studying Saito's work, we formulate that sexual and scopic pleasures are essential to defining and understanding the sexual experiences of Asian women and the problem of their representation. As such, we must reject any accusations of race traitorship, false consciousness, and complicity that can arise when looking at the works of feminist filmmakers who embrace sexual "perversity." Asian American feminist filmmakers imagine different futures beyond violence against women and other the tendency to frame women as derivative to men in perception and analyses. Machiko Saito broadens the questions by centering Asian American women's experiences. She invites us to include sexual abuse and violence against women as important matters in racial representation. She uses film to expand our ideas of what is acceptable and what must be included as viable aspects of the self. By embracing both perversity and pleasure as political and sexuality as crucial to race and identity, in film and in the audience, Saito shows us how sexuality and visuality expand the definitions of the Asian American experience.

Moreover, Saito represents explicit sex acts as sites for the recognition of oneself and one's relations within and beyond hypersexuality, but also to innovate cinematic form. Saito's experimental works articulate a racialized sexuality that is simultaneously terrorist and terrific. Her redefinition of sexuality challenges conceptions of gender and sexuality in an important way. Her films artfully provide the evidence we need to make sure the sexual experiences of women, no matter how uncomfortable and difficult, are accounted for in our definitions of racial agendas and communities. The discomfort Saito aims for is the ultimate goal for a filmmaker: to create space for subjectivities previously marked as worthless and undervalued because they did not meet the standards of normalcy for good Asian women.

In Saito's movies, the relationship between sexuality and race is not premised on repugnance, victimization, or damage. Rather, Asian American feminist filmmakers demand that we as audience, in the broadest sense, acknowledge as central different sexual practices in the experiences of gendered and racial subjects. This strongly counters the hypersexuality Asian women inherit in popular movies and stages a reclamation of sexuality as enabling and essential to any imaginings and articulations of the self. As such, her work challenges us to rise toward creative spectatorships and authorships regarding Asian female subjection. We need to imagine sexuality not as antithetical to the politics of race but as essential to its envisioning.

Saito's films enable me to imagine a more inclusive world, an agenda that informs my own filmmaking. My current documentary project speaks to lives located in the margins, similar to Saito's. It also extends Saito's work in terms of placing the margins within an encounter with those who locate themselves in the center. My documentary film, entitled *Birthright,* consists of a series of interviews with about fifty new mothers from Santa Barbara, California. As the project cannot represent all mothers, it focuses on the limits and possibilities of different forms of community as women raise their kids in unequal situations.

Mothers are frequently assumed to be natural caregivers and so are charged with the role of primary caregiver. As a result, mothering becomes an intense site of personal, social, and community pressure for women. As such, it is an extraordinary nexus in which to explore the lives of women, especially those living in California today. If motherhood is the life-altering event women describe, do they become active citizens and community organizers through their specific experiences as mothers? How are they shaped by women with different experiences of mothering whom they encounter in and out of mothers' groups, and how do they understand mothering as a unique experience?

The film raises a few key questions by using mothers' groups as an organizing device. Does the practice of mothers or new parents' groups inherently exclude some participants by including only those with the time, resources, and access to such services? Is there a privileging of particular mothers who fulfill a common understanding and assumptions of traditionally good motherhood? That is, how do financial constraints, racial concerns, gendered experiences, and sexual lifestyles shape mothering in expected and unexpected ways in the early twenty-first century, particularly in California and a community such as Santa Barbara? Also important are questions about what the women themselves share culturally across their differences. Does it benefit them equally to befriend each other as mothers? How do they transform each other's lives? For example, a single working-class mother of two has become best friends with a highly educated, successful, stay-at-home mother of two with two nannies. At the same time that they deviate radically, they also share some concerns, backgrounds, and styles of mothering. My documentary explores how a connection between these two could be possible. Perhaps they are one example of a new type of community formed around the nexus of motherhood that might otherwise not emerge in a racially and socially stratified Santa Barbara. Loaded with cultural preconceptions and investments, mothering is particularly suited to examining issues of cultural divides, social responsibility, community, and citizenship.

The film interrogates the spaces between the realities described by my interviewees, the ideals presented in popular and consumer culture, and the issues raised in the academic literature regarding mothering. In this way, a critical element of the piece is the act of talking about the most intimate aspects of private lives in public in order to address the ways in which women of various communities face challenges to motherhood today. That is, while social advancements for women are seemingly secured in a world where feminist struggle established changed definitions of motherhood and womanhood, many needs are still unmet across different identity groups, from wealthy moms with in-home care to working moms and single mothers without family support. How do women unable (or unwilling) to fulfil normalized, standard roles for mothers, such as unwed single straight moms, lesbian or bisexual moms, and working-outside-the-home moms, benefit (or not) from class-, race-, and sexuality-based contem

CELINE
PARREÑAS
SHIMIZU

porary definitions of good mothering or good gender? Some of my interviewees include such mothers, as well as those who seemingly fulfill normative definitions of good mothers.

Through the intimacies of disclosures within mothers' groups, I am interested in bringing together on camera diverse and divergent voices that may at first, on such a listing of "types," register simply as stereo- types. Some of the mothers I have identified include single mothers with abusive or absent boyfriends; low-wage working mothers, such as a nanny who cares for children other than her own; a nonprofit ser- vice worker who barely makes ends meet; a professional woman who struggles with Santa Barbara's high cost of living; a mother working three jobs; and stay-at-home mothers who struggle with absent hus- bands, volunteer commitments, and the loss of identity established in *Machiko Saito's* former jobs. But in drawing on the specificity of their stories, partic- *Experimental* ularly in shared locations where women perform mothering, such as *Movies* focus groups in the nonprofit organizations, parks, beaches, and other sites, I show how mothers transform, change, and save each other's lives in ways that redefine friendship, community, and belonging.

While my work focuses on mothers, who are also sexual beings, my work intersects with Machiko Saito's characters beyond the de- bates of sexual normalcy and perversity. We share paying attention to method and the same devotion to pressing a situation for its truths and accuracies, no matter how shocking, even in the guise of the safe and normal—the mother versus the sexually free agent. Machiko Saito and I use film to recognize our subjects—usually ones deemed unworthy—through the power of film to create love for its subject through the camera. In capturing the focus of the spectators, I hope to achieve what Loni Ding describes as the process of looking long enough at someone that the possibility of falling in love with her or him opens.[4] Through the power of film to expand our ideas of who should be loved, worlds can then transform.

Notes

This essay includes part of a chapter originally published in Celine Parreñas Shimizu, *The Hypersexuality of Race: Performing Asian-American Women on Screen and Scene,* © 2007 by Duke University Press. All rights reserved. Used by permission of the publisher.

1. See Eve Oishi, "Bad Asians," in *Countervisions,* ed. Darrell Hamamoto and San- ra Liu (Philadelphia: Temple University Press, 2000), 221–242; and Elaine H. Kim, "Bad Women," in *Making More Waves,* ed. Elaine H. Kim, Lilia Villanueva, and Asian Women United (Boston: Beacon Press, 1998), 184–194.

2. Lisa Lowe, "Heterogeneity, Hybridity and Multiplicity," in *Immigrant Acts: On Asian-American Cultural Politics* (Durham, NC: Duke University Press, 1997), 60–83.

3. For a complete interrogation of the concept of hypersexuality for Asian American women, see Celine Parreñas Shimizu, *The Hypersexuality of Race* (Durham, NC: Duke University Press, 2007).

4. Loni Ding, "Strategies of an Asian American Filmmaker," in *Moving the Image*, ed. Russell Leong (Los Angeles: UCLA Asian American Studies Center Press, 1990), 46–59.

CELINE

PARREÑAS

SHIMIZU

PART 2　BORDER VISIONS

CHAPTER 4

Framing Identities / The Evolving Self

BEYOND THE ACADEMIC DIRECTOR

Cristina Kotz Cornejo
(Emerson College)

I am currently in Buenos Aires, Argentina, working toward making my first fiction feature film, *3 Américas* (formerly titled *Soledad*). I have been working on this film for three years while making a career as a maker of short films. I make a living as a teacher and am considered an academic filmmaker, not because I make educational films, which is where the term originally came from, but because I am a filmmaker and I teach film production at the college level. What came first is obvious. I studied filmmaking at New York University's graduate film program and received my MFA in 2000 in film production.

When I was approached to write this essay about filming difference from the perspective of an academic filmmaker, I had to take a step back. Yes, I work in academia, and I realize I am an "academic" filmmaker because of that fact, but as I thought about this on a deeper level I had to ask myself, what exactly does that even mean? As a woman I have been identified as a female filmmaker. Obviously I can't deny my gender, but what if I didn't make films about women? In fact, some of my films aren't about women. Am I still a female filmmaker? As a Latina I have been referred to as a Latina filmmaker, but what would I be called if my work didn't have any relationship to the Latino experience? And again, some of my films don't directly relate to the Latino experience. My very first film, *Jewel and the Catch,* was a documentary about Los Angeles gay rights activist Jewel Thais-Williams.[1] As a gay woman I could have been referred to as a lesbian filmmaker, but *Jewel and the Catch* was the last film I made that had anything to do with being gay. So, are the labels related to my work or solely to who I am as a person? Why the labels? Why the need to categorize?

To answer these questions about my identity as a filmmaker I have to ask several basic questions. Who am I? What am I? Where do I fit in as a person? Where do I fit in as a filmmaker? What kinds of films do I make? What kinds of films are expected of me? What do I expect of myself as a person? What do I expect of myself as a filmmaker? This essay addresses how I have come to identify my work and myself. In it I examine how identity—whether race, gender, or sexuality issues—affects and influences what I do behind the camera based on the experiences that frame my life and my evolving self.

To understand who I am today as a person and filmmaker, it's important to look back at some key life-shaping experiences. My first experience with identity and labels, at least the first one I am aware of, occurred when I was a child and attending kindergarten in Scottsdale, Arizona. I didn't fully speak English because my mother, who is Argentine, spoke to me only in Spanish. I understood English because my father spoke English at home, but I was self-conscious about speak-

ing it in public. One day in class the teacher called on me and, when I didn't answer, told the class I was probably "stupid." I lived in Arizona from the time I was four until I was seven. I got along well with classmates and friends. In fact, I felt and was treated like all the other "Caucasian" children—other than the time I was called stupid.

When I was seven, my family moved to Argentina so that my father could start a business. I attended second grade and began adjusting to a new

Cinematographer Chad Davidson (left) and director Cristina Kotz Cornejo (right) on the set of *3 Américas*.

cultural and educational environment. A year later, during a military coup, my parents decided to move back to the States. For the next several years we lived in Southern California, and my experiences were generally positive. By the time we settled in the Huntington Beach community of Orange County, California, my black hair and dark tanned skin stood out in the mostly white, suburban high school of the early 1980s.

One day at school, during my sophomore year, my best friend called me a "beaner" as a joke. At the time there were few Latinos in Huntington Beach other than the migrants who worked the strawberry fields at the sides of roads. The "undocumented worker" was perceived by many to be responsible for taking work away from Americans and was viewed as a threat to American values, an attitude fueled by the push for bilingual education. Although I was somewhat aware of these

issues, I had not made any connection between my own Argentinean
cultural background and others' perception that I was "Hispanic." My
mother was certainly Latina in culture, but my parents considered our
family to be white, and I was an all-American kid. My best friend knew
my cultural background and knew I traveled to and from Argentina
during the summers. After one of my trips she asked me if we (meaning Argentineans) rode around Buenos Aires in horse and buggy. I
laughed at the ignorance of that question. When it came to knowledge
about South America, I accepted American ignorance.

But matters were getting more serious for me. Shortly after the
beaner comment, I was headed to this same friend's house on my bicycle on a slightly deserted street when I heard the sound of an approaching vehicle and turned to see a Volkswagen bug appear in the
near distance behind me. The car sped up and headed straight for me.
It looked like it was about to hit me. In a panic, I swerved onto the
shoulder and fell to the ground. The driver stopped a few feet away
and a group of guys yelled at me, "Go back to Tijuana, wetback!" They
laughed and drove away. In shock, I picked myself up and rode my
bike to my friend's house, where I said nothing of the incident, as I
was in a state of confusion. I did, however, mention the incident to
my parents. My mom innocently said, "But you're not Mexican," and
reassured me that people are ignorant. My father explained that what
happened was ridiculous because those guys didn't know any better. I
started to think that according to my father, to know better would have
meant realizing that since I was my father's daughter, I was white,
even if I looked Mexican.

This incident became for me a crucial turning point in matters of
race and prejudice. I was beginning to realize the complexity of the situation and that people were simply judging me for whom they thought
they were seeing, a Mexican. Their assumptions were only part of the
picture. Yes, I was Latina, but whether or not I was specifically Mexican did not explain why the surfers in the vw reacted to my identity,
perceived or real, in such a violent manner. I was realizing firsthand
that prejudice was not just a black and white issue, that it could include
other marginalized groups, and for the first time I was a sign of racial
prejudice.

A year later my mom and I decided it would be a good experience
for me to live with her family in Buenos Aires, Argentina, where I
would continue high school. I went to live in a country whose mother
tongue was the very one that had led to my first experience with prejudice, a country with which I felt a deep bond. Ironically, my mathemat-
ics teacher, a stern and unfriendly woman, referred to me as a *gringa*

*Framing
Identities / The
Evolving Self*

in front of my class and lectured about American kids, who according to her were all drug addicts. I was angry, but out of respect for her I said nothing. In Argentina at that time, students did not speak back to their teachers.

A year and a half later I returned to my high school in Huntington Beach and did not resume my previous friendships. Instead, I pursued my emerging interests in film, television, and theater. I worked at Disneyland, immersed myself in photography, took a television production course, and stage-managed school plays. I was chosen by my classmates to represent my school on the PBS/KCET interview show *Why in the World?* My interest in the behind-the-scenes work led me to ask the show's producer and director if I could make weekly visits to the station to observe the taping. They allowed me to create my internship.

CRISTINA
KOTZ
CORNEJO

By this time I had decided that I wanted to work in either film or TV. When I graduated from high school I went to the University of Southern California (USC). I continued my internship with KCET for another year. At USC, I studied international relations. Inspired by USC alumnus Taylor Hackford (*An Officer and a Gentleman*), who before becoming a filmmaker had studied international relations, I thought that the degree would be a good foundation for documentary filmmaking. During this time I became a student activist of sorts, protesting USC's investments in South Africa. I participated in protests at the South African consulate against the apartheid system, from which they would eventually divest. I also met and became friends with African and other international students. As was also true, I suspect, for some readers of this book, it was during my undergraduate experience that I realized I wanted to make films that addressed social injustices and influenced people in a way that mainstream media had failed to. But something else happened in my personal life that would shift my already evolving identity. I met my future partner, a young African American woman, at a piano recital on campus. She and I came out shortly thereafter. It was not an easy time for either of us on what was, at the time, a conservative campus.

After graduating from USC, I decided to pursue a second bachelor's degree in film and television at another local school. I registered for the foundation courses and enrolled in an internship with a Hollywood producer. In one of my writing classes we were given an assignment to write a short fiction screenplay. I adapted one of my favorite Zora Neale Hurston short stories, "Sweat," into a twenty-minute script. My professor returned the script to me and said it was an interesting story. He also said I should get rid of the "awful black dialect" that I had made

point of keeping in the script to maintain the integrity and authenticity of the original story. I was taken aback by his comment. Apparently
the professor was unfamiliar with Zora Neale Hurston's work, and his
comment could easily be perceived as racist; he certainly did not offer
any other explanation. Because of his advanced years, I gave him the
benefit of the doubt and continued to work on the adaptation, but after
two semesters I dropped out of the program when I couldn't register
for some required production courses. This was actually a blessing in
disguise, as I was on a journey I could not foresee. I wanted more from
a film school experience and did not see fighting to get into production
courses worthwhile. I wanted to have camaraderie with classmates,
and I wanted support for my creative ideas. In hindsight, a second
bachelor's degree was not a part of that journey, and had I forced the
issue I would not be where I am today.

I decided that if I couldn't be a filmmaker at that time, maybe I
could create an organization that would support other filmmakers,
particularly women filmmakers of color. In the early 1990s, my partner and I formed an organization called Women of Color Productions
(WOCP). We incorporated it as a 501(c)(3)[2] and decided we would create
a forum for screenings, networking, and possibly funding. Soon after
forming this organization, I began reading up on filmmakers working
outside the Hollywood system. I discovered independent filmmakers
such as Charles Burnett, Julie Dash, Sylvia Morales, Christine Choy,
and Zeinabu irene Davis. I sought out their films at local film festivals
and screenings. Upon discovering this independent film movement,
I realized I didn't want to give up my own dreams of being a filmmaker. By this time I completely identified with the plight of many
marginalized groups. I was more determined than ever to take my
college activism and put it toward something that had power. Under
the auspices of WOCP, I embarked on a documentary on Jewel Thais
Williams, an African American woman who was a leading AIDS/gay
rights activist and owner of the popular Catch One Disco. This was
my first film, titled *Jewel and the Catch*. My partner and I had come to
know Jewel through frequenting her club and attending other events
in the gay and lesbian community. I read every book on filmmaking
I could find, bought a Beaulieu Super 8 camera, wrote a loose script,
and began filming around Los Angeles, specifically at her dance club.
I had finally become a filmmaker, an independent filmmaker in Hollywood at a time before it was even popular to be independent. And
just as happens to any other independent filmmaker, my production
was fraught with technical difficulties, many of which had to do with
lighting and sound. I was shooting Super 8 sound film that was not

suitable for low lighting situations in a dark club with very loud music. I hadn't realized the problems I would face, but I was hooked on film-making. The more problems that arose, the more determined I was to finish the film.

After completing the documentary and screening it at a couple of gay and lesbian festivals in Los Angeles and New York, I decided that I wanted to formally continue my film production studies. I applied to a graduate film program and made it to finalist status. In my interview I spoke of my organization for women of color artists. A Mexican American professor on the interview committee promptly told me that I wasn't a woman of color because people from Argentina are of European descent. He knew nothing about me at that point or about my partly indigenous Argentine grandfather, whose jet-black hair and Huarpe[3] features came through in his granddaughter. I shared with him and the committee my experiences of my Latina identity, but he was unconvinced. He preferred to hold on to his own preconceived prejudices and assumptions. I suppose it's no surprise that I was not admitted to the program (although two years later I would successfully apply to and enroll at NYU Film School).

I was once again learning that identity is something that many times comes from the outside, is imposed on you, and does not come from the inside. It didn't matter that half of me was of East European descent by way of my American father and the other half was Spanish/ indigenous Argentine by way of my mother. In fact, it's that mix of ancestry that has confused a great many people in my life. I've had Algerians approach me and speak to me in Arabic. I've had Italians ask me if I'm Italian. I've had Brazilians speak to me in Portuguese. People see what you look like and see what they want to see, making their judgments on those assumptions. Unfortunately, I realized that day I was nearly run off the road that mistaken identity is not always as welcoming as someone thinking I was their fellow countrywoman. I learned that while some may embrace me because they think I am one of them, others might react with derision, violence, or indifference. People don't always take the time to get to know you for who you really are. Their preconceived ideas are based on their own frame of reference and stereotypes. We all have these prejudices and stereotypes of people. I am no different, but because of my own eye-opening experiences I am very aware of these issues of identity.

My core identity has been shaped by outside events, and these outside events have had a profound influence on the way I see the world. And the way I see the world is directly related to my work as a filmmaker. The subjects of my films, where I place the camera, and even how I frame a shot are important clues to my worldview. They speak to my existence and to my observations as an individual living outside the mainstream.

After making the documentary on Jewel Thais Williams, I was anxious to work on another project. It was the mid-1990s, and I was working at a theater in Los Angeles founded by the Mexican American actress Carmen Zapata. The theater, the Bilingual Foundation of the Arts (BFA), was started to fill a need in the Latino community for theatrical presentations written by and featuring Hispanic and Latino people. Working as the assistant to the producer and children's theater coordinator gave me insight into the theater community in Los Angeles and an "in" when it came to knowing Latino actors. I realized this would be a good opportunity to make a fiction piece with the resources that were staring me in the face.

Framing Identities / The Evolving Self

My partner, Angela Counts, a playwright, offered to write a short screenplay. I wanted a Latino story that focused on a strong female character that I could shoot in our apartment. What resulted was the dramatic comedy *Acrylics Don't Smell!*,[4] which centers on a Mexican American woman (Erica Ortega) who feels trapped by her conservative marriage to an Argentine American man and his overbearing and snobby mother. One day the main character disrupts their life by announcing her intentions to pursue her dreams of being an artist. At this time I was pretty much self-taught as a filmmaker. With the help of *The Filmmaker's Handbook,* by Steven Ascher and Edward Pincus, which I continue to use in my introductory production classes, I embarked on my first short fiction narrative video.

My partner and I hired the cinematographers, two Nuyorican (New Yorkers of Puerto Rican descent) brothers who were enrolled at AFI. We secured our locations, which included a café in Silver Lake and a USC campus building. We filmed guerilla style[5] in Echo Park and found a very talented cast through *Backstage West* and casting sessions in our living room. The crew was made up mostly of dedicated friends who threw themselves into the project. I took a week off from work, and we shot the thirty-seven-minute video over five days on a Hi-8 camera I purchased. It turned out to be a wonderful experience, a true collaborative effort. It is this experience that encouraged me to apply to the NYU film program.

While *Acrylics Don't Smell!* premiered at the Chicago Latino Film Festival, I found out I was admitted to NYU. My partner and I relocated to Manhattan, where I began a seriously intense education in film. It also when I read *Reel to Real: Race, Sex, and Class at the Movies,* by bell hooks. The essays in the book put into perspective what I had been witnessing in mainstream cinema for years, and hooks's ideas encouraged me to pursue and develop my own ideas as a filmmaker. Her writings and critiques empowered me to create stories that worked against stereotypes through multidimensional representation of situations and characters.

My first exercise in filmmaking at NYU resulted in a 16mm, black-and-white, non-sync short titled *The Man in White*,[6] about a homeless woman being led to her death by a Santeria[7] spiritual figure. I became interested in making a short about a homeless woman in a manner that I had not seen before and that would allow me to explore a style appropriate to the story. Aware of the clichés that this topic could present, I decided to incorporate the Latin American literary tradition of

CRISTINA
KOTZ
CORNEJO

magic realism, a style familiar to readers of Gabriel Garcia Marquez, Jorge Luis Borges, and Laura Esquivel. In fact, Laura Esquivel's novel *Like Water for Chocolate*, which was made into a film with the same title and directed by Alfonso Arau, is a good example of a popular film using this tradition. This style of filmmaking blends dreams and magic with everyday reality through both narrative development and visual style. I applied some elements of literary magic realism: characters who accept without question the magic elements of the world, a richness of sensory details, and time that appears absent or distorted. For example, in the opening of the film the homeless woman is immediately cast into a magical world, which is defined first by exaggerated sound design and then by the introduction of the spiritual figure also known as the Man in White. The Man in White appears to move through space and time through editing. The sound design was crucial to the film. Because the film assignment called for non-sync sound filming, I decided to create an exaggerated or heightened sound design, which also aided in placing the character in a magical world and provided that sensory detail associated with magic realism. The main character, who awakens into this world, never questions it; in fact, she follows the Man in White, who leads her from Central Park into a cemetery and into the death she was unknowingly experiencing all along. I cast a New York City actor, Mary Magdalena Hernandez as the homeless woman and Afro-Caribbean musician Wayne Eddy a the Man in White spirit.

One day it dawned on me that if I didn't achieve what I was hoping to achieve with the style of the film, then the stereotypical representations in the film could serve nothing but just that, stereotypes. I never felt that way with my two previous films because the first one was really a tribute and profile of a gay rights activist and the other was about the liberation of a repressed housewife. Neither of those themes seemed problematic to me. This film, however, made me think further about representation of people of color, especially Afro-Caribbeans. I certainly did not want to perpetuate stereotypes for the sake of making a film; this went against my reason for becoming a filmmaker. I was beginning to feel a certain pressure and concern about how I might represent certain images. On the other hand, I did not want to feel constrained as a filmmaker. I was in film school, after all, and I wanted to feel the freedom to explore stories and ideas. bell hooks speaks precisely to this issue in the essay "Artistic Integrity: Race and Accountability":

> Most filmmakers do not have to deal with the issue of race. When white males make films with all white subjects or people of color, their "right" to do so is not questioned. . . . Ironically, more than any group white men are able to make films without being subjected to a constant demand that their work not perpetuate systems of domination based on race, class and gender. As a consequence it is this work that is usually the most unthinking and careless in its depictions of groups that are marginalized by these institutionalized structures of exploitation and oppression. . . . Marginalized groups—white women, people of color, and/or gay artists, for example—all struggle with the question of aesthetic accountability, particularly in relation to the issue of perpetuating domination. Although this struggle is most often seen solely in a negative light, it enhances artistic integrity when it serves to help the artist clarify vision and purpose.[8]

I felt it was serendipitous that I would come across hooks and this book. It certainly addressed the issues and questions I was beginning to face as a student filmmaker, questions I would surely continue to face in the future. I also felt optimistic that with careful thought about what I was hoping to do, awareness of my intentions, and research on the spiritual aspects of Santeria, I could continue to pursue my ideas with the artistic integrity that hooks demands.

This issue of being accountable as a filmmaker is also a big issue I face as a teacher. As students explore their own ideas, which in most cases are influenced by popular culture, I am often faced with a resistance to understand the complexity of race and gender representation. Their exposure to and education about race and gender representation seem heavily influenced by Hollywood films and advertisements and rap lyrics, which in many cases perpetuate negative stereotypes. I address these issues in the classroom by being an example as a maker, by discussing representation in relation to student work, and finally by showing and discussing the work of filmmakers who themselves are marginalized. I approach these matters with students in the manner in which I would approach writing a script, that is, by talking about characters in their scripts as fully realized persons or multidimensional people. In other words, I try to break down the stereotypes they understand best not by negating them but by encouraging research, understanding, empathy, and learning as much as they can about the topic they are creating a film about. Again, hooks states it well in her essay on artistic accountability:

CRISTINA
KOTZ
CORNEJO

> White male artists have not necessarily benefited from the absence of certain pressures that would compel them to address their role in creating work that perpetuates domination. Filmmakers probably have more awareness than other people about the power of moving images in an age of ever-increasing illiteracy. Movies teach so much because the language of both images and words that they use is accessible. Luckily, individual white filmmakers have begun to think critically some of the time about depictions of race, gender, or nationality.[9]

I would add that a film school has the responsibility to address matters of representation in the curriculum and to make student filmmakers (most of whom are white) aware of their role and power so that they develop the awareness to think critically and to be self-reflexive in their own work and in viewing the work of their peers and future colleagues. Without such curricular mandates and pressures, student filmmakers unaware of their role and power will only continue to perpetuate the domination that hooks refers to, which leads to the type of stereotyping and prejudice that many Americans like myself experience.

This self-imposed pressure during the making of my first film in film school, *The Man in White*, led to what I believe is a truthful and engaging piece in the magic realist tradition. It is thanks to my research, my work with the actors, and the aesthetic choices I made that I am left with a four-minute film I'm quite proud of and one that continue to use in my classes as an example of a simple film done with minimal resources by someone who had never shot a 16mm black-and-white film. The title for the film came out of the spirit character's costume choice, which I decided would be white or off-white. This choice played against the contrast of the actor's dark skin and the palette of the black-and-white film stock we were required to use. Fortunately we had an overcast day when we shot in Central Park, and the spirit character stood out against some of the dark backgrounds I placed him in. I feel the suit played an important role for the spirit character giving him a sense of power and importance and thus playing against Afro-Caribbean stereotypes.

The Appointment[10] was my thesis film and another work whose main character is marginalized. In this film, based on my partner's one-act play, which I co-wrote with her for the film, the main character, Carl Meeks (Godfrey L. Simmons, Jr.), an African American copy machine salesman, is faced with the prospect of losing his job if he doesn't make a sale the day before the Fourth of July weekend. This absurd, dark dramatic comedy pits the salesman against the receptionists he thinks are keeping him from making the sale he needs to save his job. My partner wrote the original play based on experiences she had working in New York and observing how the receptionists would intercept the door-to-door salesmen who were trying to sell office equipment to them. This idea led to the play, which I read and fell in love with for its rhythmic language and power play between genders. I asked my partner if she would be interested in turning it into a short film, and she eagerly agreed. The challenge for me as a student filmmaker was deciding how we could develop the theatrical components, heavy dialogue, and a single location for the screen. We ultimately decided on breaking the film out into several locations, including his apartment, a bar, several interior and exterior office locations, a pay phone, and a scene where he's practicing a sales pitch in a storefront window. The original play had two white characters, but I decided to change their ethnicities. The rationale was that making them people of color would allow me to play with the power inequities sometimes experienced by lower-level employees, who also often happen to be black and Latino. I wanted to demonstrate how people often make judgments based on preconceived prejudices, irrational fears, and desperation.

Framing Identities / The Evolving Self

In his case, I asked myself how this man might feel facing constant rejection. Is he even happy with this line of work? Does he feel his skin color plays a role in how he's treated? What power does he think these women have over him? How does he react in this situation? Does he really see himself as powerless, or is he blaming others for his own failures? After asking myself myriad questions, many more than I have presented here, I created a character background and tried to answer these questions so when I was rehearsing and finally filming, we would see the psychological nuances and subtleties come through in the actual scenes. There is a scene in the film in the beginning that demonstrates these nuances with the most minimal dialogue. Carl enters an office and the camera in a wide hand-held shot shows his awkwardness as he confronts a receptionist, who feigns a greeting. This scene is key to who Carl is as a character and what he faces as he tries to save his job. The unsteady camera allows us to see Carl try to be friendly with an unwilling participant. His awkwardness gives us clues to his skills as a salesman. On the other hand, the receptionist's behavior allows the audience to sympathize with what Carl faces on a daily basis. In a close-up shot we see her reluctantly call her boss, who eventually shows up, only to cut off Carl in the middle of his pitch. Embarrassed and needing to save face, Carl pulls out a brochure and tosses it on the receptionist's desk. Her reaction is to move back with fear as the brochure lands on her desk. The camera stays on him as he leaves the office and the door slams, literally and figuratively shutting him out of the sale.

CRISTINA
KOTZ
CORNEJO

In the case of the co-protagonist in the film, Marta (Denise Casano), we see through Carl's interaction with her that she is unhappy with her job. And as I developed her psychological makeup, my questions had to do with her function as gatekeeper for her employer. This function in and of itself has some power, but is it a useful power for her? What does she think of these salesmen who need to bypass her in order to make a sale? Is she sympathetic or resentful? Does she resent being on the "front lines" of the office? What might be her reaction to an angry salesman? What about an angry black salesman? Her dealings with Carl become more complex than those of the first receptionist, who was able to get rid of him. With Marta, Carl feels it's his right to demand to see someone. He feels someone in that office made a mistake and he is not going to walk away—he can't walk away or he'll lose his job. The crux of the conflict takes place between Marta and Carl and develops through three separate interactions, the stakes getting higher each time. By the final confrontation, Carl's passive and awkward demeanor takes on a more menacing and aggressive nature. Obviously unaware of his previous sales misses, Marta, alone in her office with no one around, perceives him as a threat. A warm lighting plan heightens the tension and the heat of the moment. By this time in the film, the even shakier hand-held camera is in their faces. Close-ups and tight framing on the final confrontation create a strong sense of their psychological deterioration and place the viewer within that action.

As the director, I look at the layers that exist in the situation, the complexities of how race can and often does play a subtle role in day-to-day life situations, and the powerlessness that people experience in the work environment with regard to hierarchical structures. I enjoy discovering the power play and complex psychological interactions between the sexes in the writing process. As a director, I like exploring with the actors in the rehearsal process the background of the characters and how they might react to a given situation. A great deal of artistic inspiration comes from seeing what each actor brings to the role based on his or her own life experiences. Each process gives life to the story and allows me as the director to create a believable story out of an imagined situation.

Though the depiction of race in *The Appointment* was challenging in ways that reminded me of my experiences directing *The Man in White*, the main challenge was to not create a character that might be subtly stereotypical. There are no overtly racial stereotypes in *The Appointment*, but I was very sensitive to how I might be portraying a black character in a powerless situation. As a result, as I developed the script for *The Appointment*, I again asked myself many questions. How will this black character be represented? Will his weakness play into stereotypes? Will his anger play into stereotypes? My way of addressing these concerns had to do with character development, and by grounding his actions in the conflicts in the story. I also worked on the back-story of the character with the actor. For example, during rehearsals, Godfrey and I spoke about Carl's background, and together we decided that he was not suited for sales. He was an introspective person with interests in the arts and creativity who if he had his preference would be working in another field, possibly as a writer. Through these conversations we came up with Carl's personality and grounded all of Carl's actions in the story in his personality and psychology. This is a process I enjoy as a director. It is a process of discovery and analysis through discussions and rehearsals.

Since *The Appointment* I have made four other short films and videos. *Ernesto*[11] is a film that resulted from a grant program sponsored by the Partnership for a Drug-Free America and the Palms Springs International Short Film Festival.[12] It is about Ernesto (Sylvestre Rasuk), a twelve-year-old Dominican boy in New York being raised by his grandfather. Ernesto is pressured by his neighborhood friends to try inhalants, ordinary household products that are inhaled or sniffed by children to get high. The film deals with the conflicts and challenges a twelve-year-old boy feels in trying to both fit in with other kids and to do the right thing. By making Ernesto Dominican I was creating a broader representation of what we normally see in mainstream films. Ernesto is a Latino from a tough neighborhood who struggles with the pressures exerted on him by his peers. He eventually rejects the use of drugs and in fact saves his friend by taking a noble action his other friend discourages him from. The story was told from Ernesto's point of view. The subjective use of the camera allows the viewer to walk in Ernesto's shoes and experience his world. A particular sequence in the film shows two bullies trying to pressure him to sniff nail polish remover under a jungle gym in their urban neighborhood. Ernesto is reluctant to follow, but, not wanting to appear weak, he decides to join them. I had the camera at the top of the jungle gym looking down on Ernesto showing his powerlessness. As the bullies jump up onto the gym, Ernesto waits a beat before jumping himself. The camera stays on him. The viewer experiences his hesitation and reluctance. As we follow them through the gym, we settle on the hidden area where their illicit behavior is to take place. The camera is now at eye level with all of them and within the circle of action, creating an increase in tension. Once the kids sniff the nail polish remover, Ernesto takes off, realizing the error of his ways, but not before taking a hit himself. In the next scene he experiences the high caused by the chemical. A frantic hand-held camera settles onto a tight, compressed shot of Ernesto dazed and disoriented. The background sounds of an aboveground train collide with the images of Ernesto trying to recover. Key to the scene was not only the visual style achieved by shots and lenses but also the location. My director of photography, Chad Davidson, and I chose the jungle gym, which is a symbol of youth and innocence. But we wanted to show that in this urban jungle gym, youth and innocence are lost long before it's time.

After *Ernesto,* I made *Ocean Waves,*[13] a fifteen-minute digital video narrative adapted from a one-act play written by Angela Counts. It deals with an African American receptionist, Ocean Waves (Abigail Ramsay), working in white corporate America. She is approached flir-tatiously and disrespectfully by a white male executive, Dan Winters (Jeff Riebe). During a lunch break the two become involved in an un-witting game of sexual deceit, which leads them down a road neither one is prepared for involving sexual domination and subordination. I decided to stick to the play as it was written and not to break it out of its theatrical setting. I did this because I felt the language of the piece was the driving force of the story and, although many people would say that's not what cinema is about, I decided to explore this anyway. I did make one major change to the script, and that was the age of the characters. I decided to close the wide age gap between the characters. In the play, the man is in his fifties and the woman is in her early twenties. I felt this could set the wrong tone for the audience, that it could be difficult getting beyond the "dirty old man" stereotype. I also changed the piece to a darker yet comedic tone so that there would be less danger of making her a one-dimensional, buffoonish character. The play had broader comedic strokes, but I preferred to explore the darker elements of the story. In addition, I felt there was a risk with the sexual nature of the story, which subtextually references slavery and the racist notions of female black sexuality that arose from slavery. But my underlying quest for this film was to position the female and male protagonists in a seesaw game of vulnerability and power, using these tensions as the guiding force for their unconscious actions. These two characters are flawed and damaged individuals who think power in and of itself is the answer to their problems: for him, it's to exert power over women; for her, it's to exact revenge and manipulate him into submission. But the complexities of human nature emerge, and the characters' original intentions open up a new set of issues neither one is prepared to deal with.

This story was uncomfortable for some viewers, especially men (white or black). Women, on the other hand, white or black, seemed to relate to it in a way I had not anticipated, telling me they have had similar unusual and bizarre experiences related to sexual advances. I hope the film succeeds in sparking dialogue and discussion about the issues, but people seem afraid to talk about the very volatile and complex matters that involve race, sex, and power.

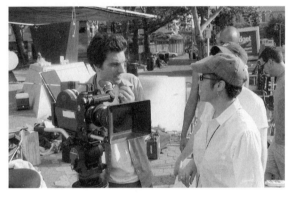

Cinematographer Chad Davidson (left) and director Cristina Kotz Cornejo (right) on the set of *The War That Never Was / La Guerra Que No Fue.*

My most recent short film is an eight-minute Spanish-language short, *La Guerra Que No Fue* (*The War That Never Was*),[14] which I wrote and shot in New York City.

It is about a roasted nut vendor, an Argentine named Diego (Darío Tangelson), who is assigned to train a new Argentine girl, Susana (Romina Poloroff), but his obsession with the Chilean competition across the street causes him to lose his

Dario Tangelson in *The War That Never Was / La Guerra Que No Fue.*

job, and he winds up working for the very competition he despises.

The idea for this story came from an article I read in the *New York Times* in 2002, "Urban Tactics: Sweet Business; Bitter Feud,"[15] which discusses the origins of the roasted nut business in New York. In the mid-1980s, an Argentine founded the business, and when the original owner died in the mid-1990s, another Argentine took it over. At about the same time, a Chilean nicknamed El Conejo (the Rabbit) arrived in Manhattan in need of work. The Argentine owner of the nut business hired the Chilean and trained him. Sometime later the Chilean decided to start his own roasted nut business. Eventually, the Chilean is interviewed on a Spanish-language show in Chile claiming he started the roasted nut business in New York. As word got back to New York, a rivalry between vendors began. The implications of this rivalry go beyond the individual beliefs of nationalism. In 1978, Chile and Argentina almost went to war over the Beagle Channel and a cluster of small islands south of Tierra del Fuego at the southern tip of South America. In fact, the rivalry goes back over a hundred years to the territorial disputes between the two nations involving Patagonia and the Strait of Magellan. This story was perfect as a comedic metaphor for war and the geopolitical issues between the two nations. It was also a perfect opportunity for me to play with some of these very serious issues through comedy and also to return to my own familial roots—Argentina. I shot the film at two locations in New York: the lot where the carts are stored, and a sidewalk across from Lincoln Center. The film opens at the lot where the vendor rivals are preparing for their day. In a detail that struck me when I first read the article, the two companies store their carts only a few yards from each other. What a perfect visual moment for the film! The opening shot in the film shows the two vendors, Chilean and Argentinean, pushing their carts very aggressively as if racing to a finish line. Without a word being spoken, the tone is set and the viewer is prepared for a comedic ride. This film has now screened at more than twenty-five film festivals and cultural centers in more than ten countries. The consistent feedback I receive is that people appreciate how such a small film can elucidate larger and complex issues of territorial disputes and nationalism. This film is an example of what I hope to continue to achieve as a filmmaker: to develop work that weaves important issues and themes seamlessly into a story without being didactic.

   This brings me back to where I started. As I mentioned at the beginning of the chapter, I am in Buenos Aires, where I am meeting with my line producer and actors to show them scenes from *3 Américas*, my first feature film, shot during the summer of 2006. *3 Américas* is a feature-length drama about sixteen-year-old América Hart Campos who is sent to live with her grandmother in Buenos Aires after a tragedy hits her family in Boston. The story deals with identity issues, family violence, loss, and self-discovery, themes that are not strictly autobiographical but are greatly influenced by my own life more than

any of my previous films to date. In the story, I explore the cross-
cultural issues that affect a teenager whose heritage is Argentinean
and whose environment is North American, specifically New England.
In dramatizing this character's challenges and opportunities, I utilize
experiences from my own life to more closely inform my film work
and the dramatic situations it portrays. *3 Américas* also poses for me
an opportunity to explore the intergenerational conflicts that confront
teens who are being raised by aging grandparents, which in América's
case is further exacerbated by the fact that these two family members
do not know each other before the tragedy that brings them together.

My goal for this film is to bring to bear all the elements I have
learned as a filmmaker and as a human being. I seek to create a work
that will actively engage the au-
dience with the protagonist on
an epic journey to claim her life
and her right to live joyfully,
free from the domestic violence
and dysfunction into which she
was born.

Production of the film went
very well. We shot one week in
Boston with a relatively small
crew, which included professionals as well as eight students
or alumni from Emerson College. The remainder of the four-week
shoot took place in Buenos Aires. My lead actor, Kristen Gonzalez,
who plays América as well as her guardian, three of my students (Pris-
cila Amescua Mendez, Tatiana McCabe, Lucia Lopez), my co-producer
(Angela Counts), my production designer (Toni Barton), my cinematographer (Chad Davidson), and I boarded a flight two days after we
wrapped in Boston and headed to Buenos Aires. The shoot continued
to go very well, considering we ran into some snags, such as scheduling problems, the loss of locations, local union issues, my having to
dismiss the local wardrobe supervisor, and a confrontation with the
Buenos Aires Police Department over shooting in front of a bank. Despite these problems, the American and Argentine crew worked seamlessly and as a cohesive unit. Though the film is not autobiographical,
it is influenced by some of my experiences, and shooting in all the
familiar places in which I grew up and my old school made this filming experience much different from that of my other films. I was connected to the storyline at a deeper emotional level, and I believe this
influenced everyone who participated in the film, particularly Kristen,

Kristen
Gonzalez as
América in
3 Américas.

who was very aware of the environment for herself as a person and for her character's journey within this new environment.

My personal journey informs my filmic explorations. More than any of my short subjects, América's story required the length of a feature film to give her time to grow into her new life in Argentina and to give me sufficient space to tell her story. It is in many ways the culmination of many years of living and making films. *3 Américas* represents my worldview, my values, and my identification with the world I live in. The journey América takes is a journey I have taken figuratively and whose construct is a result of everything I have lived and observed. It is why I have chosen to make a feature film. The long format affords me the time to develop the complexities of América's journey over time. I am able to recreate the moments in life during which we take a breather from the obstacles in our way. And I am able to solidify back-stories—the elements that give validity and believability to the story and the characters themselves—avoiding the heavy-handed imprint of the writer. I have been carefully constructing the story to allow the themes of the film to surface so that they will resonate with an audience long after the viewing of the film.

Identity is important for each of us. We all need to know who we are. We shouldn't focus on how other people see us but on how we see ourselves. There are too many factors that can influence who we become (and are becoming). Outside perceptions limit us on our journey

CRISTINA
KOTZ
CORNEJO

Still from *3 Américas.*

to self-realization and may not contribute to an accurate and true identity. When we are able to claim our own identity rather than having one imposed on us, our freedom to live life to the fullest can flourish.

My desire to acknowledge my evolving self every step of the way has opened up opportunities in my life and given me a voice for my work as a filmmaker. It is why I reject the labels people try to attach to me. Yes, I am Latina, a woman, American, and gay. And yes, I am even an academic filmmaker. I am all of these things at once, but as I define them. Labels conjure up different meanings to different people, depending on how they define them, so I also reserve the right to reject labels and what they may represent. What I do fully accept is that I am human and I am a filmmaker. I am an individual who is different from others yet connected to others in the human struggle. My films express the individuality of identity and its universality. The nineteenth-century existentialist philosopher Søren Kierkegaard has written that society and politics categorize individuals by group characteristics instead of individual differences. For Kierkegaard, those are the differences that make us who we are as individuals. I have to agree with Kierkegaard: "once you label me, you negate me."[16]

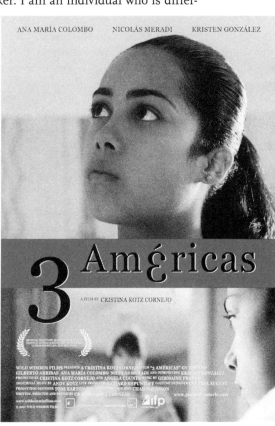

In one way or another, all my films are about marginalized people whose lives are deeply affected by their ethnicity, race, class, gender, or other life circumstances. They are characters who either choose to guide their own destinies in spite of labels and history or are thrust into a redefinition by circumstances. Either way, the characters in my films struggle to become more fully themselves. Often they must fight to reclaim their lives as well, and to pursue a better future. Long after the film is over, we might imagine, they will continue on this path, a work in progress.

Poster for *3 Américas*.

1. *Jewel and the Catch* is available from the UCLA Film and Television Archive's Outfest Legacy Collection.

2. Section 501(c)(3) of the Internal Revenue Code is the most common section under which nonprofit organizations file for tax-exempt status. For this reason, nonprofit organizations are often referred to as 501(c)(3) organizations.

3. Huarpe is a native tribe from the Cuyo (northwest) area of Argentina known for agricultural skills.

4. *Acrylics Don't Smell!* is not available for screening.

5. Guerilla filmmaking is associated with no-budget filmmakers who bypass any formal production arrangements, such as securing locations and permits.

6. *The Man in White* is available directly from the filmmaker.

7. Santeria is a religion that combines certain traditional African religious beliefs and some Roman Catholic ceremonies.

8. bell hooks, "Artistic Integrity: Race and Accountability," in *Reel to Real: Race, Sex, and Class at the Movies* (New York: Routledge, 1996), 69.

9. Ibid., 70.

10. *The Appointment* is distributed by Urban Entertainment (Los Angeles).

11. *Ernesto* is distributed by the Partnership for a Drug-Free America (New York).

12. Festival listings are available on the Web or can be found in resource books such as *The Ultimate Film Festival Survival Guide*, by Chris Gore, or *The Film Festival Guide*, by Adam Langer.

13. *Ocean Waves* is available directly from the filmmaker.

14. *La Guerra Que No Fue* (*The War that Never Was*) is distributed by OUAT! Media (Toronto, Canada) and VOY Pictures (Los Angeles).

15. Michelle O'Donnell, "Urban Tactics: Sweet Business; Bitter Feud," *New York Times*, September 22, 2002.

16. Søren Kierkegaard was a nineteenth-century Danish philosopher.

Indigenism, (In)Visibility

NOTES ON MIGRATORY FILM

John Thornton Caldwell
(UCLA)

Indigenous identities can unsettle a host of unlikely bedfellows, from globalizing corporate forces and nationalistic agendas to oppositional political schemes. Since 1978, my independently produced films and videos have consistently focused on local crises in which indigenous cultures emerged as unwanted houseguests for some coexistent, dominant culture. Indigenism, that is, proved unruly for those on both the political right and the left. And this has probably been a good thing, or at least a useful lesson, for anyone who produces cross-cultural films or is interested in alternative media and political change. In this chapter, I discuss two pressure points that have recurred in five of the films I have produced: first, the ways that "indigenism" is repeatedly put up for grabs and hijacked as a free-floating signifier, and second, the ways in which this free-floating aura has come back to bite the hands of those who seek to appropriate or adopt indigenism as their own identity or brand.[1] All of my creative works have centered on cultural investigations of one sort or another, and most have focused, at least in part, on either the systematic, strategic erasure of indigenous identity or the unruly tactical resuscitation of indigenous identity.

Although initially focused on cross-cultural migration issues and migrancy themes, five of my films—*Personas Desplazadas: The Miskito Indian Refugees* (1983), *Kuije Kanan: Managalase Tattooing* (1985), *Freak Street to Goa: Immigrants on the Rajpath* (1989), *Amor Vegetal: Our Harvest* (1998), and *Rancho California (por favor)* (2002)—ended up engaging systemic interconnections between some form of indigenous visibility (deployment) and indigenous invisibility (erasure). Acknowledging that the documentary gaze traditionally renders others in an objectifying, colonizing fashion, my approach has always been to consider my own complicity and ideological baggage when moving into any local dialogue or conflict. Blanket critical or theoretical prohibitions against representing the other are typically offered from positions of academic privilege. Most of these intellectual taboos ignore the sad fact that othering habits frequently emerge as integral parts of local sociopolitical systems and conflicts. In most of these cross-cultural quagmires, indigenism is rarely evident in any pure, isolable form or accessible to the filmmaker in a stable or clean state. Filmmakers, academics, and activists owe it to themselves and their constituents to more carefully pick apart the layers of outside interests that commonly broach, exploit, and manage indigenous racial identities in public.

Given the sometimes thick interconnections across cultures in which indigenism is an issue, my response is to try to unpack the local and regional systems of social logic (and illogic) that promote the idea

of the indigenous "problem" as innate or ultimately unsolvable. Such regional systems regularly grant indigenous groups forms of insularity that fit easily within the dominant social order, even as they efface more unruly aspects of indigenism. Before closely considering this erasure/performance dynamic in more detail in two films, I would like to briefly describe the place of race and indigenous identity in two of my earlier documentaries, *Kuije Kanan: Managalase Tattooing* (25 min., filmed 1984, released 1985, 2005), and *Freak Street to Goa: Immigrants on the Rajpath* (60 min.; filmed 1980, 1986; released 1989–1994).[2]

Managalase village elder demonstrating how the tattoo process was traditionally accomplished, years after body tattooing was outlawed by the government in a shift to a cash economy. After this legalized cultural erasure occurred, this primary visual form of male and kinship identity was reenacted for the benefit of younger generations. Siribu village, Oro Province, Papua New Guinea, 1984. (Photograph © J. Caldwell.)

Salvaging, Resuscitating, and Posturing Indigenism

Kuije Kanan (literally "thorn-hit" in the Managalase language of north eastern Papua New Guinea) most closely engaged the traditional mode of "salvage anthropology." As an ethnographic documentary on the traditional art of body tattooing among the Managalase people, the film documented the disappearing cultural practice of tattooing by having several surviving elders in the village of Kavan demonstrate and recreate the practice for the camera. Full-body tattooing was once a central part of adolescent male initiation in the villages. Thirteen-year-old boys would be housed in the darkness of womblike huts for several months (of "gestation"), during which time their skin turned lighter (to "better show up the tattoos") and their bodies were fattened up ("to look like pigs"). At the conclusion of this symbolic pregnancy, the boys would exit the huts as part of a large ceremonial "sing-sing." Many hogs were slaughtered, and blood and red paint were splattered on the boys' bodies to emulate birth. As part of a village-wide sex role reversal, women would dress like men and play the drums of men, while adolescent girls would chase after and solicit the boy initiates.

Body tattooing and male initiation were one of the crucial ways by which Managalase society maintained and perpetuated its distinctive identities, cultural practices, and social organization. Through these practices boys left the context of the mother's family and became part of the father's family. Initiate tattooing changed sibling relations by bodily connecting each boy to his newly initiated "cousin-brothers." From the point of tattooing and initiation on, male initiates lived together in the village's common "men's house" until marriage. Attracting a suitable mate was directly tied to the power and significance of one's tattoo.

Notes on
Migratory Film

The sadly predictable outcome of contact with various European

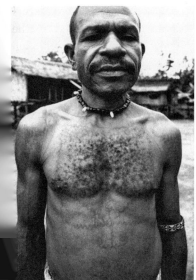 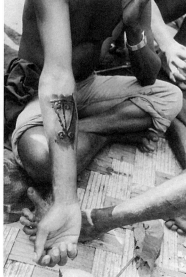

Managalase body tattooing. Left, adult male with full body tattoo as the result of collective adolescent male initiation. Right, the inked and bloodied embossed skin and surface of a young tattoo subject during tattooing reenactment in 1984. Siribu village, ro Province, Papua New Guinea, 1984. (Photographs in diptych © J.Caldwell.)

colonials, and then with the Australians who governed Papua New Guinea after World War II, was that body tattooing and male initiation were deemed economically and morally unacceptable. And so the process was outlawed and discontinued. A combination of interests—nearby plantations, missions, and the Australian government—prohibited the practice, mostly because it took the most valuable workers out of a community for inordinate amounts of time, and—worse yet—derailed their parents from productive work as well (since the parents now spent many months gathering food to bring to their sons in the seclusion huts). These indigenous practices, therefore, were simply not tolerated by the emerging, artificial, pan-tribal nation-state, which was determined to shift its residents to a cash economy. Nearby,

Return village screening of 1984 *Kuije Kanan* body tattooing documentary for the next generation, in May 2005. Kavan village, Oro Province, Papua New Guinea. (Photograph © W. McKellin.)

coffee and sago palm oil plantations paid wages to male workers who had once survived by gardening and hunting, and Australian and Chinese trading stores gladly took back those wages in exchange for new consumer goods. The last full village initiation ritual took place in 1951, shortly before the eruption of the Mount Lamington volcano; the last partial body tattooing and initiation took place in Siribu village in the early 1960s. The reenactment, demonstration, and explanation by the surviving, fully tattooed village elders for our film took place in 1984.

The disastrous impact of the tattooing prohibition is detailed elsewhere, and is beyond the scope of this essay.[3] The tattooing and initiation prohibition turned the acutely gendered system of the Managalase upside down, and so sent both Managalase familial descent lines and land claims into disarray. Both matrilineal and patriarchal functions lost logic and agency, as the Managalase struggled to participate in a cash economy of the new nation-state of Papua New Guinea. *Kuij Kanan* offers a classic example of how unruly racial indigenism was managed and rationalized away, and how such erasures precipitat unending and unforeseen social complications. The documentar represented a simple and direct attempt to allow the surviving elder to demonstrate and resurrect this culture-defining practice for other villagers, their families, and children. More than mere cultural salvage, therefore, the project can be seen as a very provisional way in which villagers visually resuscitated indigenism to help maintain and perpetuate Managalase tribal identity in the face of the sea change of consumerism that now defined the younger generations.

Freak Street to Goa: Immigrants on the Rajpath documented the lives of Western expatriates who dropped out of First World society in the 1960s and early 1970s and migrated to India and Nepal, where they remain to this day. Indigenism emerged as a secondary theme in Freak Street, although this ethnographic film does not fit easily within the traditional model of anthropological preservation. After an earlier project in Nepal in 1980, we filmed the countercultural subjects of Freak Street in 1986–1987. Originally titled The Migratory Patterns of Hippies on the Subcontinent, we followed the lives of ex-hippies as they made their annual migrations overland from the mountains and valleys of Kathmandu in Nepal (where they "summered" for six months) to the white beaches of Goa in southwestern India (a former Portuguese colony where they "wintered" for six months). Although partly drawn to the zoological nature

Four of the last surviving male elders with full body tattoos from childhood adolescent initiation, in May 2005. Siribu village, Oro Province, Papua New Guinea. (Photograph © W. McKellin.)

of this migratory habit, we intended to underscore several things as we began: first, that the United States was not the symbolic bastion of manifest destiny that the Reagan-Bush administration rhetorically made it out to be; second, that not all residents of underdeveloped nations were risking all to break into "fortress America"; and third, that intelligent, socially conscious Americans, sickened by the right-wing duplicity of the United States in the 1980s, were also permanently migrating in the other direction (to the Third World), and doing so productively. Indigenous racial identity became an issue in two ways. First, although many hippies were drawn to India and Nepal for religious reasons—and the possibility of adopting an Asian, Hindu, or Buddhist identity in the nearby ashrams—we discovered that many

Immigrants on the Rajpath. Hippie outpost in Kimdol area of Kathmandu, Nepal. Long-time expatriate, poet, and performer Eight-Finger Eddy makes the semi-annual migration between Nepal and Goa, India, to follow the weather and to avoid imprisonment for visa violations for residency beyond six months. (Photographs in diptych © 1989, J. Caldwell.)

Indians and Nepalis pretty much considered such aspirants from the United States and Europe a joke. According to this view, a white European person's identity cannot be jettisoned, since the Hindu identity (to Indians) is not something that can be opportunistically adopted or discarded like a new set of clothes.

Most of the surviving expatriates whom we featured survived in part because they never presumed to become indigenous or Indian (unlike the squads of Western Hare Krishnas regularly arriving by plane or tourist bus). Nor did our expatriate immigrants share affinities with the American "converts" to Tibetan Buddhism at temples in Nepal, like Swayambunath (converts whom some older surviving expatriates occasionally and cynically termed trust-funders). Unlike many from the "first waves," who had died from heroin use or disappeared, the four individuals we featured were all in their late forties and fifties, had locally pursued artistic businesses or artisanal production of one sort or another, and had made peace with their forever hybrid, in-between identities.

Each gave accounts of how many earlier friends had died from the harsh conditions involved in reverse migration. Complicating matter further still, we encountered indigenous peoples living and working among the hippies (such as the Newaris in Kathmandu and the Hima layan mountains) whose cultural identities freely mixed and matched elements of Hinduism, Buddhism, meat-eating, and animism.

The Western fantasy of a pure, spiritual India seemed in retrospect like a wishful dream concocted by economically privileged but politically depressed Americans. The fact that two of my filmmaking partners, co-director John Lalnunsang Pudaite and sound recordist C. Thanthieng Khobung, were indigenous Hmar people from the restricted tribal state of Manipur in northeastern India (south of Assam, west of the Myanmar border) also complicated things. As non-Buddhist, non-Hindu Indian citizens, they offered explanatory problems for local interview subjects, who freely generalized about Hindustan identities. As we filmed, it became increasingly apparent that indigenous Indian and Nepali identities were, often as not, fanciful fabrications as much as they were embodied realities. These symbolic indigenisms, popular in all kinds of cross-cultural rhetoric, proved in hindsight to be as problematic as the pan-provincial Indian nationalism that had been invented and violently imposed by the British in the nineteenth and twentieth centuries. With nationalism and colonialism apparently passé, indigenism has emerged as a favored rhetorical ploy that is used and misused by all sorts of cross-cultural

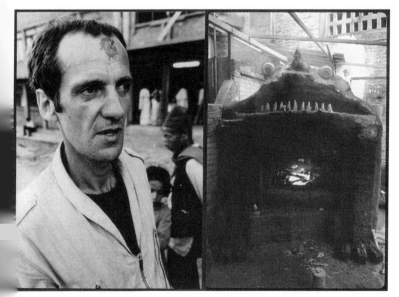

nmigrant "Woody" rode a bicycle from Germany to India and Nepal via Afghanistan. n artist and baker, Woody build a ceremonial oven-sculpture (right), which indigenous ewaris dedicated with the sacrifice of a goat, slaughtered as part of a community ɩja. Working extensively with the Newaris and locals, Woody maintains bakeries in ɔth Kathmandu, Nepal, and Goa, India. (Photographs in diptych © 1989, J. Caldwell.)

Dick Brown (left) and Jim Goodman (right), both veterans of the U.S. Army, dropped out and have permanently migrated to Nepal, India, and Southeast Asia. Dick writes and manages a Nepali band and runs a miso factory (as from-the-ground-up development work). Jim writes epic poetry (including *Mao's Long March*) and started a Nepali textile business to produce traditional "indigenous" textiles as a countermeasure against "synthetic" Western imports. Jim was last seen in the Golden Triangle area of Thailand, where he continues his work. Our sound recordist on the film *Freak Streat to Goa*, C. Thanthieng Khobung, is an indigenous member of the Hmar tribe in the Manipur state in northeast India (between Burma and Assam). (Photographs in diptych © 1989, J. Caldwell.)

players. Earnest free-thinkers invoke "their" indigenism to counter exploitative U.S. culture, European commercialism, and globalization. At the same time, the Newaris in Kathmandu Valley pretty much stayed to themselves, well versed as they are at surviving in a highly stratified, complicated, caste-driven social order on the subcontinent. The film, when completed, went on to some success on the festival circuit and broadcast in the United States and abroad.[4] Indian film critic Vijaya Mulay praised *Freak Street* as an exemplary model for reverse ethnography, given our refusal to represent Nepali or Indian culture so that we might focus instead on Western expatriation (or reverse migration) in South Asia.[5] *Freak Street* premiered the opening night of the Margaret Mead film festival in 1988, together with Dennis O'Rourke's film *Cannibal Tours*. O'Rourke's film also disregarded ethnography's classic othering of indigenes in Papua New Guinea in favor of self-critiquing Western tourists who opportunistically (and sometimes callously) celebrate indigenous identity.

Antithetical Indigenisms: Miskito Indian Refugees
(Nicaragua/Honduras, 1983–1984) and Mixteco Migrant
Workers (Oaxaca/San Diego, 1995–2002)

I became increasingly interested in issues of self-representation even as
I continued pursuing themes of migration and cross-cultural relations
in my films. In 1996, I began my involvement with nonprofit agencies in the community media and organic gardening project called La
Cosecha Nuestra, which focused on improving nutrition and establish-
ing "food security" among lower-income neighborhoods in Southern
California. One of the results of this initiative, which involved numerous nonprofit agencies in northern San Diego County, was the thirty-
minute documentary *Amor Vegetal: Our Harvest* (1998), a "collective   *Notes on*
video dialogue" by immigrant worker residents of Escondido, Califor-   *Migratory Film*
nia. My partner Devora Gomez and I completed and distributed the
film, then observed the callous ways this community's self-expression
was institutionally contained by others outside the community. This
appropriation by official institutions of collective, from-the-ground-up
self-expression underscored an important lesson for me. After *Amor
Vegetal*, I began to pursue more personal ways of speaking or filming
across cultures that might provide distinctive insights that can comple-
ment and thus support local cultural self-expressions. The rest of this
chapter traces my sometimes awkward search as a filmmaker to deal
with and understand a series of raced, cross-cultural landscapes that
surrounded the Cosecha Nuestra project. Some of these landscapes
looked like pitched battles (which were politically managed). Others
looked more benign, like creations of nature (even though they felt
suspiciously manicured).

    After the popularly supported Sandinistas overthrew the U.S.-
backed Samoza dictatorship in 1979, the new Nicaraguan government
sought to unify and develop the country by including even the remote
communities in the country's eastern regions in its development plans.
Traditionally ignored by a succession of largely corrupt federal governments, a largely independent culture had emerged over the decades
long Nicaragua's Atlantic coast in a region called La Miskitia. The
indigenous "Miskito Indian" communities in that part of Nicaragua
were different in almost every way from Nicaraguan citizens in and
round Managua. Most Nicaraguans were Spanish-speaking, Catholic whites or mestizos based in cities and towns, or campesinos who
worked in the largely semi-arid and mountainous hilly areas of central
and western Nicaragua. On the other side of the mountains, the indigenous Miskitos were dark-skinned, spoke an English pidgin dialect

Two different wars, two different decades. Top, Nicaraguan Miskito hut in Mocoron village near Contra bases along the Rio Coco between Nicaragua and Honduras, Central America, 1983. Bottom, migrant worker home of indigenous Mixteco Indians from Oaxaca near gated designer-home community in Carlsbad, San Diego County, California, 1999. (Photographs in diptych © 1983, 1999, J. Caldwell.)

rather than Spanish (from trading contacts with the British on the Gulf Coast), were largely Protestant and Moravian (rather than Catholic), and, outside of coastal port cities such as Bluefields, subsisted on a combination of farming, fishing, and hunting in the pine forests, tropical waterways, and lowlands of the eastern region. The two cultures could not have been more different, and many Miskitos reacted

to progressive Sandinista attempts to install new schools, government
centers, and clinics in the eastern region with alarm.

This widespread suspicion of the Spanish speakers from the west was almost immediately exploited by U.S.-backed "*contratistas*," many of whom were ex-soldiers of ousted dictator Samoza. While a few villages burned after initial confrontations with the Sandinistas, contra forces immediately seized on the situation by figuratively and literally throwing more matches into the fire. Contra forces quickly mobilized to "rescue" and evacuate Miskitos even as they burned other villages across the region. Opportunistically offering "protection" to the ostensible "victims," the Contras led the Miskitos north of the Rio Coco into Miskito regions of Honduras. There, on a vast and muddy plain in the lowlands, over 10,000 Miskito Indians converged on a site called Mocoron. A group of nonprofit relief agencies (including Médicins Sans
Frontièrs, Oxfam, and World Relief), under the coordination of the UN's High Commission for Refugees (UNHCR), stepped in to provide minimal housing, food staples, and potable water for the refugees. By the time my colleague and partner Joel Sheesley and I arrived in March 2003, endless rows of thatched huts and shallow groundwater wells laced the treeless and muddy landscape as far as the eye could see. "Rescuing" the indigenous Miskitos now apparently meant confining them—without their traditionally abundant natural sources of food and water in the forests—to the static life of refugee camp hut-dwellers—convenient for the Contras, but not for the Miskitos.

But the logic of this staged "indigenous" setting soon became dramatically apparent. Miskito families complained that armed squads of Contras came from hut to hut, forcibly recruiting any available male adolescents to go back and "rescue" their homeland and fight their enemies, the Sandinistas. Cut off from their traditional seasonal crops and lands, the normally invisible and mobile Miskitos became sitting ducks, static targets, for a range of political interests that quickly exploited their indigenous status. President Reagan began hammering away at what he termed the "Communist threat" the Sandinistas posed to the Americas and warned that Soviet tanks would soon be at the banks of the Rio Grande if the Sandinistas were not stopped. Reagan invoked an "exhibit A" in his call to arms against the "godless" Nicaraguans: the Sandinistas' "genocidal" killing of "innocent Miskito Indians." Cold-warrior Reagan—at least in his clarion calls in State of the Union addresses—was (rhetorically, at least) a radical "Indian rights activist." An even bigger "staging" of indigenism, however, was announced by the 82nd Airborne out of Fort Bragg, North Carolina. In two of the most dramatic media events of 1982 and 1983, the Pentagon used the Mocoron refugee camp as a backdrop. Battalions of U.S. air-

borne troops staged parachute drops as part of "Big Pine I" and "Big Pine II" for the benefit of carefully assembled international news crews, alongside the carefully positioned indigenous "victims" of the Sandinistas. This effectively provided international journalists with a kind of one-stop shopping, enabling dramatic news stories (in a single press junket away from the capitol Tegucigalpa) about American military might and political will as defined against the backdrop of Sandinista genocide against indigenous people.

Wildlife Habitat Restoration in Progress.

Please do not enter or disturb.

Pardee
Construction Company

END

Yet the Miskito refugees and the UNHCR workers were not as easily flummoxed by Washington's orchestrated media event and dramatic "proof." Our film included Miskito leaders mocking Reagan's newfound sympathy for indigenous people, and aid workers numb from trying to either justify or explain U.S. exploitation to the outside world. Of even more concern to us as filmmakers was depicting the way the hastily established and massively funded, area infrastructure around Mocoron was completed and then used. Hundreds of thousands of dollars of international relief funds were channeled in and around Mocoron to build an extensive network of roads and airstrips

Out of sight, out of mind. Making indigenous Mixteco American workers invisible by legally zoning—within suburban city limits—no-man's-lands, utility right-of-ways, floodplains, and brush-covered arroyos. Top, wall above Kelly migrant camp, Carlsbad, California. Middle, reclamation of wildlife after migrant camp eviction in Carmel Valley, California. Bottom, cul-de-sac and berm concealing migrant camp in Coachella Valley, east of Palm Springs. (Photographs in triptych © 2002, J. Caldwell.)

Ostensibly intended to provide humanitarian aid, these new airstrips
and roads from the remote port cities of Puerto Lempira and La Ceiba
provided a level of logistical expediency and efficiency never before
available to the Honduran and U.S. military along the Rio Coco and La
Miskitia. Miskito indigenism had become a free-floating signifier that
was quickly and ably exploited by the Contras, the Samozistas, the U.S.
military, and the suspect and ineffective Honduran government (at
the time the second most impoverished country in the Western Hemisphere). Strangely, indigenism became the new basis for American
military intervention even as it served as the poster child for American
foreign policy in Latin America.

Flash-forward. Exterior. Rural-suburban San Diego County, U.S.A.
1994–2002. Indigenism also circulated as a theme and a force in the
migrant worker camps that intersected the arroyos of some of the most
affluent, gated, designer-home communities in the United States: Del
Mar, Carlsbad, Solana Beach, Rancho Santiago, Escondido. Initially
intending to film counterarguments against the then vitriolic anti-
immigration rhetoric at the time of Proposition 187 in 1994, my partner Devora Gomez and I quickly discovered an indigenous community that once again didn't fit a clean binary model of left and right
politics. By the mid-1990s, more than 50,000 indigenous Mixtecos
from the mountainous regions of Oaxaca in southern Mexico had
emigrated for work in California. Like the Miskito Indians in Nicaragua, the Mixtecos of Del Mar and Escondido did not speak Spanish,
or spoke Spanish as a second language, and so were culturally cut off
from American Latinos much as the Miskitos were from the Sandinistas. Unlike the politically heralded and showcased Miskitos, however,
the Mixtecos had attained an astonishingly invisible status throughout
the sunny suburbs of Southern California. We set about to understand
how and why this invisibility had been established and maintained,
and worked on four different video productions to achieve this. Two
of the productions were completed and distributed (*Amor Vegetal* and
Rancho California), one production was used for documentation only
(*Indigenous Translator's Project* for the courts), and one was started but
not completed owing to political problems and lack of funding (*Pro-
familia*, involving video workshops on domestic abuse in the migrant
community).

Anti-immigration rhetoric demonized all migrants as "Mexicans"
and "illegals." At the same time, resurgent, flag-waving Mexican nationalism evident in the anti-Prop 187 rallies in Los Angeles and San
Diego totalized immigration in a different way—one that created a
monolithic nationalist bloc that covered over all sorts of cultural het-

JOHN
THORNTON
CALDWELL

The La Cosecha Nuestra community project in Escondido, California, used donated land, surplus meeting spaces, and logistical support from NGOs, along with fencing, compost, manure, tools, and supplies from local businesses, to create a community garden for the migrant worker community in south Escondido. The first garden coordinator was indigenous Mixteco worker Arturo Gonzales. The second coordinator was an indigenous Kanjobal-Mayan worker from Guatemala, Victor Gomez. The participatory community video *Amor Vegetal*, which included dramatizations about nutrition and cross-cultural perspectives on food and health, was produced by community members for use in local immigrant clinics and as a discussion starter in community meetings. (Photographs in triptych © 1998, J. Caldwell.)

erogeneity within the migrant worker communities. Yet the Mixteco. we interviewed in the camps saw themselves as self-governing and in digenous, not as Mexicans. A collective historical hatred had develope over mistreatment by a succession of central governments that had pi laged and punished the indigenous peoples of Oaxaca over six centurie (this included a string of Mexican governments, the Spanish coloni

empire in the sixteenth and seventeenth centuries, and the genocidal
Aztec invaders before that). Over hundreds of years, a deep-seated suspicion of any outsiders who presumed to speak for the Mixtecos had developed. This distrust, and the racial and labor caste system that continues to fuel it (with light-skinned Mexicans of European descent at the top, mixed-race mestizos in the middle, and indigenous "indios" at the bottom) was imported, largely intact, from Oaxaca via large plantations in Sinaloa to its ultimate destination, California. In this racialized system, workers in the lowest class ("Oaxaqueñitos") are marked by the darkness of their skin and short stature. In the mid-1990s,

crew bosses marketed the Mixtecos across California as "the perfect picking machines" because of their short stature. The Mixtecos' reaction to this systemic form of domination and marginalization—including their Frente Indigena Oaxaqueño Binacional's cultural strategies of "self-autonomy"— prevented extensive forms of political coalition building with other activist groups. Yet the same strategies of autonomy also encouraged and enabled Mixtecos to organize internally and binationally (across the U.S.-Mexico border) to force employers and consulates in both Mexico and California to observe fair labor, fair housing, and workplace safety laws.

One video that we produced as part of the nonprofit community garden initiative, *Amor Vegetal,* was based on collective expression, improvisational scenes, a teach-the-teacher methodology, and from-the-ground-up self-representation. This project both succeeded its goals and, to some ex-

Top, camcorder self-representations by Mixteco/Oaxacan families in Kelly migrant camp, Carlsbad, California, are featured in the hour-long film *Rancho California* (2002). Bottom, production still from improvisational filmed scenes on food security produced for the half-hour participatory health video *Amor Vegetal: Our Harvest* (1998). (Photographs in diptych © 2002, 1997, J. Caldwell.)

JOHN
THORNTON
CALDWELL

tent, failed.[6] The local chamber of commerce and conservative city government were far from threatened by the newfound presence of indigenous workers in their midst. Rather, they used the project to celebrate the fact that underprivileged "immigrants can help themselves," and to underscore the happy multiculturalism that supposedly pervades comfortable suburbs such as Escondido without burdening the taxpayer. Given the ways that indigenism was easily assimilated and thus politically written off in the *La Cosecha Nuestra* and *Amor Vegetal* projects, I changed my sights. I resumed work on a very different film that I hoped would engage the complex but sordid issues at work in completely cross-cultural environments such as Escondido.

In *Rancho California (por favor)*, I decided to shift away from any attempt at creating a pure ethnic space for expression and instead try to articulate the many material layers and symbolic boundaries used by the public to construct and assign race. What emerged, on camera and in interviews, was a very real sense that the rural-suburban landscape in the area of the camps was meticulously managed. Local housing and labor interests tended the area via roadside landscaping, zoning laws, utility right-of-ways, construction permits, subdivision gates and walls, and informally sanctioned contact zones where migrant camp workers and residents actually met on a regular basis. Essentially, these physical barriers, legal constraints, and ambiguous spaces raced the area, and showed how integrally the lives of the residents up on the hill were intertwined with the lives of the campesinos and their families in the mud and ditches of the arroyo down below. Although the Mixteco community organizers deftly deployed their indigenous identities in work, labor, and legal settings, those same identities seemed to vanish in the lush, scenic underbrush that camouflaged the camps down below the walls of the gated designer-home communities above. Several of my UCSD students from the area denied that such camps existed. These (fairly symptomatic) denials made me look for how racial identities were being conventionalized as natural phenomena in Southern California's picturesque landscape. Taking this approach to filming—visually detailing cross-cultural boundaries, barriers, and contact zones—would also clearly implicate me, as a Southern California resident, in the naturalized erasure of indigenous difference in the region. Such an approach guaranteed that my own complicity would not be covered over by the filming.

It was fairly easy to understand how the conventionalized, quasi-Mediterranean picturesque that defined the suburbs could camouflage and erase indigenous difference. After all, the adage "out of sight, out of mind" allows nearby homeowners a kind of repose that was usually unavoidable at a 7–11 convenience store or when passing a roadside hiring center for day laborers. I was far more surprised, however, at a very different landscape trope that was marshaled deep within some of the bigger nearby ranches that housed migrant workers in ramshackle huts. Behind barbed-wire fences, deep within the ravines of a sprawling ranch near Pala, I filmed a factory-like approach to migrant housing and work that seemed far more brutal than the Central American conditions the Miskito refugees faced when I filmed them during wartime fifteen years earlier. Some fifty to one hundred huts were scattered up and down one ravine. Most of these huts were propped up and tied down within a few yards of the same stream (mostly irrigation runoff) that scores of adolescent boys and young men used as a water source to bathe, wash dishes, and use in food preparation. Other men up- and downstream used the same agricultural runoff for latrines. This deleterious multitasking efficiently combined a range of lifestyle resources for the Mixtecos and cost the rancher renting the huts nothing financially. At another camp, in the mudflats on the Hedionda lagoon in Carlsbad, I came across shallow groundwater wells dug in the mud that were almost identical to the groundwater wells the Nicaraguan

eft, Arturo Gonzalez, an indigenous Mixteco community activist, organizer for "Frente
digena Oaxaqueño Binacional," and first La Cosecha Nuestra community garden
ordinator. Top right, razor wire and chain-link fencing above three migrant camps
dden in arroyos between Carlsbad, Oceanside, and San Marcos. Bottom right, sign
recting travelers to migrant camp in the towns of Arvin-Lamont, California (which
ere the sites of the 1930s "Oakie" migrant camps, whose dormitory foundations are
ill visible in present-day labor camps used by Mixtecos and others). (Photographs in
ptych © 2002, J. Caldwell.)

Miskitos dug and used throughout the refugee camp in Mocoron. If one's hut is low enough or close enough to the water table (which is almost always the case in lagoon areas), a three-foot-wide hole in the mud no more than two feet deep could easily provide a constant source of easily retrievable water that one could use in cooking, drinking, and bathing. This resource was, apparently, as important in Southern California in 1998 as it was in Nicaragua and Honduras in 1983.

Third World conditions were the norm and pervaded scores of camps throughout northern San Diego County. But by what logic had these conditions become socially acceptable in the region? A legal case against one rancher near Pala exposed the tortured paradigms that legitimized the conditions. After being threatened by legal advocates for housing his workers outside and in the dirt, the rancher provided a concrete slab, ostensibly to provide a more "humane" living space for his heretofore mud-dwelling workers. With each new seasonal crop, the rancher typically hired scores of workers. Now, however, he gave his migrant workers the confined concrete slab to pitch small tents on, at least initially. After a week or two the rancher would move the workers away into the hills and allow newer workers their portion of tent-days on the slab. When legal proceedings brought the rancher into court, the presiding judge in northern San Diego County accepted the rancher's "transitional" concrete-slab-with-tents as an "acceptable" compromise. The judge reasoned that when he served in the Marines, tents were accepted by the military as a legitimate form of housing in tactical maneuvers or war zones. Therefore, he reasoned, tents would certainly be acceptable for seasonal migrant workers of questionable legal status in San Diego County. Intended as a compromise informed by common sense, the ruling betrayed the tortured logic of the region. Yes, the Marine Corps bivouacs in tents on the battlefield, but the rancher's workers in Pala were minimum-wage, tax-paying American workers about as far away from U.S. military intervention as one could get. They certainly weren't picking American strawberries and bell peppers in a war zone.

This legal case was an exception that proves the rule. When migrants lose their cultural camouflage, they become newly visible. Such visibility tends to disrupt the local status quo, sometimes forcing local cultural paradigms to adjust to maintain legitimacy. The abject conditions of the Pala camp, once made public, easily unseated the fresh air trope of Southern California as a picturesque Mediterranean world. In its place, the courts sanctioned a new paradigm for the camps—of justly deserved hardship—apparently based on the implicit warlike conditions of California's suburban bedroom communities.

JOHN
THORNTON
CALDWELL

The various films I've discussed in this chapter all began by focusing on issues of migration and cross-cultural change. Yet during production, they all demonstrated a range of ways in which indigenous identities are performed for cultural advantage, sometimes very problematically. Looking back on the two and a half decades during which these projects were pursued suggests the complex ways in which indigenous identity is deployed and performed. Like a political football, indigenism is regularly stripped from its communal and embodied roots, and quickly becomes rhetorical grist in political and cultural wars that go far beyond any idea of essential identity or identity politics (see Table 5.1).

In the four production cases discussed here, indigenism functioned in contradictory ways: as poster child for American foreign policy (Miskitos), as an unruly enigma for organizers and crew bosses (Mixtecos), as cultural costuming and identity posturing (Newaris/hippies), and as a direct target of modernization and the rationalized economies that accompany it (Managalase). The rhetoric deployed in these instances similarly showed just how open to different uses and interpretations indigenism becomes in a cultural conflict. Indigenes are victims (Miskitos), indigenes are usurpers (Mixtecos), indigenism is nationally imagined (Newari/Buddhist/Hindu), and indigenism is reduced after government intervention to forms of cultural eye candy (Managalase). Table 5.1 details many more such flexible permutations at work in the worlds of the films discussed here. Most troubling to me is not that indigenism enters political struggle but that it has become such an integral weapon in the arsenal on both sides of many struggles. The U.S. government used the Miskitos in its 1980s political campaign, which was built on strategic racial essentialism. Yet the Mixtecos in the 1990s mastered tactical racial essentialism and what they termed bi-nationalism to confound their traditional enemies and force the application of fair-labor laws, employment rights, and occupational safeguards in the United States. Perhaps the most sobering lesson in all of this is how indigenism is used far beyond simple models of identity politics, through systematic conventions of deployment/visibility (Miskitos), erasure/invisibility (Mixtecos), syncretistic posturing (Newaris/hippies), and retrospective resuscitation (Managalase).

This very systematicity, both social and historical, deserves critical vigilance on the part of filmmakers, activists, and academics. One of my goals as a filmmaker is to force cultural issues and social problems to speak to questions other than their own, or other than those that

Table 5.1 Performing Indigenism: Cultural Politics, and Alternative Media Strategies

	Miskitos Nicaragua/Honduras *Personas Desplazadas*, 1983–1984	**Mixtecos** Oaxaca/San Diego *Rancho California*, 2002, and *Amor Vegetal*, 1997–1998	**Newaris/Hippies** Kathmandu, Nepal *Freak Street to Goa*, 1986–1989	**Managalase** Papua New Guinea *Kuije Kanan*, 1984–2005
1. Conflict(s)	Contras vs. Sandinistas, Contras vs. Miskitos, Sandinistas vs. Miskitos, U.S. vs. Sandinistas	Mixtecos vs. Mexicans, ranchers, employers, homeowners, and Latino foremen and crew bosses	Hippies vs. Western values, Indian/Nepali governments vs. street-level expatriates	Plantation and government prohibition against male initiation and tattooing
2. Role of Language	*Indigenous* creole language, *pidgin* English vs. Spanish	*Indigenous* Mixteco language vs. Spanish (*as second language*)	*Multilingual* settings in Goa and Kathmandu	*Indigenous*, plus pidgin English as trade language
3. Indigenous Community's Role	*Indigenes as handy poster child* for American foreign policy EXTREME VISIBILITY	*Indigenes as unruly enigmas* for U. S. Latino and labor organizations EXTREME INVISIBILITY	*Indigenism as a costume*, toleration of expatriates CASUAL POSTURING	*Indigenes as target of modernization* RESUSCITATION
4. Political Methods of Government	*Strategic racial essentialism*, protector of helpless indigenes; Reagan as Indian rights activist	*Calculated legal confusion* about which laws apply (OSHA, INS, fair housing, labor law, etc.)	*Strict visa limitations for expatriates*; totalitarian control of indigenes	*Rationalized efficiency*, and attempted unification under pan-tribal nationalism

Indigenes	*Transnational moral lobbying to ecumenical organizations and NGOs; agnostic political assertions*	*Binational organizing vs. U. S., Mexican government; cultural autonomy, tactical racial essentialism*	*Cultural syncretism by Newaris and Hippies, multicultural affinities*	*Gift culture payback as basis for human interactions, preemptive economy*
6. Ideological Contradiction(s)	Indigenism does not fit within binary U. S. cold war model (capitalism vs. communism)	Indigenism does not fit within binary U. S. immigration policy (legals vs. illegals)	Indigenism is *not transportable*; exotic government PR hides brutal caste relations	Indigenism as *cultural/artistic feature* guts it of social agency and force
7. Resulting Rhetoric	Indigenes as victims, protecting U. S.'s vulnerable "back door"	Indigenes as usurpers, Third World invading U. S.'s "back door"	Indigenism as imagined nation, and financial lure	Indigenes as eye candy for tourist culture
8. Dominant Media Strategies	Staged media events, airborne assaults alongside Miskito UNHCR refugee camp "stage"	Emphasize out-of-control migrant fertility, childbirth, and destruction of U. S. schools and government	Information management: government solicits tourism, but controls foreign filmmakers	Exotic as trade genre: ethnographic colonial gaze as commodity
9. Counter-Media Strategies	Show consensus exploitations in relief work, and Nicaraguan nationalism among Miskitos	Show consensus culpabilities and "little racial tactics of habitat" vs. totalizing political fixes	Reverse ethnography; made fake film for government censors; filmed secretly	Participant recreation: oral histories; elder pedagogy for youth

are typically used to frame them. Indigenous racial identity seems to be one of those issues that merit continual reconsideration, especially given the ways that indigenism is exploited and used, problematically, as a free-floating signifier. The approach I've outlined in this essay is, of course, inevitably provisional. Forcing films to confront the con-

structed and contested nature of indigenous racial identity may make it easier, arguably, to engage racism in the lived world. Racial conflict, in many of its worst manifestations, results when people opportunistically invoke or glibly marginalize indigenous identity as an innate, a priori problem. Racial categories that appear natural rather than culturally constructed and maintained, that is, may only facilitate cross-cultural solutions involving violence. Making race natural in this way severely limits the possibilities of active, critical engagement in the now ubiquitous cross-cultural spaces that increasingly define us in California and the nation.

Let's move beyond indigenism as a free-floating signifier, an exploitable cultural costume and posture, and consider it more closely and patiently: as historically specific socially constructed ways of managing and making sense of human and group behavior. The real masters of this process are as creative at deploying indigenism as any artist in any other medium: the indigenous Miskito and Mixteco activists and organizers that I met and worked with. While they mod-

Billboard colonialism. Top, Spanish-language broadcaster creates furor with white anti-immigration groups by placing L.A. "in" Mexico. Yet even indigenous Central Americans in Pico-Union district in L.A. were upset at being grouped together as "Mexicans" in the backlash. Middle, KFI fights back with nationalistic billboard of its own. Bottom, gang of white suburban youths from Rancho Penasquitos in San Diego County beat up and stab migrants in camps, then tag their huts with KKK slurs. (Top and middle photographs © Jeff Share, 2005; bottom photograph © 2002, J. Caldwell.)

how indigenism can be used tactically for cultural resistance and progessive change, the rest of us would do well to stall the strategic schemes that continually rip indigenism from its moorings in order to build suspect passing ideologies.

Notes

1. Although the terms for signs that no longer have fixed meanings—"free-float-ing signifier" and "empty signifier"—were developed by Umberto Eco, Jacques Derr-ida, and Jean Baudrillard, I prefer Alan Sekula's pragmatic deployment of the concepts as cultural images that are literally "up for grabs" and primed for endless appropria-tion and inflection by a succession of new "owners." See Alan Sekula, "Photography Between Labor and Capital," in *Mining Photographs and Other Pictures*, ed. Benjamin H. D. Buchloh and Robert Wilkie (Halifax, NS: The Press of the Nova Scotia College of Art and Design, 1983), 194. A very good summary discussion of the intellectual roots and various permutations of the idea of the free-floating signifier and the empty signi-fier in the theories of Eco, Derrida, and Baudrillard is Daniel Chandler, *Semiotics: The Basics* (London: Routledge, 2002), 74–76. A critique of these key postmodern concepts is found in Terry Eagleton, *The Ideology of the Aesthetic* (Oxford: Blackwell, 1990), 387.

2. Each of my cross-cultural projects was cooperative in different ways. I want es-pecially to acknowledge my partners, without whom each of these films could not have been completed: J. Lalnunsang Pudaite, co-director, C. Thanthieng Khobung, sound, and T. S. Hale, cinematography, on *Freak Street;* William McKellin, anthropologist, on *Kuije Kanan: Managalase Tattooing;* Joel Sheesley on *Personas Desplazadas;* Devora Gomez, assistant director and sound on *Rancho California* and co-director and story editor on *Amor Vegetal: Our Harvest;* and the La Cosecha Nuestra garden community in South Escondido, co-creators, on *Amor Vegetal: Our Harvest.*

3. Detailed authoritative accounts of these processes are contained in the research of my colleague on the *Kuije Kanan* project, anthropologist William McKellin. See "Kinship Ideology and Language Pragmatics Among the Managalase of Papua New Guinea," unpublished Ph.D. dissertation (University of Toronto, 1980), and "Hege-mony and the Language of Change: The Pidginization of Land Tenure Among the Managalase of Papua New Guinea," *Ethnology* 30, no. 4 (October 1991): 313–324.

4. These screenings included film festivals in New York, Berlin, Amsterdam, Chicago, and Hawaii; network broadcasts on SBS-Television Australia; and domestic broadcasts on WTTW-PBS Chicago from 1989 to 1994. The film was distributed interna-tionally and nontheatrically during those years by Filmmaker's Library, New York.

5. See Vijaya Mulay, "Panther Panchali (The Story of the Road)," *Jump Cut* 45 (Oc-tober 2002), online.

6. This community gardening–media project is discussed more fully in John Caldwell, "Representation and Complicity in the Suburban Campo," *Aztlan: Journal of Chicano Studies* 28, no. 2 (Fall 2003): 205–226.

CHAPTER 6

Traversing Cinematic Borders

AN INTERVIEW WITH PAUL ESPINOSA

Daniel Bernardi
(Arizona State University)

Paul Espinosa is an acclaimed documentary and narrative filmmaker. He produces, directs, and writes much of his work, which focuses on the cultural and political lives of Latinos in, around, over, under, and through the U.S.-Mexico border. The recipient of one national and seven San Diego Emmys and five CINE Golden Eagle awards, among others, he owns his own production company, Espinosa Productions; served as the director of the Office of Latino Affairs for KPBS-TV, San Diego, from 1980 to 1990; and later served as executive director for public affairs and ethnic issues.

One of his first films, *The Trail North* (1983), told the story of immigration from the perspective of one family's journey north to the United States over an extended period of time. He followed this work with several documentaries and narratives expanding on issues of Latino identity, immigration, and human rights, including *Ballad of an Unsung Hero* (1984), *The Lemon Grove Incident* (1986), *In the Shadow of the Law* (1988), and *Uneasy Neighbors* (1990), among others. His work has also addressed border politics and culture from a historical perspective, including most prominently *The Hunt for Pancho Villa* (1993), *The U.S.-Mexican War: 1846–1848* (1998), and *The Border* (2000). At the same time, Espinosa has used film to engage Latina/o artistic expression, most notably in *1492 Revisited* (1992) and *Taco Shop Poets* (2004), featured in *Visiones: Latino Art in the U.S.*, a six-part documentary series examining the range of Latino art in the United States. And he's still going at it. His most recent work, *The Price of Renewal* (2006), is an insightful documentary that examines the complex problems involving community development, philanthropy, and civic engagement in a run-down neighborhood in San Diego called City Heights, often referred to as the Ellis Island of San Diego. Tireless, Espinosa also has several projects in development.[1]

As one might tell from his body of work, a number of facts and facets make Espinosa a compelling filmmaker: his commitment to and knowledge of Latino history and life; his independence, which suggests a persistent and dedicated ethic seen in only the most successful filmmakers; and his training. Born and raised in the Southwest, Espinosa received two degrees in anthropology, a B.A. from Brown University and a Ph.D. from Stanford University. At the same time, he has always been interested in both critiquing and making media. At Stanford, for example, his work specialized in the cultural analyses of television as a communication medium capable of both degrading and enlightening audiences. The films that he produces and directs today carry on this work, as we discuss in this interview. Espinosa is an intellectual who seeks to reveal the complexity of Latino lives.

Despite being a productive filmmaker, Espinosa continues to extend his voice, vision, and community activism. After a long and successful career as an independent filmmaker in San Diego, he accepted a faculty position at Arizona State University (ASU), Tempe, in the Department of Transborder Chicana/o and Latina/o Studies. That's where we met. He and I started our faculty positions at ASU in the fall of 2004.

Community storeowner Juan Neri (left) of La Especial Produce, a mom-and-pop grocery store in City Heights, San Diego, being interviewed by Paul Espinosa (right) for the documentary *The Price of Renewal*. (Photograph by Kevin Walsh.)

I came from the Department of Media Arts at the University of Arizona, excited to work in both Chicano and Chicana studies and film and media studies at the rival institution up the road. But I was also a bit anxious. I had never worked in an "ethnic studies" department, having always been in film and media programs. I'm also no Chicano but Puerto Rican and Italian. How was I going to fit in? My colleagues in both areas welcomed me with enthusiasm. After all, they had recruited and hired me in ways that suggested a profound understanding and distrust of all kinds of borders. Still, I was somewhat anxious until I realized I'd be working side by side with an acclaimed filmmaker, especially one who challenges viewers to see things differently, just as I hope my articles and books similarly challenge readers. Our interview took place over several months, mostly through conversations across the hall, through email, before and after faculty meetings, and over lunch.

PAUL ESPINOSA: I think to really answer that question, I'd have to go back and explain the way in which my own educational experiences laid the foundation for the work I ultimately engaged in professionally.

While I was still an undergraduate student, I had an unusual opportunity to travel to Guatemala. I spent six months in the tropical jungle of the Peten, in northern Guatemala, excavating a classic Maya site. I also traveled around southern Mexico and Guatemala seeing the tremendous diversity of cultures in that region.

That experience proved to be a major turning point for me—it provided firsthand a much more powerful way of understanding culture and Latin America in general than any college class could. As a native of New Mexico, it also provided a concrete way for me to grasp that Latin America really began in the region where I had grown up.

An Interview with Paul Espinosa

When I returned to college after being in Guatemala and Mexico, I decided to major in anthropology because it seemed to me to be a powerful tool for trying to understand some of what I had been witnessing.

DB: When did you become interested in media?

PE: I went on to do graduate work in anthropology, but throughout my education, I was interested in finding a bridge between anthropology and media. One of the things which had caught my attention in Latin America was the incredible visibility of American-made media throughout the hemisphere. Whether you turned on a television or went to a movie theater, chances were pretty good that you would see a film or television show made in the United States. In most instances, the gap between the content on the screen and the reality of Latin America was glaring, both economically and culturally.

This observation about the dominance of American imperialism led me to ask various questions: what impact did so much "foreign" content have on Latin American countries, and where did media content come from in the first place? These were questions I was wrestling with as I began my graduate work in anthropology at Stanford University.

As I began to plan my fieldwork, I pondered how I could probe the relationship between anthropology and media. Anthropologists, as many of us know, typically go someplace far away, like the South Sea Islands, and study what the "natives" do. After they finish their fieldwork they return home, usually to a university in the First World, and write up their observations about "what the natives do."

I decided I would go to a "village" in Southern California named Hollywood and study what the "natives" do. I thought it could be productive to study this "village" and to train the anthropological lens on media makers themselves.

DB: What kind of reception did you get from the village people of Hollywood?

PE: When I embarked on my fieldwork, like a typical anthropologist I had a few leads and knew very little about my village. I went to Hollywood and began making phone calls. Most would lead nowhere. I learned quickly that the idea of an anthropologist doing long-term participant observation in a Hollywood studio was perceived as a slightly bizarre concept. For some reason, it was hard for people to get their heads around the idea. I gradually learned that doing long-term observation in Hollywood was going to be difficult. However, several things worked in my favor. My home institution, Stanford University, was not only a well-known institution in Hollywood, it was also highly regarded. Whatever prestige Stanford had in many people's minds was rubbing off on me.

After many, many unproductive attempts to enter a village, I finally reached a highly placed producer who seemed willing to at least entertain the idea of a visit from an anthropologist. He invited me to come by his offices and discuss my idea further. I knew that I had only made the first step in getting my foot in the door and that I would have to be careful and sensitive to how the natives felt.

I was interested, in a very general way, in how television takes cultural stories, massages and manipulates them, and then feeds them back into the general society. I suppose the oft-quoted sausage metaphor—you like eating the sausage when it's finished but you don't really want to see how it is made—comes to mind.

I ended up having unusual access to the key creative decision makers in an episodic television series—the so-called hyphenate producers—successful writers who were becoming executive producers on hour dramas in the late 1970s.

The ethnographic study I completed focused on the story conference as a key activity where television stories were created. Story conferences were meetings where executive producers met with writers on particular episodes to construct the story to be told. Although I didn't realize it at the time, this experience in Hollywood would launch me into the world of production. For one thing, I had learned a great deal about television production in the course of my study. At the same time, I was becoming aware of the constraints in commercial television and learning about a new kid on the block—public television.

As I surveyed the TV landscape in the late 1970s, another thing be-

came glaringly apparent: the way in which my own community, Mexican
Americans, and Latinos in general were imaged in the media. Either the
presentation was very stereotypical—where the only Latino characters
you saw were gang-bangers, gardeners, maids, or prostitutes—or Latinos
were completely invisible. This reality, along with a budding relationship
with the PBS affiliate in San Diego, led me to become actively involved in
producing content about my own community.

DB: Why did you elect to make documentaries? Why didn't you make
ethnographic films, for example?

PE: As I began making films about the larger border region, I wasn't
particularly focused on questions about genre. In other words, I wasn't
asking questions like, was I making ethnographic films? Was my work
part of visual anthropology? I wasn't even thinking just about documentaries, although initially most of my work was in the documentary genre
and my focus was on telling stories about aspects of the Latino experience that I believed were important for a general audience. Certainly
in thinking about my work, both in retrospect and at the time, I was
aware that it would be seen by different kinds of audiences, for example,
scholars, the general public, the Chicano community, the larger white
community, and other subsets of the public television audience.

An Interview with Paul Espinosa

In a general sense, my work is an example of applied anthropology, taking insights about culture, conflict, and change and presenting
stories with meaning for a broad general audience. Perhaps the way in
which my work has differed most from traditional anthropology (whatever that is) is in the question of audience. Instead of an interest in communicating with a narrow academic audience, my objective has been to
reach a broad public audience and inform them about relevant social and
cultural issues.

DB: Yet anthropologists have often made and contributed to the making of films that have been racist despite an often conscious attempt
not to be racist. Some examples of these are the "look at the pristine
native" films that end up crafting a division between civilization and
nature; the white man or the man or woman that has the camera and
can show the "truth"; and natives, such as *Nanook of the North*, that
are romantically constructed as being at one with nature. Your films
don't perpetuate these tropes. Why? As an applied anthropologist, how
do you avoid this history of visual anthropology, let alone the history of
cinema?

PE: I came into anthropology at a reflexive moment for the discipline.
When I began my graduate studies at Stanford, I entered that program

at an unusual point in time, when nearly 25 percent of the entering students in the Department of Anthropology were Chicano. As students from a community that had often been studied by anthropologists in ways that were often seen as uninformed, we were particularly critical of anthropology. We called attention to the privileged position that anthropologists had traditionally held—knowing that they usually came from First World countries and studied in Third World communities, which were relatively powerless in comparison to where they came from.

Laura Nader, an anthropologist at Berkeley, had coined the term "studying up" to apply to situations where anthropologists had trained their lens "up" instead of "down." Some anthropologists began studying communities that had more power than traditional indigenous communities in the Third World. These general developments in the field, along with the cultural imperialism I had seen firsthand in Latin America, were some of the elements that influenced my decision to focus my field-work on a Hollywood studio—certainly a powerful community that had not been the focus of anthropologists. After finishing my fieldwork and my dissertation, as I entered the world of production, all these ideas were part of the foundation that I carried into my productions.

DANIEL
BERNARDI

DB: What films, filmmakers, or styles from this period influence your productions the most?

PE: Maybe because of the way in which I came to make films, I have been mostly driven by content—and my internalized role as an anthropologist—with certain ideas that I wanted to communicate to audiences. I'm not really aware of having been consciously influenced by specific films or filmmakers. There are certain issues that have drawn my attention, and I have been interested in pursuing films on these topics.

I have come to appreciate the paramount importance of good storytelling. At the same time, I have also found so many absences in the media, in terms of stories about the Latino experience. I found myself wanting to pursue such stories and finding often that these stories required a kind of excavation. You had to dig down, and often dig deep, to recuperate these stories.

DB: What are some examples of good storytelling, in your view?

PE: I have enjoyed narrative films that address social and cultural issues, films like *Midnight Cowboy, The Pawnbroker, To Kill a Mockingbird, Apocalypse Now,* and many of the films of John Sayles. I find films that deal with what happens when two cultures come into contact particular intriguing, such as the films of Peter Weir—*The Year of Living Dangerously* and *The Last Wave*—or *El Norte,* and more recently *Whale Rider.* I

also like the storytelling in political documentaries such as *Eyes on the*
Prize, Hearts and Minds, The Times of Harvey Milk, Who Killed Vincent Chin?, and many investigative pieces done for *Frontline*.

I have also been exposed to a great deal of Latin American cinema. In the late 1980s I was invited to serve on the documentary jury for the Festival of New Latin American Cinema in Havana. This was a tremendous experience because I was able to see many powerful Latin American films and meet many Latin American filmmakers. It provided an immediate primer on social, political, and cultural documentaries being produced throughout the Americas and showed me the tremendous range of work and experimentation taking place in the genre.

Just a few years after that experience, I was part of a small contingent of Chicano filmmakers who were invited to Mexico for "Chicanos '90." This was a landmark event, given the way in which Chicanos have often been dismissed by Mexicans as *"pochos,"* as individuals who have somehow abandoned their *Mexicanidad* or are not quite "Mexican" enough in someone's view. We met with Mexican independent filmmakers and shared ideas and knowledge about filmmaking. We had an opportunity to present our films to Mexican audiences in various venues, both in theaters and on television, and to see firsthand that the Chicano experience as presented in our films was something that Mexicans were interested in knowing more about. These experiences opened up new worlds both in terms of contacts and subject matter. "Chicanos '90" was really part of a much larger, new relationship between Chicanos and Mexico. Mexico began to realize the importance of so-called "Mexicans in the exterior," a population that numbered in the millions and has only grown since.

D B: What is it about the border that compels you to tell so many stories about it and its place in culture? You could focus on other aspects of Latino life, other areas of the hemisphere, for example.

P E: For a filmmaker with a background in anthropology, the border has been an ideal location. It's almost as though the region is a laboratory where (at least) two cultures and societies are in contact and conflict. 's a crucible for great stories.

Although I didn't plan it in any strategic way, being in San Diego, right on the U.S.-Mexico border, turned out to be a perfect place for my interests and my background. And of course, there has never been any shortage of interesting characters and events. From the start, immigration has been a major topic of interest for me. Back in the early 1980s, and even today, the topic is often framed in relation to the issue of criminal activity. And the media contributed to this framing by generating a large amount of coverage of immigrants being apprehended at the border. The iconic image was a nighttime scene of poor Mexican immigrants, hands held high, as Border Patrol agents with night scopes and helicopters arrested them and sent them back to Mexico. To me this was a classic case of the media shedding lots of heat but no light on a topic. I believed that to gain even a basic understanding of immigration, you had to know who these people were and why they were coming north.

DB: And thus to tell their stories, right?

PE: Right. Their stories formed the background for one of my earliest films, *The Trail North,* which examined the issue of immigration through the lens of a particular family's story. This film was the result of collaboration with a fellow graduate student at Stanford, Robert Alva-

rez, who had studied his own family's journey north. In *The Trail North,* we used the narrative device of seeing Robert recapture for his son, Luis, the migration his family had made in previous generations. I was also lucky to get Martin Sheen to narrate the film, which became my first national PBS program. I was surprised to be able to reach him on the phone and even more

Paul Espinosa (right with script) rehearses actors, including Guillermo Gomez-Pena (seated at left in white), during a scene from *The Lemon Grove Incident* in which Mexican American parents gather to discuss the school board's plan to segregate their children. (Photograph by Kira Corser.)

surprised that he agreed to do it, although this was in the early 1980s, before Sheen was so well known.

DB: But after he made *Badlands,* by Terrence Malick, a terrific film. So your career was off to a good start. Where did you go from there?

PE: *The Trail North* led to a second film, called *The Lemon Grove Incident,* which was also a collaboration with Robert Alvarez. The families from *The Trail North* had migrated over several generations to Lemon Grove, a small community just outside San Diego. At the time, it was a small rural town with a growing Mexican population. It would become the site of the first successful legal challenge to school segregation anywhere in the country.

Of course, most of us know the landmark case of *Brown v. Board of Education* (1954), and when we think about school segregation, we usually think about it in black and white terms. But in fact, many early segregation cases occurred in the Southwest, and they involved not just

African American children but Mexican American, Native American, and Asian American children. *The Lemon Grove Incident* is the story of one of these cases. The film was part of a larger effort at recuperating aspects of the Mexican American historical experience, since so much of that experience had never made its way into the history books.

DB: *The Lemon Grove Incident is a powerful film. You continue working with many of its themes and issues.*

PE: Right. Within a short period of time, I found myself producing more stories like *The Lemon Grove Incident*—stories that had been only footnotes in history. One story was a fascinating portrait of one of the first Spanish-language recording stars in the United States, a man named Pedro J. Gonzalez, whose radio program on Los Angeles station KMPC became one of the biggest shows of its time.

When I first met Mr. Gonzalez in his humble home in San Ysidro and heard parts of his story, it was hard to believe that all of what he recounted had really happened. In many ways, his life was like a microcosm of the Mexican American experience in the Southwest. He had been involved in the Mexican Revolution working as a telegraph operator for Pancho Villa; then, like thousands of his countrymen, he had fled to the United States and begun a new life in Los Angeles, where he eventually had a very popular and well-known radio show. Because KMPC was a 500,000-watt station, his show was known throughout the Southwest, not just in Los Angeles.

Paul Espinosa (left) conducting a short interview with Julio Medina, narrator of *Ballad of an Unsung Hero*, during a voiceover recording session. (Photograph by Kira Corser.)

In 1934, he would be framed in a political case and spend six years in San Quentin prison before being released and deported to Mexico, due to the efforts of defense committees. When I first met Mr. Gonzalez and his wife Maria, he was already eighty-six, but both of them turned out to be great storytellers. The resulting film was *Ballad of an Unsung Hero*, a collaborative project with Lorena Parlee and Isaac Artenstein, who went on to make a feature film about Mr. Gonzalez.

DB: *Is this when you began focusing on immigration?*

PE: Yes. I produced two more films—*In the Shadow of the Law* and *Uneasy Neighbors*—examining the difficult lives of undocumented immigrants in Southern California. Both films were attempts to provide a window into the world of being undocumented for a mainstream audience.

I had the opportunity to collaborate with Hector Galan on two films for *The American Experience*. At the time, Hector and I were probably the two most prolific Latino producers for PBS, Hector having produced many shows for *Frontline*. One film we collaborated on took place in Arizona. Titled *Los Mineros,* the film was produced for PBS's history series *The American Experience,* and it chronicled the story of Mexican American copper miners' fifty-year struggle for justice in Arizona. *The Hunt for Pancho Villa,* a second film done for *The American Experience,* examined Pancho Villa's raid on the small border community of Columbus, New Mexico, in 1916, and the American expedition led by General John "Blackjack" Pershing, which spent almost a year in Mexico searching for Villa, without success. Both of these films were part of a larger effort to recapture the experiences of the Mexican American community and present those stories to both that community and the larger society.

Another major project, a feature-length adaptation of an important Chicano novel . . . *and the earth did not swallow him,* based on Tomás Rivera's novel, was a collaboration with Severo Perez on a narrative film, which was a departure for me. Although *The Lemon Grove Incident* was a docudrama, most of my previous work had been in documentary. So this film, produced for PBS's *American Playhouse* drama series, was in a different genre. However, because the story dealt with one year in the life of a young Mexican American boy and his migrant farmworker family, the subject matter was not unfamiliar.

From the time I began producing, it was clear that the national PBS schedule was practically devoid of programs dealing with the Latino experience. In short order, I realized that the films I was producing about the Southwest border region could have a national audience.

DANIEL
BERNARDI

DB: How did your work at KPBS-TV, San Diego, and with PBS both facilitate and hinder the kind of stories you tell? It's clearly provided you the opportunity to make films and reach large audiences, but has it also informed the kinds of films you made?

PE: Looking back on the work I began at KPBS, I think that I had a great deal of freedom to decide what stories I wanted to tell. Part of the reason for this freedom was that, fairly quickly, it became apparent to both me and those at KPBS that I knew as much as or more than they did about the topics I wanted to pursue.

I also quickly discovered that if I wanted to make television shows that were more than studio discussions, I would have to raise money to do that. As it turned out, I had very valuable experience with grant writ ing, and that experience was soon put to the test, as I began to generate grants to make individual films. I was able to persuade funders that the subjects I was interested in were topics that they should fund, not only for audiences in San Diego, where I was located, but for national and regional audiences. In this respect, I think I also profited from the fact that there was so little content being produced for national PBS and there was a great need to have some programs on the air.

I generally relied on my own sense of what needed to be produced and approaches that I believed would help audiences make sense of the border region. I was also certainly interested in reaching a diverse audience, both Latino and non-Latino. Public broadcasting was also a very important venue for early Chicano filmmakers. Many of the films that came out of the Chicano movement first appeared on PBS, and many early Chicano filmmakers, such as Jesus Trevino and Gregory Nava, cut their teeth on public television projects. There was a small space there for us to create work. We seized that opportunity and we struggled to enlarge that space, producing both documentary and narrative films about the Latino experience. Sometimes we worried about how many Latinos were watching PBS, because the ratings didn't always look so good, but we kept telling PBS that our shows could help them grow their Latino audience for the future.

An Interview
with Paul
Espinosa

DB: And yet if you don't raise the funds to make the film, the audience will miss out on that story. I'm wondering if you could talk more about funding. How does one go about identifying sources, securing funding from those sources, and then staying honest to vision and mission despite the necessary evil that money can bring to a project?

PE: Much of the early funding that I was able to generate for my films came directly from either the public broadcasting world or the state humanities councils. The California Council for the Humanities was an important initial funder for quite a few of my films, including *The Trail North* and *The Lemon Grove Incident*. However, I soon realized that many of the topics I was interested in were also of interest to humanities councils in other states, as well as the National Endowment for the Humanities. As I began to receive national broadcast dates for my films, I was also able to tap into national pots of money reserved for public broadcasting. One of the principal sources was the Corporation for Public Broadcasting, which would ultimately provide some part of the funding for nine of my films.

The funding from CCH, NEH, or CPB was all intended to support work for public broadcasting, and the hardest part of working with these funders was securing the funding in the first place because of heavy competition. However, once you were funded, there was little interference from the funder in the filmmaking. Of course, you had to comply with your original proposal and vision for the work, but beyond that, you had a great deal of independence.

DB: You seemed to have been quite successful at securing funding.

PE: What also happens is that the more success you have with funding organizations, the more visibility you have with these funders. One result is that when you are not an applicant in a particular round, it was not uncommon to be invited to be part of a funding panel that was reviewing proposals to that funder. Participating in this process is very valuable for a filmmaker, because you learn a great deal both about the funding organization and its interests, as well as the range of applicants out in the field. If you are reviewing proposals for a national funder like CPB or NEH, you are seeing the best proposals in the country, and that alone is very instructive in terms of learning how others are approaching stories and topics.

DB: How important was this support to your overall career?

PE: Support from public sources was absolutely key to my ability to produce the films I did. My work was not produced with commercial concerns as the primary motive. I think we desperately need to support social issue documentaries through public funding, despite the controversy that is often generated in this realm. This need is more paramount today than when I began my career, as corporate decision making has come to dominate so much of the news business. In many communities around the country, we, as citizens, are poorly informed by our local media, either print or electronic, about what is happening in our own communities, our states, or even in our country as a whole. I believe documentary films are an important antidote to this situation and need to be seen as a healthy part of the ecology of our public information landscape, if we expect to have a functioning democracy. Documentary filmmakers are often guided by an interest in public service and passionate about their subjects, and both of these elements can produce riveting engaged films that educate and inform audiences.

DB: What specifically do you look for in a project? In other words, what kinds of specific issues—historical, political, cultural, and creative— are important to you in the selection of a project? There are a lot of Latino stories out there. How do you pick the right one to film?

PE: Generally speaking, I have to be drawn to the story. To some extent, the fact that I bring a broad education about the border region to any decision means that I have some idea about how important I believe certain stories to be. For example, I know that certain historical events and individuals have been lost to history, and projects that can help to restore their importance are ones that attract me. Looking back at my body of work, I suppose that one could find an intersection of culture and history in my work. I have also been interested in collaborating whenever possible and I think much of my work bears the stamp of collaboration.

DB: Much of your work centers on challenging stereotypes and drawing out cultural complexity. How do you ensure that you don't end up reifying stereotypes and simplifying culture in the production of what will be an emotional picture that takes less than two or so hours from start to finish? For example, what kinds of things do you do to ensure you don't perpetuate negative or simplistic images of women, people of color, or even Chicanos?

An Interview with Paul Espinosa

PE: That's a little hard to answer. Whether you are reifying stereotypes or not is often in the eye of the beholder. My commitment has been to try to tell complex stories, letting individuals "speak" on their own behalf, using as much care as I can in selecting material that ends up in a final program. I think that authentic stories of real people have their own integrity. In the process of telling these stories, you end up challenging stereotypes because their stories inevitably provide a counterpoint to existing portrayals, which are often one-dimensional. I think you also have to trust audiences and their ability to see the "real deal." Sometimes this comes through in humor, where a quirky or funny line in an interview establishes that all-important credibility between the film and the audience, assuring them about the authenticity of what they're seeing.

DB: And I think your work does a great job of doing so, but still you have to boil complex lives down to an hour or two hours if you're working in the feature-length format. And you make films about diverse individuals. They're not simply Latino, Mexican, or Chicano but also women, rich and poor, rural and urban, young and old, and so on. What kinds of things or thoughts do you recommend an aspiring filmmaker consider as they tell stories in film about real people's lives? What process, intuitive or directed, do you undergo in this regard?

PE: For me, there is always a tension between a great story or individual and the larger issue which that story represents. I think all of ? love great stories and are drawn to well-told stories of interesting ?dividuals. And for the Chicano/Latino community, there is a wealth of ?scinating individuals whose stories have generally not been told. But ? you uncover these stories, I am also interested in knowing how these ?eat stories fit into the larger context of the community. How representative is the story you want to tell? Does it allow you to tell a larger story about important community issues and concerns? Is it likely to reinforce stereotypes among some audiences?

These are questions that I ask myself and that I would ask aspiring filmmakers to ask of themselves and the films they want to make. It's a dialectical process of identifying great stories and then working through a process, either internally or externally, of discovering more about how that great story fits into the larger fabric of Latino community life. Some filmmakers would regard this as a burden of sorts, and one they might not want to carry, but ultimately, if their work is going to be valuable to the community from which they come, as well as the larger society, it is absolutely critical to engage with these questions.

DANIEL
BERNARDI

DB: In what ways do your cast and crew influence the project? Describe the typical Espinosa production process and the degree to which you collaborate with other filmmakers.

PE: Producing films is inherently a collaborative process. Depending on the scale of the production, there may be hundreds of people working with you on a film. I have produced two narrative films— . . . and the earth did not swallow him and The Lemon Grove Incident. Both involved dozens of speaking parts, multiple locations, and dozens of crew members. On these films, there were many, many members of the cast and crew playing a role in bringing the story to the screen. For example, on the cinematography side, I had the good fortune to work with Russell Carpenter on The Lemon Grove Incident. Carpenter provided a wonderful sense of lighting and camera for what became a highly awarded docudrama. As you know, Russell Carpenter went on to work in Hollywood and win an Oscar for his cinematography on Titanic.

But even in the smaller scale of documentary films, I have had the good fortune to work with key individuals whose contributions have played a role in the final film. This has included crew and filmmakers who have particular skills or sensitivities to bring a story to the screen, as well as scholars or activists who are knowledgeable or deeply committed to certain stories.

DB: How do you think your work fits within the contemporary documentary tradition in general and films about the border in particular? How does it fit in the Chicano/a movement? In what ways does it spea to Latino/as specifically and U.S. "diversity" in general?

PE: The contemporary documentary tradition is so broad and increa ingly diverse that I'm not really certain where my work fits into that tra dition. In terms of films about the border, my work has been widely see by other filmmakers and audiences. At the time that I began working in the early 1980s, the amount of attention the border region was receiving was much less than it is today. As the years have passed, I have seen greater and greater interest in the border, and have had the opportunity to assist or advise filmmakers and film crews from all over the country and all over the world, as they have "discovered" the border.

I am certainly a product of the Chicano movement, and part of my work, whether consciously or not, has been inspired by the civil rights movement. Like many young people who came to know a little bit about their own community's history during that period, I became committed to trying to tell some of these untold stories. So much of the experience of the Latino community is not well covered by the media or in film. And when you look back historically, this is even more the case.

There are hundreds of wonderful stories from the past that are still waiting to be told. From a documentarian's perspective, some of those stories are disappearing with each passing year, because the men and women whose oral history would be essential to telling that story are passing on. For young students with any interest in community history, I strongly encourage them to sit down with their parents or grandparents and videotape or even audiotape their stories. These documents will be very valuable to the individual students in the future, and will probably be of value to any archival collection on the Latino community.

Perhaps because of my training, I have always been interested in speaking to a diverse audience. I have been aware of the fact that my work can speak to at least two different audiences—the Latino community and the larger, non-Latino, Anglo community. That said, I am also aware that both of these audiences are very diverse. Latinos, of course, are composed of individuals from many Latin American countries, although people of Mexican origin constitute by far the largest section of this community and my intended audience. On the non-Latino side, it goes without saying that this is a diverse audience, composed of all of the "minority" communities—African American, Asian American, Native American, and others—as well as the mainstream, white community.

I have been interested in reaching as wide an audience as possible. Some people don't think that you can speak to both, that it's an either/or proposition. But I don't hold to that theory. I have been aware that different audiences will take different things from the films you make. Some will be able to appreciate parts of the film much more than others, but that doesn't mean that a general audience won't understand your film. This speaks to the multivocality of any text, which can say different things to different audiences. As with any text, what you take from a film partially conditioned by what you bring to it.

DB: What advice do you offer your students at ASU, the ones that want to make films? Do you tell them to go to graduate school in film or anthropology (or another academic area)? Do you advise them to start now or wait until they have more formal training? What advice do you give them about making political and creative choices about real people?

PE: The good news is that there are many, many ways to make a film these days, so there is not a single path to becoming a filmmaker. I would advise students to assess their own background, skills, and temperament in considering how to enter the field. There is certainly no substitute for developing good critical thinking skills, and students can develop those skills through a variety of disciplines, including anthropology, history, literature, journalism, and others.

If students have an opportunity to gain experience on a media project, that would be valuable to them, but not so much for the actual skills they might learn, which would probably be only at the beginner's level, but, more important, these kinds of internship or entry-level experiences give students a chance to see if filmmaking is really what they want to do. The idea of making films is very attractive and sexy to a lot of young people, but sometimes when they actually experience working on a film, they decide that it's really not their cup of tea. Learning this sooner rather than later is helpful.

Students also have to develop a long view, meaning that they shouldn't just worry about how to get their first film made—usually on a topic they are deeply passionate about. The challenge is learning how to make your second film or your third film, and how to develop the stamina and the skills to have the staying power to be able to do that. I think film schools should have more discussions and training about the long view, because if you are going to be a filmmaker, particularly a documentary filmmaker, these are questions you have to think about.

DB: What are you working on now? What's next?

PE: I am just finishing a new four-hour series for PBS called *California and the American Dream* that will be broadcast in the spring of 2006. This series explores the dynamics of culture, community, and identity in California, one of the most diverse regions in the world. In the last thirty-five years, California has become center-stage for an array of issues redefining the American agenda, from changing demographics to new models of civic engagement, from the role of immigrants in neighborhood life to the democratic challenge of the initiative process, from sustainable agriculture to Native American gaming and sovereignty.

DANIEL
BERNARDI

The series represents an independent vision of a new California, a vision largely absent from the stereotyped and superficial portraits of our communities and our struggles. The series is produced by four nationally acclaimed documentary producers with longstanding relationships to ethnic communities, progressive organizations, and PBS—Lyn Goldfarb, Jed Riffe, Emiko Omori, and myself.

In the series, we argue that the experiences of California, the world's sixth-largest economy, are highly instructive in exploring the priorities of life in a postindustrial America in which "minorities" constitute a majority of the population. Each film stands alone; however, taken together, the four episodes examine a complex, daunting, but supremely crucial set of issues: Can peoples of diverse cultures and thinking come together to redefine home, community, and civic participation in ways that lead to a peaceful, prosperous society?

I am also at work on a number of other documentaries, including a documentary on San Diego folksinger and composer Ramon "Chunky" Sanchez, who has distinguished himself as a community organizer and educator of barrio youth; a film examining transnational indigenous women migrants who can no longer support themselves on their traditional lands; a documentary on the life of Antonio José Martínez, a leading intellectual and political figure who lived through some of the most turbulent years of the borderlands, when the region changed first from Spanish to Mexican control and then was conquered by the United States; and a project on the untold story of immigration through the heart of our southern border, *El Paso del Norte*, where generations of immigrants passed on their way to "El Norte."

One doesn't become a nationally recognized and, more important, a thoughtful filmmaker without support. Espinosa has received funding from the Corporation for Public Broadcasting, the National Endowment for the Humanities, American Playhouse, the John D. and Catherine T. MacArthur Foundation, the Ford Foundation, ITVS, and McDonald's Corporation, among many others. His films have been screened on PBS and in festivals across the country and around the world, including the Santa Barbara International Film Festival (where was awarded Best of the Festival), the Minneapolis International Film Festival (Best of the Festival), the American Film Festival (two Blue Ribbons and a Red Ribbon), Viña del Mar, Chile Film Festival (Special Jury Award), Cairo International Film Festival (Jury Award for Artistic Achievement), Mill Valley Film Festival, Havana's Festival of New Latin American Cinema, the Houston International Film Festival, the National Latino Film and Video Festival (Best Documentary), the National Educational Film and Video Festival, San Antonio Cine-Festival (Best Feature), the San Diego Filmmakers Showcase (Best Feature), and the U.S. International Film & Video Festival (Gold Camera Award). Traversing the border, he has lectured and also screened work in Mexico.

Notes

DANIEL
BERNARDI

This is a reprint (with minor changes in punctuation and house style) of an interview originally published in *The Journal of Film and Video*, 59, no. 2 (Summer 2007): 41–54. Used by permission of the publisher. I thank the editor of that journal, Stephen Tropiano, as well as the outside readers of the draft submitted to them for their valuable feedback on this work.

1. For more information on Espinosa, his films, and his current project, see his Web site, http://www.espinosaproductions.com/.

PART 3   GLOBAL
         IDENTITIES

CHAPTER 7 *Del Otro Lado*

BORDER CROSSINGS, DISAPPEARING

SOULS, AND OTHER TRANSGRESSIONS

C. A. Griffith

(Arizona State University)

Mexico is not simply the sweaty, sickly yellow-green of recent cinema, home to corrupt officials, drug traffickers, and one good cop who stands up against them all. It is much more diverse and complex than that, magnificent in the way that only a nation with cultures thousands of years old can be. Here in Mexico City, below Aztec ruins, tons of asphalt, skyscrapers, and the harmony of competing water and tamale vendors on their bicycles calling out their wares—*¡Agua . . . agua! Rojos, verdes, dulces, tamales! ¡Rojos, verdes!*—the subway swooshes into the station on pneumatic tires so quietly that you can speak softly to the person next to you. The shiny steel doors open and you go inside, one of millions of people moving underground every day.

But here, unlike in *el Norte*, at almost every intersection, and along dozens of spots along quiet roads at the edge of the city, is *un altar, un descanso* (a memorial), for the dead.[1] Crosses, candles, flowers, a name, sometimes several names, sometimes a photograph—these memorials mark the crossing from life to the other side. Waiting for the light to turn, watching with amazement as cars do not stop and do not care about those without steel, you feel the dead beside you. *Cuidado,* they whisper. "Don't be so arrogant. Don't be so casual with your life. It doesn't belong to you." You are in a nation haunted by legions of ghosts. The appetite for *jornaleros, domésticas,* and *maquiladora* workers[2] that the U.S.-Mexico border, poverty, indifference, and AIDS consume is unfathomable. This conspicuous consumption of souls reaps costs too great to repay. From the whole hinterland of South and Central America the youngest, the brightest, and the most hopeful—improbable in their very existence in the aftermath of the horrifying rampages of the death squads—make their way to the United States, with and without papers, with and without education, for a narrow chance at something perhaps better on the other side.

One in ten Mexicans lives in the United States.[3] The unofficial numbers are unknown.[4] Since 1993, in the border city of Juárez, Mexico, thousands of young women have disappeared. Over 430 were later to be found raped, mutilated, and murdered in the desert and alleys surrounding the *maquiladora* factories where they worked.[5] In the state of Illinois, where I lived for six years, every day thousands of Latino workers are injured without compensation, and one Latino worker dies every day while on the job.[6] In my new home state of Arizona, the official count of the 206 immigrants who lost their lives along the Arizona-Mexico border in the one-year period beginning December 21, 2005, includes three generations from one family who died of dehydration, a twelve-year-old boy who was run over by a Border Patrol truck, the named and the yet to be identified.[7] Worldwide, 12.3 million people

work as slaves or in other forms of forced labor, with 2.5 million people in forced labor as a result of cross-border trafficking.[8] And while the most painful price of this migration—exploitation, disappearance, and death—continues to rise, the arithmetic of consumption requires a heavier toll in souls for its factories, fields, homes, restaurants, and construction sites. Only the devil's accountant could rationalize this commoditization and disappearing of souls.

Del Otro Lado *(The Other Side)*

Produced in Mexico and the United States, *Del Otro Lado* (1999) is my first feature film. It is a story about love, friendship, Mexico's inability to deal with the AIDS crisis, and the problematics of U.S.-Mexico border policies. Independent in almost every way, it tries to be faithful to the Mexican tradition of melodrama, as well as to queer traditions of community building among friends, lovers, and the "family you choose." The film was adapted from a play by Gustavo Cravioto, Mario Callitzin and Josué Quino and centers on Alejandro (Cravioto) and Beto (Callitzin), a gay couple, one of whom is HIV-positive and must cross the border, leaving his family behind, to secure medical attention if he is to survive.[9] Alejandro works as a bank teller, counting and disbursing other people's money; his life's passion is writing and directing theater. Beto teaches English to the children of the rich and peppers his lessons with love sonnets by Shakespeare and Audre Lorde. Together for many years, Beto and Alejandro collaborate on theater productions and plan to adopt a child until Alejandro's T-cell count suddenly plummets. Everything they had hoped and dreamed fades into distant fantasy in the face of a disease that suddenly awakens from slumber hungry for Alejandro's bright life.

Even before I was asked to direct *Del Otro Lado*, I was haunted by the tragedies taking place at our borders. For a brief period in the 1980s, like many of my generation, I buried more friends from AIDS than my grandparents' generation had buried of old age. The unequal treatment of immigrants from Haiti, who were presumed to be HIV-positive or "just" economic refugees, compared to the treatment of immigrants from Cuba, who were presumed to be political refugees, made this nation's hypocrisy and bigotry painfully clear. If art, as Angela Y. Davis maintains, is a form of social consciousness, then haunting is certainly a useful form of purging.[10] And I am haunted by the lives and histories disrupted and shattered by recent trends in globalization, what H. L. T. Quan appropriately calls "savage developmentalism."[11] The aftermath of countless so-called civil wars and corporate gluttony: forced labor, migration, dislocation, and disappearance— exact a devastating toll around the world. It is not that constant news reports of monsoons, earthquakes, wars, and economic chaos or the millions displaced in Guatemala, China, Sudan, and Brazil do not exist, they are just harder to find after the story has been disappeared to "old news."

Though real, the specter of millions of landless peasants brutalized and massacred and struggling to survive in our world's overpopulated cities and refugee camps is difficult to fully comprehend. One face, one life, one story—real or fictionalized—somehow seems easier, more discernible, more real. From Sebastião Salgado's stunning and disturbing photo-documentary series, *Migrations: Humanity in Transition* (2000) and *The Children: Refugees and Migrants* (2000), to Stephen Frears's potent drama of migrant life in contemporary London, *Dirty Pretty Things* (2002), and Spike Lee's heartbreaking and righteously vivid, griot/oral history documentary on New Orleans after Hurricane Katrina, *When the Levees Broke: A Requiem in Four Acts* (2006), the visual representation of our inhumanity and the tenacious resilience of contemporary migrants have been rendered by artists around the world in ways not seen perhaps since the Great Depression. In this sense, art is unquestionably a form of social consciousness, and it is, as Davis argues, one "that can potentially awaken an urge in those affected by it to creatively transform their oppressive environments. . . . is special [precisely] because of its ability to influence feelings as well as knowledge."[12] If there was an artistic vision, it was this impulse for sparking social consciousness that I had hoped to render in making *Del Otro Lado.*

Del Otro Lado, like other political films, attempts to give face and voice to a community of people on "the other side" of racial, sexual, national, and cultural identities. The film is both the story of those

C. A.

GRIFFITH

who cross national borders to get to the "other side" as well as those already pushed to the margins of society because they are considered "from the other side" for being queer, bisexual, or transsexual. Experience has taught this community that there is real venom hissed and shouted in the words *atrevida, culero, pata,* and gay. Their humanity and their very lives at stake, many take their chances among the thousands crossing over to the other side. The United States has alternately reviled and offered tepid, conditional welcome to migrants from south of its borders; only in 1990, however, did it reverse its policy of excluding gay and lesbian immigrants.[13] Even with the change in law, however, to avoid persecution in their homelands, at the border, and on the other side in the United States, most gays and lesbians were forced to pass as straight as they passed through U.S. borders. Of those who left their country and migrated to the United States without papers, thousands perished in the borderlands.[14] Every soul that crossed over to the other side of life had a history and a community.

Del Otro Lado's Alejandro and Beto are sustained by an extended family of friends, mostly women. Both men, and particularly Alejandro, would have self-destructed without the forceful and nurturing interventions of their best friend, Virginia (Mara Ybarra), an actress and out lesbian who lost her partner to cancer. Alejandro's mother (Concha Mayahuel Saucedo) mends disagreements between her husband (Eduardo López Rojas) and son and performs a traditional, indigenous ceremony to protect him before he attempts to cross the border. Alejandro's rich, HIV-positive friend Sophia (Patricia Reyes-Spíndola) offers invaluable advice about how to cross the border without being marked as HIV-positive. Virginia gives Alejandro the profits from her theater performance, and even Alejandro's underpaid co-workers at the bank offer him the little money they have to help. This couple and their community represent only a small portion of the stories and lives affected by U.S.-Mexico immigration policies.

The fictionalized characters in *Del Otro Lado* represent real people, real lives, both known and unknown to the film's screenwriters. Cravioto and Callitzin, the film's co-writers, co-stars, and co-producers, are gay Mexican immigrants. At 14, Callitzin and his family immigrated to the U.S. from Mexico City. He received a full scholarship and attended Stanford University with me in the 1980's. Cravioto's immigration experience was quite different. The character Alejandro, who was compelled to cross the desert as an undocumented immigrant, resonated with Callitzin, Cravioto, and Quino. These men knew intimately the dangers and exploitation of that crossing, as well as those waiting in the United States.

The film's themes, particularly involuntary migration and symbol border crossings, speak to my body of work.[15] I was excited by the idea of representing a gay, HIV-positive Latino who is compelled to cross the border illegally in order to receive medical treatment unavailable to him in Mexico. The lead characters, Alejandro and his partner, Beto, are a loving couple living in Mexico City. Sustained by a large community of family and friends, they are also educated and hold pink-collar jobs. They are not poor, unlike many of the immigrants who cross the border without papers, yet they are not rich either. Alejandro's work suits are purchased through lay-away, and he can barely afford the ineffective medicines available to him. In Mexico at that time, only the rich had access to the life-saving drugs to fight HIV, and even they had to travel clandestinely to the United States to get them. The drugs were simply not available in Mexico, not even to doctors, for themselves or their patients. Immigrants attempting to cross the border with HIV medications would be turned back. These were not plot points to enhance the dramatic narrative; they were realities.

Se Equivoca *(You're Mistaken): The Making of Others*

Since most assume C. A. Griffith to be a white male of Welsh heritage and a distinct gringo accent, the reality of a director who is a black lesbian of Panamanian/southern U.S. heritage with a thick Castilian Spanish accent can prove quite distracting. Women directors are uncommon in the United States and quite rare in Mexico. The sight of our production unit stopped traffic in Mexico City on a regular basis. I have been told that I am the first black woman to direct a feature film in Mexico. While I speak fluent Spanish, it is not my first language. In fact, I did not learn Spanish from my *abuelita* (grandmother), Lolita Iris Griffith, who tossed her silver bangles down a Harlem gutter because they marked her as "not from here." She toiled on the assembly line at Pfizer Pharmaceuticals for more than forty years, but she dreamed and she danced—Flamenco, Bomba y Plena, Cha Cha Cha. Her native tongue, *borrado*, long forgotten, disappeared, she could no longer teach me Spanish; that I learned in school. But my abuelita taught me that losing the first part of her cultural identity as *una Latina, India y Morena* was too high a price for this country's bigotry. *Aprendi este rico idioma para ella.* I learned Spanish *for* her. At seventeen, I returned from a year abroad able to keep direct eye contact, with a passion for filmmaking and the thick Castilian accent of "Baar-THe-lona." My Spanish was so fluent that translating Roman Catholic Mass for her and her newly purchased rap single, "The Breaks," by Curtis Blow, was as easy as breathing. The accent and certain ways of saying things stuck. Also, because I am a linguistic sponge, my speech patterns adapt to their environment, and this one was full of Méxicanos with diverse regional dialects, Chicanos, and Argentinos.

From colloquialism to the lightning-fast speed of Mexico City's "*chilango*" Spanish, communication was a challenge when, at times, sleep deprivation and stress made me incapable of thinking or speaking clearly in any language. Communicating with a cast and crew who were both intrigued and discomforted by who and what they assumed I was, combined with an incredibly tight shooting schedule and a tiny, low-peso budget, pushed me to be more creative and resourceful in ways that all independent, low-budget independent filmmakers must be.[16]

Del Otro Lado was shot on 16mm film and edited on AVID for several hundred thousand dollars—most of it through in-kind services, grants, and donations. The total cash amount invested for this project constituted the smallest part of the total cost to bring this story to film. Half a million dollars will buy an impressive and sizable home in most places in the United States outside of Manhattan, the Bay Area, and Los Angeles. It is a dream budget for many small, nonprofit community service organizations. It would revive and sustain several public school arts programs gutted to feed our vast prison industrial complex. In the film world, however, $3 million would constitute a small budget. Consequently, it was a small miracle that our low-peso production was born. More cogently, though to say that *Del Otro Lado* was shot for around $150,000 cash might afford us a certain degree of low-budget pride, it would not only be inaccurate but would also effectively erase the hundreds of people who made the film possible. All of the above-the-line filmmakers (its director, writers, producers, co-stars, and many actors) worked pro bono. Also, many of the cast and crew worked for reduced rates; donated their time, talent, and expertise; brought others on-board; made the phone calls; had the meetings; gave the production extensions on bills when wire transfers didn't go through; and looked past rules, regulations, and occasionally the law itself.

After losing our principal location three times, one of the men from the grip/electric department, who had in the beginning appeared to be quite homophobic, found us an abandoned auto body shop at the city edge. It was ours if we needed. The structure was someone's incomplete thought—part of a corrugated tin roof, window frames but no glass in the windows, stained glass in the bathroom but only a trickle of water, a brick floor in places, bare earth in others. Everywhere was the dirt and debris of abandoned dreams; in places there was blue sl

where the ceiling should have been. It was perfect because it was a gift; it was perfect because it was beautiful in its own inimitable way. Our good fortune could not go unpunished. The art department "lost" key wardrobe and props and made themselves so adept at mistakes that the crew literally voted them the *pendejos* (a—holes) of the production. That night, as the rest of the crew went into overtime to get the location picture-ready, Callitzin and Cravioto found themselves in the awkward position of trying to keep the art department from quitting—not because they would be missed, but because they could not be trusted not to "lose" props and wardrobe that had already been shot and were needed for the rest of the film. Callitzin's comment to me after the meeting echoed so many conversations I have had over the years: he knew they seemed to have a hard time working for a black woman, but he "had no idea they were such racists." He was noticeably shaken. Callitzin, like others who were not "the other"—in this case, not a white male of Welsh descent—was surprised by the persistence and virulence of others' bigotry. I wondered what acrid brew of slurs or combination of rants had finally made the art department's misogyny, racism, and homophobia crystal clear. Sleep was kind that night— she came quickly and silenced my rage. Dreams transformed tangled thorns of doubt into precious visions of scenes not yet filmed.

The next morning, we drove for over an hour to a little barrio nestled in the foothills at the edge of the city. The outside was not promising—it looked like an abandoned junkyard. Inside, it had the appearance of a loftlike apartment any New Yorker would covet. Neighbors had donated clothes, plants, and whatever we needed. The grip/electric department had artfully used colored gels and plastic instead of glass windows; the couple's rickety table was made with a handmade cucoloris (patterned shadow maker) from the lighting truck with glued-on legs. Something old, nothing new, everything borrowed. We had no ceiling painted to mimic the sky; we had walls to shelter us, and the blue sky and clouds gazed down upon us between sheets of tin. At night, several neighbors wandered in wanting to know what we were doing and if it had anything to do with their soccer match lights and light bulbs fading in and out. It did. Another neighbor had shown us where to tie in inconspicuously to the city's street lamps to power our film lights. They stayed to watch for a while and asked if we needed anything. We needed a Virgin of Guadalupe for Beto to pray to and a photograph of Sub-Commandante Marcos. They gave us the Virgin, and where *el Commandante* came from I do not recall.

In classic film production fashion, the entire crew came together and did everything they could to make the production better. We had

C. A.
GRIFFITH

a rough start. Because we had to move up production by several weeks to ensure that our permits and political connections would survive the change in government, we lost Juan Cobo as director of photography (DP). A week into production, we had to fire the first and very talented DP because he antagonized the crew, disrespected the director, and didn't look at the camera tests that would have shown that the camera was out of registration. The registration problem was not caught until too late,[17] after key scenes, including ones at *El Paseo de la Reforma*, were shot. We had filmed along that famous boulevard, at the circle, beneath its towering monument to Columbus.

Envision a no-budget film getting permission to shoot all day at New York's Columbus Circle; as you can imagine, we could not get permission again. As beautiful as the images were, they were unstable. They should have been tossed and reshot but time and budget didn't allow it. Usually, when the DP goes, so does his crew. This crew, which was more accustomed to making B-movie action films with men beating and shooting each other rather than holding each other close and kissing, and who had said far too many homophobic comments under their breath, wondered if they'd be fired as well. Not members of a union, they came to work the next day, but fully expected to be fired. I told them that they were doing a great job and that I appreciated their work. I added that I understood their concerns, and not least because I had worked for years as a non-union assistant cameraperson (AC) before going I.A.T.S.E.,[18] and then moving up to DP/operator. As soon as I said I.A.T.S.E., their eyes widened and a collective *¡Que padre!* Aretha Franklin "R.E.S.P.E.C.T." vibe encircled me and buoyed us all. Apparently, they didn't know about this aspect of my professional background and this new knowledge, combined with my admiration for their artistry and hard work, earned the kind of credibility and *respecto* not often granted to first-time directors, let alone a woman director.

Del Otro Lado's line producer owned a B-movie action film production company with her director-husband; she showed us several DP reels and recommended a few to us. Juan Carlos Martín Torres's compositional and lighting choices hinted at artistry rare in such films. If he was available and could handle a gay film and working with preexisting crew, he was hired. We met on set the next day for the first time, again, a rare practice and considered rather risky.

Accustomed to the fast pace and low expectations of bad action films, Martín Torres's creativity blossomed as he worked for a director who had been a former DP, who encouraged creative collaboration, and who was impressed by his sharp eye for detail and desire for artistic excellence. Equally accustomed to a system of few rehearsals and sing takes, he was surprised by our discussions about the scenes. Soon, a huge weight was lifted from my shoulders. For the first time since we started production, I had an artist and collaborator as DP. Finally, I had the chance to focus on directing, confident that the DP understood what I was trying to accomplish and would do his utmost to make it happen and make it even better.

The art department provided the rest of the crew a chance to shine and show what production design could really do for film. In fact, the crew's transformation of the garage into the couple's apartment looked too good. I had to add a shot of Beto dusting the corrugated roof and several shots of a working-class neighborhood so that audiences might see that in quintessential gay fashion, the couple had done a lot with very little.

As is the case with many independent, low-budget films, the thematic and creative interventions of below-the-line crew were integral to the making of *Del Otro Lado*. As a first-time feature film director shooting a film in her second language, I was in the awkward position of having to exude confidence, inspire my cast and crew, and not be afraid to ask for help. I had been asked to direct the film because my artistic sensibilities were admired and my filmmaking expertise was needed to adapt this play to screen. I was not so foolish that I accepted without knowing that there would be resistance because my gender, nationality, race, and sexuality did not fit the expected profile for a gay Latino film. With my dear friend Juan Cobo as DP, I knew everything would be okay. We had worked together for many years with me as his AC. He had left the United States for his native Colombia when his career stalled here and took off there as director and DP. When we lost Cobo due to scheduling changes, I was devastated and consumed by doubt. My lover convinced me that I could, in fact, direct his film and that Cravioto and Callitzin needed me to do it because our relationship (I had known Callitzin almost half our lives, since we were students at Stanford, and we had wanted to collaborate on a project for years) was strong enough to support and challenge each other. We conscientiously and actively cultivated a climate on set that was democratic even in the context of the inherent hierarchies of film production. We encouraged and were receptive to creative brainstorming and problem solving by the cast and crew. It is an unfortunate reality that all too often, unique perspectives and artistry go untapped simply by nature of limiting such input to a person's job title. What people do for a living is never the sum of who they are and their creative or intellectual potential. McKinley Morganfield was an uneducated Mississippi sharecropper, but to friends and legions of music lovers the world over, he was the premiere ambassador of the Chicago blues and musical genius, Muddy Waters. A librarian who directed students to diverse subjects for their research would have her poetry and essays fill the shelves from New York to Berlin and Soweto—her name was Audre Lorde. A Senegalese dock worker with a grade school education would publish dozens of novels, direct some of Africa's most revolutionary and evocative films, and win countless literary and film awards (at Cannes, Burkino Faso, Berlin)—his name was Ousmane Sembene. The sad-faced woman counting out change and giving back a ticket on that crowded bus in São Paulo has dreams, skills, and aspirations we may never know.

Tapping into creative power on set is as simple as listening or sitting at a table other than with your immediate colleagues during meal breaks. On *Del Otro Lado,* many cast and crew members contributed greatly to the production. Tapping into such creativity is always a risk, however, because sometimes boundaries are crossed; ultimately, the director and producer are in charge. Fortunately, our openness to creative discussions and ideas was rewarded with a bounty of blossoms and only a few, easily trimmed thorns. It was one of our still photographers, Graciela Elizabeth Ocampo, however, who perhaps contributed the most to the creative process, as well as to the warm and intimate climate on set.

C. A.
GRIFFITH

Having a still photographer on set is vital for a production, particularly a low-budget one. The stills are used to document behind-the-scenes action and to closely match what the motion picture camera sees for use in press packages and promotional materials. That we had two still photographers but only one assistant director (AD) was odd and did not make sense except that both photographers were friends of the production. We paid Lourdes Moreno's airfare from San Francisco and Ocampo's airfare from Buenos Aires. We also covered their hotel and paid them a small salary that was more of a gesture of thanks. They came to Mexico City to help the production in any way they could. Ocampo's additional contributions in the areas of acting, production design, and props were invaluable. This is why her name breaks the pattern of alphabetical listings by department and appears at the top of the list in the film credits for the art department. Her sensuality, generosity, exquisite photography, and artistic genius were impressive and her presence on set radiated a gracious warmth and energy that helped unify the cast and crew and elevated production values immeasurably. Under most circumstances, the still photographer does his or her best to disappear on set—even their cameras are specially blimped to be absolutely silent lest the click of the shutter ruin a take. (Remember

ber, this is 1988. The cameras were still 35mm SLRs.) Most of their shots are taken during rehearsals. Ocampo's performance as the spirit of Olivia required no dialogue and was originally scripted as a few moments when Virginia simply gazed at her photograph. However, we wrote Ocampo into the script after witnessing how she enchanted everyone. As the spirit of Olivia, she appeared to Virginia in her moments of doubt, she renewed and focused her creative energies, and, most important, she provided the film's audience with a glimpse of the meaning of *saudade*—the great love that Virginia had lost and remembered with heartbreaking sadness and joy.

It is ironic but not unique that the role of Olivia metamorphosed from a photograph to an actual character in the hands of this still photographer. Independent low-budget films often depend on the kindness of strangers and friends to get made. Because we were receptive to and encouraging of creative brainstorming and contributions by all—and particularly by below-the-line crew—shooting the film was a unique experience for many of the crew who had not been taken seriously as artists in the past. The production unit forged a strong bond, and our production values skyrocketed. Therefore, despite its budget limitations,[19] multiple challenges, and the fact that the film was released with only a one-light-print telecine transfer, this rich and productive collaboration between director and the entire crew made *Del Otro Lado* a visually intoxicating film.

Del Otro Lado

Things Seen and Unseen

As much as creative control and personal voice are coveted in the arts, as unchallenged individualism they can be detrimental to the overall creative process. While there is a certain degree of authenticity to be gained, there is a danger in having a writer-actor-producer representing a personal history on screen. My experience working on numerous independent films driven by writer-directors taught me there must be someone who can and must tell the writer-director, writer-actor, or actor-director "no." If not, creative solutions are deferred to postproduction work as a means to salvage any problems unresolved during reproduction and production.

Beginning and student directors should have a safety valve—a friend, a partner, an assistant, the film's producer—present on set to support the director, but also to tell them "wait—stop and think about that again" when low budgets, stress, and inexperience combine and have the director pushing too hard, not pushing enough, or too stressed make decisions that affect the character, story, plot, and aesthetics, as well as the mood and tone of the set. If this safety valve is not present, active, and listed to, the results can be scenes that settle for cliché or stereotypes, insufficient character development or motivation, easy solutions to complex challenges, uneven performances by actors, scripted dialogue that sounds unnatural or is laden with exposition, insufficient shot coverage to edit and pace the film well—in sum, a film that is not as strong or as nuanced as it could have been, even under the circumstances in which it was shot. Unfortunately, some of this happened on *Del Otro Lado*. Such experiences are important but painful teaching and learning opportunities because regardless of how generous audiences can be with low-budget, independent cinema, the errors made are public. Also, the effort and resources required to direct, produce, and distribute a feature film remain elusive. The obstacles that excellent, even brilliant films, such as *Killer of Sheep, Man by the Shore, La Haine* (*Hate*), *Gods and Monsters,* and even *Crash* (2004), faced to get made (and in the first three cases to find distribution) point to the many challenges faced by independent filmmakers in a world where immensely forgettable Hollywood blockbusters reign and marketing and distribution budgets often equal or exceed production budgets.

Yet despite limited resources or small budgets, happy accidents and multifaceted interventions can make stories stronger and films richer, more textured and nuanced. Specifically, in our production, the representations of La Okey, a transsexual trickster spirit, in an extended argument between the couple (as they negotiated safer-sex practices and the politics of being a top or a bottom) and in the film's love scene benefited from creative interventions by the director as well as below-the-line crew.

Del Otro Lado opens with the Sioux Prayer for the Dead. The main characters are haunted and protected by the spirits of their lovers, daughters, and friends. The spirit of La Okey is the embodiment of "the other side." She is proudly transsexual, emotionally ambiguous, a voluptuous spirit that both haunts and protects the film's lovers. Apparently she is also one of the most confusing characters for audiences, who tend to wonder, is she laughing at the film's lovers, Alejandro and Beto? Is she calling Alejandro to death, or is she waiting to embrace him in her ample bosom should he find himself on the other side of life's door? Is she a dream? Whose dream does she represent—Alejandro's or Beto's? Perhaps she is Roberto Moreno, Beto's friend who died of AIDS after taking a jetliner to the United States. To all of these questions, the answer is, in fact, yes.

La Okey makes her first appearance on screen as she breaks into the lovers' ground-floor apartment by pulling out a loose windowpane

She's dressed like a 1950s movie star, in a sequined dress with shoes and a purse to die for. Originally she was scripted to appear in clouds of smoke. As a director, I felt that the actress who played La Okey, the beautiful Carla Clynes, was too glamorous, playful, and bold for such an stagy entrance. Clynes, after all, had not only bewitched many of the straight men on the crew, but she came to us from the toughest streets of San Francisco, where she regularly walked in dangerous high heels to do street theater education for Latino workers about the importance of safe sex, HIV, and AIDS prevention. And she made it clear that underneath her curve-hugging dress she was a transsexual. I thought it was much more fitting of Clynes's personality as well as the character of La Okey to mix humor and sensuality with her entrance. New to the spirit world, La Okey had not yet mastered moving through walls, but she remembered how her once physical body would break into a ground-floor apartment, and that is exactly what I directed Clynes to do. La Okey wiggles her bottom through the window, adjusts her stockings, pulls up a chair, and watches Beto and Alejandro sleep. She languidly smokes a cigarette after leaving a condom beside their bed and making her way into their dreams. The lighting effect was produced by flashing a nine-light Maxi-Brute lamp (a.k.a. a 9K PAR). This energy-gobbling light was illegally tied in to a street lamp, and it made all the lights in the small neighborhood brighten and fade ominously.

When editing the final cut of the film in our Springfield, Massachusetts, loft in June 1999, my co-editors, H. L. T. Quan and Knicole Verhoeven, noticed that the shadow of La Okey's dress looked like the devil's tail. This was a conscious choice made during production, and they expanded on it effectively in postproduction by slowing the image down in AVID; Quan then heightened the effect with a remix of Humberto Álvarez's already haunting sound track. This was just one of many examples where the creative input of below-the-line crew contributed greatly to the filmmaking process.

La Okey's later scene frames the couple's lovemaking scene, adding an unsettling quality to a scene that is both tender and highly erotic. Years ago, in New York, while helping director Anne Norda[20] shoot a short film in a room too small to do anything else, I helped her with a makeshift solution similar to the one we would use for *Del Otro Lado*. Rather than shoot the love scene from above and fight a low ceiling, she chose to prop the mattress against the wall and directed the actors to pose standing against it. The effect of lovers embracing and tumbling around each other was subtly captivating because it defied gravity. It was an effect I wanted to replicate for *Del Otro Lado*, not only because I wanted to shoot the love scene in a nonconventional manner but also because thematically, the couple's lovemaking marked a critical juncture in their relationship and demanded that the eroticism be as artfully ungrounded and synergetic as the communion of their spirits.

When filming the love scene, the unconventional choices I made as a director interpreting the scene left me as exposed and as naked as my actors. I actually had to convince my DP, actors, and AD that putting the mattress against the wall with the actors standing in front of it was the best way to film the scene not only technically but also thematically. One of the exciting things about working on that love scene years ago with Norda was that it was just the two of us. Our relationship was such that the exchange of ideas and creative problem solving was free-flowing and devoid of ego. We were willing to take risks and to succeed or fail as a result of those risks without doubting our skill, doubting our creativity, or being challenged because we were women in a male-dominated field. Moreover, we did not have to convince others to do something unconventional. Unlike other fields (from drawing, painting, and writing to science and engineering) where experimentation and risk are not only part of the process but also valued and relatively private, there are no such protections on set. Mistakes are a very public and potentially damning affair where confidence in and respect for the director can be lost in an instant. Of course, without experimentation and risk, films can become purely formulaic and uninspired. Anne Norda perhaps says it best: "It's important not to squelch those creative impulses; continue to empower people to have confidence in their vision and give yourself permission to experiment and make mistakes,"[21] particularly when directing bigger budget films with larger casts and crews.

A director should not be afraid to accept contributions from the cast and crew. People are very happy to contribute and are not asked often enough, or taken seriously. The grip or makeup person may have excellent ideas, but they are too often overlooked because they are considered technicians and not artists. Cultivating an environment in which cast and crew feel empowered to contribute has distinct benefits that can greatly improve the aesthetic and thematic content of a film. Regardless of the source, as director, you must be confident enough to accept or decline creative input and trust your own creative vision.

There is a tenuous balance that must be preserved between collaboration and leading a film as its director. Here, separating ego from ideas is ideal; this is quite a challenge in the film world. Working with creative people who recognize that they are there not to serve their own vision but the vision of the director and producer, and that th director and producer are there to serve the integrity of the story and the characters, is rare but certainly attainable. Thus, shooting our love scene in a conventional manner was not the kind of risk I was willing to take. Despite popular expectations to the contrary, shooting love scenes is tedious, voyeuristic, and mechanical work. I wanted the love-making to be sensual—something my co-stars found novel. In fact, the energy experienced on set suggested that the scene would heat up the screen.

The couple's lovemaking had been a point of conflict within their relationship. Because Alejandro was HIV-positive and Beto was not, their lovemaking relegated Alejandro to being a bottom—something he found restrictive, tedious, and lacking the surprise and playfulness of their sexual relationship before he became seropositive. The risks, Beto said, were too great to allow him to bottom for his lover. If the condom broke, Beto would run the risk of being infected. This discussion turned into an argument about Alejandro's decision to cross over the border into the United States *"como illegal,"* without legal documentation. All of Beto's fears—of being abandoned by his lover just as his family had abandoned him when he came out as a gay man, and of never having a chance to start a family with Alejandro, or of losing Alejandro to other lovers in the United States—were realized in this key moment. The couple's negotiation of safe-sex practices, of asserting their needs and desires for sexual intimacy, and fears about physical and emotional penetration were laid bare. Originally scripted for ten pages (equivalent to almost ten minutes on screen), it simply wouldn't work. As the co-writers, co-stars, and co-producers, Cravioto and Callitzin were too heavily invested in the scene, and we had disagreed about the argument scene for some time. The scene had to be cut down to two or three pages at most, and they had to trust me to do it. I cut and reshaped this argument to emphasize the emotional damage their words inflicted rather than emphasize the words themselves. I excised entire pages of dialogue, highlighting the cruelest attacks. I asked my actors to improvise and recorded audio only for most of the scene. We filmed what happens *after* a verbal argument and cut into a montage sequence using the nastiest barbs and most tender cries for help. The aftermath of this argument finds Beto alone in the apartment and Alejandro among crowds of strangers on a fast-moving metro. Their physical environment and regret for words not easily forgiven confine both lovers.

While filming the love scene, ours was a closed set. Instead of our full, tiny crew of fifteen or so, only the boom operator, DP, AD, still photographers (both women), and I were in the room. Under normal

Del Otro Lado

circumstances, the first assistant cameraperson, key grip, and producer would also have been among the key personnel for a closed set. Because a camera rig was not mounted above the talent and the lighting setup was simple, the gaffer and grip remained close by, but off set. Because the actors were my producers, they were already in the room, and we recorded the scene from the videotape monitor so they could see it afterward, along with the executive producer. I returned to my roots as AC and pulled focus for the scene I was directing. And the DP, AD, and I all adjusted the lights as needed. The still photographers and I did hair and makeup; we also spritzed the actors with water and baby oil in all the right places to mimic perspiration. I had just changed the slate and looked up to find myself between two beautiful, naked men who

were as anxious as the male crew assembled to get the scene in the can and move on. I told them to put their clothes back on so that we could film a bit of sensual foreplay. "Foreplay, oh yeah! That's great. I guess we've been watching too much porn," Callitzin laughed. We had just over 200 feet of film (about five minutes of film stock) to do it in. This was barely enough film to shoot cutaways, but it was all we had; another wire transfer had not gone through, and we

Director C. A. Griffith with Gustavo Cravioto (Alejandro) and Mario Callitzin (Beto) between takes while filming the love scene. (Photograph by Lourdes Moreno.)

were perilously low on film. Undeterred, we shot the scene. We had all seen enough films to know that two "lipstick" lesbians making love seemed to arouse everyone (straight men in particular) and some gay men. However, two men making love usually meant two men having sex—something that often arouses gay male audiences, while arousing discomforting thoughts or violent emotions in other audiences. wanted the love scene in *Del Otro Lado* to capture this lesbian sensibility and produce effects on its audiences regardless of sexual identity or gender. We shot with the little bit of film we had using half a dozen shots from one principal angle, mostly with the actors standing to create our *trompe l'oeil, sans* gravitational tension, that lent to a feeling surrender to freefalling passion. While I do not know if our goals were fully achieved, the film has been specifically admired for the tenderness and eroticism of this love scene.

Ironically, the film's gay male love scene truly smoldered and too flame *after* being recut in postproduction by three women (all women of color), editors of diverse backgrounds and a range of sexualities. Verhoeven spent most of a day rescreening every single foot of film from the love scene and all of the footage with La Okey to find unused frames. Undeterred by what we knew was insufficient coverage, we recut the scene several different ways but remained unsatisfied. We were all dangerously sleep-deprived and under deadline pressure. Our film was scheduled to premiere at Frameline, the San Francisco International Lesbian and Gay Film Festival, in less than two weeks. The festival committee had seen our fine cut and booked it for the Castro Theater.[22] A little angel at the festival had whispered in the ear of a major distributor, and they called us while were still cutting, wanting to know more. Los Angeles's Outfest booked *Del Otro Lado* and my short film *Border. Line. . . . Family Pictures* immediately after Frameline. The prefestival buzz for our little film was the stuff of dreams, and San Francisco was home to so many of us. It was vital that the film and its love scene deliver. Under intense pressure and nowhere near ready, we slept in shifts, with two of us awake and cutting at all times. Our toy Yorkie, Chula, was our salvation. She made us go outside for a walk three times a day; she sat on our laps and de-stressed us.

Del Otro Lado

    When Quan succumbed to sleep after more than forty-eight hours of editing and troubleshooting the AVID, Verhoeven and I painted her toenails the red, green, and white of the Mexican flag, with a little purple for fun. We gelled Chula's silky silver and red hair (I'm allergic to dogs with fur) into a unicorn's horn, a triple spike, and curly antlers.

Knicole Verhoeven (left) and H.L.T. Quan (right) take a break from editing.
(Photograph by C. A. Griffith.)

The AVID was breaking down several times a day. The small fortune we paid for twenty-four-hour technical support couldn't get it working. We were utterly delirious and catnapped only long enough to drive safely an hour out of town to pick up a replacement hard drive and Beta SP deck. REM sleep was a fantasy we could not afford. We pleaded with inanimate objects (the AVID hardware and software) to hold on so we could finish the film. We had to finish laying in subtitles and cut a gay male love scene so that legs would cross and uncross in the movie theater in the most delicious way. We had to find unexpected approaches to the scene and use the best opportunities provided in production and postproduction to heighten on-screen sensuality. It was overwhelming. However, once Quan found what would be the perfect music for the scene and remixed it, all the missing pieces and lingering doubt disappeared. Our edit and Quan's sound design for the love scene, with the whispering, tantalizing, pounding drums and the rising crescendo of another Humberto Álvarez sound track, was simply the amazing final layer of haunting, passionate sensuality.

In directing the scene, I was guided by the sensual and *saudade,* a Brazilian term that cannot be translated. Saudade evokes a fond but aching remembrance for something or someone who is lost. The couple's argument centers on fears of separation, combined with their best friend Virginia's longing for her lover Olivia, the memory of Olivia watching her rehearse, a stage hand doing a *limpieza* of the theater with a chalice of incense, and the murals on the theater walls recalling the history of Mexico. Its temples, conquests, and rebellions all shaped and inspired my desire to convey the rich cultural and personal histories of the film's characters and *el Districto Federal,* Mexico City itself. The scene in the theater and the couple's argument, combined with Quan's musical choice of Jésus Guillen's brilliant, sorrowful song about a man from the country displaced in the city and dreaming of belonging, remains one of the scenes I am most proud of because it represents a synthesis of conflicting emotions, the interconnectedness of friends and lovers even in times in struggle, loss, and longing. These are themes that are integral to the film and they reflect the realities of the many communities the film tries to represent.

Ironically, as much as the distinctly gendered and sensual interpretation of this scene was heralded, it was the highly charged, unapologetically sexual image of Alejandro and Beto apparently engaged in what I affectionately call Jesse Helms's delight that garnered the cover of the *San Francisco Bay Times* and the title "Queer Arts Explosion."[23] was not, as I had hoped, the alternate photo of the couple holding each other tenderly after having made love that captured the Bay Area que imagination. Word of mouth and the specter of two "hot Latino" men having sex may have drawn audiences to our sold-out premiere at the San Francisco International Lesbian and Gay Film Festival, but once there, it was the tragic and tender love story that had audience members in tears.

Unfortunately, *Del Otro Lado* is not commercially distributed, despite an unbelievably amazing prefestival premiere phone call from a major distributor, a successful national and international film festival run with several major, sold-out screenings, and, almost a year later, great interest, followed by a heart-breaking *nada* from a second major distributor. To bask in the accolades of film critics and essays published in newspapers, film trade magazines, and academic presses[24] is as dangerous as believing one's own press releases. While we lament that our film is not widely distributed, it would be a mistake to equate distribution with success. *Del Otro Lado* is not, in the end, a "commercial" film. It is a foreign language, gay, independent film with both known and unknown actors dealing with multiple controversial subject matters. Some potential distributors lamented, "If only it were in English. . . ." But the characters are Mexicans living in Mexico City: they speak Spanish. To speak English for the sake of an American audience would be a disservice to the film's principal intended audience, people in Central and South America. Shooting the film in Spanish is a decision that the writers and this director stand by, despite what it may have cost us in distribution deals and U.S. audience dollars. Other potential distributors lamented, "*pero . . . son tan gay.*" Again, representing queer sexuality openly and passionately is a decision we stand by. To represent this gay couple as a chaste, asexual pair (à la *Philadelphia*) would deny who these men were—a loving and sexual couple. Interestingly, distributors voiced few concerns with the border-crossing scenes, perhaps because both the Mexican coyote (human trafficker) and the U.S. Border Patrol were each complicit in the tragic events that took place. So, while we would like to see the film distributed, and we continue to work toward making that a reality, we hold on to the knowledge that simply to have made the film, completed it, and had screened in festivals throughout the United States, Canada, Mexico, and Europe was a miracle in and of itself. Our film has touched many people, and for that we are very grateful. Also, the many screenings at community centers, diverse conferences, and educational institutions have constituted another life for the film, one that has sparked intense discussion on themes from gay Latino identity, HIV/AIDS prevention and education, and U.S. border policy reform to the cultural work of combating homophobia.

Del Otro Lado

A Coda

Two years after Matthew Shepard's brutal 1998 murder, I found myself in Laramie, Wyoming, nauseated and struggling to breathe. Al-
titude sickness made easy prey of this body accustomed to life at sea
level. I had been invited to present *Del Otro Lado* at the University
of Wyoming's Gladys Crane Mountain Plains Film Festival as part of
the organized institutional response to the realization of homophobia and violence in the community. How does one respond to visceral
hatred of this kind? Laramie was still grieving Shepard's death and
haunted by questions that up until that moment had been left unan-
swered and were festering. Because of the brutality of the crime, Lara-

C. A.

GRIFFITH

mie was compelled to examine itself in ways that few communities
do. Jasper, Texas. Juárez, Mexico. Laramie, Wyoming. Rwanda. East
Timor. Iraq. Darfur, Sudan. New Orleans, Louisiana. Blacksburg, Virginia. These are points on a map of haunted places. These are places
where acts so cruel command our attention and crack open the deep-
est recesses of our most feared imaginings—because they are within
us all and, unless we are vigilant, they can happen again and they
can happen "here." Film, as a form of social consciousness, as a cultural artifact, has tremendous power to reconcile the irreconcilable
as it impacts thoughts, emotions, and actions. In Laramie, *Del Otro
Lado* deeply affected the audience and reminded this filmmaker that
commercial distribution is not the only or best measure of success. As
long as there are communities like Laramie, we will continue to be
haunted. And *gracias a la vida,*[25] being haunted, we will always dream
and we will always conjure.

Notes

1. The *descanso* (resting place) or *crucecita* (little cross) is a small memorial that
marks the place where a person has met a tragic death, usually in an automobile accident or while trying to cross the border. Most often found on roadsides in states along
the southern U.S. border, they are a rich Latino cultural tradition that has been adopted
by diverse communities in the United States. They are generally respected as cultural
and religious artifacts; few challenge their right to exist. In Arizona, proposals by the
police and department of transportation to destroy altars on public land (and most are
have met with strong public outcry, and so they remain.

2. A *jornalero* is a day laborer; a *doméstica* is a domestic worker or maid. The average day laborer works almost every day of the year doing the hard and thankless dirty
work of our nation in construction and manufacturing, the service industry, and private domestic work for an average of $7,000 a year. A *maquiladora* is a foreign-owned
assembly plant operated along the U.S.-Mexico border. Despite corporate claims that

maquiladoras use "competitively priced Mexican labor to assemble, process or perform manufacturing operations" (International Trade Data System, http://www.itds.treas .gov/maquiladora.html, accessed 2005), salaries of $25–$35 for a forty-eight- to sixty-hour work week, no health benefits, and brutal working conditions deny workers basic human rights. See Support Committee for Maquiladora Workers, http://enchanted-websites.com/maquiladora (accessed 2005).

3. Jorge Durand, "From Traitors to Heroes: 100 Years of Mexican Migration Policies," *The Migration Policy Institute*, March 1, 2004, cited on www.migrationpolicy.org, August 20, 2005.

4. If the number of migrants turned back from our borders is any indication, immigration has increased substantially. According to the U.S. Border Patrol (after September 11, 2001, it became a part of the Homeland Security Department), 142,500 undocumented immigrants from Mexico and other countries were arrested in 2005 (with months to go in the fiscal year), up from 39,555 captured in 2000. See Eric Lipton, "Homeland Security Chief, With Nod to Public Discontent, Tells of Plan to Stabilize Border," *New York Times*, August 24, 2005.

5. Connie Aramaki, "The Disappearing Women of Juárez: Hundreds of Young Women Are Being Killed in Mexico's Biggest Border Town," *The Santa Barbara Independent*, November 4–11, 2004, 22–27. Amnesty International, "Mexico: Further Information on Fear for Safety/Death Threats," May 28, 2008, amnesty.org/en/library/info/AMR41/026/2008/en (accessed November 20, 2008).

6. January 19, 2005, hearing, "Panel on Latino Worker Injuries and Fatalities," sponsored by Illinois governor Rod Blagojevich with testimony from workers and members of the Latino Union of Chicago, an organization that represents and advocates for the rights of day laborers. On August 9, 2005, the Illinois legislature enacted House Bill 3471, the Day Laborer Fairness and Protection Act. The legislation helps protect the state's 300,000 day laborers and "will make Illinois the most aggressive state in the nation when it comes to safeguarding day laborers from abuses at the hands of day and temporary labor agencies." Illinois Governor's Office, "Governor Blagojevich signs legislation to help protect over 300,000 day laborers. New law strengthens protections for day laborers and provides harsher penalties to unlawful agencies," press release Springfield, IL: August 9, 2005).

7. The work of Phoenix artists Katherine Nicholson and Marcia McClellan potently honored the dead in their exhibit Trespasses and Reflections, April 6–28, 2007, at the Eye Lounge gallery in Phoenix, Arizona. Using data that the faith-based humanitarian organizations No More Deaths and Humane Borders culled from the Homeland Security Department and official state documents, Nicholson and McClellan worked collaboratively for a span of several years, each year running from winter solstice to winter solstice (see www.eyelounge.com, www.nomoredeaths.org, and www humaneborders.org for further information). Their memorial to each of the 206 immigrants who died along the Arizona-Mexico border from 2005 to 2006 consisted of 206 handmade leather-bound books with fragile handmade cotton paper mixed with plants and fibers found in the Sonoran desert. Each book dangled from a fence of barbed wire and dead, bonelike cholla cacti with an attached tag bearing each person's name and age, or simply "unknown." In addition, four books with thick, rough wooden covers

and handmade, jagged-edged paper honored the dead from December 22, 2002, to December 21, 2003. These books marked each of the four seasons, and each page bore the name of the person whose body was found on that day. Seeing the four volumes and the 206 individual books not only brought life to these statistics of the dead but left one with a sense of both awe and dismay. Trespasses and Reflections was an emotional, haunting installation. The artists potently transformed the cold, white gallery walls into sacred space that honored the dead we have forgotten or long to disappear.

8. Steven Greenhouse, "Forced Labor Said to Bind 12.3 Million People Around the World," *New York Times*, May 12, 2005, cited in the United Nations' International Labor Organization report, "A Global Alliance Against Forced Labor: Global Report Under the Follow-up to the ILO Declaration on Fundamental Principles and Rights at Work, 2005" (Geneva: International Labour Office, February 15, 2007).

9. Mario Callitzin changed his name to Mario Golden. Gustavo Cravioto was diagnosed with a brain tumor and died following surgery in December 2006.

10. Avery F. Gordon, *Ghostly Matters: Haunting and the Sociological Imagination* (Minneapolis: University of Minnesota Press, 1997), 7–8.

11. H.L.T. Quan, "Finance, Diplomacy and Development: Brazilian-Japanese Relations in the Twentieth Century," Ph.D. dissertation (Department of Political Science, University of California, Santa Barbara, 2002).

12. Angela Davis, *Women, Culture & Politics* (New York: Vintage Books, 1989), 199–200.

13. In *Queer Migrations*, Eithne Lubhéid argues, "some scholars date lesbian and gay exclusion from 1917, when people labeled as 'constitutional psychopathic inferiors' were first barred from entering the United States. This category included 'persons with abnormal sexual instincts.' There is no doubt that lesbians and gay men were targeted: a U.S. Senate report related that 'the Public Health Service has advised that the provision for the exclusion of aliens afflicted with psychopathic personality or mental defect which appears in the bill is sufficiently broad to provide for the exclusion of homosexuals or sex perverts.'" Eithne Lubhéid, "Introduction: Queering Migration and Citizenship," in *Queer Migrations: Sexuality, U.S. Citizenship, and Border-Crossings*, ed. Eithne Lubhéid and Lionel Cantú, Jr. (University of Minnesota Press, Minneapolis, 2005), xii.

14. Homeland Security's U.S. Customs and Border Security (CBP) records state that from 1998 to 2004, 1,954 people died crossing the U.S.-Mexico border. While most of the deaths were attributed to heat stroke, dehydration, and hypothermia, violent deaths of immigrants along the U.S.-Mexico border have dramatically increased since 1995, particularly in the state of Arizona. The CBP attributes this directly to "unscrupulous smugglers and human traffickers [who] have moved persons into more remote, rugged and hazardous terrain with the purpose of smuggling them into the United States" and touts the 7,500 rescues it made since implementing the Border Safety Initiative (BSI) in June 1998. Its goal to reduce injuries and prevent deaths in the Southwest border region was founded on "the longstanding public safety and humanitarian measures practiced by the United States Border Patrol," but the results have been quite the opposite. Despite increased funding, millions of border arrests, and the BSI, the number of border deaths has doubled since 1995. In fact, the U.S. Government Accountability Office's (GAO) August 2006 report to the U.S. Senate is a sixty-nine-page indictment

poorly implemented and failed CBP policies. It seriously questions the data-gathering methodology and the data itself used by the CBP to assert the so-called effectiveness of its efforts to reduce border-crossing deaths. The report points to "an increase in the overall numbers of deaths occurring along the southwest border between 1998 and 2005 following a decline between 1990 and 1994." The report also cites several alarming discrepancies between BSI and National Center for Health Statistics (NCHS) mortality file data, and challenges U.S. Customs and Border Patrol Security methodology: "BSI data understat[ed] the total number of border-crossing deaths occurring within any given year." For example, in 2004, Arizona's Pima County medical examiner cited 120 border-crossing deaths. The BSI cited eighty-four. The GAO also found that from 1990 to 2003, more than 75 percent of the increase in border-crossing deaths occurred in the Tuscon, Arizona Sector as a result of exposure. Following the implementation of the Southwest Border Strategy in 1994, "illegal" immigration moved from cites such as San Diego and El Paso to desert areas, particularly along the Arizona border. In a major shift, "deaths from traffic fatalities and homicide declined" as heat-exposure deaths skyrocketed to more than double the pre-1993 numbers. According to the GAO, "The Border Patrol's assertions that its prevention efforts have resulted in a reduction in migrant deaths have not taken [important] factors into account. . . . Incomplete data may in turn affect the Border Patrol's ability to understand the scale of the problem in each sector and affect the agency's ability to make key decisions about where and how to deploy BSI resources across the southwest border." Keeping in mind the BSI's incomplete data, this excerpt from the GAO report further highlights the failures of BSI policy since its inception in 1998: "according to our analysis of the BSI data, the number of deaths in the Tucson Sector increased from 11 in 1998 to 216 in 2005." It is important to consider the potential impact of the vigilante group the Minutemen, who have gained international attention for the racist and violent statements of their founders, Chris Simcox and Jim Gilchrist. The Minutemen's armed "internal vigilance operations" units often work in collaboration with the Border Patrol at the Arizona border. See http://nomoredeaths.org/, http://www.gao.gov/new.items/d06770.pdf, and http://www.cbp.gov/xp/cgov/border_security (accessed April 28, 2007).

15. Awarded a 2004 Illinois Arts Council Fellowship in Media Arts, recently tenured at Columbia College, Chicago (2000–2006), and relocated to Phoenix, Arizona, I was recruited to help build Arizona State University's new Film and Media Production Program. A Weynex Center Residency Award for Media Arts (2009–2010) will help H. L. T. Quan and I wrap post production on *The Angela Davis Project* (working title), documentary on political culture with Davis and eighty-seven-year-old grassroots activist Yuri Kuchiyama. Recent screenplays include *Blues for the Sea*, an award-winning short and recently completed, feature-length screenplay about love and loss among a community of West African and Central American coastal migrants transplanted to the desert city of Phoenix, Arizona (winner of the Martha Muñuz Award of the Latino Screenplay Competition for its "unique portrayal of the Latino struggle"), and *Mariposa Monarca*, a short screenplay that will be a mixed-genre animation film in homage to the tenacity of migrants (both Mexican and Monarch). Told from the perspective of a Monarch butterfly, a creature who shares the same migratory path, this project is influenced by Mary Ann Peters's paintings *Recuerdo (after Tomás Rivera)* at the

Del Otro Lado

University of Texas, San Antonio. It was born out of my experience as a volunteer for the Latino Union of Chicago, an organization that advocates for the rights of contingent laborers.

As someone who should have died long ago, I find special meaning in the butterfly. A near drowning at eight; at eighteen, I felt an urgent and desperate need to get far away from the crowded Washington, D.C., Metro car I'd just entered. Moments after I'd reached the third car down, the Metro derailed, killing three and injuring dozens in the car I'd entered originally. During a camping trip at thirteen and lost in the forest during a thunderstorm, I was shot at, mistaken for a deer. I fainted. At dawn I awoke; my body was covered with butterflies. In December 2004 I survived a hit-and-run driver and the ensuing chaos of two blown tires, several 360s, and the freeway's cement divider during a Chicago rush hour. In February 2007, emergency surgery saved me from another close call. I know that life is beholden to secrets and beauty. I am more committed than ever to teaching, doing pro bono video production work for community service organizations through Q.U.A.D. Productions (a media activist production company I co-founded in 2000 with H.L.T. Quan), and completing several films and screenplays. In the winter of 2008, we finished the last conversations for *The Angela Davis Project*; we also completed principal photography on a second documentary, *América's Home*, on displacement, race, and popular resistance in San Juan, Puerto Rico. Postproduction on both films began in the summer of 2008. All these projects are imbued with *saudade* and an urgency in response to injustice. Finally, my current work reflects my intrigue with what can only be described as miracles and the intangible mysteries of life.

16. Shooting and finishing *Del Otro Lado* was a gift and a challenge for numerous reasons. First, its cast included actors with little or no film or theater experience to renowned actors such as Eduardo López Rojas (*Mi Familia*) and Patricia Reyes Spíndola (Julie Taymor's *Frida* and many of Mexico's famed *tele-novelas*). Second, Mexico's glorious tradition of *tele-novelas* and film melodramas were unfamiliar forms to me but intrinsic to the script (an adaptation from an original play) and to the culture. Third, I am not a gay Mexican man, and it was a challenge to capture gay Latino sensuality and sexuality in such a way that the gaze was not voyeuristic or shallow. Fourth, although we were originally scheduled to shoot on location in Mexico City during December 1997 and January 1998, political changes in Mexico would have made our film permit and connections useless. We were forced to move production up by several weeks. The film was shot on location, in Spanish, over a three-week period, during the end of the fall semester while I was a visiting assistant professor at Smith College and the University of Massachusetts, Amherst.

17. In a cost-saving measure, we made arrangements with the lab to screen our footage after hours, and only every three to four rolls. The lesson learned was simple and costly: regardless of budget, it is vital to process and screen the footage shot every day (the appropriately named dailies) because the money saved in lab fees is nothing compared to the cost of undetected production errors. We immediately returned screening our dailies daily.

18. I.A.T.S.E., also called the I.A., is the International Alliance of Theatrical Stage Employees. It is the largest labor union in the United States and Canada, representing

C. A.
GRIFFITH

the filmmakers we call professional stagehands, motion picture technicians, and af-
filiated crafts.

19. We could not afford to subcontract for the Spanish-to-English translation and subtitles because they were prohibitively expensive. We did them ourselves. The subtitles also cover up the time code and key code burned in at the bottom of the video transfer.

20. Originally a photographer, Anne Norda is an independent writer, producer, and director. Norda's feature films include *Red Is the Color Of* (2005), which stars Irina Björklund, Shooting Star Award winner at the 2003 Berlin Film Festival.

21. Author's telephone interview with Anne Norda, Saturday, September 17, 2005, Los Angeles and Chicago.

22. The premiere was later moved to the lovely 500-seat Victoria Theater because we could not afford a film print and had to screen on Beta SP. It was a sold-out screening, with a long line waiting to get in. We had made three mistakes, however. First, when asked by *Variety* if we were going to release *Del Otro Lado* on film—because at the time, they did not do reviews of films unless they were released on film—I naively answered that we were raising the funds to do so. Several people, all complete strangers, had come up to us after the screening to say they had sat next to the influential critic for *Variety* and he seemed to really like the film. A review from *Variety* can make or break an independent film. When an assistant called the next day from the magazine, I should have been honest, not necessarily truthful, and responded yes, the film print was being struck at DuArt lab this week. Once the review came out, we could always explain that finances fell through, as is often the case with independent films that run out of money before marketing and distribution have begun. As an example, the film on which I entered I.A.T.S.E. as a first AC, *Juice* (1992), had a production budget of approximately $3 million; the marketing budget was at least three times that amount. The *Variety* review of *Del Otro Lado* never saw the light of day. I am still haunted by what a little, harmless lie could have done for us.

Del Otro Lado

Second, the Victoria Theater offered us a theatrical run of the film. We decided against it because we were already heavily in debt and didn't know if we could fill a 500-seat theater for a week or two and do the film festival circuit (the entry fees, postage, press packages, and travel can run into the thousands). It was a great way to gain support for the film and get film reviews and possibly a distributor, but we gambled on doing it through the film festival route.

Finally, the film was officially selected for over twenty film festivals in the United States, Canada, Mexico, and Europe. We never asked for a screening fee or percentage of the ticket sales to offset our costs, let alone make a profit. In sum, we were too naive, too honest, and we didn't understand adequately how the business—marketing and distribution—end of filmmaking worked. Everyone assumed we knew these things, and we didn't know to ask when the film, print, TV interviews, and distribution talks were all so positive and success seemed within our reach. In San Francisco and Los Angeles, I was feted as one of the hot new queer directors to watch. Had I been a different kind of person, I would have believed my own press releases and fallen for the Hollywood hype. A shy person and modest by nature, I was not accustomed to swimming in the swift waters of the parties and networking sessions. This was a liability of being a director; it was expected, practically demanded. The most important invitations were for the film's director, and that happened to be me. But someone else—an agent, if we had one, or the film's co-star, co-writer, and co-producer, Gustavo Cravioto—would have better represented the film in these arenas.

23. *The San Francisco Bay Times,* May 27, 1999.

24. Please see Horacio N. Roque Ramirez's chapter on *Del Otro Lado,* "Claiming Queer Cultural Citizenship: Gay Latino (Im)Migrant Acts in San Francisco," in *Queer Migrations: Sexuality, U.S. Citizenship, and Border-Crossings,* ed. Eithne Lubhéid and Lionel Cantú, Jr. (Minneapolis: University of Minnesota Press, 2005).

25. A close translation of *gracias a la vida* is thanks to life. Like many things in Spanish, the English translation does it little justice, or poetry.

Faith in Sexual Difference

THE INQUISITION OF A
CREATIVE PROCESS

Daniel S. Cutrara

(Arizona State University)

I am a writer, a teacher, and a former Catholic priest. I have written a number of screenplays and stage plays, and have had producers secure the rights to develop two of my scripts. One of those scripts is *Kali Danced,* the focal point of my comments in this chapter. I have taught screenwriting for the past eleven years at Loyola Marymount University and Arizona State University. I have also worked as a story analyst in Hollywood, evaluating other people's creative work for major production companies such as New Regency Productions and Imagine Entertainment. For me, analyzing someone else's work is an easier task than writing an original work of substance. In fact, writing this essay, this analysis of my own creative processes, has been an extremely difficult task for me. It was not something I learned to do as a graduate student in film school. Writing this essay has been like opening up a nesting doll: inside each truth I discovered about my work was yet another truth, transforming my understanding of the experience and of myself. At times this was a torturous process, since the dolls would take on a life of their own and resist being opened; think Chucky and possession.[1] I found myself the inquisitor of a younger self whose heresy was that of having mixed motivations. Ultimately, like the author of the book of Ecclesiastes, I fear that at the heart of the nesting doll lies a simple fact about my work: "all is vanity."[2] This essay, then, is a report on the current truths I have uncovered in the examination of the creative process I undertook in the development of *Kali Danced.*

It was 1998 when I began to jot down notes and consider the tale I wanted to tell. My initial intentions were to explore a world I knew intimately, that of the Catholic priesthood, sexuality, and social justice. I wanted to be faithful in the writing to my life experience and at the same time say something new. During the development of the script, however, I had to make choices in regard to the representation of difference vis-à-vis religion, sexuality, gender, class, and national identity. The choices I made affected how open I was to discovering the truth of the characters and story I desired to tell. They were influenced on the one hand by my fears concerning Church censorship and my relationship to the Jesuit Order, and on the other by my fears in regard to my own sexual identity. The struggle with these fears led to mixed results: compromises in my creative choices for the script that I later regretted, and with those regrets the realization that if I was to be free to create, I would have to forsake the Catholic priesthood after nineteen years of religious life, which, ultimately, I did.

Why This Story?

DANIEL S.
CUTRARA

Kali Danced is about many things. Apart from my need to tell a story about forgiveness, first and foremost it is a story that deals with priests as real human beings. Most representations in the media either demonize priests, such as the dark portrayal of the Jesuit assassin in *Elizabeth*,[3] or idealize them, along the lines of the sugary Father O'Malley by Bing Crosby in *Going My Way*.[4] Most films use priests in supporting roles, similar to the representations of women, people of color, and queers, in effect denying them a fuller sense of humanity. Moreover, most media representations portray priests as either asexual or heterosexual. This is the case in *The Thorn Birds*,[5] a sizzling mini-series from the early 1980s. There is a certain irony in the fact that the star of the television program, Richard Chamberlain, was a closeted gay actor playing a straight priest, since many gay priests pass for straight. At the time I was writing my script, only the groundbreaking film *Priest*,[6] written by Jimmy McGovern, a layman offered a compassionate exploration of a priest awakening to his homosexuality.

The stereotypes of priests in film and television made it more difficult for my fellow priests and me to minister to others. The idealization raised unrealistic expectations that we couldn't meet, and the demonization dismissed whatever good we had to offer. In my script wanted to portray ordinary men being asked to mediate the extraordinary, amid the mundane and the horrific, and the challenges inherent in that activity. This was to be an exploration of vocation and faith that would portray the priesthood I knew. Given my world, the story would necessarily deal with a significant gay subculture within the priesthood that included bisexuals and homosexuals, some celibate and some sexually active. When I use the terms *bisexual* and *hom-*

sexual, I am talking about sexual attraction, not activity. You can be homosexual and celibate, just as you can be heterosexual and celibate. Many gay and bisexual priests are celibate; some are not. I think for most people, celibacy is not an easy task, regardless of sexual orientation. Finally, I use the term *queer* to include all those whose sexuality does not fit what is considered the heterosexual norm.[7] For some of us, queer is a sociopolitical statement reappropriating a word that has taken on negative connotations.[8] Sticks and stones break bones, and words do significant damage. In this case, we are dismantling one of our enemy's weapons of mass defaming.

In the 1990s my sense of the news media was that it blurred the distinction between homosexual priests and pedophiles. I wanted to make it clear that just as not all heterosexual men commit rape, so not all men with same-sex attraction prey on minors. In this toxic climate created by the blurring, my hope was that audiences would realize that most gay priests are good priests. I wanted to speak about my experience in the priesthood, about priests who fall in love with one another, who must represent a Church that refuses to accept the counsel of the American Psychiatric Association, which stopped classifying homosexuality as a pathological behavior in 1973.[9] This is a Church whose official teaching tells gay priests that ordination sets them apart, in effect making them "better" than other human beings,[10] while at the same time censuring their homoerotic desires as "intrinsically disordered."[11] These are men who are faced on a daily basis with the dilemma of supporting an institution that demonizes their most primal desires. These desires are about more than the physical. Although they are focused on the same sex, they are desires we all have for human intimacy. They provide the impetus for friendship and love, drawing us into relationships where we can discover who we are.

Context for the Process

In 1998, as an assistant professor at Loyola Marymount University, I received a summer research grant to develop the script. This was an opportunity rarely given to writers, and I wanted to make the most of it. I had eight months to come up with a draft strong enough to bring into a development workshop where I would collaborate with a director, dramaturge, scenographer, and actors. The experience was invaluable. Never before had I gone through a process that fully opened up my work to analysis not only scene by scene, but beat by beat. It was intensely rigorous and rewarding.

The Story

Here is a brief synopsis of the script. John, a Catholic priest, returns to the United States from India, where his best friend, Nick (also a priest), was mysteriously murdered shortly after a corrupt landowner's thugs slaughtered eighteen villagers from their mission. Hoping for some much needed rest, John spends a weekend at the beach with two of his friends from the seminary, Christopher and Paul. Christopher, openly gay, antagonizes Paul and John with his campy humor, goading them to acknowledge their own repressed desires. When John is not being teased by Christopher, he is confronted by Nick's ghost, who leads him in a dance of remembrance. John recalls his time in the seminary when Nick led them all in solidarity work with El Salvador. John had an affair with a woman at the same time he desired Nick, a desire that his homophobia would not let him pursue. Ordination sends them on different paths, Nick to India and John to the suburbs, until the bishop sends John to assist Nick in India.

DANIEL S.
CUTRARA

Upon John's arrival, Nick enlists his aid in organizing the mission village in a labor strike, demanding minimum wage from the landowner. Working and living together in this foreign land makes the attraction between John and Nick overwhelming, leading to a kiss that John is unable to bear. When the landowner's thugs break the village elder's arm, Nick is ready to end the strike, but John encourages him to consult the villagers. They are willing to continue, and the landowner's response is unmerciful.

At the beach, John does not want to face the final revelation of his actions and attempts to drown himself. Christopher stops him, and runs to Paul for help. The two friends hear John's confession of his betrayal. After the slaughter of the eighteen, John made a pact with the landowner: Nick's life for the safety of the surviving villagers. Christopher and Paul console John, but it is Nick's ghost that offers the final absolution: his forgiveness and continued love in spite of John's actions. While the relationship between John and Nick ends tragically for Christopher and Paul their bickering over the course of the weekend leads to what really matters, confronting the unspoken hurts that have kept them estranged over the years.

Issues Affecting the Creative Process

The decision-making process I went through in the development *Kali Danced* was more complicated than the process I had gone through with my previous scripts. Not only was I making decisions regarding the representation of difference, and thus struggling with questions of authenticity, I was making them about controversial characters in the context of a scandalous plot. This raised additional concerns beyond those of telling the best story possible with honest representations. I had to deal with the politics of writing and the politics of the Church.

I also felt conflicted about telling Jesuit family secrets, because I would be writing realistic portrayals of gay priests where some live double lives, publicly professing celibacy but privately carrying on affairs. I was very aware of my obligations as a Jesuit. I believed that because of the potentially divisive content of my script, the story had to be meaningful enough to an audience to outweigh any harm it might inadvertently cause to the Church's reputation.

Since I was exploring the gay and bisexual subculture within the priesthood, I would be potentially exposing the Church to unwanted publicity. I would be betraying the Jesuits who had given me a home where I could develop my creativity and accept my sexuality. They had paid for my extensive graduate education, my training as priest and filmmaker. My indebtedness to their generosity conflicted with my need to tell this story. I had the legal right of freedom of speech, but what moral right had I to reveal family secrets? And if the script was successful, did I want to be known as the writer who profited on scandal?

Faith in Sexual Difference

I was also concerned about outing myself. Granted, a straight man can write a story about gay and bisexual characters, but I expected my audience and my order would assume I was gay. Even though I was attracted to both men and women, I had come out as gay to my close friends and co-workers. But I had not told my family or students, and was afraid of how it would affect my relationship with them. At the same time, I needed to be myself, and I hoped that being "out" more publicly as a priest would contribute to a growing tolerance for queers in the Church and in society. The Church has its own variation on the "don't ask, don't tell" policy. Many gay priests serve in silence. They are excellent ministers, yet their lives of sacrifice are supporting a repressive institution. I believed there was an inherent injustice in this reality that needed to be uncovered.

Underlying my various concerns about the telling of *Kali Danced* was the pervasive fear of Church censorship, which in its extreme form could deny distribution or exhibition of my work. I had experienced censorship before. My first major creative project was semiautobiographical and, like many writers' first novels, probably needed to remain on the shelf. I had written the first draft of the novel as a final thesis project for my master's degree in narrative theology. Even though it was a work of fiction, I had to seek approval for publication from my religious superior because it dealt with spiritual matters such as sin and forgiveness.[12]

Before submitting the manuscript to my superior, I solicited feedback from other Jesuits. Their notes were helpful and encouraging. They seemed to agree that the work was attempting to explore the humanity of those who minister in the church. I realized, however, that because of the graphic nature of the sexual scenes, my superior could ask for revisions. No revisions were requested. My superior found the protagonist too guilt-ridden and the Church represented too ambiguously, and believed that it could be read as "gratuitously anti-Catholic." I was ordered not to disseminate the work in any form. To disobey this command would be grounds for dismissal from the order. My superior strongly suggested in his official letter of censure that teaching was my life's work, not creative writing.

That censure felt like a death. I had brought something into existence, and it was being denied life. I also felt the effects of having my voice taken away and discounted. There was an implicit message that what I wanted to communicate to others was not valued. Apparently, the complex Church I experienced and had written about with approval in my graduate studies was not the pristine Church that the hierarchy wanted to present to the world. Even though I thought my portrayal of the Church was true to my experience, I had to adhere to the dictates of my order. Jesuits take vows of poverty, chastity, and obedience. As the Franciscans are known for their simplicity of life and their embrace of poverty, the Jesuits wish to be known for their exemplary life of obedience. To obey one's superior is to obey Christ. I tried to be obedient to my superior. I shelved my novel. I took a teaching position. But I did not give up my creative work.

Over the next five years the frustration of writing to second-guess potential censors brought me to a breaking point. I had come to a crossroads, realizing that if I was to continue as a writer, I had to give myself total freedom to write the stories I felt passionate about, regardless of the consequences. That is when I received the grant for *Kali Danced*. I knew I was entering taboo territory with this script, but I had to take the risk. What I did not realize as I experienced that moment of rebellion was how truly conflicted I was, and that self-censorship would continue to influence my writing. For example, although I saw *Kali Danced* as a movie, I wrote it as a stage play, thinking that it would be less threatening to the Church and less likely to be censored. I imagined it playing before small audiences who were comfortable with gay themes and would not be scandalized.

My Jesuit friends encouraged me to bypass script approval from my superiors. They encouraged me to exhibit the work and deal with the fallout. I could always beg for forgiveness after the fact. I compromised. I moved forward with the writing and promised my workshop director and the actors she was recruiting for the workshop that we would proceed regardless of my superior's reactions. In the meantime, I submitted the script to an approval process that could take months. This time I had a new, more progressive religious superior, and I hoped a bolder one. I did not realize it at the time, but my need to have the play approved was a need to have the Church approve me as a queer. It was a need to have my homoerotic desires legitimized by the Church hierarchy. Since I was not living in total denial, I must have known on some level that this could never happen. And it did not. I was allowed the staged reading, but no other performance of the work. Living without sexual intimacy was difficult enough, being denied the full expression of my creative passion was more than I could bear. I left the priesthood.

Working Out Issues in the Creative Process

When I begin writing the first draft of a script, even though I have a preconceived ending in mind, I expect to be surprised. Invariably characters begin speaking on the page, revealing themselves and acting in unexpected ways. *Kali Danced* began as *Reunion,* the story of four Jesuit priests gathering for a weekend reunion at a parishioner's beach house. One of the priests, Frank, was happy, heterosexual, and celibate. He was like a number of priests I know, and my creative response to the movie *Priest,* where the only celibate priest is a bitter heterosexual. The other three priests in *Reunion* spanned the queer continuum: openly gay Christopher, repressed Paul, and John, a bisexual struggling with his homoerotic desires. The major conflict remained below the surface, until John's revelation at the end that he was considering leaving the priesthood.

When I brought this first draft to my writing group, they were encouraging but challenging. I had created a world and interesting characters but had not found my story yet. Actually, I had; it just was not on the page. The images of John and India and betrayal haunted me whenever I sat down to write. But I was afraid to explore them and what they might reveal about myself, even though writers were supposed to delve deep inside their psyches to uncover the stories worth telling. The script, however, had to be ready for the development workshop. This deadline triggered my fear of failure that was strong enough to overcome my other fears. I took the plunge, and *Reunion* transformed into *Kali Danced,* a tragic love story of two priests in India.

The Characters

A number of changes were made in the early drafts of *Kali Danced.* I no longer portrayed these priests as part of the Jesuit Order, partly because I was still angling to avoid censorship, partly because it was difficult enough to bring the audience into the world of the priesthood, let alone the idiosyncrasies of the Jesuits. Most people are familiar with the portrayal of the diocesan (parish) priest. Better to challenge that stock image with gay characters than to introduce them to priests who can be educators, lawyers, doctors, even filmmakers.

Frank, the heterosexual priest, was merged with Paul, because these two were performing a similar function as foils to Christopher and allies to John. By cutting Frank, I lost my response to the bitterly celibate heterosexual priest in *The Priest,* but that representation was not essential to the story. What was essential was the inclusion of a new character, Nick, John's love interest. However, by cutting the only heterosexual priest in the script, I created another dilemma. I now had four priests who were all gay or bisexual and in various states of denial and acceptance. On the one hand, in conceiving the characters across a spectrum of bisexual to homosexual, I felt that I was able to challenge some of the stereotypical representations we see in the media. On the other hand, when I brought the script to the workshop, the question for the character of Paul was, "Isn't he straight?" "Doesn't the audience need a straight character as their entrée into the story?" "How could you write about the priesthood, which isn't all gay, and not have a straight priest?" I took these questions very seriously, first, because I didn't want my script to appeal only to a queer audience, and second, because I was operating under the assumption that I could somehow accurately represent the reality of the priesthood in the Church, and had the responsibility to do so. This was in spite of the fact that on an intellectual level, I believed that given human cognitive limitations, we could not truly know ourselves, let alone the full meaning of other people, things, and the world around us. It was not until a few years later, when I encountered the works of the cultural theorist Stuart Hall that I realized the implications of these limitations in regard to storytelling. According to Hall, meaning is not only constructed in the way the artist chooses to represent things but also in the variety of ways that people may understand that representation.[13] His insight enabled me to better understand my concern regarding the representation of the

DANIEL S.
CUTRARA

priesthood in *Kali Danced*. It would have been crazy for me to try to "accurately" portray the Church and its priesthood, an incredibly complex organization that affects people in a multitude of ways. The only thing I could attempt was to be true to my own experience of it.

While writing my initial drafts, however, my inner debate revolved around whether or not the audience would see my specific characters as representative of the whole priesthood. On a practical level, I knew that media representations have an impact on viewers, reinforcing negative stereotypes or providing positive role models. For myself, when the character of Ellen came out in 1997 on the network television sitcom *Ellen*,[14] I was deeply moved. I felt validated and inspired to be more courageous and public about my sexuality, and that consequently enabled me to be more open about homosexuality in the priesthood. In the end, however, concerned about having some kind of balanced and authentic representation of the priesthood, and wanting to appeal to a larger audience, I let Paul's sexuality remain indistinct, even though the conflict between him and Christopher is best understood through a homoerotic lens.

My first incarnation of the character of Christopher was so abrasive that the gay actors who helped out with an informal reading found him offensive. Their reaction made me question the truth of the character. Christopher was coming across as a catty, unfeeling bitch—in other words, a very bitter stereotype. I realized that he was carrying a significant amount of my anger—anger at a Church and a culture that was telling me I was damned. In my subsequent rewrites I removed the bitterness and focused Christopher's anger on both Paul's sexual repression and John's denial. I also made sure the audience saw other sides of him. Christopher not only entertains his fellow priests with witty repartee and a gourmet meal, per the stereotype, it is his insight and compassion that save John from suicide and enable his acceptance of forgiveness.

In my early draft, Christopher engaged in casual sex. But after consultation with a Jesuit friend, I decided to put a spin on audience expectations and have him be celibate. This added complexity to Christopher's character, but it felt like a stretch in the script when he announces to Paul that he really is celibate. By this point the audience has seen his attempted seduction of Nick in the seminary and heard about his latest flame, Angelo, who calls him at the beach house. Although Christopher explains himself to Paul, it did not ring true. I was not comfortable with this version, but it certainly felt less controversial to portray a gay priest as not having sex, so I left it for the staged reading and addressed it in later rewrites.

Faith in Sexual Difference

Nick, the social justice priest, was the new character added to the mix. He is more than John's love interest. He represented priests inspired by liberation theology, with its radical commitment to the poor and the creation of a just society in which all people are treated with equal dignity. Nick is portrayed as decisive and uncompromising, embodying more stereotypical notions of masculinity. He comes from a family of wealth and privilege, which he rejects, yet at the same time he embodies an unconscious sense of entitlement. He is a modern-day prophet who is a little too full of himself. He embraces nonviolence and is dogmatic when it comes to issues of social justice, yet he appears to follow his own moral compass, independent of the Church or society, when it comes to sex. For me, Nick represented the best and the worst of a white male-dominated Church and the best and worst of a U.S. citizen abroad. He is willing to give his life for the poor, but he is not willing to give up power and pleasure. Nick is a modern-day version of the European missionary bringing salvation to the heathen. He can also be seen as the imperialist sacrificing to bring civilization to the "half devil and half child" of foreign lands, an arrogant sentiment captured so eloquently by Rudyard Kipling in his poem "The White Man's Burden."[15] Unfortunately, I think the challenge to the Church and the notions of imperialism that Nick's characterization evokes can easily be lost among the sexual issues.

John's portrayal is that of the passive-aggressive, self-hating bisexual who has internalized the homophobia of dominant culture. This sensibility is reflected as he recounts a religious experience to Nick's ghost:

> JOHN: I used to pray every night for God to hold me, to take me. I wanted to have the ecstasies of the mystics.
> NICK'S GHOST: You were so naive.
> JOHN: But he did. Once. One night. But then he never came back, not in that way. I don't know why. The only thing I could figure was that wasn't ready, I wasn't holy enough, pure enough.

In writing the character of John, I struggled with my impression the current sensibility among the gay community that the world didn't need any more images of the queer as a self-hating victim of society. We had gone through that stage, and now it was time to show more positive images. I decided that because of the specific circumstance of gay and bisexual priests in the Church, my representation of John was warranted. Showing priests having to grapple with a faith that condemns their intrinsic nature was important enough to explore.

Working with these characters, I began to realize how each one of 175 them had elements of priests I knew but at the same time reflected a different part of myself. I was giving voice to those parts of me that had been hiding in the shadows. Little had I known there was a Christopher inside me who enjoyed playing the queen. On one level the play became a self-dialogue and reconciliation. For me to write these characters well, I needed to understand them, and in doing so I was able to come to love them.

The Role of Women

The women in this story were all offstage; although their absence was intentional, due to the narrative, it also fulfilled a political and meta- phorical function. Their characters were not central to the plot, which revolved around the interrelationships of four male friends. Just as I cut the character of Frank, the happy heterosexual, because he was not necessary to the story, I placed the women offstage. However, I was conscious that this lack of presence echoed the marginalization of women in the Church, an injustice that deserves to be addressed in the media. Thinking about gender analytically, it is their marginalization and the devaluation of the feminine by the Church that is repeated in John's aversion to his own homoerotic desire. It is also the lack of traditional "feminine" qualities, such as mercy and compassion, that enables the rich landowner to use his power to massacre the landless villagers.

Faith in Sexual Difference

When I speak of the marginalization and devaluation of the feminine in the Church, I am referring to the religious culture created by a male-only priesthood with an all-male hierarchy. Even though Mary, the mother of Jesus, plays a key role in Catholic worship, the fact that only men can lead speaks volumes about the place of women in the Church. It has been my privilege to work with women who were much more qualified to minister in a priestly capacity than I ever was. Yet, in the eyes of the Church, my genitalia trumped whatever talent these dynamic women possessed. The Church's concern appears to be more about male privilege than how it can best care for its flock.

Three women characters fill functional roles in *Kali Danced*. During the weekend at the beach, Paul speaks to his mother over his cell phone. He has taken on a caretaker role after the death of his father, and the conversations are as much about revealing his character as they are comic relief. In their final conversation, however, she invites Paul, John, and Christopher to dinner. Paul concurs with the invitation of Christopher, in a move toward reconciliation. For me the irony inherent in this action is that it is a woman who invites the men (priests) to the table to share a meal. The altar, where priests preside at the Mass, represents the table of the Last Supper. It is normally the priest's role to invite the congregation to share in the meal of bread and wine, a meal that symbolizes the reconciliation between God and humanity.

John has an affair with a young woman, a graduate student, when he is a seminarian. The audience hears about her when he speaks to Nick, revealing his struggle regarding celibacy. He has fallen in love with this woman and, ultimately, chooses the priesthood over her. When he falls in love with Nick, he has this relationship with the woman to use as a way of denial. He can say to himself, "I've had an affair with a woman, how can I be gay?" The way he ends his relationship with the woman also prepares him for how he handles his feelings for Nick. He rationalizes the self-sacrifice of his romantic interests for the greater good of humanity. He chose the priesthood over her. With Nick, he chooses to save the village and sacrifice the man he loves.

Finally, there is a beautiful young girl from the village who dances at a birthday celebration for John. Nick teases John about her, claiming that she has a crush on him, testing to see how John will react. But John realizes that Nick is the object of the girl's affection, and knows that Nick is well aware of it. When the girl is raped and killed during the village massacre, she becomes one of the many victims that fuel Nick's resolve not to bend to the landowner's demands. She represents the beauty and innocence that are victimized by a disregard for the feminine, a victimization that ultimately unleashes a destructive response.

The Plot

Robert Mckee, the Hollywood screenwriting guru, insists that "The function of structure [and, ultimately, plot] is to provide progressively building pressures that force characters into more and more difficult dilemmas where they must make more and more difficult risk-taking choices and actions, gradually revealing their true natures, even down to the unconscious self."[16]

The structure and plot of *Kali Danced* rip away the layers of John's self-denial, leaving him naked, physically and emotionally, at the end of the script, when he must face not only the horror of his own betrayal of the man he loved but also the forgiveness offered him. After the massacre of the village, the landowner's thugs send death threats to Nick and John. John urges Nick to end the strike. Nick ignores

John's concerns and continues the strike. The surviving villagers, believing Nick to be a saint, will not openly oppose him, but they are convinced that if they continue the nonviolent resistance they will be slaughtered. They appeal to John for a solution to their dilemma. John makes a deal with the landowner that, in effect, turns Nick over to assassins.

I wanted John's motivation to be debatable. Was he betraying Nick solely to save the villagers, or was he using it as an excuse to eliminate the object of his affection? In effect, was John, as victim of Church and landowner, recapitulating their abuse of power in his relationship with Nick? Regardless of the interpretation, I wanted John's betrayal to be credible, and his character of "sound mind." This combination, however, was compromised in the writing because of the choices I made in regard to John's sexual behavior.

The following scene occurs midway through the script and is critical to the plot. It sets up the emotional reason for John's betrayal of Nick. In this scene, John can no longer tolerate his sense of helplessness in the face of the poverty and disease of the people. At the same time he can no longer repress the feelings he has living day after day with the man he desires. Yet, given his homophobia, these desires are taboo, and he can use the need to protect his vocation as a reason to not voice them, let alone act on them. For a moment, however, his defenses crack when he shares with Nick the horror of watching a patient operated on without sufficient anesthetic.

(A bungalow in India)
JOHN: They had a surgery today. (pause) They didn't give the guy enough anesthesia. The surgeon was wearing a Walkman. It was like a circus. The aide was shouting, "Take it like a man." His blood splattered on my shirt.
NICK: It could have been worse.
JOHN: What?
NICK: The power could have gone out.
(Later in the scene)
JOHN: He grabbed onto me. Grabbed onto my hands. I was begging God for the pain to end. But it didn't.
NICK: But it did.
(Nick holds out his hand.)
NICK: Take it.
(John stares into Nick's eyes. The sexual tension is very thick.)
NICK: John.

(They embrace. John begins to weep. Nick kisses John on the lips. John responds. But suddenly he pulls away.)

JOHN: No.

(John runs out.)

In this scene, John and Nick should have made love. It would have been more realistic and true to my original conception of their characters. However, after the lovemaking, Nick would have rejected John out of fear of compromising his priesthood. This would have been devastating for John, and a more serious motivation for his handing Nick over to the landowner's assassins. I held back, for two reasons. First, I thought that showing priests making love to one another would be too scandalous. The previous year, the controversial ABC series *Nothing Sacred* had succeeded in portraying heterosexual priests as fully human. However, the series' attempt to address homosexuality was censored. An episode written by a fellow Jesuit, Bill Cain, featuring a priest with AIDS was shot but never aired for fear of protests.[17] Second, and perhaps even more important, I had not come out publicly and was still grappling with those fears. Imagining the audience seeing my desire reflected in the "mirror" of the story was unnerving.

So I censored myself. The lovemaking was reduced to a kiss. This forced me to reconceive the character of John, who would now be unable to handle this brief intimacy and what it revealed about his sexuality. The consequence of this censorship was that John now had to have a degree of self-hatred that borders on the pathological. Instead of striking back at a lover who betrayed him, he had to feel the overwhelming need to destroy the man whose kiss threatened his "straight" self-understanding.

I believe that compromise is an inherent part of writing, in dealing with the ratings system, restrictions of network television, budget constraints, concerns of directors, producers, actors, and so on. For me the question becomes at what point on the continuum of compromise is the story no longer worth telling. I do not think there is an easy answer. A writer must weigh the various compensations that may accrue with the exhibition of the work versus how far it has strayed from his or her original intent, or for that matter an intention that he or she can live with.

Why India?

While rewriting the initial draft, I asked myself if the use of India as primary location was essential to the story. Since the priests as sent

narians were jailed in a protest over U.S. involvement in El Salvador, wouldn't it make more sense to place the mission work there and keep the storyline simpler? This certainly made more sense in regard to the storytelling principles I had learned and taught. But I followed my gut feeling and kept the mission in India. At the time, I had no obvious reason for this choice.

Years later, looking back on my writing process, the choice I made is much clearer. In the summer of 1988, ten years prior to writing the initial draft of *Kali Danced,* I worked for six weeks changing the bandages of leprosy patients in a Catholic hospital in Bihar. Bihar is the poorest state of India, and one of the poorest regions in the world. From my arrival in the country I had been confronted by a culture so different from the West. The interpersonal communication, cloth- *Faith in Sexual* ing, architecture, music all followed a set of rules different from what *Difference* I knew. Most unsettling was the unstable sociopolitical climate. I'll never forget picking up the newspaper in Govindpur and seeing an article that read, "'Landlord Behind Bihar Carnage' . . . If they so desire they can maim, rape, and kill at will."[18] The description of a massacre of landless villagers, men, women, and children followed. My naive American sensibilities were suddenly exposed to a country in constant turmoil. While India continued to skirmish with Pakistan over Kashmir, guerilla warfare disrupted a number of its other states.

This political and social violence was the context for my work with leprosy patients. Hansen's disease (leprosy) can be cured if diagnosed soon enough. But given the infrastructure and corruption of Bihar, hundreds of thousands still suffered from the disease. There were also cultural elements that I had not expected, including the notion of karma and the Hindu belief that leprosy was the price paid for sins in this life or a past one. It reminded me of how HIV/AIDS patients were treated by some leaders of the religious right in the United States, but the discrimination was more severe in India. Families were forced to disown those diagnosed with leprosy or face public shunning. Regardless of what caste you were born into, once you contracted the disease, you were expected to sever contact with family and friends and spend your remaining years in a leprosy colony. This oppression, however, was not the only thing I witnessed. Every day I was in India, I encountered a people's generosity of spirit and courage in the midst of this suffering.

These extreme contrasts affected me deeply. Now when I ask myself why I located much of my story in India, the answer is clear: because I wanted to write about a religion that enables the shame and abandonment of the ill. Because I wanted to write about a state that allows the rich to prey upon the poor. Because I saw the parallels between these injustices and the way in which the Catholic Church treats women and queers. I was angry, and it was my scream.

In terms of authenticity, I wasn't concerned about a realistic portrayal of India and its culture. For the story I needed a location where social injustice is starkly evident and would demand a response not only from Nick but also from John. I also wanted an exotic place where anything can happen, where John could feel free enough to respond to Nick's love and to betray him. Had I joined a long list of writers who have represented the foreign inaccurately for the purposes of their story?[19] Yes. Did I care? At the time, I was still too haunted by the images and smells of suffering to even ask the question.

DANIEL S.
CUTRARA

What was important to me regarding national identity was that Nick and John were white male Catholic missionaries from the United States. Regardless of Nick's adaptation—wearing Indian garb and learning Hindu customs—he is still "Father knows best." It is their attempts to alleviate suffering that leads to the massacre. I wanted an audience to be able to read them as representatives of an arrogant white colonial power, however well-intentioned.

I also engaged in artistic license in my representation of Hinduism and the goddess Kali. In Hindu mythology she can be understood to represent the dark side of the domestic goddess Parvati.

It is Kali who slays demons on the battlefield, yet her fury can turn uncontrollable and threaten to destroy the world.[20] This is a much more complicated understanding of good and evil than the stereotypical Hollywood good guy versus bad guy or Jesus versus Satan. When Nick returns from the village after witnessing the massacre, he recounts Kali's battle with the demon Raktabija. It is a dance of destruction.

(Nick enters the bungalow covered with blood, his shirt torn, his eyes wild.)
JOHN: Oh God.
NICK: Kali danced. She danced, the Goddess Kali. In the killing field She was drunk on blood. The blood of her victims. Her dancing was wild, it was out of control. She could destroy the whole world with her power.
(Later in the scene)
JOHN: We didn't know where you were. We brought who we could back to the clinic.
NICK: Parvati, slashed open.
JOHN: I told you to stop.
NICK: (Overlapping; remembering each person killed) You told me

what?! Eighteen. Sunil's wife, Parvati—one. Two—I didn't know him, three—the kid with the harelip, four—Chandra, the dreamweaver, five—his wife.

Nick continues his list, recalling the dead, each murder a movement in Kali's dance. Yet the dance is within Nick's soul. He is the one that is out of control, enraged at the death of his beloved villagers. Kali dances within him.

I wanted this massacre to echo the emotional damage wrought by a patriarchal Church whose culture of oppression breeds reaction embodied in the destructive nature of the feminine symbolized by the goddess Kali. John's betrayal of Nick, a parallel of Judas and Jesus, and ultimately John's betrayal of his homoerotic self are Kali's dance. This is what happens when an uncontrollable rage destroys the world of the self. Yet at the same time I wanted the back and forth between John and Nick's ghost, as the ghost forces John to remember their time in India to be a dance of healing. For it is Kali who slays the demons, and it is only in the dance of remembrance that John can face his own demons and find redemption. Was I appropriating religious symbols from another culture to tell my story? Yes, although I was not conscious of it at the time.

In terms of class, what did it mean that the only rich Indian in the script was an oppressor? The rich landowner is a faceless caricature who represents oppression. He is the privileged wealthy exploiting the poor. The landless villagers, however, are not idealized. After the massacre Nick refuses to end the strike, and because of his charisma he is able to keep the villagers united, at least publicly. Privately, a dissenting faction appeals to John to stop Nick. John makes a deal with the landowner to spare the rest of the village in return for Nick's death. Members of that faction kill Nick. What I wanted to portray was the injustice I had encountered and the violence it perpetuates in the victim. was not concerned in any ethical way about the misrepresentation of "slaveholder" who might be a good parent or loyal friend. However, I id have some concerns about the strength of the storytelling, since I elieve you do not prove you are right by demonizing the opposition.

Ultimately, the real India was not being represented in my script. I ad chosen instead to give the audience a brief glimpse into a violent nd obscure land. In effect, the real location represented was in my syche, where an archetypal struggle was being waged between the rannical father, represented by religious authority and the wealthy ndowner, and the children he consumes, represented by the poor, omen, and queers.[21]

Faith in Sexual Difference

In my current draft, I have attempted to bring greater complexity and truth to my portrayal of India. The massacres of the landless poor are placed in context with the slaughtering of landowners and their families by Communist-inspired revolutionaries. In regard to Kali, I have better grounded the representation of the goddess who is revered as a compassionate mother by millions of Hindus.[22] Her portrayal is more complex now, that of a fierce mother, concerned with healing, and destroying the demons of self-hatred. Hopefully this will prevent a simplistic reading that would reduce her to the stereotypical blood-thirsty representation found in movies such as *Indiana Jones and the Temple of Doom*.[23]

DANIEL S. CUTRARA

Revelations in the Process

During the workshop, I had the opportunity to watch actors grapple with my text in rehearsal. It was after a particularly moving reading of the post-massacre scene that I had an insight. One of the villagers who is never seen is a charming little boy whom both Nick and John befriend. He is killed in the massacre, a bullet shattering his face. When I was writing the script, the little boy functioned in different ways for me. He represented the children I had met in India when I worked at the leprosy clinic. He was the innocence victimized by the landowner. The little boy's favorite charm became a final gift to John to represent Nick's forgiveness. In the workshop, however, I realized that he was myself, a queer child who saw only perverse reflections of his face in the media. My work was speaking to me of a pain I had not known how to acknowledge.

One of the ironies of rewriting is that characters and scenes dear to us must be cut if they do not advance the story. The main function of the little boy was also being filled by the young girl. In my rewriting, her role has been expanded and the boy's has been cut. This was not an easy decision to make, but I am convinced that because he was "alive" long enough to give me that message of awareness, it enabled me to let go of his character.

Conclusions

Through this examination of my creative process, I began to explore how my representation of difference was affected by various fears concerning the subject matter, elicited by both my priesthood in the Catholic Church and my sexuality. The audience's enthusiastic response the staged reading of the play convinced me that engaging with the issues was worth the risk. Showing a subculture that exists within the priesthood, I opened up a new world for the audience. With the characters spanning the continuum of queerness, I gave voice to various parts of myself and my former order.

In the development of *Kali Danced,* I learned that just as I was not free to write the stories I wanted, I was not free as a priest to live the way I needed. John's betrayal of Nick was a betrayal I had lived too long in my own life—a suppression of my true self and nature. It took me many years to realize that sexuality is at the core of our humanity. It informs our spirituality and creativity; it is a complex, sometimes mysterious thing; and if it is not honored it will turn destructive.

I have since left the Jesuit Order and the Catholic Church, and am now rewriting *Kali Danced.* Although I am now able to write freely, I realize that censorship is not unique to repressive governments and patriarchal religious institutions and that self-censorship is not relegated to priests writing about topics scandalous to the Church. Pulitzer Prize–winning playwright Edward Albee warns us about the various forms of censorship found in the media.[24] Studios, networks, and theaters choose work based on its commercial viability and their political bias. In consequence, artists censor themselves out of fear of not having their work produced. Whether for economic reasons or the need for validation, artists may compromise their vision.

This is problematic in various ways. Culture needs the critique that storytelling can bring, in effect holding up a mirror to human foibles. But storytelling can do more than that. I believe that we should not ignore Jean Anouilh's contention, expressed in his play *The Rehearsal,* that "The object of art is to give life a shape."[25] Many of us in our attempt to make meaning out of our lives find models to inspire and challenge us in story. What happens, though, when we look to the media and see a distorted image peering back at us, or no image at all? This has been the general experience of women, people of color, and the queer community for decades.

In January 2005, PBS censored one of the episodes of its educational children's series *Buster the Rabbit.* Over the course of the series Buster visits families with diverse backgrounds, social and cultural, who demonstrate some art or craft. In this particular episode, "Sugartime," Buster visits children living in Vermont who show how maple syrup and cheese are made. Besides living on a farm, the diversity aspect for these children is that they have lesbian moms. The secretary of education, Margaret Spellings, thought that public money should not be used to promote alternative lifestyles, and complained. The episode was pulled from national distribution.[26]

It appears that what Secretary Spellings wanted to promote was a structuring of absence. In effect, by not showing healthy lesbian relationships and lesbian parenting, the media reinforce the notion that one of the essential ingredients to being a parent is heterosexuality. Censorship uses the construction of absence to create and support cultural norms.[27] I suggest that in a society where the rate of gay teen suicides[28] is much higher than straight teen suicides, it is time for this destructive absence to be filled with honest reflections of our society. We live in a multicultural world with competing values; do we pay lip service to the notion of human dignity or do we honestly value the individual experience and unique stories of every person?

Daniel Cutrara and his wife, Seline Szkupinski Quiroga, at Pompeii, Italy, in 2004.

Epilogue

I began this essay using the metaphor of the nesting dolls to speak about my reflection on the creative process for *Kali Danced*. If I may, let me extend that metaphor to life. Just when I think I know the truth about myself and the world around me, a deeper truth is revealed. After I left the Jesuits, I came out to my family as gay. They took it as well as they could given their allegiance to the traditional Christian understanding of homosexuality as sinful behavior. However, in the process of dating, I realized that my affections are driven more by the person than by the particular anatomy, since both are marvelously attractive. Much to the surprise of my friends and the relief of my family, I married a woman. Although this commitment honors our love, I am now faced with the political dilemma of passing as straight. It is a tempting option, but in a world where gay men and women are denied the right of marriage, and in effect denied full citizenship, I think it is imperative that I stand up and be counted as queer.

As for the Catholic Church, the oppression continues under Po

Benedict XVI. Vatican concerns over clergy sexual abuse, and with it a blurring of the distinction between homosexuals and pedophiles, led to the release in 2005 of a document banning homosexuals from considering priesthood.[29] The release of this document accompanied a Vatican investigation of Catholic seminaries to ensure their overall orthodoxy and compliance to this most recent dictate.[30]

In the course of this chapter, I have referred to my "current" draft of the script. A year or so after leaving the Jesuits, having gained enough emotional distance, I began a long process of rewriting *Kali Danced*. Now, with the encouragement of my producer, I am in the middle of rewriting a screenplay version. The medium I had rejected out of fear of censorship I am now pursuing. And perhaps best of all, I am restoring the heart of the story. John and Nick will make love.

Notes

1. A serial killer possesses the doll Chucky in a horror film series. See *Child's Play*, DVD, directed by Tom Holland (1988; Los Angeles, CA: MGM Home Entertainment, 1999).

2. Wayne A. Meeks, gen. ed.; Jouette M. Bassler, Werner E. Lemke, Susan Niditch, and Eileen M. Schuller, eds., *The HarperCollins Study Bible: New Revised Standard Version with the Apocryphal/Deuterocanonical Books* (New York: HarperCollins, 1993), 988.

3. *Elizabeth*, DVD, directed by Shekhar Kapur (1998; Universal City, CA: Universal Studios Home Video, 2002).

4. *Going My Way*, DVD, directed by Leo McCarey (1944; Universal City, CA: Universal Studios Home Video, 2007).

5. *The Thorn Birds*, DVD, directed by Daryl Duke (1983; Burbank, CA: Warner Home Video, 2004).

6. *Priest*, DVD, directed by Antonia Bird (1994; Burbank, CA: BV Home Entertainment, 1999).

7. Nikki Sullivan, *A Critical Introduction to Queer Theory* (New York: New York University Press, 2003), 43, 44.

8. Richard Dyer, *The Culture of Queers* (London: Routledge, 2002), 6, 7.

9. Ronald Bayer, *Homosexuality and American Psychiatry: The Politics of Diagnosis* (New York: Basic Books, 1981), 158.

10. Vatican II, "Presbyterorum ordinis," in *Vatican Council II: The Conciliar and Postconciliar Documents*, ed. Austin Flannery (Collegeville, MN: Liturgical Press, 1975), 865.

11. The Vatican and the Catholic Church, *The Catechism of the Catholic Church* (Mahwah, NJ: Paulist Press, 1994), 566.

12. The Jesuit Order is governed hierarchically. Father General, the head of the order, appoints priests to govern over their fellow Jesuits within specific geographic provinces. These superiors ultimately decide what their subjects will do and how they will do it, including where they will live and work.

13. Stuart Hall, "The Work of Representation," in *Representation: Cultural Representations and Signifying Practices,* ed. Stuart Hall (London: Sage, 1997), 61, 62.

14. *Ellen: The Complete Season Four,* DVD (1997; New York: A & E Home Video, 2006).

15. Rudyard Kipling, *The Five Nations* (New York: Doubleday, Page, 1909), 79–81.

16. Robert Mckee, *Story: Substance, Structure, Style, and the Principles of Screenwriting* (New York: HarperCollins, 1997) 105–106.

17. Eric Mink, "ABC Should Let Us See All That's 'Sacred,'" *Daily News* (New York), May 11, 1998, 78.

18. Mohan Sahay, "Landlord Behind Bihar Carnage," *The Statesman* (Calcutta), June 18, 1988, 1, 7.

19. For examples, see Ruth Vasey, "Foreign Parts: Hollywood's Global Distribution and the Representation of Ethnicity," in "Hollywood, Censorship, and American Culture," special issue, *American Quarterly* 44, no. 4 (1992): 617–642.

20. David Kinsley, *Hindu Goddesses: Visions of the Divine Feminine in the Hindu Religious Tradition* (Berkeley and Los Angeles: University of California Press, 1986), 130, 131.

21. Joseph Campbell, *The Hero with a Thousand Faces,* (Princeton, NJ: Princeton University Press, 1968), 91. In Greek mythology Kronos, father of the gods, eats all his children except Zeus, who later forces him to regurgitate them.

22. Sanjukta Gupta, "The Domestication of a Goddess: Carana-Tirtha Kalighat, the Mahapitha of Kali," in *Encountering Kali: In the Margins, at the Center, in the West,* ed. Rachel Fell McDermott and Jeffrey J. Kripal (Berkeley and Los Angeles: University of California Press, 2003), 61.

23. *Indiana Jones and the Temple of Doom,* DVD, directed by Steven Spielberg (1984; Sherman Oaks, CA: Paramount Home Entertainment, 2003).

24. Edward Albee, "Flinn Foundation Centennial Lecture," Tempe, AZ, November 16, 2004.

25. Jean Anouilh, *The Rehearsal,* trans. Pamela Hansford Johnson and Kitty Black (New York: Coward-McCann, 1961), 40.

26. Lisa de Moraes, "PBS's 'Buster' Gets an Education," *Washington Post,* January 27 2005, C01.

27. Patricia White, *UnInvited: Classical Hollywood Cinema and Lesbian Representability* (Bloomington: Indiana University Press, 1999), 1.

28. Stephen T. Russell, "Sexual Minority Youth and Suicide Risk," *American Behavioral Scientist* 46, no. 9 (2003): 1241–1257.

29. Congregation for Catholic Education, "Instruction Concerning the Criteria for the Discernment of Vocations with regard to Persons with Homosexual Tendencies in view of their Admission to the Seminary and to Holy Orders," *Vatican: The Holy See,* November 2005, http://www.Vatican.va/roman_curia/congregations/ccatheduc documents/rc_con_ccatheduc_doc_20051104_istruzione_en.html (accessed April 1 2007).

30. Laurie Goodstein, "Vatican to Check U.S. Seminaries On Gay Presence," *New York Times,* September 15, 2005, A1.

CHAPTER 9

Dead Conversations on Art and Politics

JOSÉ GUADALUPE POSADA INTERVIEWS JOHN JOTA LEAÑOS

John Jota Leaños
(California College of the Arts)

Let the atrocious images haunt us.
SUSAN SONTAG

The conversation from which this article arose takes place between nineteenth-century Mexican artist and illustrator José Guadalupe Posada (1851–1913) and twenty-first-century new media artist John Jota Leaños. The circumstances of this exchange are unusual at best: it occurred somewhere along the road to Mictlan[1] on the southern border of the ancient Mexican indigenous practice of the *Días de los Muertos*, or Days of the Dead. This cross-hemispheric exchange not only focuses on the death of art, politics, and irony in the twenty-first century, it also reflects on the dearth of such exchanges, as well as on the challenges of performing critical art within the borders of empire.

I

JOHN JOTA LEAÑOS: *Bienvenidos, Señor Posada.* It is with much respect, awe, and appreciation that I invite you back to reflect on political art practice in the age of American empire.

JOSÉ GUADALUPE POSADA: *No vengo por consentimiento sino porque me lo consiento vengo* (I return not because you allow me, but I return because I *can*). What's gone on since I've been gone?

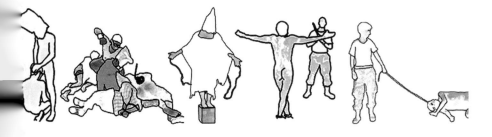

188

JJL: I would like to fill you in on the historic torture scandal that has arisen out of the American occupation of Iraq. Approximately fifty images of American torture, sexual abuse, and humiliation of Iraqi prisoners from the Abu Ghraib prison were released to the public in 2004 and were distributed globally by the media. The images released to the public are only a fraction of the dozens of photographs and hours of video that exist documenting these abuses. The U.S. Senate viewed most of this material behind closed doors, but deemed them "unviewable" and forbade their release to the larger public.[2] There is no telling when and if these images will ever become available, but evidence shows that these "captured" images are only a shadow of the abuses, including rape, murder, torture, and humiliation, that took place at Abu Ghraib

JOHN JOTA
LEAÑOS

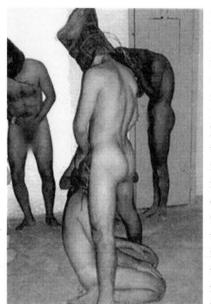

and at other detention centers in Iraq, Afghanistan, Guantanamo, and globally.[3] For the rest of the world, these images of Abu Ghraib abuses have become the face of the U.S. occupation in Iraq. The U.S. corporate media have already forgotten about them, having milked the images for all the hype and sensationalism possible but stopping short of demanding public access to the other images or doing thorough documentation and investigation of the situation and the larger implications they have for U.S. imperialism, the prison-industrial complex, ethics in a democracy, and so on. As these images are placed in the annals of atrocious war photography, they are also inserted into the photo album of the American Empire. American citizens and artists are faced with a deep and complex matrix of meaning that these images bring to the surface.

JGP: Seems pretty serious, *amigo!* (Laughs) What are you doing about it?

JJL: My art practice resides in the struggle of the symbolic arena. I engage in social critique from within the margins of institutional power challenging master narratives, employing traditional and contemporary art tactics to create platforms from which to speak, draw connections, and formulate meaning by "any media necessary."[4] The Abu Ghraib

torture scandal is the most significant U.S. war abuse scandal since My
Lai, Vietnam.

As you can imagine, artists and social critics have generated a large body of work with the release of the torture photographs. Many artists, including myself, have dedicated time to replicating, reproducing, recontextualizing, and aestheticizing these images. I believe that reproducing these images and saturating the popular consciousness with them (in an advertising sense) may help alleviate or at least challenge the widespread amnesia and the endemic optimism of the many Americans who choose not to take responsibility for or confront the horrors of life, war, and death.

Artists working with these images inevitably accept a date with the horrific and shameful. The photographs are a glimpse into the acts of exploitation and dehumanization of war, in general and the "war on terror" in particular, and they reveal a pathological culture of arrogance, ignorance, and abuse that not only saturates the U.S. military and the upper chains of command (that is, the Pentagon and the Bush administration) but points directly to the history of white supremacy, murderous imperialism, sexual domination, and, ultimately, the global exploitation of the rendered "evil," surplus, and exotic other. These acts and photographs perpetuate this truly American legacy. They are not easy images to deal with.

Abu Ghraib—
My Lai I.

JGP: Don't be such a puritanical gringo! This is what you do ¿a poco no? You confront the horrors of life with the laughter of death. (Laughs) But aren't you further exploiting, demeaning, and dehumanizing the individuals victimized in the photographs?

JJL: That's a good question. For artists committed to open democratic discourse, we have to ask ourselves critical ethical questions. The photograph has always been locked in a dangerous dance of representation. When this scandal broke, many people repeated the common mantra "photographs don't lie." Although these photos do give us a profound glimpse into American prison abuse and torture, they aren't exactly telling the truth. Photographs are muffled storytellers—they fail to tell a complete story.

Many times a photograph will reveal more about the person behind the lens—his or her intention, vision, framing, and use of the photograph—than in front of it. These considerations expose the photographer. This is certainly true with the Abu Ghraib photographs. Those who snapped these prison "memories" were trophy hunters documenting their unhappy pleasures and justifying their actions by citing orders to humiliate the hunted game from higher chains of command. The widespread and uniform practice of beatings, hooding, sexual humiliation, murder, and scatological play in Afghanistan, Iraq, and Guantanamo Bay discloses the larger dehumanization campaign within factions of the military that has established a culture of systematic sadism. Psychological detachment or "emotional distance" begins in the message system of language—naming the Iraqis "hajis," "it," and "dogs." Such an orienta-

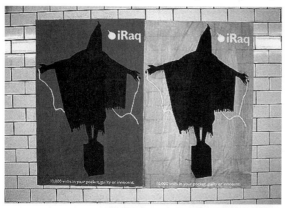

tion has in part laid the groundwork for American soldiers to treat the Iraqis and anyone deemed "enemy" in inhumane ways.

The exploitation and dehumanization that you're talking about happen in the act of torture *and* in the act of photographing. Artists face ethical issues when entering into the battle of meaning.

One of the main ethical and tactical problems in dealing with the Abu Ghraib photographs is in the lack of ability to approach the subjectivity or humanity of these victims. How do we lend them subjectivity? How do we respect their humanity in an image from which their humanity has been completely erased? How do we avoid exploiting their pain and death in order to speak to larger historical and political matters? This, of course, is not an impossible task but a challenging one that is beyond the resources of many artists. Most artists would choose to avoid

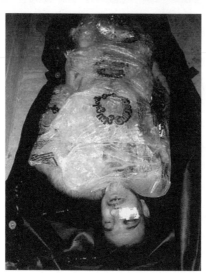

Satirical iRaq advertisement in the subway of New York City.

the maze of subjectivity of the tortured and instead speak to the torture
itself—the practices and ideologies the photographs represent—and then
move to contextualizing the image in historical, cultural, and political contexts. The photographs would then become a part of a critical
struggle of representation against the atrocities of what one might call
the Judeo-Christian-pancapitalist-military-industrial-entertainment-
prison-university complex.

Since most of us accessed these images on the Internet or on television, we were offered no insight into the exploited and tortured subjects.
The mediated message machine (I mean the corporate media) does
not offer access into subjectivity. We don't know the tortured persons'
names, ages, histories, families.
We cannot hear their voices,
their pleas, their defiance. We
only know that these people
are most likely Iraqis and that
they are being exploited and
tortured.

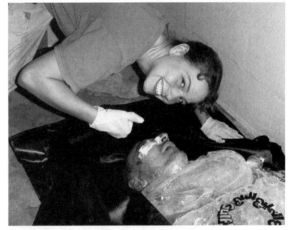

We don't even know if these
people are guilty of any crime.
(Military specialists estimated
that between 70 percent and 90
percent of the prisoners held at
Abu Ghraib were innocent of any
crime and arrested by mistake.
In the weeks following the photo
scandal, the U.S. military released more than 800 prisoners
from Abu Ghraib. International
media—the exception being U.S.
corporate media—have since
extensively interviewed many of
these prisoners.)[5]

JGP: *Pero como artista*, aren't
you torturing the prisoner by
using these images? (Laughs)

JJL: Through my cultural
lenses the artist is not torturing
the prisoner again by re-present-
ing his or her image. The image
of the person is not the person

him- or herself, per se, I believe the image and the person are ontologically separated. However, this does not mean that these images, put into different cultural contexts, cannot be dehumanizing, demeaning, insulting, and shocking. Is there a decency standard for shocking images? The audience is America, for those who don't want to look.

JGP: Excuse me for interrupting, but do you have a cigarette?

JJL: José, you're dead. You can't smoke.

JGP: ¡No importa! Lighten up a bit, will you? Y un tequilita sería perfecto también. Gracias. Anyway, what were you saying?

JJL: I was about to talk about a net.art piece that I'm working on.

JGP: I'm sorry, qué es net.art? Is that some sort of new gringo printing process?

JJL: Well, sort of, José. Net.art is artwork on the Internet that was actually an initiative by the military-academic alliance back in the classical period of twenty-first-century media.

JGP: The Internet?

JJL: . . . ehhhh . . . As I was saying, in a net.art piece that I'm working on, I have tried to demonstrate the lack of representation and subjec-

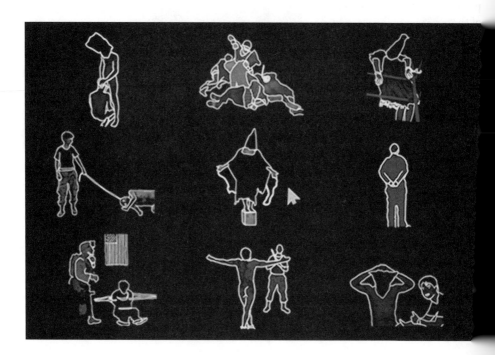

tivity that the images possess by outlining the subjects of torture and making them semitransparent, ghostlike. I ask, how do we understand these acts—the photographs and the torture—as detached voyeurs?

The digital voyeur's vantage point is somewhat determined and definitely limited—the Abu Ghraib photographs are "representations" of the horror of torture and American imperialism. How do we make them real to the passive American? What historical lessons are learned from these photographs? What do they tell us about American culture? About American military culture? About American popular culture? About American media culture?

JGP: ¡Espere! You seem to have more questions than answers, señor. And I thought I was supposed to be asking the questions! My etchings of lynchings, disaster scenes, and death scenes spoke to the brutal reality of life. What do these torture photographs speak to, cabrón?

JJL: The transformative power of these photographs is in their potential to move people, to elicit raw, unexcavated emotions. Institutional powers—the government, corporate media, and their sponsors—fear the transformative capacity of images because such emotion shocks (anger, disgust, outrage, empathy) when connected with rational understanding can potentially result in ideological shifts, political activity, and dissent. This is why the Bush administration forbade video recording or photographs of dead soldiers' coffins returning from Iraq and Afghanistan. In not showing footage of Iraqi and Afghani innocent victims (of which there are plenty), the corporate media follow the unwritten rules of hegemony.

The Face of the Occupation

It is true that the American political right cares deeply about and protects righteously *its own* image of America. This is why the symbolic arena is so sacred in the United States and why the right will fight belligerently to protect its imaginary narrative of America. Protecting a clean image of America is at the forefront of reactionary ideologies in the U.S. Conservative ideologues, led by the Bush administration, as well as the political mainstream continually frame the Abu Ghraib torture as a crime of a few "sick" individuals.

JGP: Bush! *Ese cabrón* is worse than that dictator Porfirio Diaz! Is it true that he stole those elections?

JJL: Well, the presidency was given to him through a failure of democracy and a directionless opposition.

JGP: So, back to torture photographs. Where do you draw the line?

JJL: In a video portraying the naked, hooded prisoners dancing in a Western disco, I've crossed many ethical borders in order to represent that "brutal reality" that you refer to.

JGP: What inspired you to do that?

JJL: Placing the tortured bodies in a disco was "inspired" by the U.S. military practice of blasting loud American music all night long to keep prisoners awake and forcing naked, hooded prisoners to dance. A prison in northern Iraq was nicknamed "The Disco" by American GIs because of this practice. However, this scene is hard to stomach because it seems to perpetuate exploitation and excesses.

Video still from "Disappear"

I still don't know why this is different from putting the images in a Vietnam War scene, a World War II scene, and so on. It is definitely a heavy and perverse scene, but then again, the matter is heavy and perverse.

JGP: I think gringos need to see more of that! Why don't *los gabachos* (Americans) want to see these images? *¿Son demasiado picantes?*

JJL: The Abu Ghraib images are not much worse than images of simulated violence and death seen every day in America on television, at the movies, and on the Internet. The difference between images of war and atrocity and the ever-present fictionalized representation of death, war, and abuse is that war images are for real. The anthropologist Geoffrey Gorer talks about how death in our society is treated as obscene and pornographic. Deep discourse on death is avoided and shunned today, not unlike the way pornography was avoided and shunned in Victorian times. In this case, Gorer's "pornography of death" can be translated to a pornography of torture, a pornography of imperial reality. In spite of the photographic evidence, testimonies, and official reports, most representatives from the U.S. government have declared that "the Unite

States does not use torture." Period. End of discussion. Others have passed it off on a "few bad apples" in the lower echelons of the military. The denial and rationalizations of the U.S. practice of torture and brutal execution legitimizes this practice. To confront these practices, open and active discourse is the first step. It is in the tradition of your printmaking and widely distributed broadsheets, José, that I find inspiration to use new technologies to talk about taboo ideas within the symbolic arena. José? ¿José? Where did you go?

Editor's note: At this point, the copal failed to burn and the conversation ended just in time.

II

Representation of the Dead and the Politics of Truth Telling: The Case of Patrick Tillman

In section II, nineteenth-century Mexican illustrator José Guadalupe Posada (1851–1913) continues his conversation with twenty-first-century Xicano digital artist John Jota Leaños after another round of tequila. Here Leaños discusses a *Días de los Muertos* art controversy and the use of film and animation to insert political content.

JGP: Tell me what about your troubles, *carnal*?

JJL: Trouble is easy to come by these days for those interested in practicing democratic critique of imperial dogma. In 2004, I created a *Días de los Muertos* memorial to Arizona State University graduate, ex-Arizona Cardinal football player, and fallen U.S. Ranger Patrick Tillman. Pat Tillman was a professional football player who gave up an NFL contract worth millions of dollars to enlist in the U.S. Rangers and fight the war on terror. In April 2004, Tillman was killed in Afghanistan. According to military press release, Tillman died while fighting Taliban resistance. Tillman was immediately canonized as a great American war hero and deemed imperial martyr by the government-military-media complex. This was at a time when media discourse about the war dead was, for the most part, absent, silent, and repressed. A few months later, a quiet Pentagon report released news stating the Tillman was "probably killed by friendly fire.'"[6] The Pentagon, it turns out, lied about Tillman's death.
The U.S. military is not known for admitting mistakes in public. The military, however, *is* known for media-managing heroic war narratives to promote its agendas. The Pentagon invented the Jessica Lynch rescue story that was broadcast day and night on all media outlets. After months of being silenced by the military, Jessica Lynch came out

and said, "No, none of that happened. I didn't empty my rifle and kill several Iraqi insurgents. I wasn't slapped and tortured in the hospital bed." This was precisely the type of military propaganda that surrounded the Pat Tillman story. Any criticism of Tillman or of the heroic narrative was met with angry vigilance or suppression. At his funeral, which was broadcast nationally by ESPN, one of Pat Tillman's brothers spoke at the end of the ceremony, telling the audience, "Pat Tillman isn't with God. He's fucking dead. He wasn't religious. So thank you for your thoughts, but he's fucking dead."[7] ESPN quickly edited the speech out of its broadcast.

Tillman's death by friendly fire was confirmed nearly eight months

JOHN JOTA
LEAÑOS

Days of the
Dead Memorial
to Pat Tillman.

after his death in the winter of 2004 by an investigative report from the *Washington Post* stating that Tillman died unnecessarily after "botched communications, mistaken decisions . . . and negligent shooting." The report critiqued the military for purposely distorting accounts of the events to make it appear as if Tillman had died while fighting Afghan forces. One can only speculate why the U.S. military orchestrated this complex cover-up. Tillman's death did occur on the heels of the Abu Ghraib photograph scandal.

JGP: So why did you get involved? Didn't you teach at Arizona State University? What was your commentary on this situation?

JJL: I was teaching at Arizona State at the time and I also work in the tradition of Chicana/o art making, which has a strong history of performing art in the public sphere that is often critical, sometimes controversial, polemical, anti-imperialist . . . and definitely political. Part of my job description as a Xicano artist is to comment on society and culture and to critically engage issues that may be taboo, unpopular, or culturally sensitive, and to do this in a way that raises vital questions and complicates conventional discourse especially in times of war.

Dead Conversations on Art and Politics

The Days of the Dead memorial, in the form of 500 24" × 36" posters, was simply titled, "Friendly Fire." This text is placed over the top of Tillman's Ranger portrait. On the left, there is text that reads, "Remember me?" speaking to the American culture of fifteen-minute replaceable heroes.

The text continues:

I was killed by my own Army
Ranger Platoon in Afghanistan
on April 22, 2004
I am a hero to many of you
My death was tragic
My glory was short-lived
Flawed perceptions
of myself
my country
and
the War on Terror
resulted in the disastrous
end to my life

put these posters up in downtown Phoenix and on the Arizona State University campus on October 1. A week later, local ABC and CBS *Nightly*

News did stories on this. It was then picked up by CNN and broadcast nationally over the weekend that preceded the presidential debate hosted by Arizona. By bringing Tillman back from the dead in *Días de los Muertos* artwork, I was asking the social question: If Pat Tillman's image/spirit came back to Arizona speaking to us about the tragedy of his death and the mistakes and errors of war, what would happen?

JGP: *¿Y qué pasó?*

JJL: After the artwork was aired by the media, Internet bloggers took over sending hundreds of emails to my account, to the president of Arizona State University, and to the Arizona Board of Regents, most demanding that I be fired from my job over the creation of the posters. The State of Arizona launched an investigation into my classroom activities. I received phone calls, hundreds of email messages to date, and was the subject of several right-wing blogs. The messages were filled with repulsive anger, hate, bigotry, racism, homophobia, death threats, and promises of violence. People posted my home address on the Internet and promised to visit.

JOHN JOTA
LEAÑOS

JGP: (Laughing) *¿Ah sí?* Give me some examples of the mail.

JJL: I have about sixty pages of hate mail if you'd like to see it. But, for example, one blogger instructed others in how to perform their democratic duties:

> I have found that a nice email with a little sensitivity works wonders. (Liberal pussies tend to have too many feelings. Kind of like Mr Rodgers . . .) However, if this does not work he should be hunted down (any volunteers?) and some one should KILL THE FUCK out of him. His boss should be ass-raped like he was in a Federal Ass pounding prison. This should help others decide to think before they open their cum dumpster/cock holsters and spew filth.

Others chimed in:

> Big mistake, Puto. Maybe you should get back to mowing my lawn. I mean, that IS what chicano studies teaches, right?

> You are a sick fuck. the only thought that your work provokes in my mind is "why isn't he picking strawberries" i hope you get syphilis.

> I hope you are a Mexican fag with AIDS and die soon.

JGP: (Laughing uncontrollably) Really? . . . That's horrible.

JJL: This was the general tone of the messages. It is horribly laughable, and it's great material for my next project.

JGP: Ooh. Were you surprised by the reaction?

JJL: On the one hand, I am not surprised by the overreaction of the conservative males to this artwork (over 90 percent of the hate mail I received was from men). It is business as usual on the extreme right to launch hate campaigns, ad hominem attacks, character assassinations, and witch-hunts to destroy the professions of those who breach certain ideological *fronteras.* On the other hand, that an artwork that is not slanderous, obscene, pornographic, or racist could incite such vicious reactions is revealing of the times we live in.

JGP: . . . and the times we die in . . . (Laughing) Were you scared?

JJL: Being the father of a three-year-old, I understand that many times the best way to deal with a temper tantrum is to allow it to get out of the child's system. The knee-jerk reaction to the Tillman memorial was essentially a highly orchestrated temper tantrum by conservative men on computers.

JGP: And the Tillman family?

JJL: Approaching the subject of Pat Tillman or murdered soldiers in general is serious business. We should not treat these issues too lightly because we are dealing with a dead son, a dead husband, a dead brother, a dead friend. This is serious business. The Tillman family does not want their son's image to be part of a symbolic war of ideology, but it seems this was out of their hands. After more than a year of not speaking to the media, the parents of Pat Tillman spoke very publicly and critically about the military's lies. They essentially said they cannot trust the military or this administration who, in their eyes, used the son for their pro-war agenda. It was also reveled that Tillman was against the war in Iraq and an avid reader of Noam Chomsky.[8]

JGP: ¿Entonces. . . . What . . . what . . . why were people so upset?

JJL: In dogmatic times, you get dogmatic and authoritarian reactions. Many of the more thoughtful folk were upset because I used first person. *How dare you speak for him?* This is precisely what I was asking: Who is speaking for Tillman? If we look around we'll find two (unauthorized) books have already written about Pat Tillman. A Hollywood screenplay in the works, and coming to a theater near you may be a film in which an actor will be literally speaking for Tillman. There is merchandizing galore—hats, jerseys, helmets, pins, photographs. There was constant nationalistic memorializing juxtaposing his heroic football images with his military portrait and a waving American flag. There was outright profiteering going down. The Arizona Cardinals sold tickets on his name, offering free rubber bracelets with Tillman's name and number on them for the first 10,000 fans to the stadium last season (those same bracelets were being sold for up to $70 apiece on eBay soon after).

My posters were free! But all of the branding, profiting, and pro-war usage of Tillman's image and name are OK as long as they fit into a certain ideological framework that portrays Pat Tillman as a perfect, fixed, and untouchable hero. But as soon as someone comes out and says, "Wait a second. He was killed by friendly fire. His death is tragic and revealing of a misguided war on terror." If this happens, then all hell breaks out.

JOHN JOTA
LEAÑOS

JGP: *¡Alli está el detalle!* The *pinche* hypocrisy and self-righteousness of the dictatorship!

JJL: Well, José, this is not exactly a dictatorship, but artists from Critical Art Ensemble, who are being tried as we speak by the federal government for doing artwork under the Patriot Act, think (*y con razón*) that this government is in a proto-fascist state.[9] This is supposedly a democracy, so it's vital that we put democratic precepts into practice. We must test the limits of free speech. We must encourage dissent and active participation of artists and citizens.

JGP: *Sí, sí.* But why do you think men in particular were so angry at this artwork?

JJL: The questions of gender, specifically expressions of American masculinity, are fascinating. There are the obvious connections between expressions of masculinity, the military, and football. But given the types of responses that I received—with the homophobic/gynephobic responses—the "pansy" and "fag" name calling—coupled with the racis overtones, I believe that this poster—and it *is* just another poster— disrupts white masculinity as it relates to American imperial identity. Tillman, or rather the *image* of Tillman, may be an expression of imperial white masculinity. I'm not saying that Pat Tillman, the man, was a white supremacist or that he embodied these ideals, but that his image has been ideologically constructed in this lineage. There is a strong white male war hero lineage in the American imaginary streaming fror Gary Cooper, John Wayne, and Sylvester Stallone to Ronald Reagan and Arnold Schwarzenegger (we see the line begins to blur between Hol-

lywood images and American politics). I'm sure George W. Bush would
like to write his name into this lineage as well.

The Tillman memorial could be seen as a *tactical disruption*—
disrupting fixed imperial discourse with well-placed messaging and
inciting, for better or for worse, open democratic discourse. It might
also be seen as a *tactical revealing*—revealing the underbelly of power
structures.

JGP: (Laughing) Are you serious?

JJL: No, not really. I realize, though, that this type of critique is not
tolerated in mainstream America today, as is evident in widespread attempts to police dissent.

JGP: Police? You didn't mention anything about police. . . .

JJL: José, this country has a long history of policing and silencing
dissent during times of war. From the Sedition Act of 1798, Lincoln's
suspending of habeas corpus, to the internment of the Japanese and the
McCarthyism of the cold war, from the active political harassment and
disruptions of the CointelPro Operations to the present concentration
camps of Guantanamo Bay, and everything that fell in between. The
recent Patriot Act seems to be a regressive upgrade of surveillance and
oppressive operations that is technologically driven and firmly in the
lineage of this rich, rich American history of suspending free speech
during times of war.

JGP: So the "Man" is watching over you? (Giggles)

JJL: We find ourselves in a deeply woven surveillance society that is
embedded in the cultural mythology of the West. We have the omniscient, ever-present eye of God spying on us. The eyes of mommy and
daddy watch over us. There is the myth of Big Brother. Even Santa Claus
knows when we're sleeping, he knows when we're awake, he knows if
we've been bad or good, so be good for goodness' sake!

JGP: Don't tell me you believe in that Papa Noel *mierda* (Santa Claus
bullshit)?

JJL: No, my point is that in this society we're either being watched,
we think we're being watched and thus watching ourselves (the pathos
of self-surveillance), or we're doing the watching (straddling the thin line
between voyeurism and surveillance).

There is extensive government-corporate surveillance and a strong
mythology that accompanies it. But what I'm talking about in this case is

ideological surveillance by the citizens. I'm talking about this regressi
political correctness that has emerged since 9/11/01 and the neo-
McCarthyism facilitated and fueled by digital culture that advances
extreme opinions. I'm talking about the power of bloggers and extrem
ists in digital culture, about the disembodied, detached blogger mania
blogger ire spurred by right-wing reaction to unflattering facts about t
military or the idea of their nation.

JGP: You got another cigarette? Thanks. Perhaps an uninviting offer
was made to the dead in this work. . . .

JJL: You think?

JOHN JOTA
LEAÑOS

JGP: Just joking, *jefe! ¡Dios mio!* Where's your sense of satire?

JJL: You may be right, José. However, in the context of a divided
country in the midst of two disastrous wars and in a highly contested
presidential election, I thought that serenity, confession, honesty, and
regret were appropriate tactics.

It's been said that in a time of "infinite war," irony and satire are de
The logic is this: at a time when warfields are expanding and empire i
being assaulted (in the case of 9/11), we can no longer afford the luxur
of ironically commenting on the situation from a distance. Although I
identify with the spirit of this theory, I don't agree with its conclusion.
These are severe political times, but are they more pressing than othe
moments or places in history? If we turn away from satire, humor, and
irony, we lose our perspective on our larger responsibility to humanity
and culture, *digo yo,* and we risk becoming dogmatic revolutionaries th
lead to book burnings.

JGP: Book burnings? Is that what you're talking about?

JJL: No! You're so distracted, José. Do you need another drink?

JGP: OK, OK, OK. . . . Much of your work deals with dead people. Ar
you into necrophilia? Do you see dead people?

JJL: Not precisely. I work to carry on your practice of a Day of the
Dead tradition that reimagines the dead, that is, our ancestors, as activ
participants in our everyday decisions, political realities, and social
constructions. I have turned to animation and filmmaking to speak to
larger audience around these issues.

JGP: Ay, moving pictures! I love that stuff!

JJL: Yes, many people love to look at cartoons to suspend their sens
of reality. However, I am practicing documentary animation, which

literally draws from reality within a fictitious time and space. I find this rupture quite effective. My first animation, *Los ABCs ¡Qué Vivan los Muertos!,* is a cartoon about those dead of war who have been forgotten, neglected, or, literally, left hanging. It is drawn from historical and real-life situations, such as the Women of Juarez, or the lynching of blacks, Indians, Mexicans, and Chinese in America. The ABC song is sung by dead mariachis and draws the viewer into comfortable mindsets of laughter and song while shockingly reminding them about the murderous and white supremacist foundation and maintenance of America, its doctrines, its master narrative, its ideals. It's a work about remembering your ABCs of empire, a sort of primer for understanding the other side of American history in the age of ADD, fast cuts, and historical amnesia.

I have also completed an animation called *DNN: Dead News Network,* which takes the expression "Don't fear the media, become the media!" quite literally by creating an animated dead news series that not only highlights stories that are ignored and forgotten by the corporate news networks but also offers satirical solutions to endless problems such as global warming and the U.S.-Mexico border as well as giving political projections for the upcoming (s)election.

We are at a historical moment in which alternative, do-it-yourself media, video, and filmmaking is at its height and whose conscious practice builds independent, self-reliant citizens who can begin to decolonize their learning and knowledge, thus opening a plethora of possibilities, platforms, and ways of living.

This animation cell from Los ABCs was drawn from the "trophy photo" on the night of the lynching of Rubin Stacy in Fort Lauderdale, Florida, in 1935.

JGP: *Ay,* those are good skills to exercise. But why bring up the past, *hombre?* Why not let sleeping dogs die, let *diegones* be *diegones.*

JJL: Because we still live in a democracy, José. A widely accepted strategy of controlling discourse is in silencing voices of dissent that don't take on the mainstream, militarist, imperial points of view and being silent during times of war, including the American cultural custom of being silent in the face of death (I mean real death, not simulated Hollywood video-game death). There is a silence and absence of images and discourse of the war dead, no images of coffins returning from Iraq, no coverage of the thousands of innocent Iraqis slaughtered by American forces.

Silence *es igual a la muerte*. *Silencio* equals death. The AIDS activists of the 1980s warned us of the dangers of being silent during crisis. Silence is also a space from which oppressed voices speak and are heard. We

JOHN JOTA LEAÑOS

should return to this question of silence, of imperial silence, that deafening and deadly silence that helps America pretend that it is the beacon of freedom and democracy.

So, if the solution to this imperial silence is to embrace it, to demonstrate the absence, talk about the unpopular, to articulate that which is not said, then we will not be surprised and hopefully will be prepared for the ad hominem attacks, character assassinations, threats to our lives and well-being, and witch-hunts to destroy us professionally. These are tactics of the intolerant and boisterous right, and these are the challenges of performing critical art in a time of declared infinite war. *¡Seguimos adelante!*

JGP: Let the Dead of War speak! *¡Qué vivan los muertos!*

Notes

1. Mictlan is the lowest level of the underworld where the dead reside in Aztec mythology. The dead travel far north to Mictlan guided by a psychopomp. During the Days of the Dead celebration, the dead often return to the living, finding their way with the smell of *zempazuchil* (marigolds) and by the light of the *vela* (candle).

2. As this conversation takes place, a U.S. district federal judge has ordered the U.S. government to release seventy-four photographs and three videotapes from Abu Ghraib prison to the public. See "Judge Orders Release of More Abu Ghraib Photos," www.cnn.com, September 29, 2005.

3. For the globalized practice of torture in the form of "extraordinary rendition" practices by the U.S. and other governments, see Jane Meyer, "Outsourcing Torture: The Secret History of America's 'Extraordinary Rendition' Program," *The New Yorker*, February 14, 2005.

4. To borrow from the Critical Art Ensemble's flip of Malcom X's "By any means necessary."

5. For translations and transcripts of some of these interviews with prisoners to

tured at Abu Ghraib, see Mark Danner, *Torture and Truth: America, Abu Ghraib, and the* *War on Terror* (New York: New York Review Books, 2004).

6. For a report, see "Army Finds Tillman Probably Killed by Friendly Fire: Former Pro Football Player Killed in Afghanistan," www.cnn.com, May 31, 2004.

7. See Gwen Knapp, "True Hero Athlete," *San Francisco Chronicle*, May 4, 2004.

8. See Robert Collier, "Family Demands the Truth: New Inquiry May Expose Events That Led to Pat Tillman's Death," *San Francisco Chronicle*, September 25, 2005. Also see Dave Zirin, "Pat Tillman, Our Hero," *The Nation*, October 6, 2005.

9. For information on the FBI investigation and suit against the Critical Art Ensemble, see http://www.caedefensefund.org/.

Dead Conversations on Art and Politics

PART 4   INDEPENDENT
AMBITIONS

CHAPTER 10

Neither Color Blind, Nor Near-Sighted

REPRESENTATION, RACE, AND THE
ROLE OF THE ACADEMIC FILMMAKER

Aaron Greer
(Loyola University, Chicago)

"What kind of filmmaker does not want his film viewed by a potential distributor or representative?" asked a producer's representative in Los Angeles when I expressed some reticence about sending my film to her company for consideration. "Did you make the film with the intention that it would be distributed, or not?"

The company in question represents a slate of "urban" films, the current euphemism for films featuring black and Latino characters, "urban" meaning inner city, inner city meaning ghetto, ghetto meaning black. Because I had just completed *Gettin' Grown*,[1] a film set in inner-city Milwaukee with a predominantly black cast, she concluded, sight unseen, that my film would probably be right up their alley. Theirs, however, was precisely the alley I didn't want to go down.

I had created *Gettin' Grown* partly in response to the extremely limited and limiting representations of blackness available on American screens. In fact, my film expressly critiques all the other films in her company's catalog.

Gettin' Grown features no sex, nudity, on-screen violence, drugs, or gangs. It does not star rappers, basketball players, or, indeed, "name" talent of any kind. It is a fairly unglamorous, realistic portrayal of a black child's life in a Midwestern city. By design, it has little in common with any other films in the urban film and video market,[2] making it a tough sell to distributors and by extension to film audiences. In other words, it is the type of film I became an academic to make.

At its core, the producer's question had merit. After all, film is a medium intended for mass consumption. *Gettin' Grown* could not be posed as a critique of the films currently playing on American screens if it did not find its way to some of those same viewers. And I very much wanted my film to enter the "marketplace of ideas," I just didn't want it be governed or compromised by the marketplace of dollars.

My position as an academic filmmaker allows me the freedom to straddle that particular fence. Academics have the unique ability—even responsibility—to critique, question, and create work regardless of its commercial viability, work that is truly independent of market forces. It is a luxury that allows us to challenge not just the dominant paradigms of Hollywood but also the viewers themselves on such thorny issues as class, sexuality, gender, race, and identity.

It was my interest in exploring issues of racial identity in particular that led me to filmmaking and then to the academy. Although I have been pleased to witness an increasing diversity of characters and stories in film and television, I believe that audiences in the United States continue to accept only a limited spectrum of otherness and are infrequently asked to question their own assumptions about race and identity. All too often gay men are still portrayed as fashionably dressed queens, African Americans as criminals, athletes, or entertainers, and Asians as asexual scientists or martial arts masters, because these are the archetypes with which we are most comfortable and familiar.[3] Being presented with alternative images or challenging those stereotypes directly is often disquieting for audiences and consequently unprofitable for makers, leading to a vicious cycle of rehashed storylines and stereotypical characters.

Director Aaron Greer working with actor Isaiah Matthew on the set of *Gettin' Grown.*

The raw economics of the equation cannot be discounted, since film production and distribution still demand considerable human and material resources. Although the advent of digital technologies has turned the tools of production into consumer items, this equipment, such as video cameras and desktop computer editing systems certainly remains a luxury consumer item. For the price of a broadcast quality camera and computer editing system, one can purchase used car, tuition at a state college or university, or a year of child care for example. Consequently, access to these kinds of resources—not mention intangibles such as time, creative and critical support, and stable income—contributes to the freedom academics enjoy in form style, and content, including the ability to challenge the viewers rectly about race.

In 2002, I created a short film that attempted to do just that. T inciting incident for the film was a trip I made to the Alabama Department of Motor Vehicles soon after moving to the state. As part of processing my application for an Alabama license, I was asked to declare my race and given the choice of black, white, or Hispanic. My shock at the limited options and frustration with the entire process inspired me to make the film *Not Color Blind, Just Near-Sighted*.[4]

As I began writing the film, I realized that a straight documentary or narrative account of the event would inevitably focus the critique on Alabama, specifically on the state bureaucracy and officials. As a biracial filmmaker, I was interested in making a larger statement about racial identity and the perception of race, one that would include the viewer in the critique and work to challenge viewers' perceptions. The experimental short that resulted was constructed with this in mind.

Not Color Blind is organized around a retelling of the event I described above; however, the images of me reenacting the event are distorted and animated, with shifting colors and stylized video, purposely confounding the viewer's attempts at instantly assuming a racial identity. The direct address of the voiceover is augmented by my direct look into the camera, positioning the audience in the point of view of the DMV clerk and inviting them to make the same assumptions about my identity as she did, while simultaneously pointing out the capriciousness of those assumptions through the device of the shifting colors. We hear the clerk's voice and the ambient sounds of the DMV, but my image set in an empty black space is the only plastic element of the mise-en-scène. The fact that the visual perspective of the film emanates from, but is not focused on, the clerk and the visual trappings of the state emphasizes that this is a critique of the system as opposed to the individuals or institutions.

The punch line of the narrative is that when finally forced to choose between the racial categories of W, B, and H, I choose H . . . "Honeydew."

I feel that *Not Color Blind* succinctly and effectively expresses the pitfalls of both assigning and representing race. Unfortunately, its short and experimental form means that *Not Color Blind* is unlikely to have a life outside of film festivals and classrooms (though I have been fortunate to have screenings in both venues). Furthermore, though it may successfully challenge viewers' perceptions of race, it does not directly interrogate the way race and identity are typically presented in popular media. To accomplish that, as well as to reach a greater quantity and diversity of viewers, I would need to engage the issues through one of the more popular forms of the medium, such as documentaries, music videos, or narrative films.

Representation, Race, and the Academic Filmmaker

Much of the power of narrative cinema lies in its ability to encourage us to identify with characters on the screen, often going so far as to place us in their visual perspective. In fact, we watch television and film largely to see projections of ourselves, or at least our idealized selves, engaging life in small, concentrated, typically exciting bits.[5] Consequently, our resistance—as demonstrated commercially—to seeing images of black people who are *not* engaged in glamorized sex or violence is both damning and damaging. Consider, for example, how rarely dramas or romances with black casts reach blockbuster status and what that means about filmmakers and film audiences. Films like *Antwone Fisher, Eve's Bayou,* and *Brother to Brother* have all received critical acclaim without capturing the public's imagination or

AARON

GREER

entertainment dollars.[6]

Both filmmakers and film distributors are aware of this resistance and respond accordingly, further compounding the problem and ultimately codifying an extremely narrow representation of blackness on American screens. I too was aware of this when I started writing *Gettin' Grown,* the story of a twelve-year-old African American boy in a working class Milwaukee neighborhood whose errand for his family becomes a formative rite of passage. I understood from the beginning that my decision to create a neorealist story about

Isaiah
Matthew as
Eric in *Gettin'
Grown.*

and from the perspective of a twelve-year-old child of color would severely restrict the marketability of the film.[7]

There is no one less likely to be the subject of cinematic fantasies than a working-class black child, especially one not blessed with super powers, prodigious athletic abilities, or a mission to save the world—even twelve-year-old black boys don't want to be twelve-year-old black boys.[8] Indeed, once the film was complete, I was told by several distributors, even those who professed to love it, that it would be difficult to "position the film in the current marketplace."

I thought it was important to make the film for those very reasons. I wanted to create and challenge audiences to accept images of black ness that were more nuanced and complex: images of urban life that were realistic about its challenges and dangers, without reveling in them; images of a black family that was intact and functional but faced with the same cracks and fissures as other families; and images of a child's life and concerns without invented, fantastical drama.

I began by cataloging what I considered to be the most obvious and deleterious codes and assumptions about race found in urban films, figuring I needed to identify those trends if I were to effectively subvert them. I attempted to construct the plot and characters in ways that would both utilize and undermine the audience's expectations of a black film. As I mentioned above, the story revolves around a day in the life of a twelve-year-old boy. On the day in question, the protagonist, Eric, is sent by his mother and grandmother to the pharmacy to fill a prescription. The drama in the film derives from Eric's attempt to complete the mission before dark, eluding the obstacles and temptations that beset his journey along the route. As he struggles to meet his obligations to himself and to his family, he is faced with negotiating the perilous world of adults.

My first concern related to how I would create these tensions without relying on the tired premise of drugs, gangs, and violence. It is no secret that the prevalence of crime and criminality in black films, particularly films set in urban centers, has warped our sense of what it means to be black, especially black and working class. I certainly did not want to contribute to the racialization and glorification of crime.

On the other hand, crime or the threat of crime is a fact of life in urban areas, prevalent in the depictions of other ethnic groups as well, such as Asian Americans, Italian Americans, and Latinos, among others. In making a neorealist film set in the inner city, I thought it was important to acknowledge its existence in a peripheral way without overstating its importance or glamorizing its presence. I had no intention of effecting blindness in order to create a utopian picture of urban life—this was not to be an after-school special. I also felt that I could utilize viewers' expectations themselves as an effective device for creating tension: if the viewer thinks someone is going to get shot (because someone always gets shot in these films), then I could both draw on and subvert viewers' expectations by suggesting that it could happen without actually allowing it to.

In a practical sense, my decision played out in a couple of ways. First, not one character in the film is a criminal, a drug dealer, or a gang-banger. There are no black victims or violent black victimizers. Second, there is no on-screen violence or illegal activity, except for the suggestion of two minor characters drinking and driving. Finally, and

Representation,
Race, and
the Academic
Filmmaker

perhaps most significantly, the plot does not revolve around the character committing a crime, running from crime or gangs, or otherwise focused on the crime that may (or may not) be part of the fabric of life in his neighborhood.

That said, the threat of crime and violence is part of the subtext of the film and is integrated into the narrative. In fact, the first real moment of drama involves the mother's decision to send Eric to the pharmacy by himself as nightfall approaches, a loaded decision for the mother of a black child in inner-city Milwaukee. Once she does decide to send him, we see Eric's mother warn him about walking down an "unsafe block," a route he is, of course, forced to take in the end. Later we see her worry as the clock approaches 8:00 p.m. and Eric has yet to return.

AARON
GREER

His mother's warning turns out to be prescient, as Eric does encounter danger and the threat of physical violence when he travels down the forbidden street. While pausing to talk with an uncle, who is a ne'er-do-well but otherwise harmless, Eric is suddenly threatened with handguns, introduced in a dramatic close-up. These turn out to be painted water guns with which two of Eric's friends, Will and Rashid, pretend to stick up Eric and Uncle June. The audience's expectation, drawn from the codes of urban films as well as the suggestion planted by the mother, imbues the initial close-up with tension and violence, when in fact no violence occurs. As it turns out, there was not even the possibility of violence.

This moment is intended to both manipulate and critique viewer expectations. It is also meant to serve as a statement about guns and the danger of playing with or glamorizing guns (even fake guns). This critique is taken further during a moment later in that sequence, also precipitated by the play with toy guns, when the boys react to an off screen gunshot. Again, I felt that it was important that we not see black person (or any person, for that matter) shooting the gun or being shot by the gun. The moment is certainly constructed to be tense an violent, underlined by the fast pace of the editing, the jump cuts, swis pans, and up-tempo score; however, it is meant to both acknowledge and criticize the violence that sometimes takes place without associat ing that violence directly with blackness.

The violence in the film is peripheral to the main narrative but it not the focus of the story. "Typical" narratives of crime and violen intersect the film's story only tangentially, just long enough to rec viewers' expectations of the urban crime drama and to critique ther These moments of intersection explicitly reference other black and L tino films, such as *Menace to Society* or even *Boyz N the Hood*, wh rendering those narrative models conspicuous by their near absence. Simply avoiding all reference to violence would place *Gettin' Grown* into some other, more antiseptic genre and fail to elicit the comparisons that I hope the audience will draw between my film and most black urban dramas. The limited screen and story time devoted to crime and violence and the subjugation of these images in the plot and structure of *Gettin' Grown* are explicitly meant to provide a stark contrast to the viewer's expectations.

Another set of codes I attempt to usurp with *Gettin' Grown* is the depiction of family dynamics and dysfunction in black films. Thanks to the Cosbys, the Parkers, the Jeffersons, and a few other sitcom families, we have been exposed to a variety of intergenerational, intact, and functioning black families on television (functional, that is, within the limits of the sitcom format; see George Jefferson). Unfortunately, the same is not true in a disturbingly large percentage of black films. Frequently these films feature families with an absentee parent, generally the father, and little meaningful cross-generational interaction.

Representation, Race, and the Academic Filmmaker

Employing a plot technique similar to my use of the threatened gun violence, I decided that the family in my film would contain a father, a mother, and a grandparent, but I withheld revealing the father until the last third of the film. For the first two acts of the film, Eric's family appears to consist only of his mother, his grandmother, and a fast-talking uncle. We do not see him interact with an adult male in any significantly positive way, nor do we expect to. Even though the father character, Darryl, is referred to in the first few minutes of the film, audiences generally seem surprised when he does enter the narrative and are moved by the degree of interaction and intimacy between him and Eric. The character of Darryl is often assigned more significance by viewers than his screen time or effect on the plot should warrant, because his very presence is so unexpected and out of sync with the codes of films about black folks.

In addition to constructing the plot with an eye toward transforming the images of blackness on screen, I made a number of other formal decisions, particularly with regard to casting, to oppose stereotypical representations of blackness.

Like most Hollywood films, urban films tend to feature actors who are fashion magazine attractive, thin and, particularly in the case of black women, light-skinned—one of the reasons that Halle Berry has been the "it" black actress of the last few years. The notable exception to that rule is the "Big Mama" character, who is generally neither skinny, attractive, nor light-skinned.[9] This archetypal character, who generally an overweight, wisecracking, tough as nails, older black woman, seems to be the current incarnation of the mammy characters so prevalent in films during the first half of the twentieth century.[10] One of my biggest concerns in writing the film was not to turn the grandmother character in *Gettin' Grown* into a Big Mama caricature.

I felt that casting the right actress would be key to this effort, and indeed, this turned out to be one of the most difficult casting decisions of the film, one that forced me to balance theoretical needs with the practical requirements of the plot and production (namely, acting). After auditioning a dozen actresses, we settled on two finalists. The first actress was vibrant, trim, and almost majestic, unlike any Big Mama character on film. She also performed the character of Clara, the grandmother in *Gettin' Grown*, in a way that was warm and firm,

without being foolish or overly sentimental. The problem was that she was *too* healthy and vibrant to convincingly play a sick grandmother, which is integral to the plot. The second actress was heavier and looked older (although she was in reality younger than the first), but was naturally more gregarious and wisecracking, closer in both looks and personality to the caricature I was trying to avoid.

With the support of my co-producers, I ended up casting the second actress as Clara and the first actress in another role originally conceived for a man because we were so impressed with her. We then worked with "Clara" to make her performance more complex and nuanced than the caricature typically allows. First, we decided

Original poster for the feature film *Gettin' Grown.*

that the actress would wear her hair down and uncovered in the film. One thing we really liked about the actress's look is that she wore her hair in locks, which is typically construed as a cultural signifier spirituality, earthiness, and black consciousness. By presenting the Clara character as an elderly black woman with locks, we gambled that

we could confound or diffuse one cultural stereotype by utilizing another, more positive one.

I discussed my concerns openly with the actress. I encouraged her to go forward with her interpretation of Clara, including ad-libbing one-liners—which provide some of the only comic relief in the film—but asked her to vary and modulate her performance of Clara from scene to scene. Her Clara is alternately funny, sweet, obstinate, selfish, loving, and real, thereby rendering her character more three-dimensional, nuanced, and individual than archetypical.

The structure and running time of a feature-length film allow the maker to develop characters beyond simplistic renderings. Nevertheless, narrative expedience and coherence often demand that the audience make assumptions about the characters, including cultural or racial assumptions. In fact, narrative filmmakers invite and encourage audiences to do so, as I did with my decision to have Clara wear her hair in locks. The challenge of balancing narrative efficiency with theoretical concerns becomes trickier with shorter formats such as music videos.

I recently faced this particular set of challenges in conceiving and casting a hip-hop music video. The video in question features a new artist from Alabama and a song called "Wurldwide."[11] The treatment that I pitched to the record label included images of people around the world reacting to the compelling rhythms and driving beat of the song. When the label selected my treatment, the producers returned to me for the specifics: shot lists, locations, wardrobe descriptions, and so forth. I found two of their questions to be especially loaded: *where in the world do these four scenes take place*, and *what do these people look like?* The producers thought they were simply asking for basic information to give to the designers and casting agents; from their perspective, this should not have been a particularly taxing request. I realized, however, that I had thirty seconds of screen time to present and represent foreign cultures to an audience of pop music and television consumers. How could I do that without indulging in the same sort of filmmaking practice that has led to such narrow and objectionable images of blackness? The budget didn't allow for filming on location. These "foreign spaces" would have to be created simply and cheaply in Birmingham, Alabama, without the use of green screen or computer imaging.

One of the foreign places we agreed on for a "scene from around the world" was South Asia. Without actually showing India, for example, how could I communicate to the audience in a five-second scene that someone there was responding to the music? I would have to rely to some extent on Americans' assumptions and expectations—including my own—of what India and Indians look like. I would have to represent "Indianness" not as it exists in real life but as American viewers understand it. What did that mean? Did it mean people with dark skin, hair, and eyes, wearing saris or Sikh turbans, possibly with bindi dots on their foreheads, either decked out in jewelry and wedding attire or marked by extreme poverty and malnutrition?

Intellectually I knew that those images were very simplistic and narrow representations of India. I also knew that combining any of those images would immediately and effectively signify India to the video's consumers. I decided to use a tactic similar to my hair and wardrobe choice for Clara in *Gettin' Grown,* a device that would, I hoped, both play to viewers' expectations and complicate or broaden their notion of foreignness. For this scene, I indicated to the producers that I wanted to cast a dark-haired, brown-skinned man or woman who would be wearing a sari or turban, but I wanted the scene to be set in an office or science lab, representing the reality and diversity of modern India. Furthermore, the actor should be seen reading the business pages of a Hindi or English-language newspaper, such as *The Times of India.*

The design was just as complicated with the one scene set in "Anytown U.S.A." The scene was to portray a "sophisticated" couple playing a game of Scrabble in their den. Admittedly, I initially assumed certain characteristics for this couple based on their sophistication and even on the fact that they were playing a complex word game. My first thought was that this should be an older, white, heterosexual couple. I imagined those characters to be middle class, middle-aged, and well educated, associating leisure, wealth, and literacy with suburban whiteness. On further contemplation, I realized that casting the scene that way would only perpetuate the links between class, education, and race as they are usually portrayed on American screens—a stereotype that had clearly infected my own consciousness. Instead I instructed the producers to find two black, Latino, or Asian actors for the role (in any combination of gender and race), figuring that I could kill two birds with one casting: employing more actors of color and breaking the visual link between class and race.

My position as an academic provides me with the theoretical and material support to make these kinds of choices. I believe that it is my responsibility to use that position to challenge stereotypical representations of race and identity, even when working in more popular or commercial forms. This requires recognizing not just the popular trends and portrayals of otherness but also my own inevitable assumptions and prejudices. I believe that I can meet this responsibility without creating images that are bland or bereft of cultural significance.

signifiers but instead illustrate the simplistic and problematic nature of those images. In other words, I am neither advocating nor practicing color-blind filmmaking. Instead I seek to advance the kind of image-making that acknowledges our power as filmmakers to develop audiences' understanding of the complexities of race and identity.

This requires a level of vigilance in my own work that goes beyond considerations of race. With *Color Blind, Gettin' Grown,* and the treatment for "Wurldwide," I focused most intently on complicating race and ethnic identity for the viewer, but I recognize the need to address other identity markers as well, such as gender, sexuality, class, and age. I am confronted every day with identity formations much more complex than what Hollywood typically presents on-screen. It is important that I consider these just as I consider race in creating characters and images for my films. In fact, race, gender, sexuality, class, and so forth are often so intimately linked and overlapping as identity markers that addressing one typically involves acknowledging the others.

Gender, sexuality, age, and class certainly came up in the creation of *Gettin' Grown* and "Wurldwide." Ignoring the power of those identity markers would undermine my critique of the way in which race is typically represented on-screen. Consequently, I strive to consider the totality of the character I am presenting and the person I am representing in my work. For example, *Gettin' Grown* features a scene with a group of young adults playing pickup basketball. Several young women asked to audition for one of the roles. I decided that including a woman among the basketball players would be a subtly effective means of diffusing another popular stereotype, that of the black male basketball player, and represent the growth of women's participation in pickup sports. However, I was insistent that the actress I cast be an able basketball player, capable of holding her own among the other players, so that within the scene her presence is real and effective. There is no formal acknowledgment within the scene that one of the players is a woman, no lingering close-ups or references to the fact in dialogue. Furthermore, when she makes a jump shot, she is really making the shot in one, unedited take. This is designed to communicate to the audience that this character is a real athlete and force viewers to accept a broader, less gendered image of urban basketball.

I was happy to be able to inject this statement about gender roles within the film, and felt chagrined that I did not think of it before being asked by actresses to audition for the part. As a result, and guided by my early concern with the representation of race in films, I have formulated a series of questions that I ask myself when creating any image or character:

1. What identity traits or characteristics am I assuming or assigning based on the character's role in the narrative? For example, if the character needs to be sexy or sexual in a scene, does that automatically mean a thin woman with longish hair? If the person needs to be athletic and virile, does that mean young and male?

2. Where did I get the initial idea for this image or character? Was it borrowed from other texts or inspired by an individual from my world? We often ignore complex personal experiences of the world and instead perpetuate stereotypes as a sort of cinematic or production shorthand.

3. If the character does resemble images in other texts, how much does that redundancy serve my purposes? Is it required for narrative expedience?

4. Finally, if narrative expedience does dictate that I utilize popular assumptions, archetypes, or stereotypes in creating a character, how can I complicate or undermine that stereotype by pairing it with traits or markers not normally associated with that image?

These are the tests I apply to my own films. I am certainly cognizant that this is not the approach producers, writers, or directors generally take in creating work. Most makers have to consider questions of commerce over questions of identity and theory, but my academic position affords me greater latitude when it comes to the presentation and representation of identities. I recognize the economic and practical demands of filmmaking, including the influence those demands sometimes assert on my own films, but I have the luxury of focusing more intently on the impact my work has on the world without worrying whether that focus will impact my ability to pay my mortgage. Working with students has only increased my appreciation of the power of this medium. I preach to them constantly about making careful and considered choices and encourage them to be thinking artists. I can not in good conscience demand less of myself, nor should I demand less of other makers. As academics we are both able and obligated to apply a corrective lens to our work, and we should strive to produce films that are neither color-blind nor near-sighted.

Notes

1. *Gettin' Grown* is distributed by Film Life, Inc., in partnership with Warner Bros. Home Video. For more information about the film, please visit the Web site www.gettingrown.com.

2. For a representative sampling of urban films, I urge the reader to look at

catalog of films distributed by Maverick Entertainment Group, one of the largest distributors of black and Latino films for the video market.

3. A quick survey of the films nominated for best picture awards by the Academy of Motion Picture Arts & Sciences (the Oscars) since 1994 bears out my assertion. Of the sixty-five films nominated, thirteen included stories with significant black characters. Although certainly not an indictment of these individual films (many of which I admire), the majority of those films feature black characters in the stereotypical roles of athletes, criminals, or entertainers: *Pulp Fiction* (1994), *The Shawshank Redemption* (1994), *The Green Mile* (1999), and *Chicago* (2002) all feature a black character who is a criminal; *Jerry Maguire* (1996) and *Million Dollar Baby* (2004) feature black characters as athletes; and *Ray* (2004) is about the celebrated black entertainer Ray Charles. The exceptions to this rule are the ensemble film *Crash* (2004), *Forrest Gump* (1994), and *As Good as It Gets* (1997), the latter two of which include minor but significant black characters; *The Cider House Rules* (1999), featuring a black family that works in the orchard; and the British film *Secrets & Lies* (1996).

4. To see a sample scene from *Not Color Blind*, visit my portfolio on SouthernArtistry.org or visit Big Film Shorts's catalog to purchase a copy of the film.

5. I am referencing here Laura Mulvey's seminal work, "Visual Pleasure and Narrative Cinema" (*Screen* 16, no. 3, 1975), in which she discusses the voyeuristic and scopophilic pleasure of watching our "ego ideals" on the big screen.

6. I recognize that this formula does not apply to black comedies. In fact, comedies featuring black actors are generally more palatable to consumers. Consider, for example, two black films released in 2002, *Barbershop* and *Antwone Fisher*. Both PG-13 films were produced for a little over $12 million, according to the data reported on the Internet Movie Database; however, the comedy *Barbershop* grossed more than $75 million domestically, while the award-winning drama *Antwone Fisher* made only a tad over $21 million.

7. In form and style, *Gettin' Grown* borrows from the Italian neorealist tradition, and to a lesser extent from the more recent Dogma '95 films, with an emphasis on slice-of-life stories, location filming, a mix of professional and nonprofessional actors, hand-held camera work, and a raw, documentary-like immediacy.

8. The dominant trend in live action films for and about children is a storyline featuring the superpowered or superhero child, such as *Like Mike* (2002), the *Harry Potter* franchise, Robert Rodriguez's *Spy Kids* trilogy, or his current *The Adventures of Shark Boy and Lava Girl* (2005).

9. As a prototypical example, see the Martin Lawrence vehicle *Big Momma's House* (2000).

10. Perhaps the most obvious example is Hattie McDaniel's Oscar-winning performance of a character named Mammy in the celebrated classic *Gone with the Wind* (1939), but examples abound in early Hollywood cinema. A good reference here is Donald Bogle, *Toms, Coons, Mulattoes, Mammies and Bucks: An Interpretive History of Blacks in American Film*, 4th ed. (New York: Continuum, 2001).

11. The label ultimately cancelled the video shoot because the artist never completed the full album, making the production decisions for "Wurldwide" a truly academic exercise.

CHAPTER 11

Preparing to Perform the Other

DEVELOPING ROLES DIFFERENT
FROM ONESELF

Sheldon Schiffer
(Georgia State University)

Creating performances for screen and stage where either the actor or the director is notably different from the character to be portrayed is a challenging task whose political, psychological, and cultural underpinnings have gone underexamined. Dramatic practitioners have begun to recognize that while human beings are similar enough to relate to the experiences of each other to translate the most basic aspects of character, we are still different enough to make some troubling dramatic choices when we attempt to create characters different from ourselves. The result of such errant creative work is that for some audiences, a character may appear inauthentic, inaccurate, and sometimes offensive. Recent films such as *The Interpreter* or *Brokeback Mountain*, dramas directed by prominent directors with casts playing characters ethnically or sexually different from themselves, present interesting problems of representation that are resolved (or not) in the preparation of a role. While the preparation of the actor for a role in the rehearsal process is a major step in the creation of character, I have addressed the rehearsal process elsewhere.[1] In this chapter I examine two areas of the creative process of cinematic representation of character that are especially authorial and expressive of a director's relationship with the actor: casting, and the practice of notating performance choices that often called script-scoring.[2] Both processes pose creative challenges for actors and directors who are in some way different—ethnically, racially, socioeconomically, or sexually—from the characters they portray. This chapter explores some of the questions and procedures I have developed as a director of independent film. In consequence, I reference my own work and experience dealing with this complex issue. My hope is that my account will help actors and directors develop roles that are more representational of their experiences while at the same time resisting oppressive ideologies and stereotypes.

Casting begins the process of transforming script characters into screen characters. It is the phase of production in which directors begin to use performance to tell a cinematic story. Casting also is the process during which directors make decisions that expose their impulses and interpretations regarding why their characters behave the way they do, and why real-life persons would behave similarly. But casting also implies a socially charged problem of perception: Should an actor assume that the character she will create will come from the personal experiences she brings to the role? Conversely, should a director shape the character by assuming that what he sees in the actor he casts is what the role needs? If both actor and director agree on similar character attributes drawn from the actor, then the perceptual problem is solved. But in films where difference is considerable, perception is often clouded with ideologies and stereotypical constructions of identity.

Melanie Camerman in *O-Negative.*

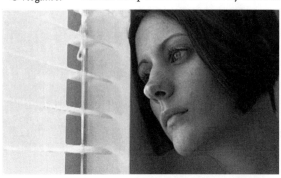

My first experiment with this problem occurred while making the film *O-Negative.* In every other film I had made every character was either Jewish, Latin American, or white. All these personas were familiar to my unconscious, as my memory is loaded with detail about people I have known in my family. *O-Negative* is about a white French woman (Melanie Camerman) hospitalized with an illness and in need of a blood transfusion. However, the woman fears receiving blood from a stranger. Her blood is the rare type, O-negative, and she has in her home country banked her own blood. But her blood cannot be sent in time to save her. Her anesthesiologist is an African American woman (Erica Douglas) who senses the French woman's fears. However, she interprets them as the fear of receiving blood from a racially different person. In the context of a preoperative surgery room, neither character is able to state directly what s

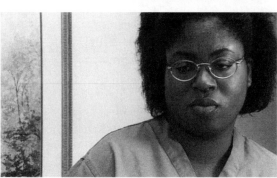

Erica Douglas in *O-Negative.*

believes. I chose to deprive the audience of any certain evidence that would confirm the nature of the French woman's fear. The audience can never know without a doubt if she is a racist or simply fearful of foreign transfusions. Likewise, I provided no certain evidence that the anesthesiologist was responding to a racist patient. What I did offer were coded characteristics in my casting choices. The French woman's pale skin, blue eyes, golden hair, and thin lips were featured quite prominently in extreme close-ups. And likewise, I cast as the anesthesiologist an African American woman with notably nappy hair, dark skin and eyes, and thick lips. Indeed, this was casting intended to comment on and trigger stereotypical understandings of race.

In *O-Negative*, I kept the judgment of the characters ambiguous, and I removed any facts that could validate the audience's judgment of the characters as racist, phobic, or reactive to race or racism. I used the cloud of stereotype and betrayed my own uncertainty to serve the theme of the film. Could I escape these stereotypical constructions without creating the desired discomfort I wanted the audience to experience? I argue that in a film explicitly about racial questions I could not, if I intend to honestly represent an ethnicity or race different from myself. If I wanted the audience to engage a racist signified that would later in the film be subverted, then my own limited experience with and significant difference from these communities at that time had to become integral to the film itself. I had to engage racial stereotypes so that the film's theme could resonate with the audience.[3]

Melanie Camerman and Erica Douglas in *O-Negative*.

The experience I have recalled with *O-Negative* examines the circumstance of a filmmaker who is both screenwriter and director. But this is not often the case. Suppose you are given a script to direct. You have to cast the characters described in the script, and some of the characters require a specific ethnicity. These specifications, if they are thoughtfully defined, cannot be altered without changing the meaning and function of the script. Character specifications that do not explicitly call for a given ethnicity may pull the filmmaker in one ethnic direction or another. But even choosing to respect the ethnic specificity of a script does not eliminate the possibility of casting actors of a different ethnicity from the characters they will play. These conditions of variability prove just how flexible ethnic identification and association can be in a film, though this is a flexibility that comes with consequence in meaning. How, then, does a director make these kinds of decisions? In what situations should a script character's specific characteristics of ethnicity, class, gender, physical ability, or sexual orientation be the same as the actor's? In what situations might the director have a greater degree of freedom to make choices based on his or her interpretation?

Now you say you have a vision of who the character is and how he or she fits into the story. Could your vision be corrupted by prejudice and stereotype? Conversely, could your vision be compromised by a desire to advocate a political agenda? If so, is such advocacy honest to the experience you, the filmmaker, are trying to represent? If not, then aren't you, as an artist, free to remake the world as you desire with all the subjective authority that directing presumes? Are not such determinations and judgments the prerogative of directing? Can or should a filmmaker visualize a thought experiment in casting? Or, if one is to succeed at making a film that diverse audiences accept as honest, are there principles of casting that one should adhere to as doctrine?

There are no certain answers to these questions. The answers are always responsive to larger questions: (1) Will the audience accept the ethnicity of a character as relevant and realistic? (2) Can the actor play the ethnic part with authenticity and believability? (3) What are the social and political dynamics implied by other characters in the script? (4) Does the character's ethnicity fit logically in the narrative? I explore each of these using examples from films I have made or studied.

Al Pacino played Shylock in *The Merchant of Venice* (2004). Although Pacino is not Jewish, he played a Jewish Shylock, as the script required. Herein lies the problem in the politics of casting. Some argue that the presentation of Shylock in Shakespeare's script is anti-Semitic and that Shylock presents a negative stereotype of Jews. Others argue that Shylock, and particularly Pacino's version of the character, portrays the conditions that Jews endured in Europe that affected behavior necessary for political and economic survival, and that whatever behavior manifested by those conditions is a justifiable result, even if that result seems stereotypical.[4] The pragmatic, opportunistic, and materialistic behaviors of Shylock were, for some audiences and critics, necessary attributes that aided the survival of Jews in his historic predicament.

Casting Pacino as Shylock created two problems typical of representing difference. First, Al Pacino was born to Italian immigrants and grew up as an Italian American.[5] This is a fact that, while

SHELDON
SCHIFFER

widely publicized, is certainly easily discovered and very much part of his star discourse. Pacino the actor is not Jewish. Therefore, he must rely on his skills at identifying what is most crudely human about Shylock, irrespective of critical and political sensitivities. Furthermore, the characteristics that Pacino and his director, Michael Radford, deem specifically Jewish must be learned and integrated into his character. Second, the audience may judge Pacino differently because of his non-Jewishness. He will be evaluated for how authentically he, a gentile, portrays a Jew. Pacino's own sensitivity toward negative Jewish stereotypes will also be scrutinized.

In my own experience as a filmmaker I have faced similar questions and problems, particularly in the production of my short film *Comeuppance* (2003), which imagines how a black woman spoken-word poet and an Orthodox Jew survive a racist encounter in the rural South. Two fearful statements from Southerners inspired the writing of this script. In the 1990s, a Jewish relative and native of Georgia warned me about driving through rural parts of northern Georgia while wearing visible symbols of my Jewish identity. A typical pendant, for example, would be a Star of David or the Hebrew letter Chi. He feared that if I were stranded alone on the side of the road, I could become a victim of anti-Semitism—a hate crime. The other inspiration came from an African American student of mine. She feared driving through Mississippi; she would not get off a rural highway to use the restroom for fear of being the victim of a hate crime. Both were aware of two very gruesome histories.

In the case of my Jewish relative, he was aware of the 1913 lynching of Leo Frank, a Jewish pencil factory manager in Marietta, Georgia, who had been convicted in a spurious trial for the murder of a white teenager, former employee Mary Phagan. His death sentence was commuted, despite published anti-Yankee and anti-Semitic remarks from the citizens of Marietta. A mob broke into the jail holding Frank and lynched him. To this day, the leaders of the mob that orchestrated the murder have not been identified by the police, and several witnesses are rumored to know details they never disclosed to authorities. However, accusers and deniers line both sides of this still unresolved hate crime. In the case of my student, she was acutely aware of the lynching of Emmett Till, the teenage African American boy who was beaten, shot, and lynched by white supremacists in rural Mississippi for allegedly whistling at a white woman. My interest in making *Comeuppance* was to explore these fears as they existed in 2001.

With research, I crafted a script that allowed for a thought experiment. I asked, what if a carpetbagging Orthodox Jewish man assumed

*Developing
Roles Different
from Oneself*

he was racially acceptable in a community of white rural Southerners, only to find out he was not? And what if the only supporting character who could reflect his predicament was a black woman spoken-word poet stranded in the same small town? Her operating assumption was that she was not racially acceptable, and so she was in a position to observe two men whose religious and racial differences drove their distrust and resentment of each other over the ownership of a house and a piece of land. She had nothing to lose, and only a poem to write. And it is the creation of her poem, and the events that she witnessed that inspired that poem, that make her the narrator-protagonist. This script provided me with the opportunity to put a method of questioning difference to the test. I had to decide which actors, if any, should be Jewish, and which should be southern.

Dennis Hughes in *Comeuppance.*

And I had to decide how dark-skinned and how much African American enculturation my protagonist should have.

While *Comeuppance* gave me the incentive to research these different ethnic communities for a contemporary fictiona story, I was also compelled to address changes in contempo rary racial dynamics. As Jew have collectively moved awa from their role as civil right comrades-in-arms with Africa Americans in the last twent years, Jews and African Amer cans have perpetrated acts racial violence against eac other. The Crown Heights rio of August 1991 were one suc

Alex Wood in *Comeuppance.*

incident that provided a common historical referent for my four ma characters: (1) Bahama, an urban, Columbia University–educate African American spoken-word poet (Tanisha Flowers); (2) Amicai New York–based jewelry dealer and somewhat backsliding Orthod Jew (Dennis Hughes); (3) Jasper, a white southern bar-diner owr (Alex Wood); and (4) Hillary, Jasper's sister, also a native Southerr and waitress in her brother's bar-diner (Julie Kennedy). In the sto both the African American woman, Bahama, and the Orthodox Je ish man, Amicai, become victims of racially motivated oppressive havior from the native-Southerner bar-diner owner, Jasper. Yet, even as they collaborate with each other to survive their unfortunate circumstances, they also distrust each other for similar prejudices.

To cast this film, I was faced with several challenges. I had to think carefully about how to evoke some discomfort in the audience through the casting choices so that they could, to some degree, identify with the hyperbolic reactions of the two male leads. Second, since both male leads behave aggressively and in ways that are less than admirable and that validate some stereotypical constructions of race and ethnicity, I had to find actors who were comfortable with the judgments they would incur, both on the set and in their private lives.

First, I chose to cast a dark-skinned woman to play the role of the African American poet, whose skin color and facial bone structure were character features that could not be easily applied to a non-African American woman or even a light-skinned African American woman. I needed a Bahama to connote a blackness that could provoke the most racist reaction in Jasper and in the audience. Here I was filming on thin ice, for these kinds of decisions have traditionally led to cinematic stereotyping. But to choose an African American woman with more European features would fail to challenge fully both the antagonist and the audience (even an African American audience). Casting required an awareness of the signification of race, and the physiology of the actors had to trigger those reactions described in the script, and therefore had to similarly trigger an expectation of those characters' reactions in the audience.

Tanisha Flowers in *Comeuppance.*

The other characters presented different issues as they included both stereotypical and archetypal features. I had to find a Jewish-looking actor who could speak with a New York accent to play the boisterous and flirtatious Orthodox Jew, Amicai. This was a problematic choice. Amicai is Orthodox, but he is not consistently observant. Alone, curious, and on the road, he drinks beer in a diner from a glass that not from a cupboard of glasses segregated for meals served without meat or milk (*fromkeit*). He flirts with the gentile waitress, Hillary, and fantasizes taking her out on a date. And later in the film, when forced under threat of death to play Russian roulette, he breaks a commandment forbidding suicide and murder by subtly positioning the gun so that, should it go off, the bullet would pass through his skull and into the body of his assailant—killing himself and his drunken hate-mongering foe. Further complicating the urban jewelry dealer, he had stereotypical opinions about African Americans. Amicai also has the ability to cautiously aid Bahama in her time of need. Indeed, Amicai is vividly Jewish in the context of his surroundings because of his character's costume, and he also has very definite sympathetic and unsympathetic characteristics. Some of those unsympathetic ones are stereotypical, though my research validates these characteristics, and thus these stereotypical and archetypical features have narrative value—principally, the signifiers that Amicai notices about Bahama serve to validate his judgment of her, and vice versa. The racist or anti-Semitic values that either character appears to accept are necessary for both of them to follow the trajectory of their dramatic conflict with Jasper, the white bar-diner owner, and with each other. The challenge was to subvert the stereotypes by putting the characters through conflicts that forced them to reflect and question their own beliefs, and to imbue these characters with other specific attributes that are neither ethnically nor racially relevant.

The actor I chose for the role of Amicai was not Jewish. He looked Jewish, certainly as Jewish as Pacino, at least from my own Jewish viewpoint. Consequentially, there are two political risks I confronted. As a Jew, I risked being accused of creating a self-hating self-image This criticism has been launched at both Woody Allen and Philip Roth for portraying Jews as weak, self-absorbed, and resentful of the religious and cultural obligations their characters inherited. Amicai's character is none of that, but he is curiously contradictory and does no practice as his faith would suggest he should. I am willing to take this criticism, as I know that Amicai comes from my own experiences o observing Orthodox Jews who would demonstrate their devotion in public and cheat their devotion in private. I also chose to present those experiences to get Jews to look at themselves, contradictions and al to consider the lifetime choice and sometimes struggle to observe as part of their cultural and religious identity. The research I did for th film indicated that indeed, observance of all 613 *mitzvot* (comman ments) among Orthodox Jews is a constant challenge. I found a su stantial body of anecdotes about persons who secretly binged durir their nonobservance or devised clever workarounds that served t convenient needs of the observer, sometimes at the expense of t spirit of the commandment. And certainly I witnessed my own fai ily members and their friends, who similarly failed to observe cons tently. My interest in this behavior with respect to Amicai is that the binges and workarounds are journeys into the worldly temptations

the gentile universe. And that universe is fraught with moral questions 231
that, without the reasoning of rabbinical scholars, can overwhelm the
observant Jew. Amicai is ill-prepared for the trouble he finds, and the
temptations that ensue.

I also ran the risk of being accused of creating an inauthentic character because the actor (Dennis Hughes) is not Jewish. The choice of a
non-Jewish actor to play the role followed this logic: Hughes's Amicai
had no inhibitions to inhibit his performance. Dennis was familiar
with Jewish culture and religion as practiced by New York Jews in particular. But he had no fears of misrepresenting Jewishness, nor was
he concerned with overrepresenting Jewishness. He was free to take
my direction and create his character from his less biased perspective,
and he could neutralize my ex-
perience of Jewishness with his
own experience as an outsider.
Could a Jewish actor offer the
same? Possibly! But how and
when would a director know?

The character of Jasper was
also challenging to cast. Jasper
is undoubtedly racist and anti-
Semitic. He distrusts Jews, he
resents blacks, and he fears the
pervasive arrival of Mexicans.
He is both the archetype and
stereotype of racially defined
whiteness. Jasper's archetype is

Dennis Hughes preps with director Sheldon Schiffer
on *Comeuppance*.

the displaced white European-American rural male reeling from loss
of power in his part of the world and threatened by the demographic
changes occurring around him. He has lost his claim to the family
and because he thinks his own Jewish real-estate agent rescinded his
id to help another Jew. That event coincides with Bahama's accidental
arrival into Jasper's small town. So, Jasper's racism is inflamed by his
circumstances as he acts out his anger with racist rationales. Casting was crucial, since the part could have been easily reduced to an
uncomplicated, one-dimensional racist. In my experience, racists are
anything but uncomplicated or one-dimensional.

To cast this part I had to find a light-skinned man who could perform an authentic southern and rural accent. He also had to be comfortable expressing hate. Herein appears the most difficult condition of
casting Jasper. The actor had to completely commit himself to Jasper's
racism without fear of betraying any of the actor's racism. If the actor

were to fear the possibility of being identified as a racist, the trust between my black and Jewish cast and crew might have eroded. Indeed,
everyone at some level carries with them some prejudicial thought and
impulse. But Alex Wood, who played Jasper, was deeply aware of the
black experience. Wood was a member of a black fraternity. He had
studied African American history and culture, and he came to the role
understanding the character from both white and black perspectives.
He had the courage to portray the rage of displaced whiteness without
fear because he had confronted his own racism. He also had the intellect to defend his portrayal. Had Wood not understood the history
of racial oppression or felt comfortable with his whiteness in contrast
to the vulnerability a black person experiences in the rural South, I
would have had to either find another actor or produce the film with
less than transparent strategies.

Finally, the character of Hillary, Jasper's sister, was less complex.
The choice to cast an actor in a supporting role with stereotypical looks
expresses another condition of casting. Supporting roles must work
with the audience's preexisting understanding of archetypes and stereotypes. For the plot of a film to unfold efficiently, supporting characters should need very little screen time to develop and make their roles
purposeful, authentic, and credible. Hillary was the only character
who did not appear to carry the cargo of racial oppression. Instead, her
blond hair and svelte looks were stereotypical characteristics that suggested her focus was on her body and, as such, her power dependent
on the way people reacted to her physical appearance. These persona
distractions made her ignorant. In her case, such ignorance was bliss-
ful. She could enjoy the hearty laughter of her Jewish patron without
suspicion. She could even fantasize about hitching a ride with him
to New York and finding a new life for herself in his big city. Therefore, Julie Kennedy was chosen for her authentic southern accent, her
blondish hair, and her figure, which supported Hillary's interest in
making a career as a fashion model in New York City. But Hillary's stereotypical characteristics are also augmented by her instinct for kindness and sympathy, which she expressed toward her enraged brother
as she appealed for him to respect the pragmatic materiality of real
estate agents (regardless of culture, race, or religion) and to soothe his
racism as misguided pain and loss.

Yes, to some degree, casting Kennedy called on stereotypical ideas
about svelte blonds. But my choice to cast in a way that validated some
stereotypical ideas was also to explore other gifts that her physical
characteristics enabled. She is the object of desire of the less than
consistently observant Amicai. Her physical attributes define her as

"shikza queen," a Yiddish expression for an attractive gentile woman (a forbidden lust interest that some distracted religious Jews might not admit to). This lure is what begins the provocation between Amicai and Jasper. Also, her brother, Jasper, tries to protect her from her own open-mindedness (which he thinks is foolish) that contradicts his racial and ethnic fears. This opens up a conversation in which her wisdom shows the contradiction in Jasper's thinking. Jasper, a small business owner and hence small-scale capitalist, cannot begrudge the rules of the game that the Jews play with him. Rather than confront her brother's racism head-on, she appeals to his capitalist ideals to get him to respect Amicai's behaviors. The stereotypical svelte blond as a narrative trope proves herself to have far more to offer than her physical attributes. The choice to cast Kennedy as a type was intentional; it is a foiling logic to draw both characters and audience into deeper discoveries about identity and appearance.

In retrospect, casting for *Comeuppance,* a movie explicitly about race, ethnicity, and power in the contemporary ex-urban and rural South, was a dicey proposition.

The film has been admired greatly by black women, black film festivals, and festivals that take an interest in issues of ethnicity and power.[6] Jewish film festivals resoundingly rejected it. Lesson learned: it is very difficult to cast films about racial and ethnic issues without disappointing or offending someone. Possibly the most awkward place to experiment with this lesson is the ethnically defined film festival, since such festivals by definition have an agenda that implies a monolithic construction of identity (however much a creative programmer might try to expand the definitions of that identity and divest himself from a monolithic construct). But these festivals are the most revealing of a community's ability to look at itself, warts, freckles, and all. In the case of *Comeuppance,* a Jew in a stereotypical business of Orthodox Jews (jewelry and real estate) is depicted, and he is a Jew who fails to observe his faith. For some Jews, observance is what defines Jewishness above all else. His own stereotyping and ignorance about African Americans are also less than admirable. It is possible that many festival programmers were simply uncomfortable with this degree of antithetical characterization. And since art is not itself social policy, the filmmaker must also confront her own reality and intentionality regardless of rejection. I have observed many Jews like Amicai, and so confront my experience at the expense of my idealizations. Many an audience member chooses to consume ethnically branded cinema to validate his or her ideas and ideals of identity. *Comeuppance* refuses to participate in that discourse. Instead, it attempts to utilize stereotypes that function as narrative tropes so that those same stereotypes are taken to their most extreme conclusions. As it turned out, black film festival programmers found that their audience was more interested in these contradictions and more directly interested in films that explore the problematics of difference. For example, *Comeuppance* screened with *Black Israeli,* a documentary about the intercultural identities of African Israelis. And in the statements from audience members and programmers, frequently the comments suggested *Comeuppance* visualizes stereotypes while examining the basic fears that allow them to frighten.

As *Comeuppance's* resounding failure in one class of ethnic venues (Jewish film festivals) was countered by a notable success in another (black film festivals), I realized that the filmmaker interested in creating work about difference is confronted with a double-edged problem. On the one hand, playing the stereotype makes use of a shorthand to be read by the viewer's unconscious eye. Evil characters or rich characters or artsy characters may need to look a certain way for audiences to read them quickly. The stereotype provides superficial codes that cue ideas efficiently in the mind of the viewer, with little screen time dedicated to observed complex character behavior. And if a filmmaker chooses to ignore this shorthand, then he must spend more precious screen time on the character. If bad guys look ordinary, what specific character codes must a filmmaker show so that the viewer associates these ordinary bad guys and their function as a nemesis through revised codes of badness? There are few choices that do not reference the stereotype. And if the stereotypical attributes are chosen, the dialectical choice is to choose them because other characters respond to those stereotypes in complex ways that evolve an audience's understanding of difference. However, the filmmaker who chooses to expand character's depth with characteristics that intentionally employ both stereotype and its contradiction risks impeding the narrative. For example, the films of John Sayles succeed for some and fail for others surfacing problems of difference while either advancing or impeding the narrative.[7] Ideally, the narrative and the character work interdependently to benefit or injure the artistic merit of the film. Of course, critics have argued that no body of films about race or difference can have artistic merit without also having political merit. It is every viewer's prerogative to determine how much political or artistic merit to give a film that represents difference and its problematic. That question best answered in a different line of research.

The balance between the political and the aesthetic is a defining hinge in the argument toward a process of filming difference. In view—and whom else can I really speak for?—what makes "good" cinema is a film that strives to develop a reality-seeking experience for the audience. Reality seeking is a subjective mode prone to dispute but open to unpredictable outcomes. For the dramatic arts, it is also a creative means that requires a very even-handed balance between allowing actors and their characters' behaviors to drive the storytelling and the somewhat omniscient interventions of the film author. A reality-seeking experience provides the experiential data that can (but do not always) provide evidence to strengthen the ideological underpinnings of multiple and opposing perspectives of characters and viewers. It does not guarantee that the rhetorical conclusions implied in the narrative that unfolds are honest or representative. It does increase the possibility that viewers will engage intellectually, will have assumptions challenged, and will experience complex contradictions inside characters and themselves. And those open-ended experiences often make the most thought-provoking films.

Developing Roles Different from Oneself

What is involved in plotting a reality-seeking performance preparation for the actor and director of a character who is diffferent from oneself? What are the methods required, and how are they ultimately brought from character research to casting and to script analysis? What follows is an exploration of the script analysis process as it relates to developing a performance for actor and director.

Script Analysis

The various well-known approaches to working with a script for the actor may not have been designed for the problem of portraying characters different from oneself, but they are certainly malleable and useful. As the actor becomes more deeply engaged in the process, however, his or her eyes and ears—all the senses—must be focused on the stimuli in the acting environment. Eventually not a synapse should be left to consider anything else during performance. That is the role of the director—to stand in between audience and actor, to collaborate in the shaping of a role for the purpose of expressing her authorial voice, and to stimulate ideas clearly through a commitment to a role, the viewer's mind. The problem of reception and expression while creating characters different from oneself must become more the director's problem at the time of production. These questions begin with casting and continue into script analysis and on into that moment when a director searches for his target audience and discovers how it likely to respond.

The period of script analysis is one of the few opportunities when neither actor nor director is rehearsing, where both are alone, and their intellect is more engaged than their emotions. It is a time when they can develop explicit strategies directed both toward the development of the role and toward seeing the role in the context of the viewers and their ideological orientation. Many practitioners of script analysis have developed schemes for moving from script to screen or stage. Among the most effective are those that schematize behaviors into a very simple system. Harold Clurman discusses his system in his book *On Directing*.[8] Subsequent performance directors have modified it. It is an approach that largely relies on written and spoken language and a basic knowledge of the parts of speech: what is a verb and a noun (most useful), an adjective and an adverb (less useful). Clurman developed a method for creating a script score that allows a director or actor, alone and scratching notes on the script itself, to do so in a methodical way that will enable him or her to speak to actors in language that focuses on specific objective-oriented actions and that helps the actor discover what stimuli to sense and why, and how to act and react.[9] Judith Weston, in her teaching and in her book *Directing Actors: Creating Memorable Performances for Film and Television*, has thoughtfully advanced Clurman's approach for the film actor and director.[10]

Weston identifies objectives for characters as needs to be possessed, essentially nouns, things sensible to the senses. These sensible nouns become physical objectives—money, a kiss, a confession. There are also more conceptual nouns that are emotional objectives—security, companionship, remorse.[11] Related to objectives are the actions that characters take to get these objectives, actions that are noted as verbs.[1] Some actions taken are very literal or physical (touch, talk, take), others are more metaphorical and can be physically executed in numerous ways (entice, engage, snatch). Also relevant are obstacles, which are also nouns and can be either sensible objects (an interrupting phone call, a gun, a door) or physical behaviors in another character (stubbornness, mania, promiscuity).[13]

This schema of words can describe one arc of action for a character also known as a *beat*. For example, a character in a script is at a job interview. The scene's longest arc of action for the job candidate might be described as follows. The candidate's superobjective might be the job or the words "You're hired." He may choose several playable verbs to get it during the interview, some literal and some metaphorical: *greet, inquire, impress, sell, question, insist, doubt*. Each one of these verbs may be played to pursue the job, and also to pursue smaller subobjectives: *smile, an inside story, a laugh*. In this way the scene can be described as a series of smaller arcs of action, each a beat, building inside the large

SHELDON
SCHIFFER

Table 11.1   237

Character Name		
Physical Objective	*Playable Action*	*Emotional Objective*
Sensible noun: e.g., a smile, a contract	Literal or metaphorical verb: e.g., chat, entice	Conceptual noun: e.g., affirmation, trust

one where subobjectives are building toward attaining the superobjective. What makes the scene dramatic are the obstacles that make the character internalize his choices, reconfigure his strategy, and then initiate a new arc of action. The obstacles in the interview will obstruct the candidate's actions to get both the chosen subobjective and the job (superobjective).

Developing Roles Different from Oneself

I developed a schema somewhat like Clurman's system for scene analysis and encourage my acting and directing students to inscribe on the script beside each hand-drawn bracketed arc of action (or beat) these simple words into a chart. (Table 11.1)

The actor and director fill in the bottom row of boxes with their choices. The actor or director can refer back to the script score to review what she planned in the preparation process. The innumerable random distractions that occur during production make a script score very useful when one is trying to create a performance that is consistent and coherent on screen.

As is true for most rehearsal methods available to an actor or director, there is nothing in this method that explicitly addresses difference and directing or performing a role different from oneself. But with a little research, the actor and director can identify specific objectives, actions, and obstacles that provide stimuli (sense data to use) for the character in ways that are unfamiliar for an actor different from the character she is playing. The method I describe was used in the film I mentioned earlier, *O-Negative*. The protagonist, a white French patient in need of a blood transfusion but who experiences discomfort and indignation at every touch from her health care practitioners, sensed bounty of racially infused stimuli. Her doctor is a black woman who appears to suspect that her patient is afraid of an interracial blood transfusion. To create this character, the actor Erica Douglas, who played the black doctor, and I worked diligently to identify the stimuli. As I am not black and do not have the internal radar to sense the racism blacks experience in the United States, I had to explore and research with the actor where she looked on the body and what she listens for in the voice of a suspected racist. I needed to find out what sense data triggered her, what subobjectives she could play for to bring her the superobjective of trust (to overcome a racist's fears), and what literal and metaphorical playable actions (verbs) she would take that would bring a racist to trust her to receive the blood of an anonymous stranger who was likely black. I also observed black people working with or for white people. I asked them about the things they looked for that suggested a white person holds racist ideas or fears, and what actions they have taken to either confront or evade the problem. I needed this information so that I could decide where to place the camera for a point-of-view shot of both the white patient and black doctor, and what scene objectives I needed to identify to achieve a performance that represented racist thought and the thoughts of a person victimized by racist thought.

SHELDON
SCHIFFER

I originally thought that the black doctor would play for simple cooperation; she needed her patient to pick up a pen and sign a form certifying permission to receive a transfusion of blood. It did not at first occur to me that the doctor would care so much if her patient was racist. That patient had no power and posed no threat. Instead, this was not her objective. She played for trust and respect, which was not a condition for receiving the blood but was a condition for her to go home and clock out of her job with dignity. Together, these two objectives physically reside in eye contact. If the black doctor could get her patient to look at her and permit human instinct to trust unconditional human help from a medical professional, then she could get her job done and heal not only the body but perhaps the fearful soul of a racist. My original script score therefore changed as I learned more from my research and exploration—a kind of research that was specific to social and political situation, yet that had multiple solutions.

As directors and actors, however, we are asked not only to represent reality but also to interpret and transform it. And so, after the research and the initial script score were completed, ideas started to flow. The next step was to consider and reconsider how to provoke an audience to think a few specific thoughts. Rather than let the audience simply sit back and observe, I asked myself what script score choices could provide some rhetorical significance to a performance. While I knew the doctors would rarely confront a racist patient, I also believed that "confront" was the right verb for the role of this doctor as she played her subtext, though her dialogue was more conciliatory. It was my rhetorical choice to challenge the audience. Although none of the dialog exposes a confrontation, she confronted in other ways. She confronted and inquired so that she could get racist evidence—a rather weighty subobjective. Ultimately, she failed to get the evidence, but the belc the-surface confrontation became the most talked-about aspect at every festival where the film has screened. Why would that be?

The balance between political and aesthetic values in a film is often played out in the tension between the visibility of an author's hand in determining a dramatic outcome and the visibility of a character's will to control her own destiny. Films that are often talked about long after their premiere are those in which the signification internalized by characters may motivate strong actions and reactions but the internalized signifieds for audience and character are left ambiguous. The appropriate amount of ambiguity gives the audience as much to internalize as the characters. A script score is a place to plan some of this ambiguous signification that is particularly relevant when filming difference as conveyed through performance. *O-Negative* was my test case.

Developing Roles Different from Oneself

O-Negative was a short film, 7.5 minutes, designed around one dramatic problem. Therefore, each object that a character senses, each facial reaction that the audience sees privately or through the eyes of a character, is intended to relate in some way to that dramatic problem. In a film where racial identity is a dramatic obstacle for its characters, and therefore an issue for the audience, visual and aural signifiers should relay a mountain of ideas, meanings that suggest clues to the thoughts of the characters, thoughts that belie either racial beliefs or a suspicion that one character believes the other holds such racial beliefs. And so, in the design of the script score and in the rehearsal process, I identified with the actors both obstacles and aids for their objectives that would stimulate racial questions in their characters' minds. The casting accomplished much of the work. Certainly the palette of flesh tones and eye color provided a stimulus for each character to internalize his or her difference. These physiological signifiers function as aids for the immediate objectives but are obstacles for the superobjectives. The doctor needs her patient's hands and eyes to help her achieve the signed permmission form for the transfusion. But those same hands are also notably white, decorated with a French manicure, something ethnically definitive, and laden with a history of colonial attitude that would obstruct the black doctor's play for dignity. Likewise, the white French patient listens to Gospel music through her headphones to give her the faith that she will survive. But this music is appropriated and voided of its cultural and historical context, a music of specific transformative endurance of the African American soul as the body it occupied survived 250 years of slavery. That connotative context implies guilt for oppression, and is an obstacle to trust. These signifiers have both personal and social meaning. On the personal level, they are attractive things that function to enable each character to give trust to the other. They are also aesthetically stimulating in and of themselves for each character. But they are also laden with social meaning that can distract each character as they achieve their immediate objectives; the social meanings of these objects can transform them from aids into obstacles to their need of trust. But as each character must take action with the other to achieve her objective, they build a relationship. The personal meanings begin to outweigh the social ones, and the obstacle becomes an aid.

SHELDON
SCHIFFER

If annotated before rehearsal, script-scoring methods may be tools generally useful for plotting the design of all dramatic material, but an actor or director informed about the dialectics of difference can provide depth to the process of filming difference in performance. What comes after script-scoring is rehearsal. A thorough discussion of how various rehearsal techniques might be adapted to address the problematics of difference is beyond the scope of this essay. Nonetheless, significant questions of filming difference through performance affect an application of the major theories that inform the processes of developing a role and a performance.

Implications

As my research for this discussion evolved, I found that acting theories and methods mostly derived from Europe and the United States seemed to ignore or were at odds with sociological theories of identity. And this had implications—presented, in fact, obstacles—for how direct films that confront race, gender, class, and sexuality. The acting approaches I have used and continue to use assume that the manipulation of specific actor attributes is the core of character development. Western acting theories put considerable emphasis on either the actor's ability to mimic observed behaviors (pre-Stanislavski and his System) or the actor's ability to tap into his or her personal memories and to use the remembered sense data transformed into physical articulations and vocalizations of his or her own body parts. Memory, physicalization, and sensing processes are contingent on specificity: the actor and her character. But very little discussion occurs around more general ideas of representing difference as perceived by the audience and its host society (differences in culture, ethnicity, gender, class, sexual orientation, and even physical ability).

The performative model offered in "the Method" or "the System" as practiced in the United States relies on a Freudian model of the unconscious. As summarized by Edward Dwight Easty in *On Meth*

Acting, an actor's ability to convey experience realistically depends on his ability to physicalize remembered sensations (called sense memory), to externalize chains of sense memories as recalled from a potent emotional experience (called emotional or affective memory), and to facilitate a personalization (or, if necessary, a substitution) of those memories that are appropriate to the character portrayed and her situation.[14] A reliance on personal memories and the Freudian model assumes that much of what we remember is what defines our character. How we use those memories is assumed to be somewhat universal across the many ways in which people are different. But what Easty, and therefore Adler, Strasberg, and Meisner (all teachers and theorists of Stanislavski's Method and members of the famed Group Theater), do not address is the problem of an actor who might lack the memories that can be transposed across a personalized cultural history of difference. While the Method proponent would argue that a substitution of a character's experience for a personal memory that is loaded with similar emotional conflicts should suffice,[15] such substitution assumes that a character's emotional experience is stripped from its social context. Some characters, like some people, have been acculturated to internalize particular attitudes and actions without having memories of their own to rationalize their actions. In historically marginalized and oppressed communities, this is a common condition. Instead, persons of these communities internalize the orally communicated memories of their family and other community members. These are not reliably transposable (or substitutable) memories because the context is not personal but social and political. The implied limitation of the Method is that if a memory is not personal, then it cannot give the stimuli necessary to yield authentic human behavior in the fiction of dramatic performance.

Another theory of role development worth examining is based on improvisational technique. Stephen Book, author of *Book on Acting: Improvisation Technique for the Professional Actor in Film, Theater & Television*[16] and a disciple of the major theorist and practitioner of improvisation technique Viola Spolin, likewise offers little to directly answer the problematic of representing characters different from oneself. Certainly improvisation technique gives many opportunities for the exploration of stimuli related to aspects not possessed firsthand by the performer or director. The variety of exercises and games that Book offers could be easily translated by choosing activities and stimuli that are loaded with signification in the problematic of difference. A challenge for future performance trainers is to take these theoretical approaches to performance and adapt them so that specific rehearsal exercises and preparation methods can address the performance problems that arise when representing characters different from oneself. The conversion of exercises would be manageable in the case of improvisation technique. Improvisation creates variables of physical and emotional attributes under specific gamelike situations. It would be necessary to limit the variables of the dozens of Book exercises to a set that is specific to what the actor or acting coach identifies as specific to the physical facts of the role or any physical facts that are similar to the role. The design of such exercises could prove the basis of a useful inquiry into what is different about a role or an actor, and in this way could provide insight into a process that might otherwise produce stereotypical choices. It is my hope that actors and directors will continue to answer the questions posed here with some of the vigor of the social sciences through experimentation and an awareness of method, which includes observation and an interpretation of the data.

SHELDON
SCHIFFER

For example, quantitative sociology looks not only at specific case studies, as do the performing arts, but also at what patterns of attributes exist in a defined sample of a population. Realistic representation of character is defined by very different means across disciplines of performance theory and social science research. But both means of seeking credible information communicate what audiences and actors think they know about people different from themselves. However biased and inaccurate, actors and audiences unconsciously sample the behaviors of persons different from themselves. Each person observes a race, class, ethnicity, sexual orientation, or physical ability and stores patterns of sense data associated with the differences noticed. These characteristic patterns are consciously and unconsciously stored, qualitatively judged, and associated with a group of persons as a set of characteristics that sometimes define a type of person (often inaccurately). Therefore, it is impossible for actors and audiences to completely evade what they think are the attributes of a character different from themselves without a combination of personal specificity and random pattern sampling. On this dual process, acting theory offers very little for rehearsal techniques, and just a little more for character research. Both trust that the unique attributes of an actor will make their way into performance without much awareness of difference, and without much concern for an audience's perception of difference.

Pattern sampling and memories of specific personal experiences individual persons different from oneself are mutated with the stereotypes that arrive into the viewer's mind through the numerous channels of cultural distribution. Every audience comes loaded with pr conception, ready to judge and embrace or reject what the filmmaker creates. But actors and directors need not see themselves as victims of a capricious audience. Instead, I suggest that actors and directors document the patterns they have sampled and compare them objectively with their personal memories, then research again what ideas the audience holds and what performances have impacted them, both in fictional media and in the news media, as well as in the historical imagination. From this documentation and research, the actor and director might consider how the performance being developed relates to what the audience has already experienced. Does the character in progress contradict or agree with a recently screened portrayal? Does it challenge the audience's imagination? Does it address a situation rarely explored? Finally, during rehearsal, the data should be internalized with exercises designed to bridge the difference so that it can become familiar. The director and actor might ask, are the objectives, actions, obstacles and aids, movements, and vocalizations uniquely advancing answers not just to personal questions about the role but also to social and political questions? The choice to film difference in thoughtful and self-conscious ways is a risky one that many filmmakers often choose to avoid for fear of failure and the extraordinary research required.

Developing Roles Different from Oneself

The adage given to screenwriters and directors, make films about things you know about, seems here to be deliberately ignored, and for good cause. But for those that subscribe to this adage I have this question: As filmmaking is a very time-consuming, even lifelong task, what better opportunity does one have to use one's time to find out about something new? Why not use life's precious hours and plentiful calories to learn about people different from oneself? For filmmakers, here are scant few hours left in life to learn at other times; why not learn while making a film? Yes, it is risky, but the personal growth opportunities are potentially immense. Very few human activities give license to find out about the intimate details of human beings. And from these details, from this learning, this growth that we ultimately share on the screen, we challenge the oppressive forces of ignorance and fear that prevent us from admiring each other's difference. We learn from the experience of shaping and witnessing a performance that the differences among us are expressions or manifestations, often brought on by conditions out of any human control, of more common characteristics of the human being. Just as often, these characteristics are not common at all. A passion to find out what aspects of human behavior are shared across categories of difference and what aspects are not is perhaps the greatest motivator for actors and directors to take the chance to portray in performance a character different from oneself. Certainly that is my attraction, and it remains a most pressing challenge in a world where cinematic representations are globalized and also carry political consequences for grave artistic mistakes.

Notes

Sheldon Schiffer, "Performing the Other: Revisiting Performance Theory for Characters Different from Oneself," unpublished manuscript (2007).

2. While script-scoring is neither standardized nor rigorously practiced by everyone in the same manner, the procedure was regimented by the play director Harold Clurman in his book, *On Directing* and is often taught to directing students of performance on preparing to direct actors. Harold Clurman, "The Director's Work Script," in *On Directing* (New York: Macmillan, 1972), 74–86.

3. *O-Negative* was screened at the San Francisco Black Film Festival (2004), the Black Independent Film Festival (2005), the Spaghetti Junction Urban Film Festival (2005), and the Dallas International Video Festival (2004). Each of these festivals explicitly screens films that address questions about race and ethnicity.

4. Ivor Davis, "Oscar-Winner Al Pacino Speaks About Shylock," online: All About Jewish Theatre: News: Artist in Spotlight, http://www.jewish-theatre.com/visitor/article_display.aspx?articleID=1131 (accessed April 13, 2005).

5. Dominic Wilis, "Al Pacino Biography," *Tiscali.film & tv*, http://www.tiscali.co.uk/entertainment/film/biographies/al_pacino_biog.html (accessed October 18, 2007).

6. *Comeuppance* was screened at the Decatur Film Festival (2003), the DeKalb County Film Forum (2003), the Independent Black Film Festival (2004), the San Francisco Black Film Festival (2004), the Santa Barbara African Heritage Film Series (2005, 2006), the Spaghetti Junction Urban Film Festival (2005), and the Urban Literary Film Festival (2005).

7. *City of Hope* (1991), *Lone Star* (1996), and *Silver City* (2004) are three films that similarly rely on stereotypes as a kind of shorthand for evolving the dramatic trajectories of their narratives. In these films, narration pauses to draw the exception to stereotype, and to provide authorial framing on how to receive those stereotypes. The length and ultimate narrative functions of those pauses contribute to the impact of the narrative's effectiveness at communicating these films' themes. For this reason, Sayles has both apologists and detractors arguing over his films' aesthetic and implied political values. Some criticize his films' narratives as tautological exercises in multiculturalism. Others celebrate his courage to open the Pandora's box of contradictions of race and class embedded in American myths and histories.

8. Clurman, "The Director's Workscript," in *On Directing*, 74–86.

9. Clurman, *On Directing*, 74–76.

10. Judith Weston, "Script Analysis," in *Directing Actors: Creating Memorable Performances for Film and Television* (Studio City, CA: Michael Wiese Productions, 199 163–234.

11. Ibid., 102.

SCHIFFER

12. Ibid., 102–103, 213–214.

13. Clurman, *On Directing*, 80; Weston, *Directing Actors*, 212–213.

14. Edward Dwight Easty, *On Method Acting* (New York: Ballantine Books, 1981).

15. Ibid., 123.

16. Stephen Book, *Book on Acting: Improvisation Technique for the Professional Actor in Film, Theater & Television* (Los Angeles: Silman-James Press, 2002).

Developing
Roles Different
from Oneself

CHAPTER 12

Cinematic Reservations

AN INTERVIEW WITH CHRIS EYRE

Yuri Makino

(University of Arizona)

Chris Eyre, the director of the 1998 independent film *Smoke Signals,* was one of the first people I met at New York University. It was our first year in the graduate film program, 1993, and I remember being perplexed by our first conversation. Chris's sense of humor was so deadpan it was hard to know if he was kidding. I soon learned that he was more often kidding than not. In fact, Chris's humor is a big part of his films. Even the most tragic of his characters, the alcoholic Mogie in his feature *Skins* (2002), finds things to joke about as his health deteriorates and death is imminent. Chris is an optimist, and this is evident in the characters he creates. They are resilient and never give in to despondency. They share their pain with family and community, often using humor to lessen the ache, and in that way they persevere—just like their director.

Our first year in the program at NYU, Chris made a short film called *Searching for Cheese.* It was a strange, allegorical film having something to do with a mouse that had all of the answers to life's questions. Although I never quite understood it, it was clear to me and to anyone who saw it that Chris had talent as a director. The film showed that he knew where to put the camera and how to move it dynamically. Visually, the film moved forward effortlessly. In his second year Chris found his subject matter with the film *Tenacity.* It was his first work about Native people and the first of many of his subsequent films to take place on the reservation. In *Tenacity,* two young Native American boys playing with BB guns find themselves in a game of chicken with a rowdy group of white kids in a 4×4 pick-up truck. One of the Native American boys stands his ground and is hit by the truck. The final shot of the film is from the truck as it speeds away, passing rusted-out cars abandoned along the roadside. The small, dark figures of the boys recede into the distance. Framed by the old cars, set on the reservation, this memorable ending is a powerful metaphor for the destruction and desertion of one culture by another.

Tenacity screened at Sundance in 1995 and got the attention of Robert Redford. Chris was invited to the Sundance Filmmakers and Writers Labs, where he and writer Sherman Alexie workshopped material adapted from Alexie's short story collection, *The Lone Ranger and Tonto Fistfight in Heaven*. The project that evolved was *Smoke Signals*. It debuted at the 1998 Sundance Film Festival, where it was awarded the Audience Award and the Filmmaker's Trophy. *Smoke Signals* was released to critical acclaim by Miramax and grossed over $6.5 million. It was the first major theatrical feature written, directed, and starring Native people.

Chris Eyre on the set of *Skins*.

A couple years after graduating from NYU I began teaching in the School of Media Arts at the University of Arizona, which coincidentally is where Chris received his undergraduate degree. In November 2004 I invited him to talk to our students and to screen *Edge of America*, a feature he directed for Showtime in 2003. The interview in this chapter is a compilation of three talks. The first was done in person the day after the 2004 presidential election, during Chris's visit to Tucson. The second and third interviews were done by telephone in December 2004 and May 2007. As a whole, I feel that the interview, in particular Chris' thoughtful and at times humorous comments, gives much insight into this imaginative director committed to telling stories about Native Americans.

YURI MAKINO: A few years ago I was developing a project based on a friend's story about a young Mexican woman who is a migrant worker and gets deported and jailed. I spent many years doing research on the project. A lot of issues came up about race. For example, can I as a non Latino person tell this story? Other issues had to do with expectations that people have of me. I often pass; some people think I'm Latina.

CHRIS EYRE: That's interesting. You have the same thing I have, which is a cross-cultural context for seeing the world. You can see that vantage point where people are quantified and how people are treated. There is a polarization where people love me for my ethnicity, or they think I'm less than human. I can have dinner with Robert Redford, fly home, and in the air something happens at 35,000 feet, which is the perception that the world has of me changes. Because when I go to rural America—last year, while I was standing in a supermarket with my wife and daughter, a woman looked at me and said, "If you are going to use food stamps, you've got to go to the other line." What is the impetus for you to look at me and decide this is something nice to say? That kind of polarization is what informs my work constantly. We're not homogenous Americans. So it informs all the time, every day and, well, it's not a big throw that you're an artist. It's not a big reach that you're expressing yourself because of your acculturation. People ask me all the time, "Are you just going to make Indian movies?" Honestly, the movies that are interesting are Indian movies. And that may sound preferential, but it's true. I mean, how many boring, stupid, dramatic stories can you see about white people? They've all been done! What's interesting is to see people you haven't seen before doing things and being in situations or conflicts that have been applied to other people. That's what interests me, because they haven't been seen, they haven't been done on a large scale. I'm happy with what I do. I don't quantify

Yuri Makino, director of *Alma.*

it in terms of I've got to tell a story about non-Indian people. I read a story and I get emotionally attached to it or I don't. Stories that I get emotionally attached to are stories about something. And when they're about something and they involve Indian people, then I'm driven to try to make them. That doesn't mean I wouldn't make a story about other people, but I don't get those scripts. I'm not sad I don't. I've become more cynical over the years because I understand the audiences better. In the years that I've been working—and I've made six features now—I realize that the audience I cater to is a minority and a thinking class, and it is a class that cares, and that's where there's some validation.

YM: I noticed, after watching your film commentary on *Skins*, that you give recognition to all the people in the film by saying who they are and their contribution to the film. I thought that was unique in the sense that most commentaries talk about the shots and the conceptualization of the film. It's clear you have a relationship with some of these people and it's not just about the end goal of having a product that is going to somehow further you.

C E : It's not uncommon for any ethnic group of people in America to understand community. That's what makes us different: we understand the concept of community, not as a generalization or as a term but as an extended family: "This person is a part of me." We have a responsibility because America is built on a separation of communities that don't interact. They draw lines and have their etiquettes. But when you talk about an inside community, I can't get away with not being personable with people. You can find this [mentality] in Asian, Hispanic, Indian, and black communities; we make minority films, but it's really about us as a family, not about us as people that were hired on to just work on this one [film]. . . . It's very personal. That's what the word *community* really means: all of us are tied together. The thing I think ethnic filmmakers understand—filmmakers like Mira Nair or Spike Lee—is that we are responsible for the community of people who come to help us. In the case of *Skins,* this is about a group of people who have been disenfranchised from the American dream, and if I am portraying them, then I have a responsibility to them. It's not just a story. I am interacting for the story. Community is a sacred and important thing. When I say, "That's James Yellowshirt. He let us shoot in his house," I know how much that meant to him.

Y U R I
M A K I N O

Y M : Does it ever make you mad that there is this responsibility?

C E : It's enriching. So no, not at all. It's totally enriching. It's like all these people feel a connectedness. . . . That's the thing about America: we don't understand our connectedness to each other. We don't understand that we are connected to the people of the Middle East. It is foreign to us because we are ignorant. These people are connected to us, meaning we have to be responsible as a participant in our own humanity for our actions with and against other people. It's as simple as when there are no jobs for people, people steal. If you are taking every glass of water in the room then I am going to try to also take a glass of water for my own family. . . . that is an oversimplified understanding of the [Middle East] conflict with Republicans. It's like, do you understand that these people don't like you because—you see, the message of 9/11 was (and we missed this message), it's the school bully. Why is this kid acti[n]g out? Why is this kid coming in the classroom and shooting other kids? Because he's been abused by us! In the Middle East and in other places in the world, we are the people taking every glass of water in the room.

And you expect them to just lie down and die? We are all connected. And that is the component that is missing in a lot of America. You are connected to those people and your actions are connected to those people and you have to be responsible, as distant as you are. You have to realize that these people are you. If you want to be a true Christian, you have to realize that these people are you.

YM: Does it ever bother you that you are held to different standards than white filmmakers, in the sense that people are going to look at you and talk about you in a much more critical context than a white film- maker who's making films that are purely entertainment?

CE: It's luggage that I've taken on. I wouldn't be happy just making purely entertainment, so it's like, it is what it is.

YM: But you could be choosing different stories. You could be making stories that wouldn't put you in that light simply by making romantic comedies about rich white people.

CE: We as a country need to be kicked, because if you want to be a true patriot, patriotism is not waving a flag on your porch. Patriotism is dialoging about how to improve where we are and what we have. Some people are threatened by that idea, and that's intriguing to me. It's like, I'm the true patriot when I made *Skins* because I'm challenging the idea of our history. Why is it that at the end of the movie, I make this guy, who is upset, want to desecrate George Washington's face? If you don't understand that connection and that history, then I think we're losing. We're losing being a vibrant, progressive community of our own. It's about dialoging to make the system better. I mean, California will have more Hispanic people than white people, and so will Texas, but at what point will the white people in those states accept that? Chris Rock said it best when he said white people are saying they're losing their populace and their right to go to college to minorities—and he responds, "If you're losing, then who's winning?" And that's the truth! White people are not victims. So get over it. The system is created for them in this country. And that's fine. But the point is, let other people have some equality without thinking that they're radicals. We're not radicals. This country, when we start to pat ourselves on the back for how progressive we are with race and religion, is at a huge deficit. If we're going to be one of the superpowers of the world—and I think we are—then we need to always examine ourselves and always improve ourselves.

YM: Did you ever feel like . . . how do I describe this? Let me just tell you in terms of myself. Sometimes I might attend a function or be somewhere with exclusively Asian Americans and feel disconnected from my father's Japanese culture. I feel at times like a little bit of an imposter, because it's a culture that I'm connected to but I didn't grow up with the traditions.

CE: Well, for me—I feel like an imposter to other filmmakers; I feel like an imposter to white people; I feel like an imposter to Native people. It's out of personal self-respect that you have to ultimately say, "Hey, this is who I am, where I am." I was working on that when I entered graduate school. But at a certain point, it really doesn't matter, because there's nothing I can do about it. So, as far as being an imposter, I've always felt like an imposter. . . . I'm ultimately a hybrid, but so is everybody else. The one thing that I don't do, because I feel it would be counterproductive to my own identity, is I don't, under any circumstances, qualify myself.

YURI
MAKINO

YM: What do you mean?

CE: I won't qualify myself to people. For example, people might say, "Well, you didn't grow up on the reservation, so that means this." Or, "How long have you known your biological mother? Doesn't that mean this?" I could, like anybody, destroy myself by qualifying myself by what I know, what I don't know, where I came from, how long, how much blood quantum . . . that qualifying of yourself is really dangerous. Sometimes I relish the fact that people want to qualify me because it makes me stronger, because I know that I don't have to do that for anybody. I'm really good at lobbying my position and my perspective. I can slice it a myriad of different ways: I'm more Indian than you because my mother has more blood quantum than you. Or that it's all based on the DNA and genetic memory (which I do believe in). Or my mother, being a real Indian, was so oppressed and poor that she did give me and my sisters away. I can slice it a myriad of different ways: by pointing out that I know this many Indian words, that I've been to these ceremonies, or that I pra every day—whatever it comes down to. But if I'm qualifying myself, or letting other people qualify me, there's something wrong. People ask me the question, and it depends on who's asking me. Because I understand what they're implying and asking. It's not like I haven't had India people ask me a leading question.

YM: Basically asking how Indian are you.

CE: Yeah, without asking. Anyway, I think there are always differen parts, and ultimately, as I was saying, I always feel like an imposter. I r ally have to try to appreciate what I contribute. I know there's a place fo me, and there's a place for what I do. It's a matter of becoming a better person at what I do, a better filmmaker. But, you know, there's a place for what I do. And I think that evolution was something that I understood, but I really wasn't going for it until I got to graduate school. It was at the end of our first year [at NYU]. Because our first year we were all kind of walking around going, "Huh?" And by the end of our first year I was like, shit, I just got to accept what I have with me and in front of me and believe in it. And believing the idea because—one of the attributes of *Skins* was, regardless of your perspective or your belief—we tried to make something. That's the most valuable part of being an artist: believing in what you're doing and going for it.

YM: Let me ask you about the word "Indian" itself. In your film *Edge of America* there's a scene where the two characters have an exchange. The actor James McDaniel refers to Irene Bedard character as "Native American," and she says "Indian," and before he walks out he corrects her and says, "black" because she's called him African American. What's your sense of the word "Indian"? In academia it's very PC to say "Native American." Is the word "Indian" used in the same ways that different cultures or subcultures and ethnic groups use words to try to take them back?

CE: Oh, definitely. I mean, I don't think it's been taken back. I think hat, probably in my vacuum, it's the groundwork for taking back (because I'm not so sure it's been taken back yet).

YM: I feel like it's still an insider word within the community—

CE: That's what I mean—maybe it hasn't been taken back yet.

YM: Because it seems like within the community people will use the word "Indian," but for me on the outside I would feel uncomfortable using that word.

CE: Let me put it this way: what makes the word derogatory?

YM: I guess it's the initial mistake—that Native Americans aren't from India. I am wondering where you think the word "Indian" is at this point in its evolution.

CE: I don't know any Indian people who call themselves Native Ameri-n. I know that Indian people do, but they might be in academia or seums—I do know that (and I probably wouldn't hang out with them).

YM: It's interesting that a word carries so much weight. I like the terms Native, Native peoples, indigenous. These words float around and seem to have less attached to them. And I think words transform at certain times, and some words have more weight than others. It's a really great point in the film because it gets at the complexity of identity and calling yourself anything (and what people from the outside call you) and claiming your own.

CE: It's a great line—she says "Indian." And he sits there for a minute and goes "black." Great line. Because all of a sudden you realize they're not part of the political correctness, status quo, "Überculture." They're two groups of minorities. They really are alike.

YM: Tell me about *A Thousand Roads.*

CE: That's an interesting movie because it's a slice of life, like a short compilation. It's kind of fun because the shorts are what we used to do in film school. It's like taking a short idea and trying to find a storyline in it. It's hard to do that in a short because it's, well, short. It was the same problem with *A Thousand Roads* in that I had to try and figure out a storyline to follow and hold on to. We shot in Alaska, Peru, New York, New Mexico, and Vancouver, and I think we found it. I hope we found it.

YM: What was the unifying theme?

CE: They're unified by this voice—I guess it's a storyteller. I say "I guess," because you never see the person. He talks over images of beautiful landscapes and nice, lush music. He becomes the voice of a storyteller who's soothing and knowledgeable, even patriarchal, who ties everything together.

YM: Does he talk in between and set up the stories, or is his voice commenting on the story directly?

CE: For the most part he talks in between and links the stories together, but whenever we needed it, he would help the story. For me, it was a real different experience because I'm used to a story, at least in concept, being told through the things you decide to shoot and not the exposition of the dialogue. Because it was a voiceover situation he is literally used as a device to move the story forward, which is taboo in narrative features. Ideally, it should be visual and should have a subtext but in this case, because it was a short, we leaned on it a bit. I was alwa conscious of it and felt slightly, "Ugh, isn't there a better way to do this? But in the end I think we came to a happy medium.

YM: How did you come to this story?

CE: It came through my agent. At the time, they weren't ready to make the movie because they were working on the screenplay. I didn't get involved because they didn't have development money for the screenplay. They had two writers and a myriad of consultants (because every time you do a Native project everyone feels like you have to have consultants for political correctness, and that drives me nuts). There is this convention—and I'm not saying I'm opposed to it, because it needs to be there, given the history of movies and the representation of Natives—this pervasive idea that for the movie to be real and authentic, they have to have Native consultants. It's not a bad idea, but for me, it's very laborious, because some Native consultants don't know anything about filmmaking and some non-Native producers don't know much about Natives. I tend to be that person who bridges the gap and says, "He's not saying we shouldn't do that, he's saying this," and "We really need to ask about this." That's been a role that I've happily taken on. I do think Hollywood productions should have people who are more knowledgeable about what it is they're representing than a writer in L.A. who just has an interest. In this case, they had a number of Native consultants because it was made for a museum. About a year later, I checked back with a friend of mine, Rick West, who is the director of the National Museum of the American Indian, and he said that the script was done. I read the script again and thought it had come a long way, and enjoyed it, and started talking to the producers, and they hired me.

YM: Did you work with the writers? What was the process?

CE: I always work with the writers, regardless of a credit or not. There are things that you're going to want changed in terms of sensibility or in terms of vision, and that's always a process of working with the writers. And there's usually a point, when you're getting into the agreement, where you know how amenable they are to making changes. Anybody who's protecting their investment—meaning anybody who's hiring you to be their director—is going to want you to put your input into the screenplay. If they don't want you to put your input into the screenplay, then you really can't care about the movie and they really aren't serious about you and your vision directing the movie. I've never had a situation where they haven't wanted me to make changes or they were apprehensive about me making changes. In this case, I added scenes and took some scenes out, but I stuck pretty close to the dialogue while we were shooting. Then again, there's not a lot of dialogue in this movie—that I am really happy with and proud of.

YM: When did the movie premiere?

CE: It played at the 2005 Sundance Festival for its world premiere, then opened at the National Museum of the American Indian in Washington, D.C., after that. It will play for, I hope, ten years or longer, every hour on the hour. We've calculated that literally millions of people will see this movie, which is pretty exciting for a theatrical run. I'm sure millions of people have seen *Smoke Signals,* but that's on videocassette and cable and available theatrically and worldwide. But this is unique because it will be all theatrical—it will be exclusive to the theater.

YM: Did the fact that this movie is screening in this venue every hour for ten years bring any special considerations?

YURI
MAKINO

CE: Everybody was thinking about how to make this movie progressive, in the sense that it is a movie about Native people, and if it does play for ten years it's going to be a little dated—and we didn't want it to feel dated. So I think the universal theme that we talked about is "eclecticness," because Native people are diverse economically and socially. So our best safeguard against becoming dated is the eclecticness of the movie. Then again, as far as props go, it'll become dated. We did pay attention to that. We had them playing video games like "Star Wars," and in ten years I'm sure that stuff will be dated. The cars will be dated. The clothing, too, but those were things we couldn't do much about. The universal aspect that makes the film timeless is its eclecticness. People are always interested in the wealth of human experience and other peoples' conflicts.

YM: I don't know anything about the stories themselves but I would imagine that the stories try to represent different classes and groups of Natives all over the world.

CE: Yes, that's right. That's the idea. It's about Native people in the Western Hemisphere. We picked the Arctic Circle, Point Barrow, Alaska. That's the story of a little girl who's about ten years old and is being raised by her mother, a single parent, in Seattle. Her mother is called up for active duty, which is one of the changes I made while we were looking at the script because I thought it was timely, and because Native people per capita have served this country more than any other group of people in America. So the mother goes into active duty and the little girl is shipped to her mother's mother in Point Barrow, Alaska. It's a foreign world to her where they ride snowmobiles and everything's frozen and there are polar bears and whales. She goes through some hard times, and her grandmother tells her she's always connected to them and this is her history. The girl eventually starts to enter the community, but she misses her mother. So she has a conflict: she's being brought back into her cultural skin, but she misses her mother.

The stories are all vignettes like that. The one we did in South America is about a healer in the Peruvian Andes who gets a visitor who says
his son is sick. They take a three-day journey across the mountains till
they get to the village of the sick boy. The boy's father and mother are at
the bedside, with the sick boy, and the healer begins to work on him with
herbs and traditional medicines. He goes through a day and a half of
trying to heal the boy, and in the end the boy dies, which is a real shock
to a lot of people. The healer then leaves—he doesn't know what to say
and is broken, just like the parents. In the end, after he leaves the boy, he
goes to Machu Picchu, the home of his ancestors, and starts to pray. The
story is really about the healer's trial. Although his practice didn't work
in this particular case, it doesn't alter his ideology and his culture. The
story is about his having this history and this culture, and the culture is   *An Interview*
not perfect.   *with Chris Eyre*

YM: It avoids romanticism, that Native healers are going to be the
answer to everything.

CE: Right. The eclecticness of *A Thousand Roads* is what makes it
human rather than something that's going to falter with time or over a
ten-year run. It has a lot of observations like that. The storyteller says,
"We have songs for everything: for breathing, for healing . . . we give our
songs to the earth . . . sometimes it doesn't feel like she hears us at all."
It's a kind of poetic vignette. And the films are all shorts; they're only
about seven minutes each.

YM: How do you usually work with actors?

CE: Until recently, I didn't realize what the trick to good directing
was. The trick to good directing is hiring good actors. As a grassroots,
low-budget, independent filmmaker, you don't always have access to
this. But it can't be overstressed. As far as working with actors, they say
that 50 percent of making a good movie is hiring the right actors. It's
really true. I don't have much rehearsal time, which makes casting that
much more critical. In the case of *A Thousand Roads*, I had no rehearsal.
To make matters even more difficult, these were real Indian people.
So we had to have an English and Spanish translator and a Quechuan
translator.

YM: This was for the Peruvian story?

CE: Yes. It would have been better if we could've found a translator
who knew Quechuan, Spanish, and English—but we couldn't find
one. . . . So I didn't rehearse with the actors, but they turned out some
of the best performances in the movie. The guy we hired to play the

healer was a healer. So he understood, even when we were translating, what we were going for. It was a visual thing. I just had to make sure that he could get to a certain place, and I did that with him in the casting session. Once I got him to that place, I earmarked it. I asked him through the translators, "Now do you know how you feel emotionally?" He said yes, and I said, "That's where you've got to get to when we shoot the movie." Then I'd go to my polite threats: "You promised me you'd get back to this." And then, "If you can promise me—because I know you can do it—to get back to this place and remember this place, then let's do this together." And the healer, and the father, and the mother, and the boy turned in some of the best performances of the whole movie. That's ironic, given the way we were working. They got it—they totally understood what we were doing dramatically.

YURI
MAKINO

YM: What were some of the things you had him do when you were casting to find out if he could do the role?

CE: I have two things that I do. When you're casting and you cast based on type and quality, you know if it's a non-actor the quality is going to be just a reflection of their reality. It's not going to be the quality of an actor. It's going to be, how real is this? And then the type, the guy has a look. It's one of those things where it just has to be. So types go out real quick, but once I get down to working with them on quality, or their being real, it's really about two things, which are (1) how much imagination do they have and (2) what kind of concentration do they have. I use those same principles when I'm casting kids. You have to know how much concentration they have, and that almost takes care of itself, because if you bring a kid in and he's not listening, no matter how good he looks, I'm not casting this kid. If he is listening, the longer you work with him, the more you're keeping your ear to the ground regarding how well he is concentrating. What is his attention span? If a kid can hold up for twenty minutes, he's got a great attention span. If it's five minutes and he's losing his attention span, I can't take the risk. So concentration is a big one. But imagination is also important, because if you say to any non-actor or kid, "Can you imagine this?" or "Do it like this" or "Can you play it like this?" and they say, "What do you mean?" that's not going to work either. So imagination is important. Usually with non-actors I have said, "Can you tell me a story or something that happened to you that's scary?" And they'll tell me a story and I'll say, "Let me see you do it without explaining it." If they say, "What do you mean?" that's fine. Then you say, "Just act it out without talking." Once you take away all that verbal stuff from them, some people really can do it in an imaginative way—using the room or whatever

they have—and some people literally keep looking at you for approval.
These are all important determining factors in their creativity, their
imagination.

YM: How about actors like Graham Greene and when you worked with
Eric Schweig on *Skins*—did you audition them or did you know they
were the actors you wanted because they fit the roles?

CE: Based on who they are you know what they're capable of. If you
research a person, even if you don't know their work that well, you kind
of know what they've done, who they are, what their best work is—and
Graham is somebody I am very proud of and have total confidence in.
He's a seasoned film actor, not to mention an Academy Award nominee.
Eric and I and Graham had some rehearsals before *Skins,* but really it's
about giving your thoughts on a certain scenario and letting them do it.
You talk in broad strokes about how to achieve something rather than
micromanaging. If they want to do it a certain way, the other thing to
realize is that it's their character. When I hired Graham to do the role of
Mogie, I don't think anybody else could have done it better. We rehearsed
Skins for three or four days. It was more of an understanding of each
other's thoughts on scenarios or situations, how to make something a
little bit more what we wanted it to be.

An Interview
with Chris Eyre

YM: Have you ever gotten pressure from the outside—from producers
or distributors—about your casting choices? Has there ever been
a situation where there was a conflict about who you were going to
cast?

CE: No, because they aren't big studio movies. So I haven't had that
problem. Probably with a big studio movie—if you're spending a certain
amount of money, tens of millions of dollars, you get into having to
insure the movie with a marquee name, and I think that's when you get
into that.

YM: What are you working on now?

CE: I'm doing a show for PBS, specifically for *The American Experience.* It's a collaboration with Rick Burns about Tecumseh, a Shawnee
leader. His idea was to band all the Indian tribes together to fight off the
colonizers' encroachment. He died on the battlefield. It'll air in 2008 as
part of a five-part series on historical tribal leaders. I'd also like to make
a period piece on Sitting Bull. That would be something new, because
I've never done a historical, Native drama. That's one of the things
that really excites me—portraying observations and ironies and digging
yourself out of a situation. For example, portray a Native leader who I

have never seen portrayed in a contemporary movie—and then have that pressure of writing a history about that person.

YM: When you say "digging yourself out of a hole," do you mean facing a new challenge?

CE: Making a movie about Sitting Bull would be a huge responsibility because I don't know a movie about Sitting Bull. It would be an opportunity to write the history—and that's a huge responsibility. That's what I mean by "digging myself out of a hole." And it's exciting.

Conclusion

YURI
MAKINO

Reconnecting with Chris through these interviews was a very gratifying experience for me. As a filmmaker who cares very much about how and who I represent on the screen, I was encouraged hearing that these are also his concerns. I wasn't sure how Chris's success would shape the decisions he's had to make as the single most important Native American filmmaker today and one of the few independent filmmakers working consistently in Hollywood. What compromises would my former classmate need to make to further his career? From seeing Chris during his visit to the University of Arizona, it was clear to me that his commitment to his community was genuine. Chris screened *Edge of America* to a packed house of 500 people, including a couple hundred exuberant high school kids from the nearby reservations. After the film and an extensive question-and-answer session, Chris patiently took the time to greet the long line of people waiting to talk to him. For an hour Chris signed autographs, smiled for the camera and responded to questions from his fans. Chris was exhausted after the long day but seemed compelled to make himself accessible to his audience. Connecting with people and making them laugh, sharing a sense of shared community, is how Chris feels most at home.

PART 5   TRUE HOLLYWOOD
STORIES

CHAPTER 13

"And Maybe There Is a Way to Give Hollywood the Kick in the Ass That It Needs"

AN INTERVIEW WITH FILMMAKER
KARYN KUSAMA

Dan Rybicky
(Columbia College, Chicago)

I first met Karyn Kusama in 1996 when we were both working as assistants to writer-director John Sayles (*Lone Star, Passionfish, The Brother from Another Planet*). We had recently graduated from New York University's Tisch School of the Arts—I from the Graduate Dramatic Writing Program, she from the Undergraduate Film Department, where her thesis film, *Sleeping Beauties*, won a Mobil Award in 1991. We lamented the paucity of soulful films being made in America, shared our similar but different family tragedies, and quickly became very good friends. A couple of months later, Karyn left the position to make her first film, *Girlfight*, about a young Latina (Michelle Rodriguez in her first role) who starts training to become a boxer. The film went on to win the Director's Award and, along with Kenneth Lonergan's *You Can Count on Me*, the Grand Jury Prize at the 2000 Sundance Film Festival.

On April 16, 2005, I attended the first-cut screening of Karyn Kusama's second feature-length film, *Aeon Flux*, which was released into theaters by Paramount Pictures on December 2 that same year. *Aeon Flux* marked the first time that Karyn had worked with a major Hollywood studio, directing a film budgeted upward of $60 million. The film, based on a popular animé shown on MTV in the 1990s, is set 400 years in the future, when disease has wiped out the majority of the population except for one walled, protected city-state, Bregna. The story centers on Aeon Flux (played by Charlize Theron), the top operative in the underground rebellion led by a character known only as the Handler (Frances McDormand), and her determination to wrest power from the leaders of Bregna, who are determined to control every aspect of the city's inhabitants, including their imaginations and their ability to create new life. But underlying this desire to destroy is the lingering question as to whether or not Aeon might have been in love with one of these leaders at some point in her unremembered past.

Karyn was born and raised in St. Louis by an Illinois-born mother and a Japanese father, and her artistic sensibility mixes meat-and-potatoes Midwestern pragmatism with an Eastern love of beauty and design. It is this combination that helped make *Aeon Flux* such an endlessly strange, aesthetically compelling viewing experience for me. Although I saw a first cut in which neither the music nor all of the special effects had been put into place, the movie is visually striking and tonally challenging in ways that most movies set in the future (especially those made in Hollywood) never are. Instead of creating a darkly lit environment of steely grays and high-tech cars, Karyn captured the total otherness of the animé series by not only having no cars whatsoever but setting most of the film in daylight. Her mise-en-scène

is a juxtaposition of angular cement structures dominating fields of colorful flowers and natural patches of green, appropriate for a film dealing with man's desire to control nature at all costs. This is just one of the provocative societal themes explored in *Aeon Flux*. A more personal one, which reveals itself through the relationship between Aeon and one of the leaders of Bregna, deals with Karyn's belief that, as she says in the course of our discussion, "Love itself wakes up parts of your brain that I don't think anything else does."

Karyn Kusama at work with cinematographer Stuart Dryburgh (left) and production designer Andrew McAlpine (right) on the *Aeon Flux* set.

The following is a slightly edited version of the interview I conducted with Karyn in her office on the Paramount lot two days after that first screening.

Stuart Dryburgh with his trusted light meter.

DAN RYBICKY: What made you choose to work in film instead of another medium?

KARYN KUSAMA: I had a highly emotional life in a lot of ways as a young person, and I think I ended up finding movies as a sort of sanctuary or as a sort of imaginative taking-off place that other arts forms weren't necessarily doing for me as strongly. I was interested in poetry and poetic forms of literature when I was growing up, but there was something about the possibilities of movies—the fact that you're its audience, whether you're sitting alone in a theater or in a packed theater, there is some kind of communal experience with the work. Unlike reading a book for half an hour and putting it down or looking at a painting and walking on, it is a one-and-a-half-, two-, two-and-a-half-hour experience that you have to commit to. I like the rigor of that. And, ironically, it is a pop form. It's a populist form of entertainment, or it can be. And I think I just found a way into storytelling through how movies were put together. There were a lot of formative movies while I was young.

D R: Like?

K K: The original *King Kong* was important to me just because it was such a crazy story made both as a popcorn movie and as one that was also quite moving. It had so many undercurrents and reflections of the fears and anxieties that were motivating culture at that point, and it still reflects fears and anxieties, particularly in relation to race and class. For me, it was really meant to be a movie where you have your soda and popcorn (or whatever the 1930s' equivalent was) and it is a communal public experience—that was very important to me, and I still think there is magical stuff in the storytelling of that movie. And then just seeing some of the first David Lynch movies, and seeing some of the best of the Altman films and the best of the Kazan films . . . there were so many kinds of movies. And then to get to high school and to start seeing movies from other countries, and start seeing current foreign films and going back and looking at Japanese films. Sometimes I'm influenced just by a sequence, or a shot, or a moment, or even by the whole puzzle-making of an entire film. I just started seeing the possibility of filmmaking as a living opera that, more than any other art form, was doing what opera did in its heyday, which was to heighten an experience of art. Even the storytelling itself can be quite heightened if you create a formal context that is very theatrical. And movies can do that. Movies can actually go there. I don't think they go there enough, or with enough balls, but they can definitely go there. And that is really exciting to me, that you can put an elevated level of emotion or intention on the screen. People get invested in that. We are pretty cynical in a lot of ways, so it's nice that there is something naive about filmmaking. As corrupted as the medium has become, the urge to make movies still feels very innocent.

D R: You went to NYU. What were the first stories you wanted to tell?

KK: I feel a bit simple in saying this, but a lot of the stories were very much about what I was experiencing in college as a young adult. They were very personal. I did some personal documentaries about an unstable group of friends in my life. The group itself was unstable, and the individuals were unstable. That was an attractive groove for me at the time. When I imagine those friendships now, I think, "Gosh, I'm glad I depicted them as I really experienced them then." Now I would look at them very differently, and I would look at my interest in chaos very differently. But it was that wildness of youth that I wanted to depict and to explore. There was the beginning of an interest in subconscious yearnings and angers and envies, and all of those things that I didn't realize I wanted to explore but I was exploring. I still hope I can make work

that feels unconscious in a way, because now that I am an older, perhaps slightly wiser, person— it's a double-edged sword to be that. What I like about some of the work that I did when I was young, as rough and awkward and crude as some of it was, is that it's completely unfettered by an intellectual consciousness of the work.

Karyn Kusama on the set of *Aeon Flux*.

DR: *Sleeping Beauties* was the first film you made that was a nondocumentary film?

KK: Actually, I made some silent movies in school that were still very experimental in feeling. The experimentation was really great for me, and I still go back to some of the things that excited me about that time period, whether it was Jonas Mekas or Stan Brakhage or Kenneth Anger or Vivienne Dick—all those filmmakers who were doing different things to push our expectations of movies. But at a certain point, I realized I wanted to take a stab at telling stories, and that was a shift I didn't expect.

DR: It's interesting that you started the interview by talking about *King Kong*. I've always said that a "spoonful of sugar helps the medicine go down." In a way, you've got to have something to hook people into what you're trying to say. For you, what was the shift?

KK: It was a personal and also a long-term ideological shift. The personal part was that people very close to me started to die. I began to see

sort of honor in the simple trajectory of a narrative that has a beginning,
middle, and end. Even though there may be questions and ambivalences
and ambiguities within those beginnings, middles, and particularly
the ends, it's still a form that people connect to on a gut level, on an
instinctual level. In many ways I was resisting the gut level because, in
retrospect, it was the youthful snobbery of not knowing any better. As I
get older, I'm learning that stories and the timeless elements of certain
stories are the things we keep returning to and still try to learn from.
It's an ongoing process that never ends. There are stories we need to tell
over and over again because we don't learn everything we need to learn
the first time around. That is what makes us animals. We can't just jump
to a higher level of understanding or cognition. We just can't. I struggle
with it, but there was a point when my life became more urgent and I
wanted to make statements that had some emotional weight, and would
also challenge the audience's collective emotional life.

An Interview
with Karyn
Kusama

DR: You mentioned earlier that you reached a point where you wanted
to make statements. What were the statements at first? As a teacher,
I often tell my students that understanding the theme of your project,
even in retrospect after several drafts or even after making your film,
can help you hone in on what the look of the film will be, and everything
else. The form will serve the function if you understand what that is.

KK: Yes, definitely.

DR: What were the first statements, even looking back now, if you
weren't conscious of them at the time? Was your first script *Take Me to
the Water?*

KK: Yes, *Take Me to the Water*. That was the first full-length screenplay I wrote. When I look at it and know it was the first movie I desperately wanted to make, and that I had *Girlfight* on the backburner brewing
as I was trying to get money for the first movie, I think of this movie and
visible X and *Aeon Flux* . . . it almost sounds pedestrian, but I do feel
that what I'm trying to get at or what I'm trying to explore in both life
and work is, to what degree are we as individuals and as a species capable
of changing? To what degree can we affect transformation within our
lives as individuals and also as a bigger living organism? Over the years
I've become increasingly uncertain of our chances for survival. I don't
mean to say that in an alarmist way. But I think that the signs are fairly
clear. It may not be in our lifetime or our children's lifetime, but we are
looking at extinguishing ourselves soon. What is that urge? What is the
urge to destroy oneself? What is the urge to destroy others? I keep going
back to it in various ways, whether it is in the Midwestern road movie

[*Take Me to the Water*], or the social realist boxing movie [*Girlfight*], or the semi-sci-fi body horror film [*Invisible X*], or something that is almost closer to straight sci-fi, which *Aeon Flux* I suppose is. I feel we are very ambivalent about our life urge. Getting in touch with it is its own trans-formative process. The fact that we want to be alive, the fact that some-times we don't. . . . I am starting to think a lot about that. This concept of existential crisis is real whether we want to say so or not, whether we respect the intellect or intellectual minds that brought those ideas into full articulation. But the fact is, regular people every day struggle with whether they want to be alive. Maybe it's not even a conscious thing, maybe I am making big assumptions about people. But evidence would support the fact that as a local society, as a bigger society, as a global society, we are obsessed with death and destruction. I think art in a way from the beginning of time has been exploring that. I am just another Joe doing that.

DAN
RYBICKY

DR: Do you feel there is any distinction between how women and men would view this? How did you end up with women in your stories?

KK: I could argue on the one hand, it's what I know. But that is a bit limiting, because I'm not sure how well I understand any woman's life beyond my own. That frees me to say if that's true, then I need to invest myself emotionally in and explore men's and women's lives as a whole in storytelling. I guess I have always been somewhat unconscious of my interest in stories with female characters. On an intellectual level, you could argue that stories with female characters are in and of themselves somewhat radicalized because we consider narrative such a masculine form. If I am going to talk about my identity as a female, however, or what the difference is between masculine and feminine as concepts, perhaps it enters more in the mix with me in how I approach form. For example, I am more interested in the circular version of a story than the linear version, and more interested in open endings than in closed, certain endings. I like the incidental moment as opposed to every detail driving the story. That might drop me into a more female idea of the world. But again, that to me is more honestly about shapes, energies, col-ors. I don't look at it in terms of ideas so much because even the concept that are easy to label as masculine, such as power and dominance, I am fascinated by and I explore over and over again. Maybe it is a call and response between concept and female identity. It is that line in between that interests me.

DR: Does it have anything to do with how one gender adopts qualitie more commonly associated with the other gender? Your films, at leas

Girlfight and *Aeon Flux*, deal with strong women, or women finding their strength, and yet trying to keep some of those qualities that we are told are masculine ones.

KK: Sure. That's definitely a component of the ongoing discussion with the world. In my mind, the feminist discussion or the feminist problem is vital because it is a humanist discussion and a humanist problem. It is profound right now because we are at a moment of visible crisis. Which isn't to say there hasn't been a visible crisis from the beginning of our existence, but our arrogance in recognizing it and doing nothing about it is most troubling. We can know what is happening halfway across the globe, whereas one hundred years ago, even fifty years ago, that was much more difficult. But we can know within fifteen minutes of investigating it through various technological means, we can understand some scope of what is being reported across the rest of the world. That is a new level of consciousness that we are not capitalizing on very efficiently. There doesn't seem to be much of an ethical discussion about access to the world and access to information. But we're all in this crisis together, and somehow the feminist movement or women in general or females as a concept, female as a concept, woman as a concept, has been about protecting the species, much more so than the men, in a way, and about being the watchdog for the ongoing survival of the species. I am sure plenty of men would say that is not true at all, but that is why the female lens right now seems so valuable. It would be valuable in any time period, but there is room for it to be sifted into culture without all the discussion. That was one of the more surprising elements of making *Girlfight*. In many ways, the narrative followed a traditional arc, and plunked itself into a traditional genre that I know and love. Yet, because the protagonist was a female who was in some way masculinized, though not at the expense of her femininity, there was a very big discussion for people. Beyond that, there was the discussion of me as the filmmaker and issues of my emotional makeup and my family history, and a desire to personalize or contextualize me as a filmmaker.

DR: How did that feel?

KK: I wonder if the urge is as great to explain a man's vision. No matter how well meaning, I question the motives of trying to explain work when we should be asking ourselves how the work works on us.

DR: I ran into a woman with a six-year-old child. She said, "I saw *Girlfight*, and it's the first thing I've ever seen that I want to show my daughter when she's old enough," which I thought was terrific. But what were you hoping to get out of this experience?

KK: I do have to say, and perhaps this is naiveté or oversimplification on my part, I wanted to make a movie with very simple—or you could argue blunt—themes. I had very plain hopes for it. I have to say, as much as I look at the movie and feel proud of what we accomplished—with the time, the money—and given my relative inexperience, the aims of it seem to be streamlined in a way. And maybe that served me really well, because in the end I just wanted to see a movie about somebody starting to live in their body, starting to feel their own physical existence and the power of that experience. That is a big theme in American life. It's big in all life: our obsession with sports. What we gloss over is the experience of knowing you're alive; we go straight for achievement, we go straight for success, winning, losing, and we get obsessed with time. The main-stream sports discussion loses the achievement of being alive at such a high level. And that was something really interesting to me for this character.

Rehearsing
Girlfight.

DR: And this character happened to be a woman. Was there resistance, and why? Did it have anything to do with the fact that it was a young woman?

KK: I think a lot of people would say, the lack of financing for the movie had nothing to do with the fact that the main character was a woman. But of course it did. Boxing is not an appealing sport to a lot of peo-ple, so that scared them off already, and the idea of a female boxer was very unappealing at the time. I think that something about her will to hurt and be hurt, the articulation of her will, was confusing for people. It's confusin to see men boxing each other, but seeing a woman want to be in the ring adds another layer of complexity. It was very difficult, actually. I do think the character being female was a short-term obstacle to the movie getting made, though it did get made eventually. The movie was about someone who has trouble communicating and has to learn how to go one step furth toward communicating a little bit better. I was trying to create a trajectory that was fairly modest in her character development because I believed th: was the most we could hope for. I know people go through major transfor-mation, but in the end, what happens to the character is seismic for her. F viewers, I hoped that the experience of seeing her change just enough to through life a little bit easier every day was a satisfying process.

DR: What were you hoping viewers would take away from the movie when you were creating it?

KK: I wasn't thinking about it at the time. There was an innocence to the experience that I hope I can retain. I was caught up in the making of it. What's interesting about movies is that, on the one hand, you are trying to put the emotional pieces of a puzzle together so that when you see the puzzle as a whole the audience says, "Ah, the pieces have fallen into place for me!" or there is some other unifying experience that leads to a reaction from them. On the other hand, as a filmmaker you look at it quite impersonally. You know the circumstances, the raw materials out of which it grew, and you know the frustrations and the egos and the agendas that went into it. It becomes quite a technical part of the process once I have gotten through the raw material and the shooting. How the movie is working becomes much more like, "Is this equation sound? Is this logarithm true?" It becomes a weird form of emotional math. That probably sounds a bit chilling, but you can only feel your way through as a filmmaker for so long, and then you have to get hard with it. In many ways, as hard as I felt I was with *Girlfight* and as hard as I feel I have to be with *Aeon Flux,* I still don't know how it works until it is in front of an audience. If I had shown *Girlfight* and viewers had said, "Wow, I really hate this movie," I would have accepted that, too. I would just have said, "Well, I guess you hate it. It works for me, but I have a different relationship to it."

DR: Do you feel your struggle to get the movie made paralleled the struggle in the film?

KK: Oh, yes. Marketing picked up on it and it threw me for a loop. I hadn't realized there would be a desire to market the movie by personalizing it and relating my story to the story of the movie. Then I realized, this is marketing, this is about creating a mythology around the work that will get people into the theater. I question whether that really works. Now, after the experience of my story being marketed for the film, I wish I could simply talk about the work as work. But I opened up my personal life, so why wouldn't others?

DR: Along those lines, one of my favorite directors, Luis Bunuel, said he was thankful he never had to make a movie with a budget over $500,000 because he would have too many choices. . . . You were saying that necessity is the mother of invention. With *Aeon Flux,* where there was more, did you find yourself having to pull back, almost as Americans do, from weighing 800 pounds because there are so many things. . . .

KK: So many Whoppers to choose from!

DR: So many Whoppers to eat! Did you find yourself having to say, "Look, this is what I want, and it doesn't matter that I can do it eight different ways and can spend eight gagillion dollars"? Were you conscious of it?

KK: I was conscious of it, but there was a balance that needed to be struck with the studio's desire to have a marketable movie with scope. The concept of scope gets formulated as "having choices." That means, *they* want to have choices. They aren't necessarily concerned that I have choices. Even if they don't mean to be insincere, they need that safety net: if the director is a disaster, if she has a nervous breakdown, if she becomes a drug addict or walks away early . . . all the things that can and do occasionally happen, they want to know they can take the movie away and make their own choices, which I would argue are often the wrong choices because of the fundamental gulf between commerce and art. Maybe that view is too polarized, but it's always going to be a challenge when you are certain of what you want, and you say, "This is what I want," and someone pipes up and says, "We're giving you money to spend on this extra choice." Sometimes it feels like a waste of time, and sometimes it's a great resource to have in a pinch.

DR: The studio can feel threatened by a creative team, which poses a challenge for the filmmaker. Do you feel that your being a woman has made it any different? Has it been harder? Easier?

KK: I will be diplomatic, because much is at stake for me. This is only my second film—it's quite a leap to go from a little tiny movie to a much bigger movie. That said, it is a much bigger leap for directors who have been responsible only for commercials or music videos that don't necessarily tell stories or have real budgets to get thrown into being accountable for (1) staying within some semblance of a budget and (2) much more crucially, telling an actual story. That is a leap that if I had half a brain I would question much more than "She told a really good story when it was a million dollars; God, she'll tell a fucking great one if we give her some resources." On the one hand, you could argue I've only made one movie, so that was part of the studios' fear, that's what powered the fear. On the other hand, if I want to get stone cold about it, being a woman doesn't make it easier when you walk into a room and you must engender confidence. It just doesn't make it easier. I wish it were different, I really do. As far as I'm concerned, the biggest difficult I have with this process so far is that part of why I got hired, part of wh anyone gets hired to direct a movie, is that you walk into the room and you're at least one of the smartest people in the room. It's tough to know that it's supposed to be the equation, but then there is this implication that others know better. There are people out there that "just know" how you can do your job so much better, yet they hire you to take something through to the end—which very few people actually want to do. People say they want to be directors, but being a director is a very hard and draining job and has many levels and stages. Yet somebody has to be the director! So, I am very happy about that, and I feel I'm actually pretty good at it. But I feel being a woman affects people's perception of your competence. You have to walk in and be dazzling as a woman. A lot of guys are frankly messes and still get the work, still get the paycheck, and still get the opportunity that so many more than competent, more than just middling-talent women don't get. I wish it were not so, and people are welcome to try to convince me otherwise. . . . I have thought about it a lot, and I don't feel confident that we are so evolved yet as a business, let alone an art form. . . .

DR: As a culture?

KK: As a culture, to be open to the fact that women come in as directors and demand all the things that their male counterparts do, and ultimately that they see the same level of opposition or submission. . . . I don't believe we're there yet. We're not there in terms of equality.

DR: Do you feel the women you have worked with at the studio have been more supportive or less supportive because you're a woman?

KK: Sometimes it's easy to say, "Let's cut the fucking crap." Then it's like two people talking to each other because there are so many women in this business who are themselves struggling with issues of power and of dominance, issues of who is in charge, issues of having a voice and wanting to be heard. That gets very messy, because it means two people coming at things from a similar oppositional position have to start talking to each other and helping each other, and that can be difficult, for many reasons. But I have had good luck with my female executives and all the women on my team who are just there for the movie. Which isn't to say that the men are not there for the movie. But the power structure is not used to a woman director walking into the room who is not wearing a power suit, doesn't have to get her nails done, and doesn't have the other costume bits of a "woman director" identity on. That's the thing that's great about being a director: you can show up to a meeting in jeans and a T-shirt because you're the director. I really enjoy that part of the process. But as a woman, it minimalizes me even more if I don't walk in with barracuda energy.

KK: Yes. I'm not a human torpedo. What is off-putting or confusing is that everyone expects a Michael Mann or Oliver Stone or Ridley Scott or David Fincher to walk in . . . there are all kinds of mythologies about male directors who have strong opinions, who can be kind and compassionate or utter dicks, but somehow get what they want. But there isn't a huge amount of precedent for women directors to walk into a room and walk out again having gotten what they wanted and needed to get their movie made. So when I go into a marketing meeting and I say, "It's really important that we don't ignore XYZ in our campaign," people are surprised that I'm speaking up at all. Believe me, I will protect the movie at all costs, and if you think I am any different from all the directors that you are scared shitless of when they walk into the room, you're wrong. Because soon you will need to be scared of me, and I'll have to show you that, unfortunately, if it comes to pass. I don't walk into the room aggressively, which may make me different, not necessarily from all male directors, but some.

DAN
RYBICKY

DR: And *Aeon Flux* came about. It is a huge leap for you. It is extraordinary to see what you have achieved at this larger level. I'm astonished by it. You were living in Brooklyn and you were given this project. What interested you about this project when you got it?

KK: Well, it's funny. I never thought I would read a story like this and say, "Oh, my god, I need to direct this movie." But what I loved about it was that its imaginative properties were advanced and refreshing. For every sci-fi moment when we needed to tell people where we are in this world, there was a moment that was a little more mysterious. It was imagining a world where people communicated telepathically through pharmaceutical boosts, where science had evolved so that all the stuff we talk about now was heightened so much more. But on a thematic level, the question of life necessitating death, of death being a crucial part of our animal existence, crucial to our having any sort of transformational consciousness, drew me in. If we don't address the patterns of life or death, and if we start to fuck around with that a little too much, or if we start to deny its gravity in the culture. . . . Westerners, Americans particularly, are alienated from accepting that we die and how we die. By being that alienated, we don't confront how much death and destruction we actually participate in. We just push it out of sight and mind. . . Even though *Aeon Flux* felt like it was solidly working in a sci-fi tradition, there was something about its lack of hardware . . . it wasn't one of those rainy all-nighttime apocalypse movies. It was actually quite bright and idyllic. There was something very familiar about that to me. It was very timely, and the world portrayed didn't seem far from the world we live in right now, with the refreshing exception of the lack of cars.

DR: Why do you think you got the job? What did you want to bring to filming it?

KK: One of the first things I talked about—and I'm sure it sounded pretty snotty of me—is that movies are not beautiful enough. They are just not good lookin' enough, and they should be. That's the great thing: you can train your eye on a subject and always find room for the pure pleasure of aesthetics. There are a lot of great filmmakers that I love that might argue with me. Particularly in sci-fi we are so accustomed to the gray, rainy, dark, apocalyptic world. Great movies have been made in that tradition, but I thought, "God, what's so awesome about *Aeon Flux* is that you can create a very beautiful surface of a world and start to peel away at it." On an aesthetic level that was really interesting to me, so I prepared a lot of imagery for the studio to say "here is my concept of the past," and "all these books here are reference books," "here's a direction we can go with weapons," "here's a direction we can go with furniture," "we should feel light and never see where it is coming from." We just started talking in those kinds of ways about the story. There is an incredible level of existential romance to the story. That is very unusual for this genre. It's just unusual to have what I felt could be a moving examination of love as a transformative energy. Love itself wakes up parts of your brain that I don't think anything else does. I tried to show them the movie in terms of at least the references that I drew from in thinking about it. I thought really specifically about architecture and about how to make this movie, now that you've seen at least an object that exists. This was banging around a long time as an unmakeable script. Because it was a movie that would be very easy to make for around $200 million the way it read originally on the page, or $150 million, or $100 million. When I first started, our initial budgets were $110 million, and that is not what the studio wanted to spend on such risky material. I had to imagine how to do the movie very practically. I had originally suggested to shoot the movie in the capital of Brazil, which is Brasilia. No one had heard of it, so I showed the pictures and said that to me, this was the landscape of the film. It just helped to set the tone, even though we didn't end up shooting in Brasilia; it helped set up the shapes of the imagery. It was really about the tension between a very hard sense of line and an obsessive use of circularity. I suppose it is easy to argue that a pretty obvious kind of symbolism. But to me it was a tension in the movie that would be supported by that kind of aesthetic.

DR: There is a tension between looking and feeling modern and also having an Eastern influence, and also—beautifully with certain colors and moments—almost a sort of *Logan's Run* aspect, which creates its own tension and makes the overall aesthetic into something that I believe really good art is, which is uncanny. I find there is an uncanniness to what the aesthetic is, which is what I look for, the unspeakability of it. They were into it?

KK: They were. I think what they were into was that I had no chance of getting the job in anyone's eyes. And I came in and I said, "Look, I know I have no chance of getting the job, but I would like to show you what I would do with the movie." And I talked about the script in detail. I said, "This needs to change and this needs to change, and I think we can really work with the strength of this storyline and this trajectory and on this theme and why don't we amplify that. . . ."

DR: Then you came out here and were working with the screenwriters. What do you feel your addition to that process was?

KK: Sometimes it was literally talking about plot and saying, for instance, "I really think Oren and Trevor should be brothers. I think it would thematically solidify the movie." Or, at the time, "I really think we should lose the flying cars, because in my mind this culture shouldn't have any cars." And "What if Bregna wasn't just a city, but a walled city, where, once you were there, you couldn't escape because the natural world had become its own force to be reckoned with now that we are much more frightened of the power of the natural world because it's been unattended to for four hundred years?" When you think of one percent of the human population or less flocking to one little area of the world because they've heard there might be a cure to a food-borne illness, and they all stay there and survive and procreate, what if the rest of the world became unnavigable and uninhabitable? It became that thing about the themes of nature and human nature and how they're opposed and how they're similar—all of that stuff having narrative manifestations. That was a fun thing to work on. For me as the director it was nice to work with the writers to clarify the direction of the tone. Initially, there was stuff in the script that was much more in tune with the animated series—more quips, more jokes—and to me the story couldn't handle anything too lightweight. Once it took off, it needed to be as serious as the world it was imagining. So we shed that tonally imbalanced stuff.

DR: What kind of character is Aeon Flux?

KK: Morally ambiguous. She is sort of like a human spider, a big, strange-looking, hard-looking, angular beast . . . and there is somethin very sexy about her, very sexual, but also something quite cold. She is interesting because her body is a magical thing, she can do so much with herself. The series is quite experimental, it would be fair to say. At the end of every episode she dies. There is a lot of interesting formal stuff that it's doing, that kind of format for an animated series—it was really trying a lot of interesting things. So we hoped in adapting it to a longer form with real people playing those characters that we could riff on things that were happening in the series by actually making them part of the story. For instance, the mysterious open-ended Aeon Flux dying in every episode and miraculously being back for the next episode was something we attempted to address in a larger way in the scope of the story of the movie.

Karyn Kusama with *Aeon Flux* script supervisor Trudy Ramirez.

DR: Were those concepts in the script? Was that storyline there of the pregnancy? And Oren was trying to kill off the people?

KK: Yes, it was. We made t much clearer that there was his personal vendetta that Oren ad against the chaos of nature, r the order of nature, but the rder was beyond his control. e made that a lot clearer. The regnancy became important n the plot level because, when I first read the script, it brought to mind ur natural inability to truly grasp a great many simple concepts in life. ife and death, being and not being, choice and no choice, voice and no ice. There was something about the pregnancy that was also about how man nature wants so much to create order in the world. And there are ings like pregnancy, for instance, that remain so mysterious to us. As uch as we understand its mechanisms, there is stuff about the world at is still so mysterious.

DR: And unknowable and uncontrollable. And what's been interesting in general in talking to you, I know I have been taking this gender angle. . . .

KK: I like that, the "gender angle."

DR: But when we talk about it, I know what you're getting at is that obviously a female eye to you is in some ways not only necessary but in this culture also important, because we've heard other stories so much that there is still a desire to hear more stories from more women, without a doubt just in the spirit of balance. So again, it's very interesting in this film that Oren, in a sense, is killing women.

KK: Oh, yes, it's very clear.

DR: Is there an underlying sense that women's ability to give life is being taken away?

KK: Yes, and a sense that that ability to give life is very frightening in and of itself. And I still believe that. There is something subtle that we worked into the movie, where when Trevor is in the Relical space and he calls up the test group that Una was in, and he sees all these faces staring at him and he starts to put together that they've each been murdered. There is this sense of gravity to me about one lone man looking at these women's faces and knowing that they're all gone. We are not at all alienated from that experience. When I think about it, wars in general are exacted on men and women in very specific ways. With women you sexually humiliate them, then kill them; with men you kill them, then rape their wives and their children and kill them right in front of you. The dehumanizing thing of war—it sounds like a big lofty idea, but I was hoping to do something small with it. Sometimes you just need to see faces to understand that death is not an abstraction. It is an actual, real, material experience.

DR: Your desire seemed ultimately to bring in this masculine structure. Why was that? Is that again in the spirit of balance? You can understand the cyclical quality of things, what was that?

KK: Well, it's just been something I've really been thinking a lot about. Lately, I've been thinking about Don Seigel, and how he made some really interesting movies by committing to genre. In his case, he was pretty macho about it. He was really good with westerns. He was really good with crime and vengeance movies. He was really good with sci-fi. You could probably argue that *Invasion of the Body Snatchers* is one of the great science fiction movies, one of the great movies of all time, in terms of the questions it asked and still asks about us as humans. He wanted to make movies that reached people, but he was very shrewd about how important it was to put the cloak of genre on what was in front of people so that they were comfortable on the way in. And then he started to make people less and less comfortable. And genre is the masculine tool that I would like to experiment with to exercise my eye, exercise my voice, because I don't know if there is any such thing as a purely feminine or masculine voice. I'm feeling like there is a way to find the masculine and feminine strains of yourself in your work, and to me I like the classical Hollywood narrative. It can be great. They're just so often not great because it's very hard to do. It's very hard to tell a good, satisfying story. We are less and less interested in stories in filmmaking anyway. It's always a challenge to tell a story that's engaging and challenging and maybe leaves something open to the imagination of the viewer. So anything I can do to flex those instincts to express something personal. . . . Lately I've been wrestling with the idea that I've been drawn to frankly Hollywood movies. But if that means I stand a chance at telling a story that actually reaches people and does sort of slip in through the back door with interesting themes or subversive politics, I'll do it. Because I really think in a way, genre say, for instance, with sci-fi is the thing that lets everyone sigh a breath of relief and suddenly feel like, okay, we can talk about a totalitarian government, or we can talk about the concept of disappearances, we can talk about a culture in which there is no sort of articulated complexity. All of a sudden that is doable.

An Interview with Karyn Kusama

DR: In terms of funding this film and the future of funding, what kind of influence or control have funding sources had over cultural and gender representations in your work?

KK: Well, for instance, if I am going to make *Aeon Flux* at a studio, could have been asked the question, "She's going to be sexy, right?" It was very clear she had to be sexually attractive. She had to be a sexual fantasy. And it was also pretty clear—and it's still a war I feel I have to fight with the studio—everyone believes that teenage boys are the audience you need to cater to first. That means that everyone else gets second fiddle, and the teenage boys don't get great work in front of them either, given the way the studios view them, which is awfully sad for them. It was really important that everyone be attractive. Before we cast Charlize, there were many names in the air, and much of the casting process revolved around whether three guys in a room thought she was sexy. It's as if their fantasy was the only thing that really mattered.

DR: What about the editing or marketing? Is it the same kind of thing: will the poster show what kind of babe she is?

KK: Yes, that's really important. People are pretty craven. Short of using the words, "Is she fuckable?" they come very close.

DR: Interesting. Two last questions. What effects, if any, are you hoping viewers will walk away with?

KK: I remember when you asked me about *Girlfight*, "How did you expect people to feel about it?" and I said I didn't know. What I learned is that it is an interesting experiment to have an idea of what you want people to walk away from a movie feeling. In this case, I hope people think about themselves differently in terms of their own mortality and ask themselves if there are currents or fragments that their life offers them that seem related to another period of time. Is there a sense that we may be each more than one person? Is there a sense that we are capable of more than one life? Is there a sense that we are part of a trajectory? I guess I would love it if people looked at each other after the movie and felt they were humbled by the unknowable.

Girlfight's Michelle Rodriguez (right) and Karyn Kusama (left).

DR: Instead of scared of it?

KK: Yes, yes! Maybe, in some secular way, reverent about our animality, our animalness, our aliveness—reverent and honoring that. Again, in a secular way. It is not within the framework of organized religion that I am talking about souls or energies or reincarnation or any of these things that do pulse through the movie. I just hope that people look at each other with more forgiveness.

DR: In a sense, it's not just to be humbled by the unknowable but to approach the unknowable with hope instead of with fear, which is such a huge problem right now.

KK: It's just huge! I guess I would love it if people walked out and felt freer to imagine their life in transit, freer to imagine that that's possible free to imagine that they are still living beings capable of change. It is easy to believe that we are stuck. And it is easy to actually be stuck.

DR: And to be excited by the prospect of that change instead of being just plain terrified. What do you want to work on next?

KK: I am in a little bit of a genre lust moment right now. A part of me would love to go on to another movie that was big and challenging in the same way that *Aeon Flux* was. So, there is a sci-fi thing kicking around, much more overtly political than *Aeon Flux*, that interests me. In general, I am interested in what pulp is to people, how you can mak something that feels just shy of trashy feel like it's ripping your guts out. I want to experiment with that. . . . Soap operas and pornography are the most exciting things happening in our culture right now. Is there a way to take the melodrama, soap operas, porn films, action movies—to take those corruptible forms and corrupt them with my own sensibility? I use the word "corrupt" in a very loose way. But is there a way for me to infect denigrated forms with my own sense of politics, my own sense of hope, my own sense of lyricism and personality, and bring a sense of identity to those genres that is often missing, which is why we consider them trashy? I guess I feel that high art is not reaching people right now. And it goes in cycles. And maybe there is a way to give popular entertainment a real kick in the ass. It needs it.

Cut to April 14, 2007. I spoke with Karyn almost two years after our first interview to fill me in on what had transpired in the interim.

In June 2005, Karyn screened a second cut of the film, incorporating the concerns and notes of the studio, the producers, and her creative team. This time the film was screened in front of, as she put it, "more of a test audience." The people in power at the studio seeing the film at this screening were "basically a completely new group of people—the third administration to take over creative control of Paramount" since Karyn had become involved with the project in preproduction.

"Because they were seeing the film at that late a stage," Karyn told me, "they didn't feel any particular investment in it, because it really represented a previous regime of executives. And I think the attitude toward the film after the testing process was very negative. People were very, very scared of what the movie in this form—a form that at least I could stand by—was. I was encouraged to what is diplomatically called 'take a step back.' " This ultimately meant that her main editor and composer were fired, and the lead producer, Gale Ann Hurd, was told by the new administration to do her own cut of the film.

Karyn spent the summer overseeing the addition of visual effects while Hurd and the new editor she hired did a completely different cut of the film. Karyn was somewhat aware of what was going on and would have attempted to be more involved, but she felt the direction that the new regime, under the new president Gale Berman (formerly the head of Fox TV), wanted to take the film was "so not the right thing to do" that there was no way for her to be supportive of the process. "It was a very difficult time for me because I felt so certain that there were elements of the direction they wanted to go in that completely undermined the original intentions—everyone's original intentions—of what the movie should be."

Why did the studio want to recut it? Karyn says:

There was a set of twin fears: one, is the pace too leisurely? and two, is the film too emotional? And I think when we had originally all been talking about the movie, the fact that it was a love story was key to setting it apart from other films of its kind. The fact that there was an emotional component that was actually satisfying was a really important part of the equation. So to prep and shoot and cut a movie toward that end, and then be told, "That's the thing we want to get rid of" . . . well, it was basically like they wanted to cut the heart, or the brain— or the brain-heart—out of the movie.

DAN
RYBICKY

The people I was working with would completely disagree with me. They would say that members of the test audience said they didn't like the romance, that it was too sentimental. But you have to believe in the testing process to even take those results seriously. And, for me, I used the testing process more to really figure out when do people just not understand at all what's happening, who the key characters are in relation to other key characters—and when is that not a good thing.

The most important part of the testing process to me was to see when the movie didn't have emotional weight. The studio, on the other hand, saw this as an opportunity to "fix their broken movie." I don't think that kind of situation is ever helpful. The fact is, I shot a certain amount of footage, I shot a certain kind of footage—and I was told over that agonizing summer, when the movie had essentially been taken away from me, "Well, Karyn, you've got to remember: it will still be your movie." But what they were looking to do [by recutting it] was to make a completely different movie from the movie I wanted to make. I liken the shots that you have available to use in a film to an expansive alphabet of sorts. You can take twenty-six letters and spell the word "love" or you can spell the word "hate," and those words mean totally different things. It's still the same alphabet though, right? So basically what the studio was saying was, "It's still your alphabet, now we'll just be rearranging the meaning entirely from the movie you intended to make." That was a key disconnect that did not register with the studio. And if it did, they might have had second thoughts.

But, Karyn says,

I don't think they really cared. There was a very brutal, incredibly dismissive attitude toward the film. A lot of that had to do with posturing, because it's very important for a new administration to distinguish itself from the old administration, and that involves rejecting most of the movies that were developed during the old administration's regime. It doesn't benefit you to support the movies from the old administration because the industry at large says, "Well, if it's a success, it's because something was working about the old administration." And if it's a failure, you can still blame it on the old administration and kind of prove your worth by letting everyone know there's a good reason that the old administration was replaced.

Karyn says the new administration wanted to make the movie faster and colder and less emotional:

But instead of saying "colder" they would say "cooler." They wanted it to be a "cooler," hipper movie. But in my mind, the footage was never there to make the movie they imagined. It just wasn't that kind of movie. I'm not saying the movie doesn't have incredibly cool sequences and fresh ideas. It does.

The movie that the first administration loved that I pitched to them was like a daylight noir, not one filled with steely rain and gray surfaces and all night. There were already so many movies [like that]. I thought, why not depart from that kind of paradigm and try something a little bit different? I said right from the start that this would be a movie in which there are no vehicles, that this movie would be anti-hardware, that technology had advanced to the point where it was purely organic. People really responded to that on an intellectual and emotional level. They felt, "This is fresh, we haven't seen this before."

But in making the film less romantic or emotional—and, of course, ster—Karyn thinks, "part of what this third administration was do-g, even if they weren't aware of it, at least you could accuse them of —I do—was to make the movie a disaster. I think there might have en some shred of an instinct to ruin the movie as a self-fulfilling ophecy, so then they could say, 'look what a failure the old adminis- tion was, what a shitty movie they produced.'"

Looking at it now, Karyn feels the movie she made is so signifi- ntly different from the movie that was shown in the theaters that e still grapples with the fact that the distributed movie exists with r name on it at all.

Why? She says:

The film was reconceived narratively so that huge chunks of story that help you understand the tone of the world, some of the gravity of the issues at hand, and the emotional height that the film could reach—all of those narrative elements were excised. For instance, things that give you a sense of that world are gone—gay characters were completely removed. And everyone said, "It's not because we want to remove gay characters." But in fact, the studio people repeatedly said during the recut, "What are we gonna do about the gay guy?" So I do feel there was a desire to destroy anything that made the world more distinct. That included an unapologetic freedom in sexuality that was a very important part of the original series. In general, anything that anyone felt vaguely uncomfortable with was removed. If you take any movie out there and randomly test it, I think you'll find lots of things make lots of kinds of people uncomfortable. That's the nature of art, or the nature of any text, whether you think of it as art or not. So there was a very mercenary attitude toward how to treat the strengths of the film. It was as if the whole conception of the movie were turned upside down, and the strengths of the film became its weaknesses and had to be addressed as problems, when in fact those were the things that everyone should have been fighting to preserve because the people who would innately like the movie and liked the series would want the romance, would want to feel emotionally satisfied, would not be threatened by characters who might be gay or have uncertain sexualities. They would appreciate the epic tone. All of that was excised in service to "please more people." But in doing that you end up appealing to no one.

DAN
RYBICKY

Ultimately, Karyn feels *Aeon Flux*

was always a weird, fringe title and a movie that was not necessarily easy to sell in any environment with any amount of money. And what they did was make it as hard as it could be to reach the people who might have appreciated it the most. I would say that characters being gay, characters genuinely falling in love—the entire Aeon and Trevor storyline—was watered down to a steely "couple on the run" narrative thread, as opposed to an epic romance that you felt had somehow survived centuries of misery and centuries of self-deception. And granted, this is not necessarily a storyline or a movie—even in the form that I would have been most proud to have it seen in—for everyone. The movie was never meant to be, for instance, a shoot-'em-up action movie. But what they did when they were recutting was look at all the second unit footage. So every time a gunshot goes off, every time somebody gets killed—there was just an *obsession* with making action sequences feel bigger than they actually were ever meant to b

Or if there was an action sequence that in my opinion was designed to be operatic and function on a more existential level—in which you're watching characters move, watching bodies in space, and it's not so much about a constant exchange of gunfire—all of the stylistic choices on my part to make the action more distinctive were removed. Huge plot issues that tied into a bigger thematic thread about the concept of life asserting itself in the most stunted conditions, particularly expressing itself through pregnancy—all of that was cut.

At the end of what Karyn describes as "an agonizing summer," the studio screened the movie everyone thought they wanted:

That movie was eighty-two minutes long, which isn't even long enough to release into the theaters as a feature—and it was . . . I mean, one executive who shall remain nameless said to my agent, "You know, I really hated Karyn's version of the movie, but I think I might hate this version even more." That was his vote of support! I think what they realized in attempting to reconceive the movie once it had already been shot by a director who had a point of view is that they had dismantled nearly everything about the movie that might make it marginally make any sense. Storylines were eliminated, completely switched around in order—whole new chunks of voiceover were written that made very little sense, although ironically they had been written to explain everything.

Although Karyn thinks the movie that was eventually released is still fairly incoherent, she thinks it's fair to say that the movie they recut and screened at the end of the summer was "a complete fucking mess."

After giving lead producer Gale Ann Hurd nearly four months to produce such a disastrous cut, they gave Karyn two weeks of working round-the-clock to try to fix what she had broken. "It's a very hard thing to realize that, as much as I wanted to try to make the movie better, at this point there was a 'losing battle' feeling about the whole thing because the studio was so stubbornly attached to certain ideas that I just thought didn't work fundamentally and still don't think work fundamentally."

Karyn spent every waking moment of those two weeks working with an editor whom she hadn't even hired, someone whom the studio had hired but with whom she had a good creative relationship and liked a lot as a person. But the studio was nervous. Every producer and two studio executives—a total of seven people—would sit in the room with her while she worked with the editor. "They said to him, 'Don't ever be alone in the room with her,' as if I was going to hypnotize him! Honestly, I think the fact that I might develop a good relationship with this completely new team that was hired to be averse to all of my ideas scared them. They literally had to keep watchdogs on me at all times. It was so truly, truly small and sad to experience. Very sad."

The movie that ended up in the theaters, according to Karyn, "was probably about twenty-five minutes shorter" than the movie she would have distributed and, even beyond those twenty-five minutes being cut out, she says that "almost every single scene was, if not altered, actually kind of mangled in some way."

Karyn says the film "wasn't a huge success theatrically, but it did do business and certainly wasn't a failure." It has done very, very well on DVD. But one of the things they did, as she said, "to put the nail in the coffin" was pull all of the critics' screenings so that no critic could see it before it opened. There were no reviews in the paper on the Friday the film was released. Karyn: "That was a way of saying to the critics, 'we have a stinker on our hands that we're so embarrassed by that we're pulling it from you, and you can now decimate it.' And many critics didn't even write about the movie. They wrote more about the fact that they didn't get to see it in their usual professional environment and how pissed they were about that. It was very petty, because they had to go to an actual theater and see it with regular people."

I asked her what she learned from the experience. She said,

> There's a quality to working in the studio for the first time that oftentimes for me felt a little bit like a kind of unconscious hazing process, and part of that was tied in to the fact that I wasn't necessarily always so flexible with the number of people one had to answer to. The sense of always having to address your movie as a product was actually difficult for me. I didn't understand that what I really had to do was spend more time putting on a happy face, and that that's part of the process. It's a very gifted social animal who knows how to both work that system and get a movie that they're proud of out of it. And don't know if I am that social animal. I think that's probably not one of my strengths as a director, which could be very damaging to me i the long run. I always took people at face value, which turned out to be a big mistake. I always assumed that we were all in this together and that the power hierarchy was ultimately meaningless, because i sort of is. But that was a big mistake, too. I was naive about how the system really functions.

Karyn says she wouldn't change the way she directs a movie or tempts to creatively conceive of it all the way through to the end. Bu interpersonally, the pecking order is really distinct in a studio system situation, and the pecking order is one of status. I treated everyone the same, and I don't think that served me very well. I'm ultimately not looking to kiss anyone's ass—and I wouldn't do that in the future—but next time, I would probably be more cautious and more mindful of people's perceptions of their own roles in those kinds of studio environments. If people feel like they're the big cheese and their title is big cheese, I guess you just have to let go and treat 'em like the big cheese. That's just how the system works. I guess I was just more optimistic that we could all get along both personally and creatively. I just didn't realize that that was not so easy to do in this environment.

Dan Rybicky at work.

Has she given up? Thankfully, no. "I think sometimes you can make a movie in that system and be really successful and make a very interesting movie. I think those movies tend to have at least on the surface a more pop sensibility. For example, *The 40-Year-Old Virgin* is sort of a triumph of subversive comedy reaching the masses, but that movie had a real hook, which is a forty-year-old virgin."

Karyn still does believe that there are smart people at all of the studios and has no doubt they are capable of trying to push through interesting work. But the experience has definitely influenced her. "I think the movies I want to make now would probably get made at lower budgets and in circumstances where there's at least an attempt made to preserve some kind of creative voice and creative consistency in the process."

I asked Karyn if and how *Aeon Flux* has affected her career.

The fact that the movie was basically dumped by the studio and that they telegraphed some notion that the movie was a failure to the outside world—I don't think it helped me. But I also feel unless you are part of what's viewed as a colossal failure—or unless you're part of something that's viewed as a colossal success—everybody else falls into the same pool. Ultimately, I'm just another person that wants to keep making movies as opposed to fighting an uphill battle every step of the way or walking down Easy Street. I don't know many people who walk down Easy Street, but, you know, I'm certainly not one of them.

If Karyn were to make a movie in the studio system again, she says she would just want to be sure that the movie she wanted to make had that same sort of pop element as *The 40-Year-Old Virgin*, what she calls "a more accessible component," so she wouldn't go into it feeling like it was an uphill battle every step of the way. "With *Aeon Flux*, I probably went in there with a fairly brainy surface. I mean, I like to talk about ideas, I read books and look at art. I like to use what I read and see as references in how to talk about a movie. And I think the first adminis-

tration responded to that. But by the time we got to a third administra-

tion, I was just perceived as an intellectual or a snob. And in the end, I don't think there's any shame in being intellectual. And, as for being a snob, I think I just have high standards. I don't think that remotely makes me a snob. I think it's much more snobby to assume that audiences are just plain stupid and need to be spoon-fed every detail of a movie or they'll just walk out catatonic and ask for their money back. That, to me, is snobbery."

So maybe, as Karyn told me two years ago, there is still a way to give Hollywood the kick in the ass that it needs. But based on her experience of making *Aeon Flux*—and the troubles that ensued between production and distribution—it seems like Hollywood and the studio system are still doing their own share of ass-kicking. Unfortunately, it's the directors and the audiences—as well as the films themselves—that are hurting from the bruises they leave behind.

CHAPTER 14

From Selena *to* Walkout

AN INTERVIEW WITH

MOCTESUMA ESPARZA

Kathryn F. Galán

(Executive Director, National Association

of Latino Independent Producers)

"When you struggle against something, you grow," says preeminent Latino film and television producer Moctesuma Esparza. Growth and struggle define Esparza, a first-generation Chicano from East Los Angeles who has become an esteemed businessman, filmmaker, and Latino advocate.

Those who know Esparza's work think of him as the man who brought us *Selena,* with the then explosive new talent Jennifer Lopez, or as the producer behind *Gettysburg* and *Gods and Generals,* plus great HBO films such as *Introducing Dorothy Dandridge, The Disappearance of Garcia Lorca,* and *Walkout,* directed by Edward James Olmos. Some know of his work developing the Sundance Institute with Robert Redford, and his support and training of new Latino/a film, television, and documentary makers through the National Association of Latino Independent Producers, or NALIP, an organization he helped found. He is an activist involved in the education, business efforts, and media representation of the Latino community. Through these accomplishments and others, Esparza has defined himself as an agent for social change. His strategies for positive impact on and in his community keep him grounded in a difficult profession and serve as both challenge and inspiration to a new generation of filmmakers.

How would he characterize his approach? Audacity. Fearlessness. willingness to fail. I spoke to him in his office at Los Angeles Center Studios in the summer of 2005 as he completed his twenty-ninth feature film, and as NALIP began its seventh year as an organization that supports the professional development of Latino/a film, television, documentary, and new media makers. Esparza has long coached filmmakers to cultivate their own capacity to persevere, to withstand rejection, and to stick to a course without concrete results, sometimes for a very long time. A visionary who continues to make commitments that keep him focused on his path, Esparza spoke about his journey and his plans for the future, reiterating his challenge to students and colleagues: *Do the impossible.*

KATHRYN GALAN: You have just completed production on *Walkout,* an HBO film that draws from activist and media experiences that occurred at the very beginning of your career. How did you begin your journey as a film producer?

MOCTESUMA ESPARZA: I started off in the entertainment industry as a political activist, as an organizer for the Chicano movement and the Chicano student walkouts. I was eighteen years old, a freshman at UCLA, and my job was to act as liaison with the media for strike committees that were organizing student strikes in East Los Angeles. It was 1968, and I came in at the culmination of four years of conversations and efforts to impact the public schools in a positive way. The problem was an over 50 percent dropout rate, a devaluation of Latinos in the schools and of Mexican Americans in general, and a lack of Latino/a presence in the curriculum with respect to our existence in the country, or of Latino contributions to the history of this country. During these four years, we did surveys and asked questions of students, plus had communications with other organizations, such as US, CORE, and the Black Panthers, but no one else was paying attention to our particular situation: lack of educational access. Latinos were at the bottom of the barrel, and ironically, thirty-five years later, we still are. Latinos still have the lowest educational attainment rates, the highest dropout rate, and the lowest college participation rate per capita of all ethnic minority groups, with the exception of Native Americans.

KG: You graduated from Lincoln High School in East Los Angeles. How was your personal education, on the eve of this conflict, and how many of you went on to UCLA?

ME: I was one of four who attended UCLA; from an original class of over 300, only 150 in my class actually graduated. I had managed to take advantage of an excellent curriculum that was beginning to disappear in the early 1960s—Lincoln High School originally served a more Italian American population, and as it transitioned to being Mexican American the school district cut back on all of the arts in their budgets. I was a theater arts major in high school and loved the arts—I had been in plays as an actor, a singer, and a musician, and was also a photographer; I also wrote for my high school newspaper. So when I went to UCLA, although I became a history major, I had an arts background, so I was asked to be a media liaison by the strike committee. That led me to being the radio host of a show called *La Raza Nueva* for seven years—the voice of the

Chicano movement on KPFK Pacifica Radio. Everyone who was involved in the movement at one point or another in either a leadership or a cultural role passed through that program. I also ended up being a photographer for *La Raza* newspaper and on the editorial board. All of these elements led me back to media. Also, while I was a student at UCLA, I participated in a research study on the images of minorities in media. Of course, we were able to document that the images were virtually nonexistent, so we recommended to the university that there be more people of color in the School of Journalism, and in film school.

While I was there, I wrote a proposal to create a program called Ethno-Communication at UCLA, which for the very first time introduced a significant number of Asian Americans, Native Americans, African Americans, Latinos, and Chicanos to the film school. There were thirteen in the first class, and I became a member of that class of '71.

KG: As a film major with roots in history, you also had an interest in documentary filmmaking?

ME: Yes. For my graduate thesis, when I went back to UCLA to complete a master's, I made a documentary called *Five Lives* (*Cinco Vidas*, 1972) about five individuals in the barrios of East L.A. I was very fortunate with that piece: I sold it to NBC and won an Emmy. It grew out of my first student film about a moratorium protest against the war called *Requiem 29*.

KG: In 1970?

ME: 1970, August 29. There were a good fifty thousand people who marched in East Los Angeles, and the event turned into a huge police riot that swept throughout the community, the riot in which *L.A. Times* journalist Rubén Salazar was killed and that ended in the burning of Whittier Boulevard. That led me to graduate film school and my thesis. An African American professor, Eliseo Taylor, convinced me that, as an organizer, I already had the skill set to be a producer—I could organize projects, marshal resources, and get things done. What I had to *contribute* was as a producer, so that clearly became my career path.

KG: From early on, you saw your work at UCLA organizing the student strikes in 1968 as having potential for a narrative. What was it about the incident that indicated it might be a good film?

ME: When over twenty thousand students went on strike, this was really the spark for the entire urban civil rights movement for Chicanos. The event reverberated across the United States: there were strikes of Chicano students all over Texas, in Denver, in Chicago, and beyond. I knew then that we had done something that was historic. Early in my career as a filmmaker, in the early 1980s, after I began doing narrative films with an emphasis on historical material, I started thinking about making a movie about the student strikes. It's taken me since 1968—twenty-eight years—to finally get this movie made. It's been in development at HBO for the last five and a half years, and has been something that I have been pursuing actively for the last two years.

Until the country woke up to the fact, after the 2000 census, that Latinos were a major part of the economy and population of the United States, we continued to be out of sight and out of mind of all of the power centers of the country—media, politics, finance, commerce, culture. After the realization that we were a significant population, I saw there was an opening to tell this story. People needed to understand where we came from, and how Latinos were now in the crucial position of determining the outcome of elections and influencing the economy in powerful ways. Prior to that, the fact that Latinos were largely Mexican Americans concentrated in the Southwest put us outside the East Coast power centers of New York and Washington and the intellectual centers of Boston and Philadelphia. We were invisible to that community, invis-

KATHRYN F.
GALÁN

Walkout, produced by Moctesuma Esparza, chronicles his true-life story as an organizer for the Chicano student walkouts.

ible to the opinion makers, and, on the West Coast, largely ignored by
the studios and the networks.

KG: So you were here on the West Coast, amidst a Chicano concentration, and made the decision to penetrate media "invisibility" or lack of
representation through narrative storytelling. How did you begin?

ME: I was very fortunate in that I had several very impactful teachers
who guided me in this path, Fernando Flores being among the most important. Fernando is a philosopher and currently a senator in Chile, the
former Minister of Interior of the Allende government. I was his philoso-
phy student for a number of years in the early 1980s, and the key lesson
I learned from him was that I had to take responsibility for other people
listening to what I had to say. I had to learn how those folks listened and
then speak to their listening. To attain that, I had to learn their vocabulary. I had to learn the vocabulary of the entertainment industry, I had to
learn the vocabulary of finance, I had to learn the vocabulary of narrative
filmmaking in order to understand both the decision-making process
and the emotional process that those in charge of studios and networks,
who have the authority and power to give the financing I need to make
the movies I want to make, go through.

*An Interview
with
Moctesuma
Esparza*

Given that I had my own agenda, I now have a career of having made
sixteen to seventeen long-form programs, feature films, and scores of
documentaries and short films, almost none of which fit into the classical,
commercially viable, Hollywood mainstream genres. They have all come
from outside that context: an entire career. And I have achieved that by
listening for the openings and being able to present to Hollywood projects
and packages they could understand and were willing to make, because
I understood they had viability from Hollywood's perspective. So, to get
The Milagro Beanfield War made, I had to have a star—that was Robert
Redford. Having that star transcended the limitations of the subject
matter, that is, Mexican Americans in New Mexico who are struggling
to retain their land rights and their traditional way of life. That does not
sound like a very commercial movie! But given the extraordinary piece of
literature it is based on plus a movie star, I was able to get it made.

KG: You did that film through kind of a unique partnership, right?

ME: The first ten years of my career I spent making documentaries
and learning my craft. I then made a decision to move over to long-form
fictional or dramatic works. I made my first film with the machinery and
infrastructure that I had as a documentary filmmaker. It was called *Only
Once in a Lifetime*. I partnered with Alejandro Grattan, and it ended up
being a well-crafted movie that no one ever saw.

KG: Why not?

ME: Because we did not make it for an audience, for the market—we made it for ourselves! And I didn't understand that when I made it! It was a very rude awakening. And certainly, if there was an audience for that movie, we didn't know how to reach it. Plus, we didn't know that all of the marketers didn't know how to reach it either, which was more important. Even if we *had* known, if the marketers didn't know and the distributors didn't know, then that movie was doomed the day before we made it. So it was a very important lesson that I learned about making a movie for an audience that marketers and distributors could reach.

After I recovered from the economic debacle of that movie, I set about to build alliances because I realized that to be successful in a mass-market medium, I needed to have alliances with other people who agreed with what I was proposing to do and who supported it. I started with the National Council of La Raza. I went to Raul Yzaguirre, who was the executive director and president, and proposed to him that we needed to impact the country by changing the images of Latinos, by transforming our images from stereotypes to true, three-dimensional human portrayals. I suggested that we could do that by taking our literature and dramatizing it. NCLR assisted me in getting a grant from the National Endowment for the Humanities, and I went about seeking out the advice of many experts and confirming my feelings about specific literary works. We identified a number of literary works, from *With His Pistol in His Hands* by Américo Paredes (which became *The Ballad of Gregorio Cortez*), to *The Milagro Beanfield War, Chicano,* a novel by Richard Vasquez, *Pocho,* and a few other literary works. I set about to acquire the rights of those works and create screenplays of them so that I could then go about the process of packaging and marketing these to Hollywood to get them made.

Two of those five projects I was able to realize within a short period of time. By building relationships, by building alliances, by working with broad-based community organizations, and by following the established paths of getting material developed and produced in Hollywood, I managed to do what people had thought was impossible.

KATHRYN F. GALÁN

KG: Your interest did not remain solely with Chicano/Latino stories. Coming from a history background, you've also tackled some large non-Latino projects. How did you come to work on *Gettysburg* and *Gods and Generals*?

ME: After I produced *The Milagro Beanfield War* and *The Ballad of Gregorio Cortez,* I founded a partnership with Robert Katz in 1984. At that point I was developing a story about apartheid in South Africa, an

I met Robert through the writer-director of that project. Robert indicated that he could raise a significant amount of the budget from South Africa for the project, so we partnered on it, then, later, on a few other projects that he brought me, or that I brought him. Over a year's period, we established our partnership. What motivated me to develop the project on South Africa was a deep interest in portraying on film what it is to be human—what humans are capable of, what is both sublime and corrupt about human behavior—and through that to explore the human condition, which I thought was a further affirmation of creating human portrayals of Latinos.

In creating human portrayals, my ultimate goal was to study what it is to be human. As a history major, I had a tremendous interest in how we come to be who we are through the paths that we've taken. Reading the Michael Shaara novel *Killer Angels* was a powerful experience, and I desired to produce that movie. Ron Maxwell brought the material to us. Robert Katz and I immediately committed to it, so we became his partners, and together we worked to achieve it. Prior to this I had done a movie with Whoopi Goldberg called *The Telephone,* and one with Eric Roberts, Janine Turner, James Earl Jones, and Red Buttons called *The Ambulance,* so I had gone through the process of proving to myself that I could make a commercial genre movie that still had heart and social content. That led me on this path of becoming a filmmaker who focused on Americana history biographies—at this point, I think I am one of the most prolific, active producers in that genre.

KG: So it's pedagogical as well as about following your personal interests?

ME: Yes. Because I myself am learning about these themes and topics, I am able to explore how to present them to a mass audience.

Along with the lesson that I learned about producing a movie knowing that you have to have an audience, it was also very clear to me that film at its most successful is both art and commerce. All of my endeavors need to have both art and commerce together. Movies, to be successful, must entertain. That is, in fact, a very noble pursuit: to entertain. We all need to escape to other lives and times. The power of film is so profound that, in the deep recesses of our mind, in the cortex, the experiences on-screen are as powerful, emotionally, as the experiences in our lives. There is very little discrimination in what we experience in a dark room and the emotions we experience in our daily lives. It is cathartic and enlightening, and entertaining. The pursuit of that entertainment is very powerful and very worthwhile. So yes—I made a commitment to learn how to make movies that entertained and that also taught me about different aspects of the human condition.

> KG: In your biographical films, you took on a very commercial and successful idea in the Selena story, which, as I understand, was an exercise in excellent producing just to obtain the rights. How did you come to that story?

ME: Selena's death was macabre and fit the tabloid criteria for exploitation. As a consequence, I felt that if Hollywood was going to be interested in her story, it was going to be interested more in the sensational part of her death than in whoever she might have been. At first I was not really interested in pursuing it; my daughter, who is a fan of Selena,

pushed me, over a six-month period, to make a movie about Selena, to learn about Selena. She constantly sent me her music, gave me a documentary quickly made about her plus a couple of short biographies that were written about her. In reading and consuming these materials, I was convinced by my daughter that there was a story there. And that the story was a story of family—a family that was pursuing the American dream against great odds and that, through tremendous sacrifice, achieved this dream in the United States.

That story held a tremendous amount of dignity, honor, value, and affirmation for all Latinas, in particular, because this was also a story of Latina empowerment, of Latina independence from the powerful, patriarchal Latino father. Selena achieved all these things yet stayed true to her family. So that was the story that I became deeply interested in because I saw the ability to explore all those themes and present three-dimensional human images of Latinos and family to the American public. Also, to explore themes that were important to Latinos, such as the emancipation of Latinas and the breaking away from negative, historical quasi-cultural patterns that we hold ourselves in. So, after my daughter convinced me, I found out that Abraham Quintanilla lived in Corpus Christi, made a few contacts, got his phone number, reached out to him and wrote him a letter showing my interest.

At that point, Abraham had already entertained scores of offers, and I was literally the last person who called him. I discovered that he was already in contract negotiations with a very prominent Hollywood producer. What I chose to do at that point was to offer my services to educate Abraham on the industry, on what was possible and what could be achieved, and discover what his concerns and needs were. In that process I learned that Abraham was very concerned about the exploitation that was going on around his daughter: people stealing her image, her material, her songs, and making everything from T-shirts to pirate albums of her material to calendars—all sorts of stuff. They were a family under siege and in mourning, and they felt like everyone was trying to take advantage of them. What I realized was that if I was to make this movie and be of service to the family, I needed to do something that was completely unorthodox for a Hollywood producer. So what I offered to do was to partner with Abraham and give him full control and veto power over the script, the director, and the casting of the lead role.

KG: Wow, who let you do that?

ME: I just did it on my own, which is why it's completely unorthodox and not what people do!

KG: Not when there are millions of dollars riding on a production.

ME: Right. And so I basically gave myself to them as their resource person in achieving their goals, while maintaining the integrity of the process. I knew that, having done this, no studio would underwrite a movie where the life-rights holder had all of those powers. But I also knew there was a way to satisfy the studio, which was by going to them after I had attached a director, developed a story that the family approved, and come up with a group of actresses that the family accepted. *That* I could bring to a studio. So when I started marketing the project, I had reached agreement with the family about who would direct, who would write, and a group of actresses to play Selena who would be acceptable to Hollywood.

KG: How difficult was it to find that right actress?

ME: I had a group of actresses who were pre-approved, and we also had the option of finding someone who was unknown. We actually went through a process during which some eighty thousand young ladies auditioned for the role. Several of them were competent actors who had never worked professionally but ended up being in the final nine who did full screen testing. We went from eighty thousand to two hundred to fifty to a final nine. Of the nine screen tests we did, four were of amateurs. Of those four, several of them went on to have careers in Hollywood. I'm very pleased about that. We cast one young lady to play Selena as a young girl who had never acted before. We found her in the open casting calls in San Antonio. There was another young lady whom we found in casting sessions in Miami who had never acted before, and we actually cast her as Selena for a little while before we ended up with Jennifer Lopez. She ultimately didn't get the role, but she spent a number of months out here and became a professional actress as a consequence.

KG: While you've been working to transform images of Latinos in the culture, you have also done national advocacy work and activism for the community in order to impact the landscape at large. How did you come to find that we had a need for the National Association of Latino Independent Producers?

ME: In the 1970s and again in the 1980s, I was part of efforts to create national organizations of Latinos in media, and those efforts, for various reasons, were not successful. (One was HAMAS: I was not an active participant in organizing that group, but I was a supporter. Another was JUSTICIA, organized by Ray Andrade back in the late 1960s, along with several other organizations.) It was clear to me that, until we had a national organization that could focus on creating opportunities for Latinos behind the camera, we would not be able to have a huge impact in front of the camera, because the *producer* is the motive behind writers and directors in creating projects and creating stories and scripts, which then become the platform for actors to fulfill their careers. Although there were media organizations, such as Nosotros and the National Hispanic Media Coalition, no one was focusing on providing networking, mentorship, and career training to Latino producers.

In 1998 there was a crisis in the Latino media community: the one organization that was providing minimal funding for producers working in the PBS world—the National Latino Communications Center, member of the Corporation for Public Broadcasting minority consortia—had not provided any funding for three years. So there was a great deal of controversy about that and a great deal of dissention among Latinos active in the PBS world. That led to a national conference in San Francisco in 1999, for which I was one of the organizers. The outcome of that conference was a declaration by those in attendance that there was a need and desire for a national organization, and NALIP was born there.

KG: That was six years ago, now. Have you seen any changes in the field?

ME: When we started NALIP in 1999, there had not been any series on television in the previous ten years that were Latino-themed and had gone beyond a pilot level or a couple of episodes. There had not been hired any vice presidents of diversity who would focus on increasing diversity within studios and networks. And there had not been any organized support by studios or networks to develop Latino films. Since that time, during the past six years, there have been eight series, including *Resurrection Blvd., Brothers Garcia, American Family, The George Lopez Show,* and *Greetings from Tucson,* and scores of people have been hired

KATHRYN F. GALÁN

at the networks in beginning positions, as well as a number of Latino creative executives. Although you can still count these Latino shows and executives on one or two hands, they did not exist six years ago. I'm convinced that this came about as a consequence of the advocacy and educational work done by both NALIP and the National Latino Media Council, of which I am also a founder.

KG: What do you foresee for the next five or six years?

ME: I think that progress is going to accelerate and there is going to be an explosion, largely because there is a large group of young Latinos who are graduating from college and choosing this as a profession. They are getting trained and being sought out by the networks—obviously, in entry-level positions, but they will accelerate their progress and begin to have an impact on the face of Hollywood, as is occurring in supporting roles on many television series where, six years ago, there was almost no one in supporting roles, with the notable exception of Jimmy Smits and Cheech Marin.

KG: You also seek to have impact in other areas. You founded an organization called the New America Alliance. Why?

ME: Because I understand that societal power resides largely in economic power, I became an entrepreneur. I was successful as an entrepreneur in developing cable television systems in East L.A., Boyle Heights, and San Bernardino, and I used that, again, as a platform to create training opportunities for Latinos. I created a studio in East L.A. back in 1980, where it was not standard to have a state-of-the-art public access studio, and quickly had over forty producers who produced weekly programs—more than cable systems ten to twenty times our size. Many of those young people went to work at the various television stations and started their own shows. Quite a few of them are working at KJLA, a television station here in Southern California that has a Latino/Chicano English-language format. Others have gone to work in other companies, or come to work for me.

That venture also led me to establish a new company called Maya Cinemas. My first modern multiplex theater opened July 29 in Salinas, California, and there are five more in progress. The goal of Maya Cinemas is to create a national movie chain that is both Latino-centric and mainstream in nature and character. This will allow me to do several things: (1) do economic redevelopment by creating jobs and entertainment centers in Latino communities throughout the country and (2) invigorate and create again a Latin American Spanish-language film presence in the United States that was very strong in the 1920s, 1930s, 1940s—all the way up to the 1980s.

KG: So Maya Cinemas' films will be in both English and Spanish?

ME: In fourteen-, fifteen-, or sixteen-screen multiplexes I can devote one screen to a Spanish-language film and have the rest all be Hollywood mainstream. Or I can dedicate one screen to art films. In Bakersfield there are no art theaters but there is a university, so there is an appetite for art films.

KG: How many theaters are you planning?

ME: I'm planning to do forty different theaters, five hundred screens at least, over the next five or six years.

KG: Only in the Southwest?

ME: All over the country. New York, Chicago, Florida, Tennessee, the Carolinas—wherever there's a significant Latino population. And this will allow me to assist in distributing or giving a platform release to English-language, American Latino–themed independent films. That is part of my plan as well.

The goal is both to create a transformation of Latino communities by providing retail redevelopment, entertainment venues, new jobs, and revitalization and to bring in mainstream Hollywood films on 90 percent of the screens and Latin American Spanish-language films or American independent Latino films on 10 percent of the screens.

As an entrepreneur, I was fortunate, again, to be a founder of the New America Alliance, which is the leading Latino business organization in the country, an association of the most successful and most prominent leaders. I was honored to be elected chairman of the organization for three years. The goal of the NAA, which requires a very substantial net worth plus $10,000 a year in annual dues and significant giving, is to support the transformation of our communities by creating access to capital, by supporting political capital and human capital in our communities and by creating a new ethos for philanthropy. We're talking about having those who have succeeded give back to our communities in a strategic way, in a way that leverages their wealth to empower our communities.

KG: Why do we need separate organizations both in the high levels of power and leadership, with something like New America Alliance, and in a very specific field, like NALIP, in order to make these transformations? Why does it have to be Latino and separate as opposed to working within existing structures and associations?

ME: First, we're not a part of the other associations, and being a single voice in those associations is a very lonely, difficult thing. I have been there. Although you can find support, transforming those organizations is more than a single individual can do. By bringing together many Latinos of like mind who have achieved success or who have a single common interest, the numbers and the resources become strategic and powerful unto themselves and can then have an impact on other organizations to become more diverse and equal. It isn't any different from what Jews have done, or African Americans. It's what the Irish and Italians did, what the Asian communities are doing, and Iranians, who have come here and created their own circles, culturally, educationally, and economically. It is what people do. They first go to what they know and where they are comfortable and then branch out.

KG: What do you do to stay balanced and focused on these commitments while working in a business that is far from tranquil or logical?

ME: I follow several disciplines as best as I can. I follow a dietary discipline (I've been a vegetarian for thirty years) and a meditation practice, plus a spiritual life that includes Native American traditions as well as Buddhist traditions. I've chosen to live in my community: I live in East L.A., certainly in a home that is lovely, but within my community, and I stay connected to my community just by living there. Every day I drive through it and see my neighbors, see the schools and the kids, and I participate in the cultural life of my community. I am the chair of the Latino Theater Company, and I have started a charter school in a Latino community for the arts and business (Los Angeles Academy of Arts & Enterprise). I actively support Latino candidates and other candidates who are progressive. All of these things I have found to be vital to maintain any kind of perspective and grounding in my life.

KG: Any other advice to the young media artists out there or for young Latino media makers?

ME: Listening to your own thoughts and words is extremely powerful in discovering who you are. The more you listen to yourself—and the more you *take responsibility for how other people hear you*—the more you are able to become the master of your own life.

Moctesuma Esparza's twenty-ninth film, *Walkout,* premiered in March 2006 on HBO and is now available on DVD. Directed by Edward James Olmos (*American Me*) and starring Michael Pena (*Crash*), Alexa Vega (*Spy Kids*), Laura Harring (*Mulholland Drive*), Yancey Arias (*Kingpin*), and Efren Ramirez (*Napoleon Dynamite*), the film depicts the 1968

An Interview with Moctesuma Esparza

student strikes that launched Esparza's career in both activism and media. The film had a sneak premiere at the Seventh Annual Conference of the National Association of Latino Independent Producers in Long Beach, March 9–12, 2006. Just seven days after its airing, it inspired the walkout of 500,000–1 million students and workers who protested proposed immigration legislation. Esparza has since founded Maya Releasing to distribute Latino-themed projects to the art and general market.

NALIP is now in its ninth year, and Mr. Esparza serves on the executive board to institutionalize the National Signature Programs critical to the maturation of Latino/a film, documentary, and television makers. These programs include the Latino Writers Lab, which works with screenwriters for ten days each spring and fall; the Latino Producers Academy, held each August to advance documentary rough cuts to completion while providing narrative film producers and directors with mentoring and lab time to rehearse, shoot, and edit scenes from works in progress; the Latino Media Market, which programs executive meetings with funders and broadcasters for select advanced projects during NALIP's annual national conference; and the *Latino Media Resource Guide,* which publishes contact information and credits on 2,500 Latino/a writers, producers, directors, and craftspeople in order to improve employment and create community. NALIP prints an e-newsletter twice each week, *Latinos in the Industry,* to support communication amongst Latino media makers, share opportunities, and celebrate successes. NALIP has over 1,200 members, and maintains an informational Web site and national events calendar at www.nalip.org including regional Web pages for chapters and their local professional development workshops.

KATHRYN F.
GALÁN

CHAPTER 15

Negotiating the Politics of (In)Difference in Contemporary Hollywood

AN INTERVIEW WITH
KIMBERLY PEIRCE

Denise Mann
(UCLA)

Kimberly Peirce, the writer-director of *Boys Don't Cry* (Killer Films/ Fox Searchlight, 1999), became the toast of the town after her lead actress, Hilary Swank, won both a Golden Globe and an Academy Award for her performance as the transsexual Brandon Teena and after Chloë Sevigny was nominated in the supporting actress category for her role as Brandon's girlfriend. *Boys Don't Cry* is a fact-based dramatization of the events leading up to the tragic murder of Teena Brandon, a Nebraskan teenage girl living as a young man.

After Fox Searchlight picked it up at Sundance, the film went on to win critical accolades at several major film festivals, including Toronto, London, Venice, and New York. The film represents a radical effort by a woman director (already a rarity in Hollywood) to challenge the stereotypical views typically associated with representations of sexual difference. Peirce's accomplishment is that much more profound when considered against the backdrop of a Hollywood system governed by a complex and multifaceted web of institutional and cultural tensions. Our conversation traces the challenges she faced as a newly anointed "auteur," as a woman director, as a New York-based independent-minded director, as a former Sundance "labbie," and, finally, as an openly gay director whose socially conscious films grapple with the politics of sexual identity.

Making *Boys Don't Cry* outside the Hollywood studio system was probably Peirce's first and last experience of true independence, given that first-time filmmakers typically operate below the radar of the Hollywood system; however, after her film's high-profile win (for actress Hilary Swank) at the Oscars in 1999, Peirce became increasingly subject to the often Draconian development, financing, and production rigor associated with the Hollywood mainstream; therefore, when Peirce and I met in late September 2004, we talked about her transition from being a New York–based independent filmmaker to working within the Hollywood system proper. We talked first about her breakout independent film, *Boys Don't Cry*, and then shifted to *Silent Star*, which at the time she believed was going to be her next feature project. As it turned out, Peirce's *Silent Star* would not survive the Hollywood development-production machinery. There are many possible explanations for this, the most likely being that the project broke several of the cardinal rules that prevail in Hollywood today: by telling a self-referential story about Hollywood history, a topic that is viewed to be of limited interest to those outside Hollywood; by focusing on a disreputable hero, who plays two women against each other; and finally by showing the seamy side (vs. the glamour) of the entertainment industry and, more to the point, by showing the Hollywood film industry succumbing to a Foucauldian disciplinary impulse as it instituted the Production Code to protect its economic interests.

DENISE
MANN

Notably, Peirce's next film, *Stop-Loss*, is based on a politically sensitive topic of a different sort: the war in Iraq while the battle is still being waged. Hollywood has been notoriously gun-shy about making films about unpopular wars until sufficient time has elapsed to make it palatable to the mainstream audience. In contrast, at the time of this writing, a number of Iraq-themed projects by well-known male writers and directors, among them *In the Valley of Elah* (Paul Haggis) and *Redacted* (Brian De Palma), were released to disappointing box office numbers. *The Invisible World* (Ridley Scott) and *Stop-Loss* were both about to be released.

Contemporary filmmakers like Peirce become immersed in the complex sets of negotiations and compromises that inevitably accompany participation in the Hollywood entertainment industry, which makes the task of interviewing them challenging. My goal at the start of the interview had been to extract evidence of the series of adjustments that any independent filmmaker must make as he or she moves from the margins to the Hollywood mainstream, and in particular to trace Peirce's cultural legacy as part of the New York "downtown cinema" movement that some media scholars argue can be traced to the American avant-garde underground filmmaking tradition of late 1960s[1]; however, as we spoke, I realized that her career trajectory was uniquely colored by her status as a woman director and as a gay director—in other words, as someone who had studiously positioned herself as an outsider at the same time she was struggling to navigate the notoriously "insider" world of Hollywood studio filmmaking.

DENISE MANN: Once you finished writing *Boys Don't Cry*, and you knew you had something wonderful, did you take it around to the studios?

KIMBERLY PEIRCE: I took it around to the studios before I had something wonderful. We took it around to the studios with the first draft, and they didn't get it. I worked on it, worked on it, worked on it, and went to the Sundance Lab. And people kept being intrigued by it but never knew what to make of it. At some point, I remember, Andy and I were telling ourselves, "This is not going to get made, but let's just work on it tonight." One studio did get hold of it. MGM called me and said, "We are going to greenlight it." So I quit my job, only to realize they weren't gonna greenlight it! It was a disaster. I realized there was no way the studios were going to make it. So when we got some private money, even though it wasn't enough, we decided to move forward. The whole idea of a studio scared us, made no sense to us. Plus, once we realized how good it was, and that it was very gay, very violent, and very much about identity in a very particular way, the idea of changing it [to accommodate the studios] was not appealing to me. It was not even comprehensible to me to bring in outsiders and change my perspective. After I had been to the Sundance Labs and had a draft that was starting to work, I became protective of it because I had started to realize I just wanted to make it, and I did not care if it opened in just one theater. I did not have any big ambitions in that regard.

An Interview with Kimberly Peirce

DM: I understand you also took it to Miramax?

KP: Christine [Vachon, president of Killer Films] was friends with them, but to us, Miramax was Hollywood. It is so big. When Christine told me, "MGM likes your movie, they want to make it," my first thought was, "Ooh, Hollywood!" I had never been there and I bought all these new clothes, and I went out there, and I was at the studio. I never aspired to be a studio director at that point, so if they wanted to make my movie, that's great, but if they didn't, that was okay too.

DM: After Sundance Film Lab, what was the process like?

KP: Very depressing. I love Sundance, they were amazing . . . grad school [Columbia University] took it a certain way, and then Sundance took it a whole other way. I got to work with all these amazing people. Sundance there was so much excitement. Everybody loved it, and I was doing great and I thought, "Oh my God, my movie is going to get made." I think I experienced a good year and a half of utter depression after Sundance. And I think that is the experience most of the labbies go through, because you have all the support and then you go back and you start rewriting and you start making it work, and then there was no money anyway. I was working on it every day of my life. Christine was doing her best. These movies are hard to make; it was a tough topic. . . .

DM: Then you and Christine spent a year and a half hustling to try to get independent financing.

KP: Yes, we went everywhere. I had gone to one of the European festivals and talked to, oh, my God, eight people a day for six days. We went everywhere, and every time there was a chance to talk to somebody, we did. Ultimately it was just not destined to be made in the system.

DM: How ultimately did you get the money?

KP: Ultimately [it was] the guys who worked down the hall from Christine, who had known about the project for years. John Hart said, "Oh, that movie, we will do that." It was John Hart and Jeff Sharp. And I was thinking, those guys had this project three or four years ago. What took them so long? Anyway, they took me out to lunch and started hustling me. Will you cast this movie star? And I was thinking, I've worked too hard on this, and it can't be that movie star. I knew we needed to keep looking to find someone who could play the part and pass as a boy. We went back and forth. We were fortunate to finally find Hillary. Ultimately they gave us the money we needed to get going. They didn't give us all the money. Literally seven days later the film was happening.

DM: What was the initial budget that Hart put in?

KP: The movie was budgeted at $1.7 million. I thought we were going to get $1.7 million, and we got on set and it ended up being only $700,000. I didn't know at the time we were short. John Hart probably didn't like the project that much. He's a good guy. I accepted the fact that it was only $700,000. I did not know then that it simply couldn't be done for that little. I just know that literally I would interview an AD [assistant director] and he would turn white. People on the set were throwing up and basically freaking out. And I was thinking, what's the problem? My producers kept telling me, you just have to shoot seven pages a day. I think, fine, I'll do that. I didn't understand that shooting seven pages a day on our film was nearly impossible. That first day they stopped us from shooting and said, well, you will finish up those scenes at the end of the shoot. And I was thinking, oh, fine. Then someone else came up to me and said, "You don't understand. If you don't finish up those

scenes and they save them all for the end day, you will never get to do it."
I freaked out and said, "I can't lose those scenes. That's crazy." The next
day I went over by five hours and I got everything done, plus the stuff
I had missed. Everybody said, "What are you doing? You can't go over
five hours." And I said, "I have to make my movie. What are you talking
about?" At the end of the week, they called me to say the Independent
Film Channel loves the dailies, and they are going to put in a million
dollars. I thought, oh, my God, we're rich, we're rich. And then someone
told me, "You don't understand. We were going to shut you down if the
Independent Film Channel didn't like your dailies." So the fact that they
liked the dailies, the first week, changed everything.

DM: At this point IFC stepped in and gave you a million dollars and you
got your magic number. You got to make your movie. When you were
saying "they," were you talking about Christine and her group or was it
another "they"?

KP: Christine was in charge of production. Hart had put in a certain
amount of money. Between the two of them, I did not know we did not
have enough money.

DM: They were probably trying to shelter you in the hopes that everything would work out once they had dailies to show to other investors.

KP: It was a very daring move for them to take a first-time director and
put themselves in a situation where it was do or die, for everybody. People
were working eighteen-hour days, getting sick, working under budget.
People just gave and gave and gave. I can't believe what they gave me,
but I think they saw how much I was also putting into it. I would love to
work that way again. I mean not in such extreme circumstance, but with
that sense of commitment and devotion. I suspect it's different when you
re working within the studio system because there are so many added
pressures weighing on you. I don't know if the art comes from the same
place. I think the bottom line must be the pressure you put on yourself.

DM: Christine Vachon's reputation is that of a goddess for independent-minded filmmakers like you. Can you talk about the relationship
and what role she played in the process?

KP: I shot a short version of the Teena Brandon story for my graduate
thesis film. The producer was someone I had hired three weeks before
because another producer walked out. I had saved $11,000, which for
me was like a million dollars. I gave it to her. I don't know what the hell
she did, but at the end of the shoot I hadn't finished the rape scene, or
the ending. I had $8,000 in car rental bills and $2,000 in tickets, and I

didn't even drive. My dailies were being held by Duarte. My girlfriend at the time knew Christine. Christine had heard I was doing the Brandon Teena movie, and since she also wanted to do a Brandon Teena movie, she met with me. I walked in and said, "I can't even see my dailies." She said, "I will help you get your dailies out of the lab." That was just magic to my ears. She looked at them and said, "I can help you finish the short or I can give you $200,000 and you can make a feature." $200,000! Well, that was like $10 million, and I said, "Okay, I'll make a feature from the short." While we were in Amsterdam, trying to sell the movie, I had this epiphany. I called her up and said, "Christine, I know this wasn't the plan, but I don't think we should write around the short, because I will be taking actors who are good, but who were hired for this short. I just think you will be wasting resources if you do it that way. I just think we should let go of the short because it was only $30,000, and we should write the feature version of the movie from scratch." And she said okay.

DM: Did Christine come up with the $200,000 to start over?

KP: Christine, like most producers doesn't actually put money into movies; she raises money from other sources to make movies. I told all my friends I had $200,000 to make the movie. We are going to be rich. We are going to make a feature. I am going to be a motion picture director. Well, that $200,000 never materialized and then the budget was $400,000, and that $400,000 never materialized and the budget was $800,000, and I kept walking around thinking, I am going to make an $800,000 movie, but in reality, we had no production money for quite a long time.

DM: She was trying this whole time, obviously, to raise the money.

KP: She was absolutely trying, and Christine again handled it perfectly. The only way Christine could keep me rejuvenated and interested was to keep on saying we are going to do it. The money is going to come in. But she was flying by the seat of her pants. But that is the only thing you can do in this business.

DM: That is her job as producer—to be the eternal optimist and cheerleader.

KP: Right. It was hard for me over the years to sustain the energy, bu the good thing for me is I just love writing and every day I would just go home and make the script better. A lot of people were saying, "Don' make it better 'til it's gonna go." Thank God I didn't listen, because when we finally raised the money, I was ready. The same thing happen with Silent Star. There have been a couple of years when nobody was interested, but I kept telling myself, "If I go home and work on it because I really like it, then if it ever happens, I'll be ready."

D M: How did John Hart and Jeff Sharp raise the money?

K P: Christine is a producer-producer. These guys are producers who have access to equity money. They raise money. They get people to invest. Christine does not really do that. She is a producer.

D M: Has she worked with them on other projects?

K P: Yes, a lot of them.

D M: And where does John Sloss come in?

K P: John was Christine's lawyer, the film's lawyer, and my lawyer.

D M: Did he bring money into it?

K P: No, but after it turned out the $1.7 million was not enough and we ran out of money, it was like living through triage. I came back to New York with most of the movie shot, not all, and in the editing room. I was told, "Okay, in nine weeks we need your director's cut." After seven weeks the movie was still four and a half hours long. People loved the movie. I could tell they were getting it. But it was way too long. They said, "You have to edit a trailer together. If we can pre-sell the movie based on the trailer, we'll get more money to finish." So I said, "I have to edit the trailer before I am even done with the movie?" "Yes. It's hard enough to pre-sell a movie when it's done." So I said, "Fine." I edited all day, and we went to Sundance, where Christine created a bidding war. And thank God, because she pre-sold it for $5 million. It was a promissory note and a negative pickup by Fox. My only fear throughout this entire process was that the film would die. So every time we went through phase where it was hemorrhaging I would think, shit, this is the breaking point that the movie can't survive. But then somebody would come in and build a little bridge for it.

D M: Then Fox Searchlight came in and you had the $5 million?

K P: We didn't have $5 million. We had the promise of $5 million. The way they keep you on budget is to say, "We are buying it at this price. So our budget cannot suddenly go up." So we were still wrangling, arguing that we need more.

D M: Did the money that you got allow you to go back and do reshoots?

K P: Yes, we begged and begged and begged for reshoots. Ultimately, got a portion of my reshoots and more editing time. That is the thing that saved us. We hired a guy called Lee Percy. He is a brilliant editor. He edited *Reversal of Fortune;* he edited *Kiss of the Spiderwoman.* My first editor was wonderful, so all justice to her. But this guy just came in and did an amazing job.

Lee just came in and really knew what he was doing. Lee is also going to edit *Silent Star.* I invited him to my birthday party in New York last week and when I told him the story [for *Silent Star*], he said, "This sounds like *Reversal of Fortune.*" I told him we were studying that film when we were writing this one. Lee came in and just had an eye for what was needed. Also, because of his stature in the industry, people have respect for him so when he said I needed more time to edit, I got it.

DENISE
MANN

DM: How did you find him?

KP: Serendipity. He happened to have just finished a job, I happened to have let my other editor go, he happened to love the material. He is an out gay man. He is so established. Everything, all the stars were just lined up and he was just so amazing.

Transition from N.Y. Indie to Hollywood Director

DM: After *Boys Don't Cry,* you were described by *Variety* as "a heavyweight indie filmmaker" and the second indie director of such caliber to be signed by DreamWorks in the space of two months, the first being Todd Field. In another *Variety* article you are linked to David O. Russell, Paul Thomas Anderson, Alexander Payne, Sophie Jonk, and Wes Anderson as rebellious and maverick storytellers comparable to independent filmmakers from the 1970s' Hollywood Renaissance.[2] Has the shift from being an independent filmmaker who is under the radar to the next big thing in Hollywood changed your way of working?

KP: I don't think so. I am just trying to do good stories, good characters. If they happen to be bigger movies, that's fine, but if you gave me a amazing movie that was a million dollars, two million dollars, I would do it in a second. The hardest thing is finding good scripts. We are all s desperate for good material.

DM: Why do you think you are being singled out for that film (*Boys Don't Cry*)? Was it because of all the awards (Academy Award and Golden Globe wins for Hilary Swank and nominations for Chloë Sevigny; Independent Spirit "Best First Feature" Award nominations for Peirce and the producers, Christine Vachon, Eva Kolodner, John Hart, and Jeff Sharp)? Or was it because such a small-budget movie attracted interest from such a wide audience?

KP: *Boys* crossed over. *Boys* was a Fox Searchlight movie that crossed over into a mainstream audience, and that's symbolically significant. Plus, it wasn't just one performance, but the film had five performances [that were admired]. Even though it was a small budget, it was a big story. It was a well-rounded story. I think people saw that and said, "Oh, she knows how to tell a story." If you look at my development slate, there are several big characters, big movies.

DM: Yes, I want to talk about the fact you are currently developing both types of films—bigger budget, star-driven or genre-driven studio films like *Silent Star* (DreamWorks), *Dillinger* (Warner Bros.), and *Childhood's End* (Universal), as well as smaller character studies like *Ice at the Bottom of the World* (Newmarket Films).

KP: Yes. I don't have any prejudice that way about the size of the budget or the release. I just want the material to be good. If it doesn't feel personal, relevant, good, human, and compelling, then I am not going to look further. There was a reason we all went into films. For me, it was because it is the most exciting art form in the world.

DM: Do you think you are being allowed to make more "difficult" movies, based on their belief that you might be their next breakout auteur?

KP: I think there is a certain trust, and I think I have proven that I have pretty good taste. That helps. *Dillinger*. That's a money-maker. That is a big-budget studio movie. *Childhood's End* is a big-budget studio movie. *Ice at the Bottom of the World* with Newmarket is a different kind of movie. Berney [Bob Berney, president of Newmarket Films, distributor of *Monster*] loved it. And if Berney loves it, he'll do it. What's great about him is he doesn't have to make these tent-pole movies. He is not under that kind of pressure because his operation isn't that big.

DM: Do you think there is more pressure in today's marketplace for "specialty distribs." to look for films that have the potential to cross over to a mainstream audience?

KP: The studio [Fox Searchlight] came in after *Boys* was already perceived as successful, so it wasn't as big a risk for them. But would they really want to do something at that level of darkness at a bigger budget? You really can't make *Boys* for too much money.

DM: So there's a definite relationship between budget and risk, even for "specialty distribs."?

KP: You can only be as dark as what the budget will allow. It's ultimately a business. At the end of the day, they [the studios or specialty divisions] only want an auteur if they can produce awards that allow them to make money, or if they make a film that lots of people want to see, so once again, only if they can make money. So filmmakers are perceived as difficult when they are focusing on their vision, if that vision doesn't make money.

DM: Do you have final cut?

KP: Yes. I have final cut up to a certain budget.

Filming Gender

DENISE
MANN

DM: Can you discuss your attitudes or sense of responsibility regarding representations of gender, ethnicity, class, and other aspects of "difference" in your films? You are known for your complex, contradictory representations of individuals at the margins of society and for undermining stereotypical views of gender, class, and ethnicity. Does the material you field from agents and producers explore these concepts in the same way that you would have? Or are these scripts driven more by genre and other marketplace concerns?

KP: The scripts I am offered by the agency tend to be nothing like what I would do. If you look at that pile of scripts over there [pointing to a pile in the corner of the room], that's a small portion of the total. I have just been in this house a week and a half, so that's just the beginning. Generally, the projects I read are not very culturally sophisticated about gender. I was living in New York City, in a queer culture, with transgendered people. We were not so much ahead of the times, as we shared certain sensibilities. We had all moved to that place because we shared certain views. As a result, these people were setting the trends for the culture. Anybody who does not fit into the mainstream leaves the mainstream and goes there. So we were already on this cutting edge. It shocked me that the mainstream liked the stuff that I had been writing about while I was back in New York. I feel fortunate that I was part of a movement that was ahead of the curve.

DM: According to *Variety*, "Transgender-themed films have found greater acceptance in both gay and straight film festivals. The problem is typically finding distribution after the festival appearance."[3] Have things changed for the better since *Boys Don't Cry* was released and succeeded with a mainstream audience?

KP: My movie was not perceived as a transgender movie, I think. The same thing with *Silent Star*. If *Boys* had been perceived first as a transgender movie, it wouldn't have done as well. They [Fox Searchligh weren't excited by that; they knew it also delivered on the basics: a good story, good characters, good actors. The same thing is true of *Silent Star*. It is not just a movie about silent films. It's a murder mystery. In other words, it's going to be a lot of fun.

DM: Was *Boys Don't Cry* championed by gay and lesbian groups?

KP: Completely.

DM: Do you feel the film helped open the door for films about non-heterosexual sexuality?

KP: Sure. I don't think it was seen primarily as that kind of movie, but sure, I think it made the subject matter less scary [for a broader audience].

DM: For instance, depictions of gays have moved into the mainstream via prime-time TV shows.

KP: You used not to be able to talk about the gay person who lived down the block. Then you used not to be able to talk about the trans person down the block. Now you are talking about the gay-trans person, and now, I was reading in the paper today, you are talking about kids who are naturally hermaphroditic. Suddenly, people are no longer afraid to talk about this stuff.

DM: And to what do you attribute that change?

KP: Other people broke down the door for me, and I stepped through it. Then I broke down the door for other people. Once you start talking about something, and once you know people who are that way, you humanize it. That was what I wanted to do with *Boys*. If I can make a film about this weird thing and give this person their humanity, people will no longer think it is a weird thing.

DM: Who preceded you, by knocking down doors?

KP: Many of my influences were straight males: Scorsese, Hawks, Ray, and Welles. And in terms of the gay thing, who opened it? Christine. I think Christine opened doors. I think Todd Haynes opened doors. Maybe not with the mainstream. I think Ellen DeGeneres opened doors there. When Ellen's show came out it became easier to cast gays. To be gay now is not a freak show. Eight years ago it was still treated as a freak show.

DM: What kind of material are you attracted to? Is it always about gender?

KP: I do tend to like male protagonists.

DM: You tend to like male protagonists?

KP: I tend to write female but I tend to get attracted to male stuff—men who are weirdly effeminate. Because people don't write women the way I think about them.

DM: Tell me more.

KP: Brandon was completely my type of woman, that woman-man thing. You were not going to find that anywhere else. That came from my weird group of friends. Mary [from *Silent Star*], she's a girl who gets a gun. You know, she behaves very much like a male. She's a very assertive female.

DM: In contrast, most films don't depict assertive or aggressive women?

KP: They just don't. You need a strong protagonist. In most films the protagonists are men because they are considered stronger than women. When they show a strong woman on screen, they tend to be "feminist strong." That image of feminists from the 1970s. I don't understand that. I don't know what they are doing. The portraits of strong women I prefer are more for my generation. So they are behaving more like a kind of male.

DM: Can you name some examples?

KP: I loved *Monster*. I thought that Charlize did a great job with that role. I like *Mildred Pierce*. But if you're talking about female characters in contemporary, mainstream films, there are not many that I like.

Women Directors

DM: I want to turn to the issue of women directors in today's Hollywood. In a 2000 *Variety* article, the journalist talked about your role as one of a small handful of talented, powerful women directors working in Hollywood today.[4] Have things improved for women directors, even though the numbers are still far lower than for men? *Variety* lists you, Sofia Coppola (*Virgin Suicides*), Patricia Rozema (*Mansfield Park*), and Jennifer Goodman (*The Tao of Steve*) as "redefining films made for and about women." Since the article was written, Sofia's second film, *Lost in Translation*, Catherine Hardwicke's *Thirteen*, and Patty Jenkins' *Monster* came along. Perhaps things are improving as recently as the past year or two, given the greater opportunities each of you have had to make bigger movies. In the article in 2000, you said you believed

"We are on the cusp of a transition" in terms of the film industry's acceptance of women as directors. Do you still feel that way? You also said innovative executives like Mike De Luca (first at New Line, then at DreamWorks, now an independent producer) and women studio heads like Stacey Snider at Universal and Nina Jacobson at Disney represent a "changing of the guard" in Hollywood. Do you think that these executives being in charge of the studios have anything to do with it?

K P: No, I don't think that having a woman executive changes anything. They are still just doing their job. These women have been wonderful to me. And I know many women in the industry that are so smart and good at what they do. And they are incredibly nice to me and give me every opportunity that they can; however, I certainly don't think their agenda is to make it a more female-driven market. That's ultimately a good thing. Their agenda as businesspeople is to do good business. I don't know that there is a lot of room to be socially political in a business. But they do what they can. What you are finding is more girls are being encouraged at a younger age to do the things that previously only boys did. Girls are now given cameras, and go to film school [in large numbers]. We are seeing more women's talent coming to the fore, simply because girls are now being given greater access.

D M: But women have been attending film schools for the last twenty or thirty years without much progress made in terms of the numbers being allowed to direct, for instance.

K P: Oh, it's behind. It's like civil rights, or gay rights. It's all behind. But what I am saying is that people are relating more to women's stories and women are feeling more empowered to tell their stories. I think women's stories are making more money.

D M: Do you attribute the shift in part to a film like *Titanic*, which prompted the studios to start focusing on the young female audience?

K P: I attribute it to women with strong stories who are making strong movies. Look at me, look at Patty, look at Sofia. These are women who have strong stories to tell, and if you notice, they are telling female-centered stories. My film was about a pretty masculine girl, but it was still a girl. So what you have is a good crop of storytellers.

D M: Do you think "male indie auteurs" are treated differently than "women indie auteurs"? Many of today's top women directors, such as Sofia Coppola, Patty Jenkins, and Catherine Hardwicke, are winning awards and are much admired as women directors but thus far have been focusing on films primarily in the "prestige" arena—that is, making films for a certain price, for older, sophisticated audiences, which are distributed by special division movies rather than big studio movies, which are mostly directed by men.

KP: Name a movie.

DM: *Lost in Translation, Monster, Thirteen*. Perhaps it's too soon to argue that these women won't be gravitating to big studio movies. Hardwicke, for instance, is making *Lords of Dogtown* at a major studio, Columbia, and with a relatively big star, Heath Ledger. Plus, like you, she has several big movies in development, including a historical costume drama, *Vivaldi*, with Imagine Entertainment. It felt significant to me that you were offered *Memoirs of a Geisha*, for instance, but that DreamWorks ultimately went with a male director, Rob Marshall (*Chicago*). Do you think the current generation of women directors is getting offered the same big, expensive movies as the men?

KP: You'd have to ask them, but I believe each of these other girls is being offered the same scripts. If you look at my scripts, they are being offered to everybody.

DM: Do you think Sofia is?

KP: I don't think Sofia is. She is writing her new script now.

DM: What about Patty Jenkins?

KP: I don't know. I am friends with Patty. I adore her. I think Patty is figuring out what she is going to do. I don't think Patty is against doing a big movie. It's funny. I talk to Patty about this all the time. If you have done a personal, intense movie, you say, "Now I want to do a big movie." And then you look at the big movies and you say, "Oh, my God, they aren't about anything." I am offered those all the time, but then I say, "Oh, my God, I don't want to take that on."

DM: So you feel as if you are getting the same great scripts that men are at this point in your career.

KP: Oh, yes. I am shown the scripts. Are they ultimately going to choose director X, who has done ten movies and is bigger than I am? Sure. And that tends to be a man.

DM: Because they have been around longer and got more cracks at the bat?

KP: Yes, because they have been around longer and have got more cracks. Whatever inequities there are in the system, they tend to go to the people they know. I don't want to say more qualified, because I think the talent is the same. I understand why the men tend to get the job.

Developing Silent Star *at DreamWorks*

D M: Let's talk about your next movie, *Silent Star.* I understand that DreamWorks has committed to making it?

K P: *Silent Star* is a project I have worked on for a while. DreamWorks decided three months ago that they wanted to make it in the winter [2005].[5] From that point on, you are on this collision course, trying to get the script in, get the casting done, get everything ready to go by then.

D M: How did you find the material? Did someone bring it to you?

K P: My writing partner from *Boys Don't Cry,* Andy [Bienen, now a screenwriting professor at Columbia University], who is one of the writers on it, brought me this story right after *Boys* was finished; and I felt it was this amazing "greatest unsolved Hollywood murder mystery." There is a Web site called Taylorology that has eight thousand pages with every single article ever written about him [William Desmond Taylor].[6] There was also an A&E special, an E! Entertainment special, and tons of books [on the topic]. I have half a room full of research [from this project]. The unique story angle that we brought to the project is we figured out who committed the murder. There was a murder, a cover-up, and a conspiracy.

An Interview with Kimberly Peirce

D M: How did you confirm your findings?

K P: Based on historical record. We got the police records. We interviewed Kevin Brownlow, who wrote many of the silent-movie books [books on Chaplin, Pickford], and several other books about early Hollywood. Then we went to the Library of Congress and to the Will Hays archives. We went everywhere. When we started [putting together the facts about who we thought had committed the murder], Kevin thought our version made sense. Something similar happened during the writing of *Boys Don't Cry.* When you finally get to know a character really well, a true character, and you go back and discover something new about them, then when you start looking back at everything that happened to that person through this new lens, it starts becoming obvious that this is probably what happened. I don't believe in fictionalizing. The reason I'm drawn to true stories is because I love the idea that there is a basic truth in there. That if I look hard enough I will find it. We were skeptical for four months. But then, every time we read everything this person did or wrote, we were thinking, oh, my God, that person killed him.

DM: So who did it?

KP: You know the story, right? William Desmond Taylor, Paramount film director, was killed. Found dead in his bungalow. Mary Miles Minter, who was the greatest star of the day, and Mabel Norman, a beautiful comedian and heroin addict, were both there. Both their careers were destroyed by this incident. They both had been involved with him. It could have been the drug dealers, because he was clearly involved in the drug trade. It could have been Mary's mother. It could have been somebody from the studio. Our theory is that it was Mary. Hollywood [during this period, in the early twenties] was in trouble because of the Fatty Arbuckle scandal. In response, Adolph Zukor decided that he needed an icon of innocence. Since Mary Pickford had left him, he

DENISE
MANN

decided, "I'll make another one." So he went out to the vaudeville circuit and did a nationwide search. Like *American Idol*. He brought all these girls in to determine who could be America's next sweetheart. He chose this girl, Mary Miles Minter, who had been tripping around vaudeville with her mother. He said, "I'll make you the greatest star of the day. I will put you in twenty movies. You have to sign this contract saying you won't fall in love, you won't get married, that you won't have sex." She said yes. Essentially he created this cauldron of desire because she fell in love with Taylor, but she was under a binding contract not to fall in love, not to have sex. So our version follows the escalation of the love triangle between those three people, Taylor, Mabel Norman, and Mary Miles Minter, until Mary, to free herself, finally kills Taylor, and the studio covers it up for her.

DM: Why does she kill him? Was it because he wouldn't commit to her over Mabel?

KP: She killed him because of their Pygmalion-like relationship in which he had essentially "created" her. He gave her access to a whole new language of love. He opened her up by introducing her to a sensual life she'd never experienced. Here was this girl who had been on the road for most of her life, who had been worked to death by her mother, and what he did was touch her. He opened up a part of her, artistically, romantically, and sexually, that she has never experienced. When Zukor finds out that Mary, his prized possession, has fallen in love with Taylor, that she has broken the "rules," he is enraged. Zukor tells Mary about Taylor's secret past, thinking she will leave him. Instead, she is even more enraptured. The more Zukor tries to destroy him, the more she makes it her life's mission to save Taylor, to the point of running away with him. Taylor does not have the courage to leave his Hollywood life for her, so she kills him. Her actions are covered up by several "interested parties"—by Zukor, by the studio, and by her mother. I was out to lunch with [producer and now Universal Focus co-president] James Schamus, and he said, "Look at *Mildred Pierce,* it's one of my all-time favorite movies." And I did, and I realized, oh, my God, that's the structure of my film. So our story is told in the same way as *Mildred Pierce.* It's a melodrama about love and familiar relations framed around a detective story. Her first confession, that her mother did it, is told to a plant. That person turns Mary over to Zukor, who, along with her mother, confronts her and says, "Don't you ever dare do something like this again." In other words, they both agree to cover up the confession. Eventually, years later, she breaks free from the control of both her mother and Zukor and goes directly to Will Hays, who perpetuates the cover-up. That is essentially what prompted Will Hays to take over Hollywood [when Hays became the head of the MPPDA and initiated self-censorship of the industry through the Hays Office].

DM: Is this part of the story, the cover-up by Zukor and Hays, publicly known?

KP: No, but it is all implicit in the research. We all know that Hays wielded huge power over Hollywood and that Zukor was in his confidence.

DM: Clearly there are a lot of strands to follow in this story and a lot of social conventions that are being examined and critiqued. Which aspects of this story were the most important to you—the repressed love story, the corruption inherent in the business practices of early Hollywood, the Hays Code, or the mother-daughter relationship?

KP: All of it, but I especially love the mother-daughter story. I have wanted to tell a mother-daughter story for a long time. For me it's about the repression of sexuality. If you repress something, if you repress a human being, if you repress identity, if you repress sexuality, it will come back to haunt you. It will ultimately explode.

DM: Mary appears to be reacting to each of these forces rather than actively pursuing a goal. Do you see her as a heroic character?

KP: Mary is a ticking time bomb. Zukor thinks that he can control Mother Nature, so it becomes like a Frankenstein story in that regard. Zukor thinks that he can be the puppeteer for all these people. Mary was the center of this effort. Mary picked up a gun and shot Taylor, and it was the smartest thing that she could have done because it was the only way to stop Zukor. It was a dramatic, brilliant act of freedom.

DENISE

MANN

DM: Who are your biggest advocates at DreamWorks?

KP: I told Steven Spielberg [DreamWorks co-principal] the story, and he really loved it. Also, Walter Parkes [then co-head, DreamWorks] loves it. In other words, really smart people—the people who have the power to make the movie—get my story. It's like mobilizing an army—getting everyone to see the same movie as you do.

As forthcoming as Peirce had been when describing her work, she became evasive when asked to talk about the ways in which she too might be caught up in the complex, often indecipherable social-sexual hierarchies that prevail inside the Hollywood culture of production. I questioned her version of Hollywood as a place that provided complete creative autonomy for talented and uniquely original storytellers. And yet, despite my prodding efforts to expose the more jaded, cynical version of Hollywood that I knew existed behind the PC version she was presenting, she remained upbeat and cheerful, even celebratory about her many allies within the system, including not just famous auteur directors like Quentin Tarantino, Robert Rodriguez, and David Russell, who had embraced her as one of their own, but also the "suits" her agent, her producers, the studio executives, and the studio heads who were each portrayed as smart and supportive, in equal measure. That is, until I turned off the tape recorder and asked one last time whether she felt that women directors faced additional challenges in Hollywood. As I had before, I gave her my list of examples of women filmmakers—Allison Anders, Tamara Jenkins, Lisa Cholodenko, Lisa Kreuger, Julie Dash—whose careers I felt had been derailed or hadn't fulfilled their early promise.[7] I pointed out that not as many women filmmakers seemed as adept as some of their counterpart male directors at simultaneously reinforcing their status as authentic, aesthetically experimental indie auteurs and as commercially viable directors of cross-over hits. Neither were they able to simultaneously satisfy devoted cult following and reinforce the commercial publicity machinery underlying the dominant media industries; for example, Tarantino had simultaneously delivered another one-two punch set of indie art house hits with *Kill Bill* volumes I and II (2004, 2005) and managed to widen his already substantial celebrity (apparently without tarnishing his cult status among his fans) by appearing as a guest host on *American Idol* during the 2005 season.

Peirce agreed that she felt it is more difficult for women directors who are trying to straddle the line between indie, low-budget, personal filmmaking and the studio production world of bigger budgets and more high-profile material. I was frustrated that I hadn't got her observations on tape, but I also realized that these are subtle distinctions, difficult to articulate in any meaningful way without sounding ungrateful. After all, here was a woman who had broken through the anonymity facing the thousands of equally passionate first-time directors by winning Academy Award recognition for not one but two of her actors; and yet, she feels it can be a vicious cycle for woman directors who aren't the beneficiaries of the long Hollywood tradition of celebrating mostly male director-auteurs. Women directors don't seem to be given the same latitude as their male counterparts to develop their craft, make mistakes, and thereby discover a path that allows them to balance their personal creative goals with the political and economic goals operating in Hollywood.

Sensing her nostalgia for the heady days of "guerilla filmmaking" in New York while making *Boys*, I asked why she hadn't decided to do her second film with the same producers—Christine Vachon and Eva Kolodner. Peirce told me that she hadn't realized at the time how unique producers Vachon and Kolodner were in their "take no prisoners" approach to making politically charged independent films. Instead of staying within the protective and supportive environment for independent-minded filmmakers, for which Vachon is best known, Peirce had opted to use her new-found leverage to explore the challenges of working within the commercially driven, product-oriented environment of Hollywood. Peirce earnestly believed she could operate within the system and still remain true to her independent roots as writer-director making films about gender identity. Eight years later, she has just now had the opportunity to direct her second movie.

While *Silent Star* ultimately fell through for budget reasons, in many ways, adhering to her independent roots had put her in a position to get *Stop-Loss* made. Her passion for the topic even extended to the world at large when she appeared before Congress in 2008 to speak about the Stop-Loss Compensation Act. After working on this interview, I fully expect that Peirce will be able to survive the Hollywood system and am hopeful that *Stop-Loss* will give her the type of critical accolades and commercial success needed to allow her to make her politically challenging films. After all, Peirce is, like her characters, quietly tenacious.

An Interview with Kimberly Peirce

Notes

1. This telling phrase, from the margins to the mainstream, is taken from an excellent recent anthology, *Contemporary American Independent Film: From the Margins to the Mainstream*, ed. Chris Holmlund and Justin Wyatt (London: Routledge, 2003).

2. Marc Graser, "De Luca Pops for Peirce," *Daily Variety*, November 6, 2002; Charles Lyons, "Rabble Rousers," *Daily Variety*, June 19, 2001.

3. Robert Abele, "Jumping on the Trans Express," *Daily Variety*, July 12, 2001.

4. Gregg Kiday, "Indie Helmers Redefine Chick Pics," *Daily Variety*, November 29, 2000.

5. As of July 2005, *Silent Star* still had not officially been given the green light.

6. See www.angelfire.com/az/Taylorology.

7. For a more detailed discussion of women directors working in contemporary Hollywood, see Christina Lane, "Just Another Girl Outside the Neo-indie," in Holmlund and Wyatt (eds.), *Contemporary American Independent Film*, 193–209.

CHAPTER 16

Televising Difference

AN INTERVIEW WITH PARIS BARCLAY

Kevin Sandler

(Arizona State University)

*"I get a feature film every week
and 95 percent of them are black
[in theme]. It's true that I am
black, but I also went to Harvard
and have some experience with
Caucasians. I've directed* NYPD
Blue—*having won two Emmys
with it—and* ER, The West
Wing, *and many other shows.
So you would think I'd start to
get some scripts that reflect those
experiences—police dramas and
so forth. Nope, I get B.A.P.S. and
Booty Call."*

PARIS BARCLAY

met Paris Barclay in November 2005 at the Academy of Television
rts and Sciences Foundation Faculty Seminar, an annual five-day
ries of discussions, presentations, and interactions between college
ofessors and the Hollywood production community. He immedi-
ely struck me as one of the most articulate and passionate media
ofessionals I had ever encountered. At the seminar, Paris spoke of
iginality, knowledge, and wisdom as the cornerstones of success in
e entertainment business. For students, he believed these founda-
ns should be grounded in a well-rounded media arts curriculum,
e in which theater, music, new media, and journalism join film and
evision in an interdisciplinary *pas de deux.*

Paris's advice mirrors that of his own career. At Harvard, where he
duated in 1979 with a B.A. in English and American literature and
guage, Paris wrote thirteen musicals, revues, and plays, including

the score for two Hasty Pudding Shows. After graduation, he achieved success writing and directing television commercials, directing music videos for New Kids on the Block, Janet Jackson, and LL Cool J, and composing plays, two of which were produced off-Broadway. In the mid-1990s, Paris's career turned to film and television as he directed the feature film *Don't Be a Menace to South Central While Drinking Your Juice in the Hood,* the HBO film *The Cherokee Kid,* and episodes of ER, *The West Wing, The Shield,* and NYPD *Blue,* for which he won two Emmys for directing. He co-created the 2000 series *City of Angels* and served as co-executive producer and principal director for *Cold Case.* Currently he is the co-executive producer and principal director for HBO's new series, *In Treatment,* starring Gabriel Byrne, Dianne Wiest, and Blair Underwood. He also recently returned to his roots in theater, writing the book, music, and lyrics for *One Red Flower,* a musical adapted from the 1985 best-seller *Dear America: Letters Home from Vietnam.*

KEVIN SANDLER

Despite working within the constraints of broadcast television, Paris demonstrates that commercial media artists can produce socially conscious entertainment. Issues of discrimination, intolerance, and injustice regularly permeate his multicharacter episodic series Combined with a bittersweet mixture of hope, affirmation, and just ness, Paris's dramas display complex and nuanced forms of storytell ing not often seen in prime time. His progressiveness also extend to the inclusion of diverse casts in front of and behind the camera, a well as his commitment to increasing the employment of women an

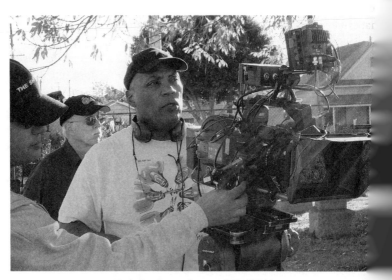

Paris Barclay on the set of *The Shield.*

minority directors by the television networks through his work with the Directors Guild of America, now serving as the first vice president of the board. For his charitable and community service, Paris received the Stephen F. Kolzak Award from GLAAD for his work toward eliminating homophobia, and was given the Founder's Award from Project Angel Food, a nonprofit organization that delivers meals to people affected by HIV/AIDS and other serious illnesses. He also was honored in 2007 with the Directors Guild of America's Robert B. Aldrich Award for his service to the guild.

I spoke with him by telephone from the set of *Cold Case* on April 21, 2006.

KEVIN SANDLER: You've been quite busy these last few years directing episodes of *Cold Case, Numbers, House,* and *The Shield,* writing a musical, *One Red Flower,* as well as writing and producing *Hate,* a pilot for Showtime based on the activities of a hate crime unit in the New York City Police Department. Where did this interest in entertainment begin for you?

PARIS BARCLAY: I think it goes back to about seventh grade. Around then I wrote my first original musical, and I performed it in the basement of the Ascension Catholic Grade School in Harvey, Illinois, along with a few of my friends. It only had a couple original songs. And since I couldn't actually write down songs at that point, we sang the new songs and lip-synched to various recordings of songs that I chose for the musical—which was called *Time for Living.* It was about a warlock who needed a second chance—of course, I played the warlock. And where that came from I have no idea, other than from watching too much television. So I think I can trace my first attempt to actually create something from hours and hours of sitting in front of the television and whiling away the time and learning about life—basically from *Bewitched.*

KS: From private school through Harvard, you continued to write many musicals and plays, particularly the music for the Hasty Pudding show. How did your education prepare you for an artistic career?

PB: That's interesting. I went to a small private high school called LaLumiere—at that time LaLumiere School for Boys—in La Porte, Indiana. And at LaLumiere, since there were only one hundred students, we were encouraged to do everything—to play sports, to excel in academics, and also to be involved in the arts. A couple of the teachers there thought I had some sort of artistic talent, so they encouraged me to write plays. I was also at that point involved in a musical group called The Time. John Roberts, our current Chief Justice of the Supreme Court, was a classmate of mine and was in the singing group. We also were cast in a play together, *You're a Good Man, Charlie Brown*. I played Snoopy and he played Patty—remember, this was an all-boys school at the time. And I think these experiences sort of fanned the fire. Then by the time I went to Harvard I didn't really want to go to class as much as I wanted to learn more about writing and composing. So I eventually chose to concentrate my studies around English and music, which seemed the best way to get through school while doing the least amount of real work. As you mentioned, I wrote a lot of musicals and directed plays through my Harvard years—hardly ever went to class except my screenwriting class with William Alfred and a couple of other seminars. I wrote a musical version of Machiavelli's *The Prince* with my roommate Arthur Golden, who would go on to do much better. And then I went to New York hoping I could be a black Stephen Sondheim. You can see how well that worked.

KEVIN
SANDLER

KS: Yet you ended up primarily working in television. How did that happen?

PB: It wasn't really what I chose. What I thought I would do was, I'd come to New York and I would write these musicals that everyone would love and they would recognize me as an enormously talented musical theater person—and I could make a living in the process. As it turned out I did do a couple of musicals, which were produced, but I couldn't make a living. I mean, I would make about $500 or I would lose $1,000 getting the whole thing done. And so I survived working in advertising as a copywriter. And from working through a number of agencies in New York, including Grey and BBDO, I eventually started directing television commercials, which eventually led me to directing music videos. Then my music video reel was seen by a young writer-producer named John Wells, who had the enormous foresight to hire me to direct a television series he had just created called *Angel Street*. This was back in 1992, and that became my first job directing television. Fortunately for me, I ended up doing two out of the six episodes that were made. The show wasn't a success, but my directing of it was a success—and John Wells remembered me when his next show, a little medical show called *ER*, went on the air. And then I got to direct that, and that led—well, one thing leads to another, and before I knew it I was in the game.

KS: What commercials were you involved in prior to *Angel Street*?

PB: I worked on a lot of what we called "packaged goods" clients. I would do a lot of things for Folgers, I was part of the team that worked on the campaign we called "Great Restaurants of the World," which yo may remember as: "We've replaced this coffee with instant coffee—see if you can tell the difference."

KS: I remember those commercials.

PB: I didn't actually create that campaign but I was one of the team that continued to make what we called "pool outs" of it, where we would go to Tavern on the Green and different restaurants and do different versions of it. I had clients like Scott Paper for Viva paper towels ("as absorbent as THIS sponge!") and Crisco ("Crisco home cookin'!"). I also worked from IBM's business-to-business computer division, which I'll make a movie about someday, it was so deep and strange. The first time I did a commercial where I really felt I was making a difference was when I wrote a commercial for the American Foundation for AIDS Research in 1986, a new organization at the time but now a beacon in the fight against AIDS. Elizabeth Taylor was the head of it, along with Dr. Mathilde Krim. It was to be Ms. Taylor's first television commercial ever. Days before shooting, we had a little disagreement with the director, so I had to go out to L.A. to film Elizabeth Taylor for the spot. She was late, but could not have been more gracious to the crew. It ended up airing on ABC only once, because there were too many complaints about the tag line had created (that Ms. Taylor said at the end of the spot): "AIDS: It's nobody's fault . . . and everybody's problem." Apparently people disagreed with both parts of that statement. I still stand by it. Folks just could not separate the affliction from the afflicted. It probably didn't help that it showed a series of people playing Russian roulette, the gun right to their temples. That became my first directing gig.

An Interview with Paris Barclay

KS: And music videos?

PB: In the mid- to late 1980s, I was one of the very few African-American directors who had directed anything. So I was approached by a gentleman named Joel Hinman to create a company that would do music videos and commercials, with the primary idea to provide opportunities for more minorities behind the camera. We called this company Black & White Television (weren't we clever?) and we said, well, if we give jobs to African Americans and other people of color behind the camera and in different various crew positions, they can gain experience, and then they can go out and get all kinds of work in the world. That was incredibly liberal and very cute for us to have that idea, but it lost a lot of money in its first season—I mean, the first year of the company we lost thousands and thousands of dollars trying to get this company to work. The second year we were a multi-million-dollar company. It just exploded.

KS: Concerns about race, then, even back in the music video days, played a role in the choice of projects that you did as a producer or director?

PB: I was lucky because one of the first major music video clients I worked with was James Todd Smith, a.k.a. LL Cool J. I did seven music videos with him: "Big Ole Butt," "One Shot at Love," "Jinglin' Baby," "Around the Way Girl," "Mama Said Knock You Out," "Strictly Business," and "The Future of the Funk" compilation. "Mama Said Knock You Out" was an enormous success, a black-and-white, *Raging Bull*–inspired video that took an MTV award for Best Rap Video and two Billboard Music Video awards. But also I did groups like Kid 'n Play, Brand Nubian, and R&B artists like Vesta Williams. Eventually I broadened out to do Bob Dylan; Harry Connick, Jr.; Was (Not Was); and New Kids on the Block. Then I became known just as a director who could direct anything, not just people of color, not just hip-hop. So that actually ended up being quite great for me. See how easy this all was?

KS: Did you have a lot of control over the representation in music videos at that time?

PB: That's a really great question. I miss the control we had in the music video days. In the music video days you would get a song in the mail, or sometimes through a messenger if they were in a hurry, and they would say, write a concept. And you would have to write a description of what the music video would be in two or three pages, submit it with a budget, and they decided whether or not you'd get the video. Then you'd refine that concept with the artist and the label, and then you'd shoot it with relatively little interference (I mean, usually there would be some person with the record company on the set but they trusted you—more or less). It was very unlike either advertising, which is micromanaged by a million different people, or television, which has a ton of bosses as well. So I was in heaven in the music video days, although I didn't realize it at the time. We got to see what we created a few weeks later, and pretty much it would be what you'd imagined.

KS: Did you feel that you needed to somehow shape the content of music videos in a way so they would be acceptable and playable on MTV at that time?

PB: Absolutely. For the African-American audience, the biggest outlets were BET or *Yo! MTV Raps*, the rap show on MTV at the time. They were the two major outlets. so you really had to target each video, and you had to make sure that it matched their standards and practices.

LL Cool J's "Around the Way Girl," for instance, almost didn't make it on MTV: half of it was shot on video and MTV just had a policy against showing music videos shot on video. It wasn't that it was sexist—which it was—or misogynistic—which it kind of was. That stuff was fine. It was that it was shot on video, and they thought it looked terrible. They wouldn't play it until the record became a number one R&B hit, and eventually they had to add it to their play list. The single went gold. So there.

KS: Knowing that it was sexist and misogynist, did that bother you at the time?

PB: I knew you would go right for that, so that's why I threw it out there. No, because at the time I thought my job was to represent the artist more than to represent myself. That has evolved as I have become someone who creates his own projects. But as I began working in music videos, I took the song and I interpreted it in a way I felt would represent the artist and sell more records—I was not as concerned particularly with the content of the song. Sometimes a little bit, but—LL Cool J['s song] called "Big Ole Butt" comes to mind. It was about his love of women's behinds and the-bigger-the-better—years before "Baby Got Back." My mother felt the whole video was incredibly sexist—which it was—but I thought it was actually quite funny, and Todd (that's what we called LL back in the day) loved it because it represented his point of view. But I wouldn't do that video today.

An Interview with Paris Barclay

KS: What projects, then, represent the kind of representations and themes that you are gravitating toward now?

PB: The project called *Hate* that James DeMonaco and I created last year for Showtime was one of the most significant pilots I have ever done. I had hoped that it would become a series but it only ended up being a pilot because Showtime wanted to do other shows like *Huff* and *Weeds* and more power to 'em. But what we had done was look at the real hate crime team of the New York Police Department and created a story about how those crimes are investigated, the politics of those crimes at the highest level of the police department and the mayor of New York, and how they affect the public as well as how they affect the detectives themselves. And we used a conceit in that show where you can actually hear the detectives' thoughts while they were talking. The thoughts were overlapping what they were saying. And we thought that was fascinating because it helped reveal when their thoughts were in harmony with what they were doing and when they were absolutely dissonant with what they were doing—or with what they were saying. And I thought that was just one of the best things I had ever done in my life. I was gravely disappointed that it didn't go further.

> KS: You know, there's a line in that show by Marcia Gay Harden, the Chief Jackie Mantello character, when she says to the press, "I think hate breeds in an atmosphere where intolerance becomes the norm, where ethnic groups are demonized, where people are denied rights because of their sexual orientation. When the government appears powerless, hate crimes grow." These words seem to sum up many of the themes you're dealing with—in terms of race, class, and gender—these last five or six years of your career.

KEVIN
SANDLER PB: Interesting thought. I wrote that speech for Marcia Gay Harden and it has been in every draft—the show probably went through fourteen drafts before it was done, but that speech pretty much remained intact because I thought thematically that was what the show was about. I'm pleased it pricked up your ears, as Joe Orton would say if he were alive. I feel that hate crimes in particular and intolerance in general is the area of society where the mass media could do the most good. Before that I was heavily involved with sexism—I really gravitated toward projects that dealt with that—and racism too. In the mid-1990s I did a show for HBO called *The Cherokee Kid* that was purportedly a comic western starring Sinbad and Burt Reynolds, but I loved it because it was the first time the mass media dealt with black cowboys in a setting that young people could see and enjoy. So I figured this was genius: it was fun, Sinbad had a built-in audience (he was very popular at that time), but it's also telling a historically based story about black cowboys and their place in society and in the Old West (which I thought was an undertold story). That was a passion of mine, too. I guess I have evolved toward tolerance—even before September 11; I've basically become insanely repetitive on this tolerance thing.

> KS: Obviously everybody needs to make conscious choices in terms of choosing the script they want to direct or the project they want to develop in terms of race, sexuality, gender, and other issues. How are you conscious of representing people of color, of whites, of the working class or gender, in perhaps a single episode of, say, *The Shield* or *The West Wing*? What would be a good example of a situation in which you might have thought, "This is how I am going to put my mark on this particular episode"?

PB: Let me backtrack a bit. Whenever I create a show, I always try to do what John Wells taught me, which is to find the overarching theme of the show. He always said the theme of ER is compassion—it's the id

that if you come into this county hospital there are going to be doctors
who will present a compassionate face and care for you. The theme of
The West Wing, in John Wells's mind, is patriotism. It wasn't really that
it was left or right—although most people felt that it was both left and
right—but the show was really about how patriotic these people were
in the way they worked for the president, the hours they put in, and the
amount of commitment they gave to it. With *Hate,* we were dealing with
tolerance (or the lack thereof). So I've always tried when I create a show,
to look for an overarching theme. But sometimes I'm working on a show
where I have not been the creator and I have less actual personal control.
A perfect example is *Cold Case,* which has a lot of episodes dealing with
socially relevant situations. Last season I came in and directed an episode called "Strange Fruit," which revolved around a 1968 lynching of a
teenage boy whose body was discovered by one of our detectives when he
was a child. I was very moved by the original setup, and I asked, what is
this going to really be about? How is this story going to tell me something new or take me to a different place? Fortunately, it had been written by the producer, Veena Sud, and she was open to some of the ideas I
had to address some of these issues. So it represented for me a different
view of the assimilation or the attempted assimilation of African Americans into a basically white culture in the 1960s, and how that can have
negative consequences if it's misperceived by the majority, in this case
the white majority, who began to loathe these people because they were
taking their jobs. So the whole story eventually revolved around an issue
that is current today, the new assimilating minority struggling with the
majority and taking their places, and how that—in this particular case—
leads to a tragic death. But had we redone that show this year, people
would have seen the immigration struggle in it, because the theme
continues to play out in so many different ways. So in that particular
case, we were able to refine the script, to shape it, and with casting and
how we put the whole show together, we made that finer point through it
that made it relevant to today. It did very well, and the NAACP recognized
with an honor this year, so I can't complain.

KS: Were there any stylistic choices you made in "Strange Fruit" to in-
terject your own personal voice into a show that already had a preexisting narrative and visual style?

PB: We made the killing much more protracted and much more
brutal than the show ever does. I think of the episodes we had done:
never did a killing that's taken that long and has been shown that
specifically, from the binding of the hands to the dragging of the feet
the actual hanging off the tree; we've just never done that. We don't

normally make you suffer through it; it's usually a shotgun, a knife off camera, or someone gets hit over the head with a blunt instrument. But in this particular case we—or I—thought the brutality of it helped show viewers that lynching in and of itself is an animal activity. It's not human, it's subhuman. Without that it wouldn't have the same impact.

ᴋꜱ: How are you capable, though, of representing race and gender in a socially conscious way if you come in as a director-for-hire for all these shows? Is that in any way possible?

ᴘʙ: It's very possible. I came in on *The West Wing* as a director-for-hire, and either the first or the second episode had a gay Republican. The first thing I said to Aaron Sorkin was, "Do these people exist?" I was joking, because I know they do. But my whole goal is to understand, how can this person be completely realized as a three-dimensional person? It's not really about my particular agenda, because virtually everything that this character said I disagreed with. I just wanted to make sure he came off as real as everyone around him. In my work, I just want to make sure that even if an African-American person's a killer, or a gay person is a Republican, I just want to make sure I can see their humanity. That's what I work toward. That's using television to its best advantage, because it's tough to shove a particular agenda down people's throats; they tend to resist that. It's too obvious, too blatant. So I gave up on that whole concept a while ago, and what I try to do now is show humans that viewers can relate to (even if they disagree with them so there's some way to get under their skin and maybe provoke some thoughts and consciousness, and in some way maybe shake down the stereotypes we may have of people. Even presenting gay Republicans, to me, is interesting and refreshing for both gay and straight people: to see a different point of view that's not necessarily that of a consistently Democratic-voting, liberal, San Francisco–dwelling, well-furnished, well-heeled, Fire Island maiden.

ᴋꜱ: Do you feel personally obligated or responsible for portrayals of this sort as an openly gay African-American director?

ᴘʙ: I do. I don't have a posse of other people doing this, so I feel tha if I'm actually near the center of influence on any of these things, I wa to be felt, and I want that to be known. I normally don't object unless I feel that the character is superficial or stereotypical. I had an experience working on ɴʏᴘᴅ *Blue* where David Milch, who is the best writer television I have ever worked with, bar none, created a character for ar episode who was a lesbian and whose lover had been murdered. In the first scene, when the detectives come in and the body is still there, she

seemed very cold to me. There was no feeling that they had any kind of
relationship at all: she wasn't teary and she wasn't in shock. I knew she
wasn't the murderer, which is the only thing I thought might explain
why she was characterized in this way. So I said, "David, this doesn't
seem like this person is really her lover. It doesn't seem like this dead
person is the equivalent of your wife to you. Are you trying to seed a
suspicion that this woman killed this other person, and the relationship is not significant?" He said, "No, that wasn't my intention at all."
I said, "Well, maybe there could be something in that scene that tells
you there was actually love and affection between these two women."
And he huffed and puffed and was exasperated somewhat, but he sort of
knew I was right. So he took me into the writing room. David goes to lie
down and looks at a monitor (he doesn't actually type—he dictates the
script from the floor to a typist across the room). We went to the scene,
and he found a moment in which the photographer pulls off the sheet
from the dead woman's body to take a picture, and he inserted into the
script that the woman who is being interviewed at that moment begins
crying hysterically. And that moment (I call that little activity a rhetorical "can opener") popped her open and showed she was withholding
all that emotion until the body was revealed, or until in some way she
felt her partner had been violated, and that made her crazy. That made
the scene work for me, and it also made her more human, and made us
realize where she was. I love that he was able to do that. I mean, he was
really glad, because it made things deeper, richer, and more interesting
for the detectives, but at the same time it was more true to the character,
and she ended up being more human. So that's one way I can influence
things even if I am not the writer.

KS: Are there times when you had to compromise your vision or your
opinion of a particular scene in terms of the cast, the script, or the
direction because of pressures from the producer or the studio?

PB: There are times. Not too many, considering how many times I've
been up at bat. There were people cast in *The Cherokee Kid*, for example,
that I personally would never have cast but were marquee names, and
they made it very difficult for me to do my job. But because I don't actually pay for these things, I have to listen a little bit to the folks who do—
in this case, HBO—and they've had a little bit of a history of success also.
Don't get the opportunity to make a movie with them if I don't listen to
them. Normally, if it becomes too abusive or too painful, then I just don't
do the project. I find a way to extricate myself from it.

KS: Was that similar to the situation with *City of Angels*?

PB: I reached an agreement with Steven Bochco and company that I wouldn't talk about aspects of that production, but I can talk in general about when I'm in a position on a project and feel I am unable to influence the outcome: I become frustrated, and I have to find a way out. If I cannot be a positive force, then I am in the wrong place, and I know that I have to go.

KS: Bochco and director and executive producer Kevin Hooks were quoted in the paper that they had to make *City of Angels* a more user-friendly show, to make the show a bit more accessible for the second season. Were you expected to make creative changes to the show to broaden its audience appeal beyond the core group of black viewers in the first season?

KEVIN
SANDLER

PB: From the beginning I had always hoped it would be a show with broader appeal, and I hoped it would have a very eclectic cast. You're not going to be on CBS for long if you don't have a big audience. It just doesn't work that way. I can't just sit down and say, "I'm going to do a show that's just for lesbian women," and expect that it's going to be on the number one network in terms of eyeballs, which is CBS. That's just not going to happen. There just aren't that many eyeballs that are lesbian women or men who want to see lesbian women in shows—that's why *The L Word* is on Showtime. But now if I'm going to do that show (and I was one of the co-creators of it) I would also like to show you something about African American people that you don't know—their intelligence, their dignity, but also the fact that they can be slimeballs and creeps just like everybody else, but with real reasons to do that. And that's one of the reasons why it's very important that villains are as well portrayed as heroes.

KS: It was considered to be a "black show," especially because it had more black viewers than white viewers. Does the industry still use the term "black show" to describe shows, and how does this affect the type of pilots that are being made?

PB: The industry definitely still uses the term "black show" and generally doesn't produce them. And as time goes on they will produce fewer and fewer shows with primarily African-American casts. Right now we have only the four big networks and a fifth network, CW, the morph of UPN and the WB. UPN used to have a business model that call for doing shows geared to an African-American audience. But now tha they have merged they're going to go for the broadest audience and fig for that big demographic that the other big four are getting. So I think actual shows for African Americans will be found on other cable chan nels, somewhere down the line, or will be produced by some enterpris ing person—someone like Reggie Hudlin who can turn BET into a rea production entity. But it's not going to happen in the networks now. They think there's not enough money in the black people business, basically. And they're really wrong.

K S: Is this why the networks focus on shows with integrated casts rather than developing shows whose chief protagonists are people of color?

P B: Absolutely. With an integrated cast of some sort you have a chance at getting the broadest possible audience, and also you get more advertisers supporting it, because advertisers want to—how shall I say this nicely—they want to sell the most things to the most people. So they're going to want the show that has a diversified cast, like the cast of *Without a Trace,* for instance, or *C.S.I.*

K S: What does it take to get white audiences to sample a show that has minorities, in your opinion?

P B: It would have to be written by one of three people I know in the world who can write in such a way that it would gain a critical mass and the characters would be universal enough to appeal to them. But none of them are currently interested in doing such a show.

K S: Which writers are you speaking of?

P B: One would be David Milch, who can do just about anything and could actually write a show with a black cast and make it a success.

K S: He created *Deadwood.*

P B: Yes. He's the creator of NYPD *Blue.* I think Tom Fontana could write that show. I was moved in the way he created characters in *Oz,* among other shows. And there's a relatively little-known writer who probably could do it, named David Mills or David Simon—Mills is African American, Simon is not—who wrote a really great series called *The Corner.* Simon went on to do *The Wire,* which is currently the best show on television with a largely although not exclusively African-American cast. Simon could probably write that show in such a way that it would have a lot of appeal. But those are the only people I know in the world who could do that.

K S: I'm assuming these people are not writing these stories because the networks aren't buying them?

P B: Or they're not interested. Or they don't have a great concept for such a show.

K S: This point might now be moot, but in 1999 the NAACP declared the fall season to be a virtual "whitewash." Not a person of color was a lead in twenty-six new series, and few minorities appeared in secondary roles or ensemble situations either. Then *City of Angels* came the following year, which was one of the first broadcast network dramas with a predominantly African-American cast and crew. It's now 2006. Do you think network television shows have become increasingly inclusive or racially diverse, or better yet, do you feel the television landscape—which would include cable as well as broadcast—has become increasingly inclusive and racially diverse?

PB: Generally they have become more inclusive. The current thinking is, let's get as many different people as possible and stick them in front of all three cams. Let's have a show that's got a black guy, a Latino guy, a beautiful blond chick, some buff white guy, and let's see if we can get as many people as humanly possible to watch the show. It's all about commerce right now and it's hardly ever about art or politics.

KEVIN
SANDLER

KS: Is it still about having a white male or female heterosexual lead to star in these ensemble dramas?

PB: Absolutely. You can't do anything else. Why would you even think about it? When we did *Hate,* we were a little insane to make one of the leading characters bisexual. The network thought we were just on crack. We were doing it for a network that we thought would be open to a bit more diversity; the lead was an awfully handsome guy, and we thought, well, maybe if the girls like him and the guys like him, who knows what But that wouldn't happen on a major network right now. They would say that person would be off-putting and it couldn't happen. Even an African-American lead is rough without a second lead that gives him some support. On *The Unit* right now Dennis Haysbert plays the lead, but Scott Foley is right there to help him look not quite so black.

KS: Are networks providing more employment opportunities for women and minority directors or are minorities still underrepresented in those realms?

PB: They are still underrepresented, and substantially so. Unfortunately, there are also fewer people working more; in other words, there are fewer African-American directors like myself who are successful, and they are working more. That makes the numbers look better than they really are, if you follow my meaning. If I do ten shows a year, that not as good as ten different African-American directors directing show It might be good for me, but it is not as good for the industry and it is not as good for people having careers. But the numbers, statistically, l the same. So if the numbers still look bad, you can see what's happening: the veterans are being rewarded, and more and more new people are being excluded from coming in. That's the real disaster. And it's worse if you're a woman. If you're a woman, you can just about forget about it. A woman of color probably has a one in seventy-five shot of ever getting a job directing a network television series.

KS: You were a co-chair of the African American Steering Committee of the Directors Guild of America, and now you're the first vice president of the D.G.A. board.

PB: That's really where my powers to influence diversity lie. In my role in the D.G.A. and also as co-chair of the Diversity Committee, we meet with show runners regularly; at least once a month we've got a meeting. For instance, last time we went to ABC and met with the creators of *Desperate Housewives, Lost,* and *Grey's Anatomy* all together. I talked about the importance of diversity. I talked about how some of them had very little experience before they were given the opportunity to create these great series, and we feel they have an obligation to bring new people along. It's not always an argument that's welcomed. Sometimes we've had relatively heated debates: "Why do I need to bring diverse people along? How does that help my show?" We patiently point out that without people giving you a shot you would be nowhere. That has certainly been my experience. Without John Wells seeing my reel I would probably still be in advertising, living somewhere in Nyack. But because of the opportunity he gave me, I have a whole other life, and I've been able to influence and bring other people along with that. So we're trying to remind them they have a responsibility. They still say, "Well, we're not going to bring in new people just because you say so, and hurt our show." So we say, "You're not going to hurt your show, and in many cases you're going to find new talent, you're going to develop them, they're going to help your show, and they're going to become people that you brought to the fore, and that's a good feeling." As you know, we don't win that argument often enough.

KS: Was Alfre Woodard on *Desperate Housewives* a result of such discussions?

PB: I don't know why she's on *Desperate Housewives.* She must have really been in financial need or something, because the part is thankless. I used to watch *Desperate Housewives,* and when I heard she was coming on I said this is great, because they're going to give her something that's worthy of her talent, and won't that be interesting. Then, after a few episodes, I realized that wasn't happening, and then I became depressed and just stopped watching the show altogether. The D.G.A.

doesn't normally get into casting because actually casting the shows are doing pretty well on. Black people are actually proportionately represented in terms of the cast on network television shows. It's behind the scenes where we don't get any love.

K S: What shows do you feel are the most successful in terms of behind-the-scenes and in-front-of-the-camera employment of minorities?

P B: One of the most successful ones I know of—because I'm on it—is *Cold Case*. I'm looking at this year's schedule of directors and I can tell you that even though the show is not particularly a show full of people of color, thirteen of twenty-three episodes were directed by African Americans, Latinos, or women—which is better than 50 percent. Now why do you think that is?

K S: I guess just opportunity. Is that what it really is about?

P B: Part of it is opportunity, part of it is because I am here (and I do four shows automatically), and part of it is because a couple of directors were given opportunities, like Kevin Bray, and he hit the ball out of the park, and now he's returned for a couple more episodes. We had a new director named Nicole Kassell who's only done one feature film. She's a young woman from New York; she did a feature film called *The Woodsman*, starring Kevin Bacon, in which he plays a pedophile. She did an episode that was so fantastic, people wanted to hire her and keep her around all the time. And she wasn't getting any opportunities anywhere else. For some reason we were doing it—we were willing to give people opportunities, and now we've found three or four new directors that we're pretty excited about. So that's what happens: we hunt and we meet—I've probably met with fifty directors this year, and if you meet fifty directors you're going to find some great people of color and women that you can give opportunities to.

K S: What future projects are you working on now?

P B: By the time this interview is published, they will either be dead running on the air. But one of them is a half-comedy, half-drama that I think represents my voice at its very best.

K S: Is it broadcast or cable?

P B: Broadcast. And I also want to do a family show. I want to do a family show with a different kind of family. I am a gay man with a house, husband, and two adorable young adopted kids. There might be some room pretty soon to do a show that's not unlike my actual life.

KS: Do you think broadcast will be receptive to that?

PB: Probably not. But I might be able to figure out some way to make it tasteful to them. That's the other thing—in something like *Hate,* at least we gave them a procedural drama in a police detective mode as a way for them to get into the whole theme of it, and then a way for us to slip in our point of view in different corners of it.

KS: If you're doing a comedy about a nontraditional family, what would you have to do to make it desirable to networks?

PB: If you want to exist on a network you have to have something that allows them the comfort to sell it to advertisers. So there would have to be some element of it, probably a central, non-gay character. For instance, let's say I am going to do two gay partners and their kids. There will probably have to be another character, a mother or a close friend, who really is the voice of the show and a central character whom you can hang the story on, rather than telling the story through a gay man's point of view, so that you can get away with all those other stories. Just baldly going with two gay guys dressed in L.L. Bean and their babies is probably not going to be enough for them to sell all the goods they want to sell.

An Interview with Paris Barclay

KS: Do you have to have a character in a comedy who kind of states the morality of the show, so it can be easily digested by mass audiences?

PB: I don't know if they have to state the morality of it, but as David Milch said, you always have to have an audience surrogate somewhere. An audience surrogate in his point of view—this is from his analysis of all dramatic television—can be done a number of different ways, but there needs to be someone whom the audience can see the show through. In *NYPD Blue* it was the character played by Nick Turturro in the pilot. It was his first day, he was just beginning, and he was looking the world with fresh eyes the same way that the viewer was. He eventually became more of a minor character as David Caruso's character took off. In the very beginning of the first pilot episode he was the eyes to that world, and you always need that—you always need some sort of leverage to get into it. I think we would need that to make it work.

KS: And that person needs to be somewhat comforting and not threatening?

PB: Yes, unless you're dealing with HBO, in which case that person can be very likable and also very bad, like Tony Soprano. But Tony Soprano is highly unusual and highly successful, and is a great alchemy of great writing and a terrific actor in a role that only a couple of different people could do. It's really "don't try this at home" territory.

> KS: You talked about writing for broadcast. Do you see that as a greater challenge than, say, writing for HBO, or do you have relationships in broadcast that lend you to be developing pilots for those networks?

> PB: I tend to work in broadcast a little bit more because (a) it's more lucrative and (b) there are more opportunities. I don't fully understand what HBO is doing at this point, and I don't know if they do. They're losing their biggest hit shows, and I don't know if they're creating new things to replace them—shows that have the same kind of excitement as the shows they've had. I think they have lost their way a bit, which is too bad, because it makes less appointment television for me. I don't see *Big Love* as a new improvement over *Six Feet Under*.

KEVIN
SANDLER

> KS: Are you pursuing any more of the short-term programming that you did at NBC in 2003, those one-minute movies? Is that a lucrative business?

> PB: Funny that you should ask. I just started discussions about that very subject. When we did that, two or three years ago, cell phone and iPod technology wasn't at the level that it is at now. A couple of networks and studios have talked to me about redeveloping the idea of short, interstitial films that can be deployed on the Internet as well as on people's mobile devices—"mobisodes," as we call it. I'll probably be getting back into that. One of those mobisodes is being developed into a pilot for NBC so even a show came out of it, which is kind of awesome.

After my interview with Paris, I shared the transcript with my Medi[a] Industries graduate class when I taught at the University of Arizon[a]. In a semester that ended with a bleak account of the contempora[ry] landscape by political economists, Paris demonstrated to them th[at] filming difference still was possible, if perhaps a bit more difficult f[or] broadcast television in the wake of the UPN/WB merger into CW. Whi[le] further concentration and conglomeration of the U.S. media may [af]fect diversity in mass media, nascent technologies such as cable, [In]ternet, and cell phones are narrowcasting content to audiences a[nd] advertisers that increasingly embraces difference, dispels stereotyp[es] and challenges conventional ways of thinking. Paris traverses the televisual realms, having reached a point in his career where he c[an] selectively choose and develop those series he wants to be invol[ved] with. John Wells gave him his opportunity, Paris made the mos[t] those opportunities, and now he uses those opportunities to make a difference.

This conversation with Paris inspired me to write a book about *The Shield,* a television series for which he directed three episodes. Together with my co-author, Daniel Bernardi, we observed the shooting of the seventh season and conducted interviews from August to November 2007. It soon became clear in our investigation that many other cast and crew members, executives, and marketers also complicated social ideologies about race, sexuality, and class during the production of *The Shield.* Individuals like creator Shawn Ryan, writer-producer Adam Fierro, cinematographer Rohn Schmidt, FX president John Landgraf, and director Gwyneth Horder-Payton were consciously aware of—if not deeply rigorous about—filming difference in their respective artistic capacities. In fact, Horder-Payton was a student of Professor Vivian Sobchack at UCLA. While these artists may not use the same paradigms as scholars, they are equally as concerned about representation and the meanings their work might bring about. *The Shield* book, among other objectives, explores this relationship within a climate of ethnographic collaboration, offering a theoretical and methodologically nuanced approach to production studies. Like Paris, we hope to use this given opportunity to make a difference and to bring new insights to authorship, media texts, and audiences.

Selected Bibliography

ESSAYS BY AND INTERVIEWS WITH
FILMMAKERS—GENDER, RACE,
SEXUALITY, CLASS

Compiled by Chiara Ferrari
(California State University, Chico)

Abbott, Rebecca. "The Avant-Garde in American Film: An Interview with Stan Bra-khage." *Sacred Heart University Review* 9, no. 1 (Fall 1988): 33–45.

Abrash, Barbara. "Matters of Race: An Interview with Orlando Bagwell." *Cineaste* 30, no. 1 (Winter 2004): 34–35.

Acker, Ally. *Reel Women: Pioneers of the Cinema, 1896 to the Present.* New York: Continuum, 1991.

Alba, Victoria. "A Conversation with Lynn Kirby and Trinh T. Minh-ha." *Artweek* 30, nos. 7–8 (July–August 1999): 18–19.

Anton, Saul. "A Search for Roots and Identity: An Interview with Tiana Thi Thanh Nga." *Cineaste* 20, no. 3 (1994): 46.

Areu Jones, Cathy. "Cheech Marin's New Vision." *Hispanic*, October 2001, 48–52.

Aufderheide, Pat, and Debra Zimmerman. "From A to Z: A Conversation on Women's Filmmaking." *Signs: Journal of Women in Culture and Society* 30, no. 1 (2004): 1455–1472, http://www.journals.uchicago.edu/SIGNS/journal/issues/v30n1/300118/300118.text.html.

Auster, Al, and Leonard Quart. "Counterculture Revisited: An Interview with John Sayles." *Cineaste* 11, no. 1 (Winter 1980–1981): 16.

Badt, Karin Luisa. "'I Want My Films to Explode with Life': An Interview with Mira Nair." *Cineaste* 30, no. 1 (Winter 2004): 10–15.

Barbash, Ilsa, and Lucien Taylor. *Cross-cultural Filmmaking: A Handbook for Making Documentary and Ethnographic Films and Videos.* Berkeley and Los Angeles: University of California Press, 1997.

Belton, Don. "Isaac Julien: Britain's Leading Independent Filmmaker." *Outlook* 4, no. 4 (Spring 1992): 15.

Beltran, Mary C. "The New Hollywood Racelessness: Only the Fast, Furious, (and Multiracial) Will Survive." *Cinema Journal* 44, no. 2 (Winter 2005): 50–67.

Berry, Chris. "On Questions of Difference." *Cinemaya* (India) 23 (Spring 1994): 40–43.

Bielby, Denise, and William T. Bielby. "Women and Men in Film: Gender Inequality Among Writers in a Culture Industry." *Gender & Society* 10, no. 3 (June 1996): 248–275.

Binfield, Marnie. "An Interview with Lourdes Portillo." *Velvet Light Trap* 55 (Spring 2005): 33–38.

Birringer, Johannes. "Homosexuality and the Revolution: An Interview with Jorge Perugorria." *Cineaste* 21, nos. 1–2 (1995): 21.

Biskind, Peter. *Down and Dirty Pictures: Miramax, Sundance, and the Rise of Independent Film*. New York: Simon & Schuster, 2004.

———. *Easy Riders, Raging Bulls: How the Sex-Drugs-and-Rock 'n' Roll Generation Saved Hollywood*. New York: A Touchstone Book, 1998.

Bobo, Jacqueline. *Black Women Film and Video Artists*. New York: Routledge, 1998.

Bobo, Jacqueline, and Ellen Seiter. "Black Feminism and Media Criticism: *The Women of Brewster Place*." In *Feminist Television Criticism: A Reader*, edited by Charlotte Brunsdon, Julie D'Acci, and Lynn Spiegel, 167–183. Oxford: Clarendon Press, 1997.

Boccino, Joan. "A Talk with Barbara Hammer. Part One. Personal Reflections." *The Empty Chair*, November 1993, 10–11.

———. "A Talk with Barbara Hammer. Part Two. Reflections on Work." *The Empty Chair*, December 1993–January 1994, 10–12.

Bourdier, Jean-Paul, and Trinh T. Minh-Ha. *African Spaces: Designs for Living in Upper Volta*. London: Africana Publishing Co., 1985.

Brakhage, Stan, and Bruce R. McPherson. *Essential Brakhage: Selected Writings on Filmmaking*. Kingston, NY: Documentext/McPherson, 2001.

Brownworth, Victoria. "Out in the World: An Interview with Barbara Hammer." *Metroline* 18, no. 1 (January 1995): 18–19, 21.

———. "Reel Women: The Iconoclastic Art of Barbara Hammer." *Deneuve* 5, no. 5 (October 1995): 44–47.

Caldwell, John T. "Critical Industrial Practice: Branding, Repurposing, and the Migratory Patterns of Industrial Texts." *Television and New Media* 7, no. 2 (2006): 99–134.

———. *Televisuality: Style, Crisis, and Authority in American Television*. New Brunswick, NJ: Rutgers University Press, 1995.

Campbell, Loretta. "Reinventing Our Image: Eleven Black Women Filmmakers." *Heresies* 16 (1983): 59–62.

Cancela, Lorena. "Feminist Filmmaking Without Vanity or Sentimentality: An Interview with Sue Brooks." *Cineaste* 29, no. 2 (Spring 2004): 18–21.

Cantrill, Arthur, and Corinne Cantrill. "Nick Deocampo: Independent Filipino Cinema." *Cantrills' Filmnotes* 59–60 (September 1989): 5–10.

———. "Philippine Independent Film and the Mowelfund Film Institute." *Cantrills' Filmnotes* 61–62 (May 1990): 4–6.

Carroll, Rebecca. "Spik(e)ing the Indie Film Punch." *The Independent Film & Video Monthly* 27, no. 6 (July–August 2004): 41–47.

Carson, Diane, Linda Dittmar, and Janince R. Welsch, eds. *Multiple Voices in Feminist Film Criticism*. Minneapolis: University of Minnesota Press, 1994.

Chute, David. "John Sayles Interview: The Writer-Director of the Winning *Return of the Secaucus 7* Talks About His Struggle to Go Hollywood and Still Make His Own Movies." *Film Comment* 17, no. 3 (May–June 1981): 54.

Ciecko, Anne. "Representing the Spaces of Diaspora in Contemporary British Films by Women Directors." *Cinema Journal* 38, no. 3 (Spring 1999): 67–90.

Crowdus, Gary, and Dan Georgakas. "Thinking About the Power of Images: An Interview with Spike Lee." *Cineaste* 26, no. 2 (2001): 4–9.

Crowdus, Gary, and Dennis West. "'Cheech' Cleans Up His Act." *Cineaste* 16, no. 3 (1988): 34.

D'Acci, Julie. "Leading Up to *Roe vs. Wade:* Television Documentaries in the Abortion Debate." In *Feminist Television Criticism: A Reader,* edited by Charlotte Brunsdon, Julie D'Acci, and Lynn Spiegel, 273–289. Oxford: Clarendon Press, 1997.

Dash, Julie. *Daughters of the Dust: The Making of an African American Woman's Film.* New York: New Press, 1992.

Davis, Zeinabu Irene. "Woman with a Mission: Zeinabu Irene Davis on Filmmaking." *Voices of the African Diaspora* 7, no. 3 (1991): 37–40.

Deocampo, Nick. "Homosexuality as Dissent/Cinema as Subversion: Articulating Gay Consciousness in the Philippines." In *Queer Looks,* edited by Martha Gever, John Greyson, and Pratibha Parmar, 395–402. New York: Routledge, 1993.

Desmond, Jane. "Ethnography, Orientalism and the Avant-garde Film." *Visual Anthropology* 4, no. 2 (1991): 147–160.

Don, Abbe. "Making the Political Personal." *Artweek,* April 1985.

Dorment, Richard. "What's Up Front: Movie Happenings: Movie Maverick: Mario Van Peebles." *Interview* 34, no. 5 (June 2004): 52.

Dougherty, Cecilia. "Stories from a Generation: Early Video at the LA Woman's Building." *Afterimage* 26 (1998): 8–11.

Dow, Bonnie J. *Prime-Time Feminism: Television, Media Culture, and the Women's Movement Since 1970.* Philadelphia: University of Pennsylvania Press, 1996.

Dowell, Pat. "Demystifying Traditional Notions of Gender: An Interview with Sally Potter." *Cineaste* 20, no. 1 (1993): 16.

Dunye, Cheryl. "Original Gangsta." *Filmmaker—The Magazine of Independent Film* 12, no. 3 (Spring 2004): 42–43, 45–46, 100–101.

Dyer, Richard. *Now You See It: Studies on Lesbian and Gay Film.* London: Routledge, 1990.

The Editors. "An Interview with Rachel Raimist." *The Velvet Light Trap* 53 (2004): 59–65.

Ehrenstein, David. "Out of the Wilderness: An Interview with Sally Potter." *Film Quarterly* 47, no. 1 (Fall 1993): 2.

———. "Warren Sonbert Interview." In *Experimental Cinema: The Film Reader,* edited by Wheeler Winston-Dixon and Gwendolyn Audrey Foster, 265–272. London: Routledge, 2002.

Ellerson, Beti. *Sisters of the Screen: Women of Africa on Film, Video and Television.* Trenton, NJ: Africa World Press, 2000.

Feder, Elena. "In the Shadow of Race: Forging Images of Women in Bolivian Film and Video." *Frontiers* 15, no. 1 (Winter 1994): 123–141.

Felperin, Leslie. "Interview: Spike Lee." *Sight and Sound* 13, no. 4 (April 2003): 15.

Florence, Penny. "Lesbian Cinema, Women's Cinema." In *Outwrite: Lesbianism and Popular Culture,* edited by Gabriele Griffin, 126–147. London: Pluto Press, 1993.

Foss, Karen A. "Trinh T. Minh-ha." In *Feminist Rhetorical Theories*, edited by Karen A. Foss, Sonja K. Foss, and Cindy L. Griffin, 227–256. Thousand Oaks, CA: Sage Publications, 1999.

Foster, Gwendolyn Audrey. "Barbara Hammer, An Interview: Re/Constructing Lesbian Auto/biographies in Tender Fictions and Nitrate Kisses." *Post Script: Essays in Film and Humanities* 16, no. 3 (Summer 1997): 3–16.

———. "A Tale of Love: A Dialogue with Trinh T. Minh-ha." *Film Criticism* 21, no. 3 (Spring 1997): 89–115.

———. *Women Film Directors: An International Bio-critical Dictionary*. Westport, CT: Greenwood Press, 1995.

———. *Women Filmmakers of the African and Asian Diaspora: Decolonizing the Gaze, Locating Subjectivity*. Carbondale: Southern Illinois University Press, 1997.

———, ed. *Identity and Memory: The Films of Chantal Akerman*. Carbondale: Southern Illinois University Press, 2003.

Fregoso, Rosa Linda. "Chicana Film Practices: Confronting the 'Many-Headed Demon of Oppression.'" In *Chicanos and Film: Essays on Chicano Representation and Resistance*, edited by Chon A. Noriega, 168–182. New York: Garland Publishing, 1992.

———, ed. *Lourdes Portillo: The Devil Never Sleeps and Other Films*. Austin: University of Texas Press, 2001.

Friedman, Lester D. "Interview with Peter Wollen and Laura Mulvey on *Riddles of the Sphinx*." *Millennium Film Journal* 4–5 (1979): 14–32.

Friedrich, Su. "Radical Form: Radical Content." *Millennium* 22 (Winter–Spring 1989–1990): 118–123.

Fusco, Coco. "Las Madres de la Plaza de Mayo: An Interview with Susana Munoz and Lourdes Portillo." *Cineaste* 15, no. 1 (1986): 22–25.

———. "Visualizing Theory: An Interview with Isaac Julien." *NKA: Journal of Contemporary African Art* 6–7 (Summer/Fall 1996): 54–57.

Gaines, Jane, and Michael Renov, eds. *Collecting Visible Evidence*. Minneapolis: University of Minnesota Press, 1999.

Gallagher, Steve. "Bizarre Love Triangle: Interview with Richard Glatzer and Wash West." *Filmmaker—The Magazine of Independent Film* 10, no. 1 (Fall 2001): 68–7, 84–87.

Ganguly, Suranjan. "Stan Brakhage: The 60th Birthday Interview." In *Experimental Cinema: The Film Reader*, edited by Wheeler Winston-Dixon and Gwendolyn Audrey Foster, 139–162. London: Routledge, 2002.

Garrett, Stephen. "Sundance '99: No Man's Land." *Filmmaker—The Magazine of Independent Film* 7, no. 2 (February–April 1999): 82–83, 108–109.

Geffner, David. "New Realities." *Filmmaker—The Magazine of Independent Film* no. 2 (Winter 2003): 69–71, 102–104.

Gemunden, Gerd, Alice Kuzniar, and Klaus Phillips. "From Taboo Parlor to Porn a Passing: An Interview with Monika Treut." *Film Quarterly* 50 (Spring 1997): 2–

Georgakas, Dan. "From Stella to Iphigenia: The Woman-Centered Films of Michael Cacoyannis." *Cineaste* 30, no. 2 (2005): 24–31.

Georgakas, Dan, and Gary Crowdus, eds. *The Cineaste Interview II: Filmmakers on Art and Politics of the Cinema*. Chicago: Lake View Press, 2003.

Georgakas, Dan, and Lenny Rubenstein, eds. *The Cineaste Interviews: On the Art and Politics of the Cinema.* Chicago: Lake View Press, 1983.

Gever, Martha, John Greyson, and Pratibha Parmar, eds. *Queer Looks: Perspectives on Lesbian and Gay Film and Video.* New York: Routledge, 1993.

Glicksman, Marlaine. "Spike Lee's Bed-Stuy BBQ." *Film Comment* 25 (July–August 1989): 12–16.

Gold, Heather. "Film: Desperately Seeking Jewish Women." *NCJW Journal* 14, no. 1 (March 31, 1991): 9.

Goldovskaya, Marina. *Woman with a Movie Camera: My Life as a Russian Filmmaker.* Austin: University of Texas Press, 2006.

Goldstein, Lynda. "Getting into Lesbian Shorts: White Spectators and Performative Documentaries by Makers of Color." In *Between the Sheets, in the Streets: Queer, Lesbian, and Gay Documentary,* edited by Chris Holmlund and Cynthia Fuchs, 175–189. Minneapolis: University of Minnesota Press, 1997.

Goumarre, Laurent. "Catherine Breillat: Double Remake." *Art Press* 272 (October 2001): 58–59.

Griffin, Ada Gay. "Seizing the Moving Image: Reflections of a Black Independent Producer." In *Black Popular Culture,* edited by Gina Dent, 1983. New York: New Press, 1998.

Grundmann, Roy. "Black Nationhood and the Rest in the West: An Interview with Isaac Julien." *Cineaste* 21, nos. 1–2 (1995): 28.

———. "'Encouraging the Experimental': An Interview with Jim Hubbard." *Cineaste* 19, no. 1 (1992): 51.

———. "New Agendas in Black Filmmaking: An Interview with Marlon Riggs." *Cineaste* 19, nos. 2–3 (1992): 52.

Grundmann, Roy, and Judith Shulevitz. "Minorities and the Majority." *Cineaste* 18, no. 3 (1991): 40.

Hale, Sondra, and Terry Wolverton, eds. *From Site to Vision: The Woman's Building in Contemporary Culture.* Los Angeles: The Woman's Building, 2007.

Hallas, Roger. "The Resistant Corpus: Queer Experimental Film and Video and the AIDS Pandemic." *Millennium Film Journal* 41 (Fall 2003): 53–60.

Hammer, Barbara. "An Interview with Barbara Hammer." *Wide Angle* 20, no. 1 (January 1998): 64–93.

———. "Invisible Screen: Lesbian Cinema." *Video Guide* 10, no. 5 (November 1990): 14.

———. "Lesbian Filmmaking: Self-birthing." *Film Reader* 5 (1982): 60–66.

———. "Risk Taking as Alternative Living/Art Making: Or Why I Moved to the Big City." *Millennium Film Journal* 22 (Winter–Spring 1989–1990): 127–129.

———. "Women's Images in Film." In *Women's Culture: The Women's Renaissance of the Seventies,* edited by Gayle Kimball, 117–129. Metuchen, NJ: Scarecrow Press, 1981.

Hankin, Kelly. "Lesbian 'Making-of' Documentaries and the Production of Lesbian Sex." *The Velvet Light Trap* 53 (2004): 26–39.

Hardy, Ernest. "Young Soul Rebels: Negro/Queer Experimental Filmmakers." *Millennium Film Journal* 41 (Fall 2003): 23–30.

Harrell, Andre. "The *Baadasssss* Actress Interview: Joy Bryant." *Interview* 34, no. 5 (June 2004): 62–67.

Harris, Thomas Allen. "About Face: The Evolution of a Black Producer." In *Black Popular Culture,* edited by Gina Dent, 234–242. New York: New Press, 1998.

Hartouni, Valerie. "Fetal Exposures: Abortion Politics and the Optics of Allusion." *Camera Obscura* 29 (May 1992): 131–151.

Haug, Kate. "Femme Experimentale: Interviews with Carolee Schneemann, Barbara Hammer, and Chick Strand." *Wide Angle* 20, no. 1 (January 1998): 1–19.

———. "An Interview with Barbara Hammer." *Wide Angle* 20, no. 1 (January 1998): 64–93.

———. "An Interview with Carolee Schneemann." *Wide Angle* 20, no. 1 (January 1998): 20–49.

Hayward, Carl. "Interview—Carolee Schneemann." *Art Papers,* January–February 1993, 9–16.

Hemphill, Essex. "Looking for Langston: An Interview with Isaac Julien." In *Brother to Brother: New Writings by Black Gay Men,* edited by Essex Hemphill, 175. Boston: Alyson Publications, 1991.

Hladki, Janice. "Decolonizing Colonial Violence: The Subversive Practices of Aboriginal Film and Video." *Canadian Woman Studies* 25, nos. 1–2 (Winter 2006): 83–88.

Hoberman, J. "Explorations: Our Movies, Ourselves." *American Film* 8, no. 1 (October 1981): 34–36.

Holmlund, Chris. "When Autobiography Meets Ethnography and Girl Meets Girl The 'Dyke Docs' of Sadie Benning and Su Friedrich." In *Between the Sheets, in th. Streets: Queer, Lesbian, and Gay Documentary,* edited by Chris Holmlund and Cyn thia Fuchs, 127–143. Minneapolis: University of Minnesota Press, 1997.

hooks, bell. *Reel to Real: Race, Sex, and Class at the Movies.* New York: Routledge 1996.

Hubbard, Jim. "Introduction: A Short, Personal History of Lesbian and Gay Exper mental Cinema." *Millennium Film Journal* 41 (Fall 2003): 5–12.

Jaafar, Ali. "Rushes: Interview: Paul Haggis: Shooting into the Sun." *Sight and Soun* 15, no. 8 (August 2005): 5.

Jackson, Cheryl. "Interview: Lourdes Portillo." *The Squealer,* Spring/Summer 1991,

Jackson, Lynne, and Jean Rasenberger. "Interviews: The Passion of Remembrance: A Interview with Isaac Julien." *Cineaste* 16, no. 4 (1988): 23.

Jaehne, Karen. "Melvin Van Peebles: The Baadasssss Gent." *Cineaste* 18, no. (1990): 4.

James, David. "Carolee Schneemann." *Cinematograph: A Journal of Film and Media* 3 (1988): 36–38.

Johnson, Harriet McBryde. *Too Late to Die Young: Nearly True Tales from a Life.* N York: Henry Holt, 2005.

Johnston, Trevor. "Sayles Talk—John Sayles in Interview, on His Most Recent F *Passion Fish* and His Career as Director, Writer and Actor." *Sight and Soun* no. 9 (1993): 26–29.

Juhasz, Alexandra. "So Many Alternatives: The Alternative AIDS Video Moveme *Cineaste* 20, no. 4 (1994): 32.

———. "So Many Alternatives: The Alternative AIDS Video Movement: Part 2." *Cineaste* 21, no. 12 (1995): 37.

———. *Women of Vision: Histories in Feminist Film and Video.* Minneapolis: University of Minnesota Press, 2001.

Julien, Isaac. "Black Is, Black Ain't: Notes on De-essentializing Black Identities." In *Black Popular Culture,* edited by Gina Dent, 255–263. Seattle: Bay Press, 1992.

———. "Confessions of a Snow Queen: Notes on the Making of *The Attendant.*" *Cineaction!* 32 (Fall 1993): 5.

———. "Interview." In *Struggles for Representation. African American Documentary Film and Video,* edited by Phyllis R. Klotman and Janet K. Cutler, 36–37. Bloomington: Indiana University Press, 1999.

———. "In Two Worlds: An Interview with Isaac Julien." *Sight and Sound* 9, no. 7 (July 1999): 33.

———. "Performing Sexualities: An Interview with Isaac Julien." In *Pleasure Principle, Politics, Sexuality and Ethics,* edited by Victoria Harwood and David Oswell, 124–135. London: Lawrence and Wishart, 1993.

———. "Queer Questions." *Sight & Sound* 2 (September 1992): 34–35.

———. "'Who Is Speaking?' Of Nation, Community, and First-Person Interviews." In *Feminisms in the Cinema,* edited by Laura Pietropaolo and Ada Testaferri, 41–59. Bloomington: Indiana University Press, 1995.

Julien, Isaac, and bell hooks. "Critical Reflections." *Artforum* 33, no. 3 (1994): 64.

———. "States of Desire: Interview with Julien." *Transition* 53 (1991): 168–184.

Julien, Isaac, and Colin MacCabe, eds. *Diary of a Young Soul Rebel.* London: BFI Publishing, 1991.

Julien, Isaac, and Laura Mulvey. "'Who Is Speaking?': Of Nation, Community and First-Person Interview." In *Framer Framed: Film Scripts and Interviews.* New York: Routledge, 1992.

Julien, Isaac, and Jon Savage. "Queering the Pitch: A Conversation." *The Critical Quarterly* 36, no. 1 (Spring 1994): 1–12.

Juno, Andrea, and V. Vale. *Angry Women.* San Francisco: RE/Search Publications, 1991.

Kaplan, E. Ann, ed. *Feminism and Film.* Oxford: Oxford University Press, 2000.

Kissel, Laura. "Lost, Found and Remade: An Interview with Archivist and Film Artist, Carolyn Faber." *Film History: An International Journal* 15, no. 2 (Spring 2003): 208–213.

———. "The Research Value of Amateur Films: Integrating Amateur and Found Footage into a Film Production Course." *The Moving Image Journal* 2, no. 2 (Fall 2002): 153–157.

Klotman, Phyllis Ranch, ed. *Screenplays of the African American Experience.* Bloomington: Indiana University Press, 1991.

Kopple, Barbara. "True Tales from the Global Crisis ("Pandemic: Facing AIDS")." *Filmmaker—The Magazine of Independent Film* 11, no. 4 (Summer 2003): 54–57, 92.

Koresky, Michael. "Mule Variations." *Filmmaker—The Magazine of Independent Film* 12, no. 4 (Summer 2004): 46–48, 85–86.

Larkin, Alile Sharon. "Black Women Filmmakers Defining Ourselves: Feminism in Our Own Voice." In *Female Spectators: Looking at Film and Television,* edited by E. Deidre Pribram, 157–173. London: Verso, 1988.

Lauzen, Martha M., and David M. Dozier. "The Role of Women on Screen and Behind the Scenes in the Television and Film Industries: Review of a Program of Research." *Journal of Communication Inquiry* 23, no. 4 (October 1999): 355.

Lebow, Alisa. "Lesbians Make Movies." *Cineaste* 20, no. 2 (1993): 18.

Levy, Emanuel. *Cinema of Outsiders: The Rise of American Independent Film.* New York: New York University Press, 1999.

Liebman, Stuart. "There Should Be No Scissors in Your Mind: An Interview with Helke Sander." *Cineaste* 21, nos. 1–2 (1995): 40.

Lucia, Cynthia. "Progress and Misgivings in Mississippi: An Interview with Connie Field and Marilyn Mulford." *Cineaste* 21, nos. 1–2 (1995): 43.

———. "Redefining Female Sexuality in the Cinema: An Interview with Lizzie Borden." *Cineaste* 19, nos. 2–3 (1992): 6.

———. "Saying 'Yes' to Taking Risks: An Interview with Sally Potter." *Cineaste* 30, no. 4 (Fall 2005): 24–30.

Lutkehaus, Nancy Christine. "'Excuse Me, Everything Is Not All Right': On Ethnography, Film, and Representation: An Interview with Filmmaker Dennis O'Rourke." *Cultural Anthropology* 4, no. 4 (November 1989): 422–437.

MacDonald, Scott. "Carolee Schneemann's Autobiographical Trilogy." *Film Quarterly,* Fall 1980, 27–32.

———. *Critical Cinema: Interviews with Independent Filmmakers.* Berkeley and Los Angeles: University of California Press, 1988.

———. *Critical Cinema 2: Interviews with Independent Filmmakers.* Berkeley and Los Angeles: University of California Press, 1992.

———. *Critical Cinema 3: Interviews with Independent Filmmakers.* Berkeley and Los Angeles: University of California Press, 1998.

———. *Critical Cinema 4: Interviews with Independent Filmmakers.* Berkeley and Los Angeles: University of California Press, 2005.

———. "The Filmmaker as Visionary: Excerpts from an Interview with Stan Brakhage." *Film Quarterly* 56, no. 3 (Spring 2003): 2–11.

———. "His African Journey: An Interview with Peter Kubelka." *Film Quarterly* 5 no. 3 (Spring 2004): 2–5.

———. "Illuminations: An Interview with Andrew Noren." *Film Quarterly* 44, no. (1991): 30–43.

———. "Interview: Peggy Ahwesh." *Millennium Film Journal* 39–40 (Winter 2003): 1–

———. "An Interview with Carolee Schneemann." *Afterimage,* March 1980, 10–11.

———. "Putting All Your Eggs in One Basket: A Survey of Single Shot Film." *Afterimage* 16, no. 8 (March 1989): 10–16.

———. *Screen Writings: Scripts and Texts by Independent Filmmakers.* Berkeley and Los Angeles: University of California Press, 1995.

MacDonald, Scott, and Yoko Ono. "Yoko Ono: Ideas on Film: Interview/Scripts." *Film Quarterly* 43, no. 1 (Autumn 1989): 2–23.

Maira, Sunaina, and Rajini Srikanth, "Visualizing Three Continents: An Interv with Filmmaker Mira Nair, June 3, 1996." In *Contours of the Heart: South Asians Map North America,* edited by Sunaina Maira and Rajini Srikanth, 129. New York: The Asian American Writers Workshop, 1996.

Martin, Michael T. "I Am a Storyteller, Drawing Water from the Well of My Culture: Gaston Kabore, Griot of the African Cinema." *Research in African Literatures* 33, no. 4 (Winter 2002): 161–179.

Masilela, Ntongela. "Women Directors of the Los Angeles School." *In Black Women Film and Video Artists,* edited by Jacqueline Bobo, 3–19. New York: Random House, 1998.

Mask, Mia. "Looking Beyond Race: An Interview with Jennifer Fox." *Cineaste* 25, no. 1 (1999): 32–35.

Massood, Paula J. "The Quintessential New Yorker and Global Citizen: An Interview with Spike Lee." *Cineaste* 28, no. 3 (Summer 2003): 4–6.

Mayne, Judith. "Interview with Midi Onodera." *Quarterly Review of Film and Video* 20, no. 1 (2003): 53–62.

———. "Lesbian Looks: Dorothy Arzner and Female Authorship." In *Feminism and Film,* edited by E. Ann Kaplan, 159\180. Oxford: Oxford University Press, 2000.

———. *The Woman at the Keyhole: Feminism and Women's Cinema.* Bloomington: Indiana University Press, 1990.

McCluskey, Audrey T. "Melvin Van Pebbles [*sic*]: Renaissance Man." *Black Camera—A Micro Journal of Black Film Studies* 15, no. 2 (Fall–Winter 2000): 1–3.

———. "Revelations of the Spirit: An Interview with Filmmaker Booker T. Mattison." *Black Camera—A Micro Journal of Black Film Studies* 18, no. 1 (Spring–Summer 2003): 1–2, 12–13.

———. "Telling Truth and Taking Names: An Interview with Spike Lee." *Black Camera—A Micro Journal of Black Film Studies* 19, no. 1 (Spring–Summer 2004): 1–2, 9–11.

McGilligan, Patrick. "A True-Blue Red in Hollywood: An Interview with Paul Jarrico." *Cineaste* 23, no. 2 (December 1997): 32–39.

McHugh, Kathleen. *Indiscretions: Avant-Garde Film, Video and Feminism.* Bloomington/Indianapolis: Indiana University Press, 1990.

———. "Irony and Dissembling: Queer Tactics for Experimental Documentary." In *Between the Sheets, in the Streets: Queer, Lesbian, and Gay Documentary,* edited by Chris Holmlund and Cynthia Fuchs, 224–240. Minneapolis: University of Minnesota Press, 1997.

McMahan, Alison. "Women Film Pioneers on Video: An Interview with Jessica Rosner." *Cineaste* 26, no. 1 (2000): 60.

Mellencamp, Patricia. "Making History: Julie Dash." In *Redirecting the Gaze: Gender, Theory, and Cinema in the Third World,* edited by Diana Robin and Ira Jaffe, 99–126. Albany: State University of New York Press, 1999.

Menasche, Louis. "Woman with a Movie Camera: The Films of Marina Goldovskaya." *Cineaste* 24, nos. 2–3 (1999): 85–86.

Mercer, Kobena, and Isaac Julien. "Racism and the Politics of Masculinity." In *Male Order: Unwrapping Masculinity,* edited by Rowena Chapman and Jonathan Rutherford, 112. London: Lawrence & Wishart, 1996.

Miller, Denene. "Spike Lee." *Interview* 30, no. 10 (October 2000): 17.

Minh-ha, Trinh T. "An Acoustic Journey." In *Rethinking Borders,* edited by John C. Welchman, 1–17. Minneapolis: University of Minnesota Press, 1996.

———. "Difference: 'A Special Third World Women Issue.'" *Feminist Review* 25 (Spring 1987): 11–36.

———. *Framer Framed.* New York: Routledge, 1992.

———. "Mechanical Eye, Electronic Ear and the Lure of Authenticity." *Wide Angle* 6, no. 2 (Summer 1984): 58–63.

———. "On the Politics of Contemporary Representation." In *Discussions in Contemporary Culture,* edited by Hal Foster. Seattle: Bay Press, 1987.

———. "Outside In Inside Out." In *Questions of Third Cinema,* edited by Jim Pines and Paul Willemen, 133–149. London: British Film Institute, 1989.

———. "Questions of Images and Politics." *The Independent* 10, no. 4 (May 1987): 21–23.

———. "The Triple Bind." In *Available Means: An Anthology of Women's Rhetoric(s),* edited by Joy Ritchie and Kate Ronald, 378–381. Pittsburgh: University of Pittsburgh Press, 2001.

———. "Who Is Speaking? Of Nation, Community, and First-person Interviews." In *Framer Framed,* edited by Trinh Minh-ha, 191–210. New York: Routledge, 1992.

Minh-ha, Trinh T., and Tessa Barringer, eds. "Strategies of Displacement for Women, Natives and Their Others: Intra-views with Trinh T. Minh-ha." *Women's Studies Journal* 10, no. 1 (March 1994): 5–25.

Minh-ha, Trinh T., and Nancy Chen. "Speaking Nearby: A Conversation with Trinh T Minh-ha." In *Visualizing Theory: Selected Essays from V. A. R.,* edited by Lucien Taylor, 82–91. New York: Routledge, 1994.

Modleski, Tania. "Our Heroes Have Sometimes Been Cowgirls: An Interview with Maggie Greenwald." *Film Quarterly* 49 (Winter 1995–1996): 2–11.

Moran, James M. "Gregg Araki: Guerrilla Filmmaker for a Queer Generation." *Film Quarterly* 50 (Fall 1996): 18–26.

Morrow, Bruce. "An Interview with Isaac Julien." *Callaloo* 18, no. 2 (1995): 406–415.

Mottram, James. "Paul Haggis: Director's Chair." *Film Review* 660 (August 2005): 76–80.

Mullen, Harryette Romell. "Cinema of the Oppressed: An Interview with Francis Newman." *Callaloo* 27, no. 3 (Summer 2004): 715–733.

Muñoz, José Esteban. "The Autoethnographic Performance: Reading Richard Fung Queer Hybridity." *Screen* 36, no. 2 (Summer 1995): 83–99.

Negrón-Muntaner, Frances, and Rita Gonzalez. "*Boricua* Gazing: An Interview with Frances Negrón-Muntaner." *Signs: Journal of Women in Culture and Society* no. 1 (2004): 1345–1360.

Noriega, Chon A. "Between a Weapon and a Formula: Chicano Cinema and Its Contexts." In *Chicanos and Film: Essays on Chicano Representation and Resistance,* edited by Chon A. Noriega, 141–167. New York: Garland Publishing, 1992.

Noriega, Chon A., and Ana M. Lopez, eds. *The Ethnic Eye: Latino Media Arts.* Minneapolis: University of Minnesota Press, 1996.

Ono, Yoko. "Yoko Ono on Yoko Ono." In *Experimental Cinema: The Film Reader,* edited by Wheeler Winston-Dixon and Gwendolyn Audrey Foster, 221–224. London: Routledge, 2002.

Parmar, Pratibha. "Filling the Lack in Everyone Is Quite Hard Work, Really." In *Queer Looks: Perspectives on Lesbian and Gay Film and Video,* edited by Martha Gever, John Greyson, and Pratibha Parmar. New York, London: Routledge, 1993.

———. "'Woman, Native, Other.'" *Feminist Review* 36 (Autumn 1990): 65.

Pearlman, Bari. "Unorthodox Behavior. Interview with Sandi Simcha Dubowski." *Filmmaker—The Magazine of Independent Film* 10, no. 1 (Fall 2001): 78–81, 87–88.

Penley, Constance, and Andrew Ross. "Interview with Trinh T. Minh-ha." *Camera Obscura* 13–14 (Spring–Summer 1985): 87.

Petrolle, Jean, and Virginia Wright Wexman, eds. *Women and Experimental Filmmaking.* Urbana: University of Illinois Press, 2005.

Pierson, John, and Mike Spike. *Slackers & Dykes: A Guided Tour Across a Decade of American Independent Cinema.* New York: Hyperion Press, 1997.

Porton, Richard. "Elusive Intimacy: An Interview with Patrice Chereau." *Cineaste* 27, no. 1 (Winter 2001): 16–19.

Quart, Leonard. "Raising Questions and Positing Possibilities: An Interview with Mike Leigh." *Cineaste* 22, no. 4 (1997): 53.

Rabinovitz, Lauren. *Points of Resistance: Women, Power & Politics in the New York Avant-garde Cinema, 1943–1971.* Urbana: University of Illinois Press, 1991.

Rahmani, Avira. "A Conversation on Censorship with Carolee Schneemann." *M/E/A/N/I/N/G Journal,* November 1989, 3–7.

Ramirez Berg, Charles. "The Mariachi Aesthetics Goes to Hollywood: An Interview with Robert Rodriquez." In Charles Ramirez Berg, *Latino Images in Film,* 240–261. Austin: University of Texas Press, 2002.

Rashkin, Elissa. *Women Filmmakers in Mexico: The Country of Which We Dream.* Austin: University of Texas Press, 2001.

Redding, Judith M., and Victoria A. Brownworth. *Film Fatales: Independent Women Directors.* Seattle: Seal Press, 1997.

Renov, Michael. *The Subject of Documentary.* Minneapolis: University of Minnesota Press, 2004.

———, ed. *Theorizing Documentary.* New York: Routledge, 1993.

Reynaud, Bérénice. "An Interview with Charles Burnett." *Black American Literature Forum* 25, no. 2 (Summer 1991): 323–334.

Rines, Jesse Algeron. "Integrating the Film Industry's Craft Unions: An Interview with Grace Blake." *Cineaste* 20, no. 4 (1994): 30–31.

———. "The Political Economy of Black Film." *Cineaste* 21, no. 3 (1995): 38.

———. "Stimulating a Dialog Among African-American Viewers: An Interview with Daresha Kyi." *Cineaste* 20, no. 3 (1994): 43.

Rombau, Esteve, and Casimiro Torreiro. "This Film Is Going to Make History: An Interview with Rosaura Revueltas." *Cineaste* 19, nos. 2–3 (1992): 50.

Rich, Ruby B. "In the Eyes of the Beholder." *Village Voice,* January 28, 1992, 60, 65.

———. "Isaac Julien: Filmmaker." *Out-Look: National Lesbian & Gay Quarterly* 1, no. 3 (Fall 1988): 68–69.

Rose, Jacqueline. "Sexuality and Vision: Some Questions." In *Vision and Visuality*, edited by Hal Foster, 121. Seattle: Bay Press, 1988.

Rosenberg, Jan. *Women's Reflections: The Feminist Film Movement.* Ann Arbor, MI: UMI Research Press, 1983.

Ross, Matthew. "The Divided Self." *Filmmaker—The Magazine of Independent Film* 13, no. 3 (Spring 2005): 54–57.

Salas, Fred. "Not Just the Pyramids and Menudo: Interview with Lourdes Portillo." *Motion Magazine*, December 6, 1998, http://www.inmotionmagazine.com/lp.html.

Sanchez-Padilla, Beverly. "Interview with Lourdes Portillo." *Tonantzin* (San Antonio, TX: Publication of the Guadalupe Arts Center) 3, no. 2, 1986.

Sandals, Leah. "Noam Gonick: Interviewed by Leah Sandals." *C Magazine* 87 (Fall 2005): 28–31.

Sanford, Christy Sheffield. "Interview with Carolee Schneemann." *Red Bass: Journal of Politics and Art* 14 (1989): 16–23.

Saynor, James. "Young Soul Rebels." *Interview Magazine*, January 1992, 24.

Schlesinger, Tom. "Putting People Together: An Interview with John Sayles." *Film Quarterly* 34, no. 4 (Summer 1981): 2.

Schneemann, Carolee. *More Than Meat Joy: Complete Performance Works and Selected Writings.* Kingston, NY: Documentext, 1997.

———. "Notes." *Performing Arts Journal*, Fall 1977, 21–22.

———. "Notes from the Underground, A Female Pornographer in Moscow." *The Independent*, Winter 1992, 23–25.

———. "The Obscene Body/Politic." *College Art Journal*, Winter 1991, 28–35.

———. "Selected Text and Drawings from the Performance Work Dirty Pictures." *Heresies* 23 (1989): 54–55.

Seckinger, Beverly, and Janet Jakobsen. "Love, Death, and Videotape: *Silverlake Life.*" In *Between the Sheets, in the Streets: Queer, Lesbian, and Gay Documentary*, edited by Chris Holmlund and Cynthia Fuchs, 144–157. Minneapolis: University of Minnesota Press, 1997.

Sharp, Saundra. "Interview with Charles Burnett." *Black Film Review* 6, no. 1 (1990): 4–7.

Shimizu, Celine Parreñas, and Helen Lee. "Sex Acts: Two Meditations on Race and Sexuality." *Signs: Journal of Women in Culture and Society* 30, no. 1 (2004): 1385–1402.

Silberg, Jon. "A Scandal in Suburbia: Interview with Todd Haynes and Edward Lachman." *American Cinematographer* 83, no. 12 (December 2002): 54–56, 58, 60, 62–65.

Sklar, Robert. "The Lighter Side of Feminism: An Interview with Marlene Gorris." *Cineaste* 22, no. 1 (April 1996): 26–28.

———. "Rediscovering Radical Film Style: An Interview with David Riker." *Cineaste* 24, nos. 2–3 (March 1999): 6–9.

———. "Sex, Violence, and Power in the Family: An Interview with Francois Ozon." *Cineaste* 30, no. 4 (Fall 2005): 48–50.

Simonds, Cylena. "Spontaneous Combustion: An Interview with Barbara Hammer." *Afterimage*, December 1993, 5–7.

Sitney, P. Adams. "Interview with Stan Brakhage." In *Film Culture Reader*, edited by Adams Sitney, 201–229. New York: Praeger, 1983.

Smith, Gavin. "Toy Stories. Interview with Sadie Benning." *Film Comment* 34, no. 6 (November/December 1998): 28–31+.

Stephenson, Rob. "Interview with Trinh T. Minh-ha." *Millennium* 19 (Fall/Winter 1987–1988): 122–129.

Stiles, Kristine. *It Only Happens Once: Selected Letters and Performances of Carolee Schneemann*. Baltimore: Johns Hopkins University Press, 1998.

Strand, Chick. "An Interview with Chick Strand." *Wide Angle* 20, no. 1 (January 1998): 106–137.

Taylor, Rahdi. "Daughter of the Diaspora: An Interview with Filmmaker Julie Dash." *Third Force* 1, no. 5 (December 31, 1993): 12.

Thompson, Clifford. "Showing Complexity in Documentary Portraits: An Interview with St. Claire Bourne." *Cineaste* 26, no. 3 (Summer 2001): 36–37.

———. "St. Clair Bourne: Documenting the African-American Experience." *Cineaste* 26, no. 3 (Summer 2001): 34–35.

Torres, Hector. "A Document Title: A Conversation with Lordes Portillo." *Film & History* 34, no. 1 (2004): 66–72.

Unterburger, Amy, ed. *Women Filmmakers & Their Films*. Detroit: St. James Press, 1998.

Vekic, Natalija. "Ready for a Challenge: Sally Potter: Always Says Yes." *MovieMaker* 12, no. 59 (Summer 2005): 106–107.

Velasco, Juan. "The Cultural Legacy of Self-Consciousness: An Interview with Lourdes Portillo." *Journal of Latinos and Education* 1, no. 4 (2002): 245–253.

Walters, Ben. "Hong Kong Dreaming. An Interview with Christopher Doyle." *Sight & Sound* 15, no. 4 (April 2005): 86.

West, Dennis. "Filming the Chicano Family Saga: Interview with Director Gregory Nava." *Cineaste* 21, no. 4 (Fall 1995): 26.

———. "'Strawberry and Chocolate,' Ice Cream and Tolerance: Interviews with Tomás Gutiérrez Alea and Juan Carlos Tabío." *Cineaste* 21, nos. 1–2 (1995): 16.

West, Dennis, and Joan M. West. "Borders and Boundaries: An Interview with John Sayles." *Cineaste* 22, no. 3 (Summer 1996): 14.

———. "Not Playing by the Usual Rules: An Interview with John Sayles." *Cineaste* 24, no. 4 (September 1999): 28–31.

Williams, John. "Daughters of the Diaspora: A Filmography of Sixty-Five Black Women Independent Film- and Video-Makers." *Cineaste* 20, no. 3 (1994): 41.

———. "Re-Creating Their Media Image: Two Generations of Black Women Filmmakers." *Cineaste* 20, no. 3 (1994): 38–43.

Willis, Holly. "Uncommon History: An Interview with Barbara Hammer." *Film Quarterly* 47, no. 4 (Summer 1994): 7–13.

———, ed. *Scratching the Belly of the Beast: Cutting-Edge Media in Los Angeles, 1922–1994*. Los Angeles: Filmforum, 1994.

Willis, Sharon. *High Contrast: Race and Gender in Contemporary Hollywood Film*. Durham, NC: Duke University Press, 1997.

Wilton, Tamsin. *Immortal, Invisible: Lesbians and the Moving Image*. London: Routledge, 1995.

Wyatt, Justin. "Cinematic/Sexual Transgression: An Interview with Todd Haynes." *Film Quarterly* 46 (Spring 1993): 2–8.

Zahed, Ramin. "Confessions of an Indie Toon Queen: Interview with Joanna Priestley." *Animation Magazine* 19, no. 3 (March 2005): 22.

Zheutlin, Barbara, and David Talbot. *Creative Differences: Profiles of Hollywood Dissidents.* Boston: South End Press, 1978.

Zimmermann, Patricia. "Fetal Tissue: Reproductive Rights and Activist Amateur Video." In *Resolutions: Contemporary Video Practices,* edited by Michael Renov and Erika Suderburg, 304–332. Minneapolis: University of Minnesota Press, 1996.

CHIARA

FERRARI

Contributors

DANIEL BERNARDI is director of film and media studies at Arizona State University. He is the author of *Star Trek and History: Race-ing Toward a White Future* (1998) and the editor of *The Birth of Whiteness: Race and the Emergence of U.S. Cinema* (1996), *Classic Hollywood, Classic Whiteness* (2001),and *The Persistence of Whiteness: Race and Contemporary Hollywood Cinema* (2008).

CHRISTOPHER BRADLEY started out as a professional actor, moving between New York, Los Angeles, and Europe doing stage, television, and films. He was then accepted into the master's program in screenwriting at UCLA, where he won several awards, including the Alfred P. Sloan Fellowship in Screenwriting. In addition to his acting and writing, he has taught screenwriting for UCLA's online Professional Program and is currently teaching screenwriting as well as producing and managing distance learning courses for the College of Liberal Arts at Arizona State University.

JOHN THORNTON CALDWELL is professor and chair, Department of Cinema and Media Studies at UCLA. A scholar and filmmaker (M.F.A., Cal Arts; Ph.D., Northwestern University), Caldwell has authored and edited several books, including *Televisuality: Style, Crisis and Authority in American Television* (1995), *Electronic Media and Technoculture* (2000), *New Media: Digitextual Theories and Practices* (2003), and *Production Culture: Industrial Reflexivity and Critical Practice in Film and Television* (2008). His critical and theoretical writings have been featured in *Television and New Media, Cinema Journal, Genre, Quarterly Review of Film and Video, Emergences: Journal of Media and Composite Cultures, Medie Kultur, Film Quarterly, Aura,* and the *Los Angeles Times*. In addition, he has contributed chapters to numerous books, including *Television after TV; Mediaspace; The New Media Book; Issues in Contemporary Television; Film Theory: An Anthology; Television: The Critical View; Living Color: Race, Feminism, and Media;* and *American Television: History and Theory*. Caldwell is the recipient of awards from the NEA (1979, 1985), Regional Fellowships from the AFI/NEA (1985, 1988), and awards from state arts councils (1984, 1985, 1989). His films have been screened in museums and festivals in Amsterdam, Sundance, Paris, Berlin, Toulouse, Mexico City, Taipei, San Francisco, New York, Palm Springs, Santa Cruz, Hawaii, and Chicago and have been broadcast on SBS-TV Network/Australia, WTTW-Chicago, WGBH-Boston, WNED-Buffalo, and WEIU-TV-Illinois. He is the producer-director of the award-winning documentaries *Freak Street to Goa: Immigrants on the Rajpath* (1989), a film about the migratory pattern of hippies in India and Nepal, and *Rancho California (por favor)* (2002), a troubling look at the migrant camps that house indigenous Mixteco workers in the arroyos of Southern California's most affluent suburbs.

DANIEL S. CUTRARA entered the Jesuit Order in 1981 with a B.A. in political science from the University of Florida. He was ordained in the Roman Catholic priesthood after extensive studies, including graduate studies at the Jesuit School of Theology at Berkeley, California. After working in a leprosy hospital in India and an inner-city parish in the United States, he turned to storytelling as a way to make sense of the social suffering he witnessed. He received his M.F.A. in film production and writing at the University of Southern California. After completing the degree, he worked as a story analyst for Imagine Entertainment and New Regency Productions while teaching screenwriting at Loyola Marymount University. In 2000, he left the priesthood to pursue his writing aspirations. He is currently assistant professor in film and media studies at Arizona State University. His latest screenplay, *Kali Danced,* is in development with Cape Cod Productions.

CHIARA FERRARI is assistant professor of communication criticism in the Department of Communication Design at California State University, Chico. She is currently co-editing a volume on contemporary Italian media in the era of globalization. Her work examines the negotiations between the local and the global in the international import and export of television programs. In particular, she focuses on dubbing, analyzing how audiovisual translations allow national elements to be introduced within globally distributed programs.

KATHRYN F. GALÁN is the executive director of the National Association Latino Independent Producers (NALIP), a nine-year-old professional arts organization committed to supporting Latino/a film, television, and documentary makers, and to increasing the quality and quantity of images by and about Latinos. NALIP's national signature programs include the Latino Writers L, Latino Producers Academy, Latino Media Resource Guide, Latino Media Market, and "Doing your Doc" development workshops. She has produced a number of films, including *French Kiss* with Meg Ryan and Kevin Klein, *Squar, A Warrior's Tale* with Adam Beach and filmmaker Xavier Koller, and *Daybr* with Cuba Gooding, Jr., and Moira Kelly. For three years she partnered with Meg Ryan in their producing company, Prufrock Pictures. Prior to that was a vice president of production at Walt Disney Co.'s Hollywood Pictures (The *Joy Luck Club, The Marrying Man*) and spent seven years as head of production for Atlantic Entertainment (*Valley Girl, Teen Wolf, A World Apart*).

AARON GREER is assistant professor at Loyola University, Chicago, where he teaches courses in film studies and production. He is also an award-winning filmmaker whose work has screened at festivals around the world, including the Tribeca Film Festival and the American Black Film Festival. Greer has been awarded a fellowship by the Alabama State Council on the Arts and had his work selected for recognition by both the University Film & Video Association and the Broadcast Educators Association. His feature film *Gettin' Grown* is distributed by Warner Bros. Home Video, and his current feature project, *Fruit of the Tree,* has been selected for the Tribeca All Access Program, designed to help foster relationships between film industry executives and filmmakers from traditionally underrepresented communities.

C. A. GRIFFITH is an independent filmmaker and associate professor at the School of Theater and Film, Arizona State University. Raised in Washington, D.C., at age sixteen Griffith spent a year in Barcelona, Spain, where she learned Spanish and gained a passion for filmmaking. She is a graduate of Stanford University (B.A.) and the University of California, Santa Barbara (M.F.A), and co-founder of QUAD Productions, a nonprofit production company dedicated to producing grassroots, progressive media. She and H.L.T. Quan (School of Justice and Social Inquiry, Arizona State University) are completing two documentaries: *The Angela Davis Project* and *América's Home* (working titles). *The Angela Davis Project* features conversations between Davis and Yuri Kochiyama, an eighty-seven-year-old community activist and former confidante of Malcolm X, and examines cultural activism as intellectual and political work. *América's Home* explores community displacement, race, empire, and popular resistance in San Juan, Puerto Rico. Griffith's awards include a Wexman Center Residency Award for Media Arts (2009–2010), an Illinois Arts Council Fellowship in Media Arts, the Panavision/Kodak University Outreach Program Grant, the Vision in Color Award of the New England Film/Video Festival, and the Martha Muñoz Award of the 2007 Latino Screenplay Competition. Griffith directed, co-edited, and co-produced her first feature film, *Del Otro Lado* (The Other Side), in 1999. One of the first black female professional camera assistants and cinematographers in the film industry, she has worked on award-winning PBS and BBC documentaries, including *A Litany For Survival: The Life & Work of Audre Lorde* (cinematographer), *Branford Marsalis: The Music Tells You* (camera operator), and *Eyes on the Prize II*; feature films such as *Juice;* and music videos from Tracy Chapman and Public Enemy to The Rolling Stones. Her written works have appeared in *Black Feminist Cultural Criticism, Black Women Film and Video Artists, The World Good*, and the journals *Meridians, Signs,* and *Calyx.*

LAURA KISSEL is a documentary filmmaker and associate professor of media arts at the University of South Carolina. She has received numerous fellowships and grants for her work, including a Fulbright Award (2006), a MacDowell Fellowship (2006), and funding from the South Carolina Humanities Council (2003 and 2008). She was named the South Carolina Arts Commission's Media Arts Fellow for 2007–2008. Her documentary work explores issues surrounding landscape use and meaning, the representation of history, and the use of orphan films. Her nonfiction work *Cabin Field* has been honored with three festival awards, including the Jurors' Citation Award at the 2006 Black Maria Film and Video Festival. Her media projects in progress include a documentary about disability rights and a documentary on South Carolina cotton and globalization. Kissel received an M.F.A. degree in radio, television, and film from Northwestern University in 1999.

CRISTINA KOTZ CORNEJO was raised in Buenos Aires, Argentina, and the United States. She is an independent filmmaker whose feature-length film *3 Américas* was twice semifinalist for the 2004–2005 Sundance Screenwriters Lab and was in the official script competition at the 2003 International Festival of New Latin American Cinema in Havana, Cuba. She is the recipient of 2004 and 2007 Moving Image Fund grants from the LEF Foundation. She was also selected for the NALIP Writers Lab and was invited to attend the Sundance Institute's Independent Producers Conference with *3 Américas*. Her short film *La Guerra Que No Fue / The War That Never Was* (2004) has screened in more than ten countries and at twenty-five festivals, and is distributed by OUAT! Media and VOY Pictures. Her personal documentary, *My Argentine Family / Mi Familia Argentina* (2003), premiered at the 2003 Rhode Island International Film Festival, and her digital short *Ocean Waves* (2002), which has screened at various U.S. festivals, received the Award of Merit from the University Film and Video Association. In 2000 Kotz Cornejo was awarded a grant from the Partnership for a Drug-Free America to direct *Ernesto* (2000) which premiered at the Palm Springs International Short Film Festival. Her short film *The Appointment* (1999), developed under the advisement of Spike Lee and Nancy Savoca, was awarded a Warner Brothers Pictures Production Award, a Dean's Post Production Award, and three NYU Craft Awards and is distributed by Urban Entertainment. She earned a B.A. in international relations from the University of Southern California and an M.F.A. in film production from NYU's Tisch School of the Arts. She is an associate professor of film production at Emerson College, Boston.

JOHN JOTA LEAÑOS is a social art practitioner who utilizes all and any media to engage in diverse cultural arenas through strategic revealing, tactical disruption, and symbolic wagon burning. His practice includes a range of new media, public art, installation, and performance focusing on the convergence of memory, social space, and decolonization. Originally from Pomona, California, he identifies with the mainly hybrid tribe of Mexitaliano Xicangringo

Güeros called "Los Mixtupos" (mixt-up-os). Leaños's work has been shown at the Sundance 2006 Film Festival, the 2002 Whitney Biennial in New York, the San Francisco Museum of Modern Art, the Museum of Contemporary Art in Los Angeles, and the Massachusetts Institute of Technology. Leaños is a Creative Capital Foundation grantee and has been an artist in residence at the University of California, Santa Barbara, in the Center for Chicano Studies (2005), at Carnegie Mellon University in the Center for Arts in Society (2003), and at the Headlands Center for the Arts (2007). He is currently assistant professor of social practices and community arts at the California College of the Arts.

YURI MAKINO received her M.F.A. from the Graduate Film Program at New York University and a B.A. with highest honors in film studies and German studies at the University of California, Santa Barbara. She lives in Tucson, Arizona, where she works as an independent filmmaker and is associate professor at the University of Arizona. Makino's most recent short film, *Alma*, won the Best Director award at the 2007 Reel Sisters of the Diaspora Film Festival in New York and Best Narrative award at the 2007 University Film and Video Association Conference. She is in the development stage of a feature-length version of *Alma*, a film about a nineteen-year-old Chicana who discovers she is not a U.S. citizen and is jailed in a maximum-security prison. *Alma*, co-written by Makino, was awarded semifinalist status at the 1999 Sundance Institute Feature Film Lab, the 2000 Roy W. Dean Grant, and two grants from the Amazon Foundation. *Tokyo Equinox*, her poetic documentary about visiting her estranged Japanese father, has had more than two dozen festival screenings, and *Llama Walks*, a personal documentary about her mother, won the Best of Arizona Award at the 2003 Arizona International Film Festival and an Honorable Mention at the 2003 University Film and Video Association Conference. In 1999 Makino was awarded the Arizona Commission on the Arts Visual Fellowship for *Umeboshi* (Pickled Plums), a film about a Japanese-American girl facing the complexities of cultural identity and familial ties. To produce her current work, *111 Degrees Longitude*, Ms. Makino received a Hanson Film Institute grant and an Artist Project grant from the Arizona Commission on the Arts. This poetic documentary about what it means to call a place home is a collaborative piece being produced with Montana filmmaker Cindy Stillwell.

DENISE MANN (M.F.A. and Ph.D., UCLA) is associate professor and head of the UCLA Independent Producers Program in the Department of Film, Television, and Digital Media and teaches in both the M.F.A. and the M.A./Ph.D. programs. Mann is routinely asked to deliver talks on the contemporary Hollywood entertainment industry in Asia and Europe, including the Tokyo International Film Festival, the Shanghai International Film Festival, the Beijing Broadcasting Institute, Shanghai University, Paris 1 Pantheon Sorbonne, and Institut National de L'Audiovisuel (INA). She is the author of *Hollywood*

Independents—The Postwar Talent Takeover (forthcoming) and co-editor of *Private Screenings: Television & the Female Consumer* (1992). She has published articles on television and consumer culture in a range of journals and has served as associate editor of *Camera Obscura*, a journal of feminism and film theory, for six years.

DAN RYBICKY is an artist and writer who recently became a tenure-track professor in the film department at Columbia College, Chicago. His story "Picky" was published in Front Forty Press's *Short Stories Illustrated by Artists*, which won a 2007 USA Book Award. His stage work has been produced in different venues in New York City, including Soho Rep. He recently wrote a screenplay for independent producer Andrea Sperling (*Pumpkin; But I'm a Cheerleader*) and has worked in different capacities for Martin Scorsese and John Sayles. He is completing a documentary about his relationship to Ed Noonan, the head architect-developer of Tryon Farm, a conservation community located in Indiana.

KEVIN SANDLER is assistant professor in the Film & Media Studies Program at Arizona State University. He teaches courses on the contemporary U.S. media landscape, with an emphasis on censorship, animation, and convergence. He has published articles in *Cinema Journal, Animation Journal,* and various edited collections. He is the author of *The Naked Truth: Why Hollywood Doesn't Make X-Rated Movies* (2007), the editor of *Reading the Rabbit: Explorations in Warner Bros. Animation* (1998), and co-editor with Gaylyn Studlar of *Titanic Anatomy of a Blockbuster* (1999). He is currently working on *Scooby-Doo* for Duke University Press and *The Shield* for University of California Press.

SHELDON SCHIFFER was born in Los Angeles and lived in New York and Atlanta. He grew up with Chasidic Jews in West L.A. and African Americans in Inglewood and Compton, California, and was raised speaking Spanish with his Central American grandmother. He studied theater and film at the University of California, Santa Cruz, and received his M.F.A. degree from UCLA's School of Theater, Film, and Television as a director. He is an associate professor of film production and acting at Georgia State University.

CELINE PARREÑAS SHIMIZU works as a filmmaker and associate professor in Asian American film and media and women's studies at the University of California, Santa Barbara. Her publications include articles in the *Yale Journal of Law and Feminism, Theatre Journal, Signs* and *Wide Angles,* and the book, *The Hypersexuality of Race* (2007). She is an internationally screened and award-winning filmmaker whose new work, *Birthright* (2002), is on the transformative power of womanhood through mothering.

Index